World War II and the West

Gerald D. Nash

WORLD WAR II AND THE WEST

RESHAPING THE ECONOMY

University of Nebraska Press   LINCOLN AND LONDON

The paper in this book meets the minimum requirements
of American National Standard for Information Sciences—
Permanence of Paper for Printed Library Materials,
ANSI Z39.48–1984.

Library of Congress Cataloging-in-Publication Data
Nash, Gerald D.
   World War II and the West.
   Bibliography: p.
   1. World War, 1939–1945—Economic aspects—
West (U.S.) I. Title.
HC107.A17N373 1990   978'.033   89-4935
ISBN 0-8032-3303-5 (alk. paper)

To Marie

Contents

Illustrations

Illustrations

Preface

AS AMERICANS undertake to reshape their economy in the last decade of the twentieth century, the historical experience of previous generations who faced similar problems becomes more relevant. A knowledge of that experience may not provide specific answers to contemporary issues, for each age faces unique problems. Yet it is instructive to know something about the process of economic restructuring. Beyond details, such an understanding can provide a sense of confidence, a sharing of a common heritage for a new generation that seeks to cope with economic issues under difficult and often frustrating conditions.

The reshaping of the economy that Americans undertook during World War II was not the first such restructuring in the national experience. Throughout the last two centuries Americans have responded to technological, economic, environmental, and political pressures by reorganizing their economic ideas and institutions. That was as true in the nineteenth as in the twentieth century and occurred at least once every generation. The process was often painful, sometimes bumbling, and marked by sharp economic fluctuations. In a democratic society such as the United States the process of restructuring the economy was particularly complex because explicit national or regional planning was never popular. Governments at all levels usually did not publish detailed plans with clearly articulated goals. Nor did they provide rigid institutional mechanisms to carry out the myriad of details required by comprehensive plans in the hands of a large corps of bureaucrats. That, Americans believed, was more suited to Fascist, Nazi, Communist, or totalitarian regimes. Even those who admired the centralized planning programs of democratic countries like Sweden had little inclination to imitate that experience.

Rather, in the United States such restructuring has been accomplished through a complex process of cooptation. This has meant the close interaction of groups representing private enterprise—such as business, agriculture, and labor—with a wide range of governmental agencies in all branches—legislative, administrative, executive, and judicial. Out of this welter of conflicting interests public policy has emerged, representing an imperfect consensus on economic goals and on the best means for their implementation. The lack of clear direction in such planning in a participatory democracy was often frustrating, was not always economically efficient, and yet was accepted by many Americans as part of the price to be paid for maintaining political freedom along with a viable economy.

The primary purpose of this volume is to examine this process within the context of the American West in World War II and to analyze the influence of that conflict on the economic life of the region. The war compressed the experience of one generation—or about three decades—into the short span of just four years. The wartime experience is therefore particularly instructive for observing the American people at work undertaking the restructuring of their economic lives. And in the West such a reshaping was more visible than elsewhere in the United States because the region was America's "Third World," its youngest and most underdeveloped section. The economic effects of the conflict thus were more dramatic in this region than in the older and more fully developed areas of the nation. If the West was not quite a tabula rasa, nevertheless the changes were more revealing here than elsewhere. In 1940 the western economy was still characterized by its colonial aspect as an exporter of raw materials to the industrialized Northeast and Middle West. But in 1945 the West emerged from the war with a burgeoning manufacturing complex, a bustling service economy, and a bevy of aerospace, electronics, and science-oriented industries that heralded a new phase of economic development with the rise of a postindustrial economy. In four years the war had transformed a backward colonial region into an economic pacesetter for the nation. And the pattern created by the war dominated the western economy for the next three decades.

In tracing these momentous changes I have used a historical approach that focuses on people, on the individuals who were involved in shaping entrepreneurial as well as public policies. I have not attempted to write an institutional history, an ideological tract, or an econometric history or to calculate cost-benefit ratios. My mode of analysis does not preclude other approaches that could be fruitfully applied to the subject. Nor have

Preface

I tried to be exhaustive. Certain important topics, such as agriculture or water policies, are not intensively covered in this volume. My purpose has been to make an initial foray into a neglected subject and to raise questions others may wish to explore in greater depth or from varying perspectives.

In writing this book I have incurred many debts. A Senior Fellowship from the National Endowment for the Humanities allowed me to complete much of the archival research that was necessary in view of the paucity of secondary works. It made it possible for me to exploit the riches of the National Archives in Washington and of Federal Records Centers such as those in San Bruno and Laguna Hills in California. Manuscript collections at the University of Montana, the University of Texas, the University of Wyoming, the Nevada State Archives, the Colorado Historical Society, the Oregon State Historical Society, the Bancroft Library, the Henry L. Huntington Library, the Franklin D. Roosevelt Library, and the Harry S. Truman Library were essential to the study. I express profound thanks to the highly professional and devoted staffs of these institutions. To my wife I owe thanks for encouraging me to finish what came to be a long-term project. For all errors and imperfections I alone bear responsibility.

CHAPTER 1

Introduction: Reshaping the Western Economy

WORLD WAR II left an indelible imprint on the economy of the American West. No other event in the twentieth century had such far-flung influence. Domestic mobilization diversified the western economy, as yet underdeveloped in comparison with the older and more heavily industrialized Northeast and Middle West. In four short years it accomplished a reshaping of the region's economic life that would have taken more than forty years in peacetime. As westerners sought to catch up with the rest of the nation they found that federal expenditures in wartime provided the capital they had lacked for so many decades. Government funds now helped to boost manufactures, even if a significant portion went directly into the aircraft and shipbuilding industries and into the expansion of many kinds of military installations. The federal government also created new industries such as aluminum, magnesium, and synthetic rubber production. At the same time it built a vast new scientific complex for the West, establishing major new laboratories at Los Alamos, New Mexico, and Hanford, Washington, and the future Jet Propulsion Laboratory at Pasadena, California. The Office of Scientific Research and Development also awarded numerous contracts to western universities for special projects. These facilities did much to spawn new technologically oriented industries in the region.

Such a reshaping of the economy spurred other changes. It encouraged an influx of new settlers, particularly to the Pacific Coast and the Southwest, and did much to stimulate expansion of service industries and financial institutions. And the unprecedented growth of the armed forces increased the federal presence in the western economy. Scores of new military installations, whether storage facilities, arsenals, airfields, or testing and training centers, added another dimension to the economic life

1

Introduction

of the area. Proximity to the Pacific theater of war contributed to the growing importance of the West in the broader context of national security policies. And as the Orient assumed greater prominence in American diplomacy, the trans-Mississippi West acquired a new geopolitical importance.

The result of such changes was a diversification of the western economy on an unprecedented scale. In 1940 the West was still characterized by a colonial economy. The region's primary emphasis was on the extraction of raw materials to be sent for processing to the older East, where the region also secured its manufactured goods. Agriculture, livestock, and mining were the major industries of this underdeveloped area that constituted America's "Third World." But the forces unleashed by World War II wrought momentous changes by 1945. The West emerged from the conflict with a more developed and diversified economy. In addition to raw materials, the region now boasted expanded manufacturing facilities, rapidly growing service establishments, and pioneering technologically oriented industries such as aeronautics, electronics, and atomic energy development. The presence of recently established science and engineering operations now gave the West a cutting edge that was to make it an economic pacesetter in the postwar decades. In four short years westerners had undertaken an impressive reshaping of their erstwhile colonial economy.

But to comprehend the significance of these remarkable changes one needs to place them in a broader national as well as regional historical context. Since the founding of the Republic, Americans have been wont to reshape their economic lives about once every generation, with surprising regularity. In fact, the concern of Americans with restructuring the economy in the 1980s and 1990s has been only a more recent manifestation of what had already become, by 1940, a well-established cyclical pattern.

By the eve of World War II, four major swings in economic restructuring had taken place on the national level. The first took place between 1775 and 1815 when Americans transformed a dependent colonial economy based on trade into a more independent economy founded on greater self-sufficiency. The second restructuring occurred between 1815 and 1860 when Americans turned their agricultural economy into one in which manufacturing played an increasingly important role. Sometime between 1860 and 1920 Americans effected the third restructuring when they created large corporations that dominated the process of extensive industrialization, converting the erstwhile agrarian society into an industrial civilization. By 1920 resulting economic changes prompted the fourth

Introduction

restructuring during which Americans built a consumer economy characterized by mass production and distribution.

This consumer economy lasted until the 1970s; its decline has led Americans to undertake another restructuring in the last two decades of the twentieth century. At no time has the process been painless, for each phase has been characterized by a significant depression, whether in the 1780s, the 1830s, the 1870s and 1890s, or the 1930s.[1]

These broad national trends obviously affected westerners, although their area also had unique characteristics. Since the trans-Mississippi region was not settled intensively until the second half of the nineteenth century, its economic development lagged behind that of the older East. At a time when the Northeast was enmeshed in the third restructuring—undergoing the rise of industrialization and big business between 1860 and 1920—the West was still largely undeveloped, not unlike the Northeast during the first restructuring in the early years of the nineteenth century. Between 1880 and 1940 westerners built a colonial economy based on the export of raw materials. With the coming of the railroads in the 1880s and the ending of the Indian wars, the West was integrated more closely into the national economy. During the next fifty years or so westerners embarked on a slow economic restructuring in the hope that they would achieve greater diversification and independence. Certainly the development of commercial agriculture and a few manufactures helped them to attain these goals, but to most westerners the process of change seemed painfully slow, particularly during the Great Depression. By 1940 the western economy resembled that of the East in the 1860s. Most westerners thus were aware not only that they were "colonials" but also that they still needed to catch up with the economic development of the older regions, the South excepted. Somewhat unexpectedly, World War II provided them with that opportunity. It was a major turning point—a watershed—in the growth of the western economy during the twentieth century.[2]

How did westerners accomplish this mighty leap, this reshaping of their economy in the course of World War II? The process was complex, but the main engines of restructuring were the federal government and private enterprise. The federal investment in the West between 1940 and 1945 was large, about $40 billion. These dollars flowed westward through government contracts for thousands of goods, but primarily for ships and planes. Federal largesse also affected the West through the establishment of a vast network of military installations such as army camps and supply depots. The presence of more than three million military personnel did much to boost the region's service industries. And since most of the new

3

science installations in the West were federally owned and operated, they brought additional public money into the area.

If Washington provided a substantial portion of the new investment capital that sparked the reshaping of the West, private enterprise—individuals and corporations—did much of the actual work. That meant big business had a major role in the process while small business played only an auxiliary part. Their respective functions in reshaping the region's economic life led to chronic disagreements during the war years. When peace came, big business emerged with its influence enhanced.

The range of federal expenditures in the West was wide: vast purchases from business and agriculture; wage and salary payments to civilians as well as to military personnel; investments in new manufacturing facilities; disbursements for public projects such as dams, roads, and highways; and transfer payments, subsidies, and grants. In addition, benefit payments to farmers, social welfare recipients, and large-scale conservation and reclamation projects also contributed to the flow. Federal spending was not only important for its immediate, direct impact, however. It was also significant because in 1940 it triggered the rejuvenation of a depression-wracked economy. Consequently it had what economists designate as a multiplier effect. Federal funds revitalized many spheres of the economy and accelerated the general pace of economic activity, in classical Keynesian terms.

California was not a typical western state, but it starkly reflected the significant impact of federal spending as revealed in selected economic indicators. The value of its manufactures tripled during the war, increasing three times as rapidly as the national average. Personal income of Californians doubled in the war years, as did also their per capita income. California's share of federal revenues also rose sharply, from $15.1 billion in 1942 to $50.2 billion in 1945. Federal spending in California ballooned from $1.3 billion in 1940 to $8.5 billion five years later. Personal income climbed so rapidly because the federal government contributed fully 45 percent of the state's personal income during the war years, compared with only 8.5 percent a decade earlier. The wages the federal government disbursed in the state also mushroomed, from $216 million in 1940 to $2.1 billion in 1945—a tenfold increase.[3] Perhaps the effect of federal expenditures in other western states was not quite so dramatic as in California. It is true that most did not receive the large-scale aircraft and shipbuilding contracts that went to the Pacific Coast states. Still not a single western state was left untouched by the sudden increase of federal spending.

Utah provides a case in point. Here was a state that lacked the West

Introduction

Coast's extensive shipyards and airplane factories. Nevertheless, its economy was profoundly affected by the federal presence. Contemporary travelers commented on the sudden sprouting of a new network of military installations and the large new Geneva Steel Works near Provo. Federal spending spurred a tripling in the manufactures value of the state between 1939 and 1947, an increase similar to that of other Rocky Mountain states.[4]

Many new federal military installations now dotted the Utah landscape. One of the largest of these was the supply depot at Ogden. Although the depot was first established in 1935, the army and the navy did not expand it until the war years, when they spent more than $100 million for permanent facilities. That sum exceeded the total value of Utah's farm production in 1942 and was twice as great as the assessed valuation of Ogden's real estate. As the largest quartermaster depot in the United States— and a prime supplier for American forces in the Pacific area—it employed six thousand people and constituted a city in itself.[5]

Nearby was Hill Air Force Base, which the air force began building in 1935 at the suggestion of General Hap Arnold, who was stationed in the area. Between 1938 and 1942 the army completed construction at a cost of $30 million. The base provided not only supplies but also repair shops for the air force. During the war as many as twenty-two thousand people were on the payroll, which by 1950 had grown to $22 million annually.[6]

Farther south, the Tooele Army Depot grew to be one of the largest in the nation. It generated 8 percent of all income in Utah. Between 1941 and 1945 the War Department allotted the Tooele facility (which had first been established in 1920 as an ammunition depot) $52 million in an ambitious expansion. A vast storage facility, it contained 902 igloos to hold explosives, 31 large warehouses, and a tank repair shop. Covering an area of forty-four thousand acres, the Tooele depot had ample space for the storage of armaments and thousands of military vehicles. During the war it employed five thousand people annually and had a payroll of $4.3 million.[7]

In the western part of the state the air force built the world's largest military reserve at Wendover. Located on the famous salt flats straddling the Utah-Nevada border, this great expanse covering 3.5 million acres was used by the army as a bombing range and a training school for pilots and bombardiers. Thousands of crews for B-17, B-24, and B-29 bombers received their training here. Wendover Air Base also left a unique heritage. In 1945 air force personnel there received the world's first atomic bomb, delivered from Los Alamos, and loaded it onto the *Enola Gay* for its historic mission to Japan.[8]

In the barren wastes of southern Utah the armed forces built special centers catering to chemical warfare needs. One was the Deseret Chemical Depot, which the army built in 1942 some twenty miles south of Tooele for storing chemical warfare materials. Another was the Dugway Proving Ground, eighty-five miles southwest of Salt Lake City, which the Chemical Warfare Service used for toxic chemicals testing. Covering 850,000 acres, it was larger than the state of Rhode Island. More than four thousand people built Dugway, and about one thousand were employed there once the facility opened. One of its prime tasks was to supply flamethrowers and incendiary bombs used mainly in the Pacific theater.[9]

In addition, several smaller installations dotted the Utah countryside and channeled federal money into the state. The Clearfield Naval Storehouse, constructed in 1942 fifteen miles south of Ogden, cost $37 million. It provided a wide range of supplies for navy bases on the Pacific Coast and for the Pacific Fleet. By 1944 it employed 7,600 workers. Kearns Air Base was somewhat smaller. After the war the army sold it as surplus, and private developers turned it into a townsite; by 1960 it had grown into a community of seventeen thousand people.[10]

The historians of Utah's defense installations have estimated that altogether the federal government spent about $650 million building military facilities in the state during the war. In addition, Congress authorized another $250 million for privately operated defense plants. Of the latter, the Geneva Steel Works and the Remington Arms Ordnance Plant were the largest. Payrolls in five counties affected by these enterprises rose from $100 million to $250 million annually during the war. Utah's experience was not unique. The state epitomizes the extraordinary influence federal expenditures had on the economies of most western states.[11]

The changing western landscape now also revealed a mushrooming of new science installations. Southern California witnessed the rise of an impressive science complex. The California Institute of Technology in Pasadena began innovative research in rocketry under the direction of Charles C. Lauritzen in what was to become the Jet Propulsion Laboratory after the war. Between 1941 and 1945 this was a manufacturing as well as research facility, concentrating on rocket motors and projectiles. In La Jolla the Scripps Institute of Oceanography expanded its operations to provide vital information on ocean currents for the armed forces. It created a new operation at Point Loma primarily for submarine detection studies. At the University of California in Los Angeles aviation medicine became a specialty with the concurrent growth of America's air power. In Berkeley the Lawrence Radiation Laboratory rapidly became one of the nation's leading centers for research on nuclear fission. Its director, Ernest O. Lawrence, a Nobel Prize winner in 1939, worked closely with leading physicists to develop an atomic weapon. In the Pacific Northwest, the Boeing Company developed highly sophisticated research facilities and research teams, which also stimulated the Applied Physics Laboratory at the University of Washington. The cheap power available from Grand Coulee and Bonneville dams was one reason administration officials decided to establish the world's largest plutonium-producing plant at Hanford, Washington.[12]

The war quickened scientific activity elsewhere in the West as well, funded almost entirely by federal funds. The University of Texas worked on the development of airborne fire-control testers while at Rice University in Houston researchers worked on special problems of nuclear chain reactions. The University of New Mexico conducted tests with V-1 rockets. A major industrial contractor in New Mexico, the Zia Corporation, built a vast nuclear and rocket experiment facility that in later years became the Sandia Corporation, operated by the Western Electric Company. The Lovelace Clinic in Albuquerque specialized in aviation medicine. Of course the most significant new science facility in the Southwest was the secret Manhattan Project in Los Alamos, New Mexico, which became the headquarters for building the atomic bomb.[13]

The total effect of these varied scientific complexes was to direct several more billions of dollars into the West. In addition, as noted by Bernard Jaffe, a contemporary science writer, this extraordinary federal effort moved "the center of gravity of scientific talent in the United States . . . westwards." That left the region in 1945 with a new science complex, one bound to affect the civilian economy. The new science facilities provided additional institutional channels for the westward flow of federal money.[14]

Contemporaries readily became aware of this new phenomenon. "During the war scientific research was conducted on a scale never before contemplated," a congressional report noted in 1945.

> Before the war, the Nation spent between $300 millions and $400 millions a year on scientific research, of which approximately one-fifth was provided by the Government. During the war the total shot up to more than $800 millions a year (excluding $3 billions for atomic energy) more than three-fourths of which consisted of Government expenditures. Private expenditures on research declined about one-half while Government expenditures increased by nearly ten times. . . . During the period 1940 through 1944 the Federal Government spent nearly $2 billions in research and development. Nearly half of this took the form of contracts to private industrial laboratories.[15]

In short, through extensive contracts with private businesses, through military installations, and through the new science complexes—to name only a few of the myriad programs administered by the federal government—vast amounts of public funds were channeled westward. There they had an enormous effect, invigorating almost every facet of the western economy as the war progressed. The infusion of federal dollars set the region's mordant economy humming at breakneck speed.

But the government was not the sole energizer of the American people in wartime, for private enterprise also played a major role in reshaping western economic life. Its functions were carried out to a considerable degree by large corporations, which had already become the dominant institutional form used to promote economic expansion. Yet most Americans still clung to the ideal of economic equality, at least in theory, leading to continued support for small business firms as well. Indeed, the small-business person had an important symbolic function within the ideological framework of American democratic values, particularly in a war that highlighted a clash of ideologies. Sometimes the vision represented more hope than reality. Still, policy makers during World War II struggled to maintain the ideal and to strike a balance between the roles of big and small businesses, between theory and reality.

Wartime mobilization clearly accelerated economic concentration in the West, as in the nation. Goods manufactured by the one hundred largest corporations in the United States increased from 30 percent of the total goods produced in 1941 to a whopping 70 percent two years later. In 1945 the champion of small business, Senator James E. Murray of Montana, bewailed this tendency.

> [I] was aware of the increasing concentration taking place in manufacturing and was greatly concerned with what this concentration portended for competitive enterprise in the postwar period. Manufacturing is the pivotal point of our modern industrial economy which determines in considerable measure the level of economic activity. What happens in manufacturing directly influences the level of national productivity, employment, and the degree of competition which will prevail in the economy as a whole.
>
> Wartime business casualties reached alarming proportions. Government figures indicate that there were over one-half million fewer businesses in 1943 than in 1941. Most of this reduction in number of businesses was due to the sharp decline in new businesses. New small business has ever been the seedbed of American expanding enterprise. But, the years of war failed to produce the normal needed expansion. On the contrary, it saw great increases in the concentration of the American economy and startling developments of those monopolistic controls and practices which recent economic history has shown mean curtailed opportunity for successful independent business.[16]

Murray then summarized his position clearly: "The relative importance of big business, particularly the giant corporations, increased sharply during the war, while the position of small business declined. Although small

Introduction

business increased its actual production and employment during the war, the gains made by big business were much greater." The one hundred largest corporations secured 75 percent of all war contracts issued by the federal government.[17]

Such a ratio also held true in the West. Of the one hundred largest prime war contractors in the United States, twelve were west of the Mississippi River. Most of these were involved in aircraft manufacture and shipbuilding. The aircraft manufacturers listed among the top one hundred were Consolidated Vultee (no. 4 in rank), Douglas (no. 5), Lockheed (no. 10), North American Aviation (no. 11), Boeing (no. 12), and Northrop (no. 100). From the shipbuilding industry, Kaiser ranked no. 20, Todd no. 26, and Calship no. 49. The Anaconda Mining Company was no. 58, the Standard Oil Company of California was no. 75, and the Western Pipe Steel Co. of California was no. 89. The big four of western mining—Kennecott, Phelps-Dodge, Anaconda, and American Smelting and Refining—accounted for 82 percent of the mineral production in wartime but, except for Anaconda, did not rank among the one hundred largest contractors. Similarly, of the one hundred largest corporations operating government facilities, the airplane and ship builders were dominant.[18]

Federal policies during the war tended to favor big business over small. Army and navy procurement officers, especially, regularly preferred large enterprises over small firms in part because they believed big businesses could secure faster deliveries. As the Small Business Committee of the U.S. Senate noted in 1945:

> Government agencies relied especially heavily upon the industrial ability and know-how of the giant concerns. . . . In many government quarters it was felt that the big firms were best equipped to operate the new Government-owned facilities, since they were experienced in operating their own big plants. It was believed that volume production could be obtained most quickly . . . by the big corporations which were in a position to provide patents, engineers, production men, and general technical ability.

Thus, 83.4 percent of the value of privately operated but publicly financed industrial plants was in the hands of only 168 corporations.[19]

The federal government's major instruments for expanding industrial production in the West were varied. The most important was the Defense Plant Corporation (DPC), a subsidiary of the Reconstruction Finance Corporation. The latter was managed by Jesse Jones, federal loan administrator, who had a reputation of being partial to large rather than small enterprises. The DPC expended more than $7 billion to build new plants in wartime. The army and the navy also spent about $1.5 billion each in

9

constructing new manufacturing facilities. About $500 million was disbursed by the U.S. Maritime Commission, almost half of that in the West. Of the one hundred largest privately operated government facilities in the United States, eight were in the West, with an estimated value of about $767 million (of a national total of $9.3 billion).[20] As a region, then, the West was still behind the East. But wartime mobilization accelerated its efforts to catch up. After all, in terms of economic development, the West was still the new kid on the block.

But the acceleration of economic concentration in the wartime reshaping of the West alarmed the champions of small business. Many of these individuals came from the West. After all, business in the region was characterized by small rather than large firms. As noted earlier, no more than a dozen of the one hundred largest government contractors were headquartered west of the Mississippi River. Many westerners also feared that economic concentration in the East would perpetuate their colonial status and stymie their hopes for greater self-sufficiency and economic diversification. The West thus played a prominent part in the movement to bolster the role of small business in American society. Indeed, most westerners viewed the war as an unusual opportunity to throw off the shackles of economic dependence.

Between 1940 and 1946, therefore, western leaders actively promoted the cause of small business in the national as well as regional economy. In Congress they included Senators James E. Murray of Montana, Joseph C. O'Mahoney of Wyoming, Pat McCarran of Nevada, and at times Harry Truman of border state Missouri. In the House, Representative Wright Patman of Texas was active in the movement. At the same time, prominent New Dealers were eager to continue the antimonopoly policies espoused during the second Roosevelt administration. Interior Secretary Harold Ickes and his staff were among the most outspoken and persistent advocates of western economic independence through the stimulation of small enterprises. The antitrust crusade was also supported by Assistant Attorney General Thurman Arnold, a former mayor of Laramie, Wyoming, and by his successor in the Department of Justice, Wendell Berge. Assistant Secretary of State Adolph A. Berle, one of the nation's leading experts on corporate concentration in the United States, acted behind the scenes with advice for small business advocates. Of prime importance also was Maury Maverick, a former congressman from Texas. As a vice-chairman of the War Production Board (WPB), and especially as chairman of the Smaller War Plants Corporation from 1943 to 1945, he was in a strategic position to further small business participation in the war effort, particularly in the West.

Introduction

Between 1941 and 1945 these men formed a cohesive network and worked in various ways to promote their cause. From their perspective, wartime agencies such as the War Production Board, the Defense Plant Corporation, the Department of War, and the Department of the Navy were bastions of big business whose activities required constant vigilance.[21] The nation may have been involved in a global conflict, but westerners at home were also fighting for the greater economic independence of their region.

Perhaps the most persistent advocate of small business was Senator James E. Murray of Montana. Although personally affluent and financially secure, Murray had a lifelong concern for small business stemming from his Jeffersonian vision of an egalitarian society. That led him to join the battle to gain a greater place for small business in American life. First elected as a New Deal Democrat in 1934 he once told a reporter: "I have long been concerned with the problems of small business because in my state—with the exception of one giant copper monopoly—almost all business is small business. I have lived with them. I have worked with them." The contrast between big and small business may not have been as gross in most western states as it was in Montana, yet the state was not wholly atypical for the region.[22]

During his second term in the Senate Murray asserted himself more fully. Inspired by a plank in the Democratic Party platform of 1940 that promised special aid to small business, he wrote to President Roosevelt in July of that year. Murray noted that he hoped to establish a Senate Committee on Small Business to recommend remedial legislation. Roosevelt gave Murray his full backing. In addition, the issue transcended party lines. One of Murray's most enthusiastic supporters was Senator Robert A. Taft, the conservative Republican from Ohio. Although at different ends of the political spectrum, they both believed in private enterprise and competition and had an aversion to monopoly.[23] Thus Murray experienced little difficulty in September 1940 in securing approval of his plan to establish the Special Senate Committee on Small Business. Murray became its first chairman and promptly appointed James Mead, former secretary of the Billings, Montana, Chamber of Commerce, as executive secretary. As the committee's staff grew over the years Murray also selected Dr. Dewey Anderson to direct research. A former Stanford University professor, Anderson had served as executive secretary of the Temporary National Economic Committee during the New Deal's antitrust phase from 1937 to 1941.[24] Clearly, direct links existed between the New Deal's Temporary National Economic Committee and the wartime Senate Committee on Small Business.

11

Introduction

The Murray Committee became intimately involved with the economic development of the West. Of the more than ninety-nine volumes of testimony it compiled between 1941 and 1946, over two-thirds were directly concerned with economic conditions in the West. As a senator from copper-rich Montana, Murray had a special interest in the western mining industry, as well as in the economies of California, Nevada, Arizona, and, of course, Montana. The extensive hearings he conducted for the thousands of people in small businesses throughout the West provided a forum at which they could air their special problems and concerns. For many of these people it was their only means of direct communication with highly placed federal officials. Unlike big business corporations who had representatives and lobbyists in Washington, many small western business interests had no such option and often felt isolated, frustrated, and helpless.[25] The committee also sent out thousands of questionnaires to business people throughout the West asking them to relate their most pressing problems. Murray believed in grass-roots democracy. In addition, he intervened on behalf of small businesses with federal agencies such as the War Production Board and the Reconstruction Finance Corporation. He was also skilled in sponsoring legislation to remedy complaints, whether these concerned confusing bureaucratic rules, termination of federal contracts, or the disposal of federal surplus properties. And among his achievements for small business he was also proud to point to his part in the creation of the Smaller War Plants Corporation (SWPC).[26]

The origins of the SWPC lay in the increasing concern of many people in small businesses that they were receiving only a very small fraction of the flood of new government orders. As early as the summer of 1940 one of Harry Truman's close friends, Lou Holland, a small sprinkler manufacturer in Kansas City, Missouri, expressed his fears. He wrote to Truman, "It does not seem to me as though we are getting our share in the defense program." Holland was also chairman of the Mid-Central War Resources Board, a consortium of small businesses seeking contracts. Truman noted approvingly, "You are just as right as you can be about our not getting our share of the defense program."[27] The flow of orders to Pacific Coast plants also concerned Holland as he viewed the drain of skilled workers from Kansas City to the Pacific Coast. Said Holland: "Harry . . . all told, we have sent about twenty-five hundred boys out there since January 1st . . . to take jobs for the Consolidated Aircraft Company on the Pacific Coast. . . . Those boys are not going there by choice—they would prefer to stay here, but we cannot offer them jobs in this area." By January 1941 Truman was more alarmed and wrote Holland, "The little fellow will just be receiving the crumbs off the rich man's table." In fact, Truman now decided to bring up the problem directly with the president. As he reported to Holland: "I paid a visit to the President . . . for nearly half an hour. . . . I told him we were not interested in getting the crumbs from the table of the big fellows. . . . I don't know whether I made any impression, or not, because the President is always courteous and cordial when anyone calls on him, and when you come out you think you are getting what you wanted, when nine times out of ten you are just getting cordial treatment."[28]

Truman was not alone in his concern. One of the prominent members of the National Defense Council's Advisory Commission, Chester C. Davis, expressed similar fears. Speaking to the Southern Governors' Conference on March 15, 1941, Davis said:

> I was somewhat shocked a few days ago to see a tabulation of the distribution of defense orders to date. . . . Included in the tabulation were $ eleven and a half billions of prime contracts awarded between June 15 of last year and February 15 of this year. . . . Of this vast total . . . 80 per cent has gone to 62 companies (mostly in the East). There is rich food for thought in these figures. I believe they are closely related to the mediocre success we have had in apportioning . . . this new defense industry to the states.[29]

Truman became increasingly agitated about this trend. "I am still fighting the old gang tooth and nail," he wrote to his confidant, Lou Holland. "I have succeeded in creating a faction in the War Production Board who believes as I do. . . . I fear very much that Nelson [chairman of the War Production Board] is passing on his powers, and that Somervell [chief of army procurement] is very shortly going to be the head of the Gestapo, and then we will be through for good. I am going to fight to the last ditch, however."[30]

Meanwhile, Senator James Murray took it upon himself to try to do something about the problem. Starting in December 1941, his Small Business Committee began to hold hearings on the one-sided flow of war orders to big business. A succession of witnesses expressed their fears that the war might decimate small entrepreneurs. James Ingrebretsen of the Los Angeles Chamber of Commerce complained that in his county the large corporations, mostly aircraft manufacturers, had secured more than 80 percent of the new contracts issued by the government in the amount of more than $2 billion. On the other hand, small businesses in the area were experiencing real difficulties in securing priorities for scarce materials from the Office of Production Management (OPM) and its successor, the War Production Board. Often they had no option but to close down.[31] On the basis of such evidence Murray issued a scathing report chastizing the OPM for ignoring the interests of small business. Since Murray had little confidence in that agency, or in the WPB (created in February 1942), he urged the establishment of a new division within the WPB expressly for the purpose of securing war contracts for small business. By March 1942 Murray, in cooperation with Representative Wright Patman, had drafted legislation to create the new agency.[32]

The Murray-Patman Act of 1942 creating the Smaller War Plants Corporation was enacted unanimously by both houses. The measure allocated $150 million to this new government corporation, whose primary purposes were to make loans to small businesses so that they could convert to war production, and to secure government war contracts for them. The law provided that not the president but the head of the WPB appoint the chair of the SWPC. And the act stipulated that the SWPC chair report to Congress and the president every sixty days on the progress made in garnering contracts for small enterprises. Although this measure gave a boost to small businesses, it did not require procurement agencies to seek them out or to award them contracts. Murray always considered the agency to be within his sphere of influence and directed its management from behind the scenes. At the outset, however, he was unable to appoint one of his protégés, C. W. Fowler, a close friend and Montana businessman, as chairman, although he was able to place him on the board of directors.[33]

Instead, Senator Truman's influence prevailed as Donald Nelson appointed his good friend Lou Holland as chairman of the SWPC. During his ten months in office westerners especially were dissatisfied with his poor performance because he accomplished virtually nothing. Small businesses received very few contracts. Senator Murray was furious and publicly roasted Holland at hearings of the Small Business Committee. When Murray asked Holland point-blank why he could not do better, the Missourian could only answer meekly, "But this is a tremendous job." Murray confided to one of his staffers, Bertram Gross, that he considered Holland a "klutz."[34] Congressman Wright Patman was even more vehement. In a strong and rather frank letter to Roosevelt he said: "The Smaller War Plants Corporation to date is an absolute failure and flop. It has deceived the small businessmen of the country, and so far as helping them is concerned, has been a fraud and a hindrance. . . . Lou Holland . . . is not big enough for the job. I think he is an honest, sincere person but does not have any more executive ability than a section foreman of a medium-sized machine shop. . . . Generally, the whole organization is referred to, here in Washington by those who know, as a bunch of fifth rates." He went on quite pointedly, "It is my hope that this organization will be cleaned out immediately."[35] And cleaned out it was. Within two weeks Holland submitted his resignation. And to add insult to injury the Senate Small Business Committee in January 1943 issued a scathing report in which it deemed Holland's performance totally unsatisfactory.[36]

Roosevelt was himself concerned about the issue and took a direct hand in selecting Holland's successor. In a memo to War Stabilization Board Director James F. Byrnes, the chief executive was unusually candid, "This Small Business problem has baffled me, as you know, for nearly two years." And with great frankness he added, "We have not met it—and I am not sure that it can be met." Clearly frustrated, he asked: "What would you think of the rather wild idea of putting Joe Kennedy in charge of the Smaller War Plants Corporation? He *might* do a good job with it and he *might* do us no harm."[37] Byrnes thought about the suggestion for a few weeks and then replied, "I believe Joe's appointment to be all right, but if you have determined not to talk to him about it, Robert Johnson who is the head of Johnson and Johnson Surgical Dressings Company of New Brunswick, New Jersey . . . sounds good." Johnson had been serving as vice-chairman of the SWPC under Holland. Meanwhile, Byrnes talked to Kennedy about the position, but he reported that Kennedy "reached the conclusion that there was no possibility of his rendering a service in that office. . . . He doubts that anyone could accomplish anything of value to small business. . . . He said that if he felt that it was possible for him to be of any service that he would undertake the job, but he is convinced that he could not accomplish anything and he could not accept it."[38] Donald Nelson also tried to persuade Kennedy, but to no avail. That left Johnson as the prime candidate.[39]

Johnson was acceptable to Murray and Patman. He had been a boyhood friend of the president's and had some experience with small business enterprises. Since Johnson was a colonel in the army reserves, Patman believed he could be more effective with procurement officers in the armed services if he had higher rank. Consequently Patman pressured Byrnes to seek a promotion for Johnson. "His Army uniform is helpful rather than harmful in dealing with the procurement agencies," Patman wrote Byrnes. "If he were a brigadier-general instead of a colonel, it would give his position more prestige. I hope that you can recommend to the President that he increase his rank for him to do a better job in the position he holds." The suggestion fell on favorable ears, and Congress quickly approved Roosevelt's recommendation for promotion.[40]

Unfortunately, during the next six months Johnson indicated that he too was not quite up to the challenges of the position. He did contribute by creating an organizational structure for the SWPC, organizing field offices around the nation, and appointing local advisory boards. But he failed to accomplish the corporation's prime objective of securing more war contracts for small businesses. By July Murray's man on the SWPC board, C. W. Fowler, was reporting to the Montana senator that by and large the agency was still highly ineffectual. Quite often Johnson met opposition from Nelson and the WPB, who were loath to use small business services unless they were absolutely essential to the war effort.[41] Meanwhile, the Senate Small Business Committee kept a close watch on Johnson and stalked his every move. In fact, Murray even appointed a special subcommittee on complaints, under Senator Tom Stewart, to do nothing but solicit criticism of Johnson and the SWPC. Stewart reported to Patman in no uncertain terms that he considered Johnson "to be a complete flop." By the summer of 1943 the movement to unseat the newly appointed general was well under way. Since Johnson also suffered from bleeding ulcers, he handed in his resignation in September.[42]

At this point Murray and Patman wanted a proven professional. Their choice was Morris L. Cooke, a highly regarded industrial engineer who had served the New Deal very capably as head of the Rural Electrification Administration. Roosevelt liked the suggestion and virtually promised the job to Cooke. As the president wrote to Byrnes about the Cooke appointment: "I think this is a rather good idea. Cooke is an awfully good man and has done quietly and efficiently a great many small jobs for me. What do you think?" Byrnes was receptive and thought that since the Senate Small Business Committee had complained so loudly about the SWPC's performance, Cooke's selection might be a good way to stifle such criticism in the future.[43]

But this time Nelson balked, although he was willing to follow the president's orders. He preferred one of his subordinates, former Congressman Maury Maverick. Murray was a little cool to Maverick at first. As E. M. "Pa" Watson, the president's administrative assistant, reported to Roosevelt, Murray thought that "Maury is a nice fellow and a good Democrat but hasn't sufficient background. . . . He is too political minded." Although Roosevelt had promised the job to Cooke, he was willing to go along with Nelson's preference for Maverick. But to avoid personal embarrassment, the chief executive insisted that it appear Nelson was making the appointment on his own.[44]

And so, in October 1943, Maury Maverick from Texas became the third—and the most successful—chairman of the SWPC. An avid New Dealer, he worked closely not only with Murray and Patman but also with Thurman Arnold, Wendell Berge, Joseph C. O'Mahoney, Adolf A. Berle, Luther Gulick, and others in the group of antimonopolists concerned with economic concentration. Maverick was especially sensitive to the economic needs of the West and made them one of his special concerns. A human dynamo with a sparkling personality, he brought fiery passion to the cause of small business in the West. Soon after his appointment, in fact, he embarked on an extensive trip to the Pacific Coast where he spoke in major cities including Los Angeles, San Francisco, Portland, and Seattle. Everywhere he espoused the gospel of western economic diversification and promised to use the resources at his disposal to stimulate the awarding of new government contracts to small businesses in the West. During the first sixteen months of his administration he completely revitalized the moribund agency. In that time the SWPC awarded more than $2 billion in prime contracts to small businesses and another $500 million in subcontracts. Under Maverick, small business in the West finally received some of its due.[45]

Reshaping the western economy in wartime was obviously a complex process. As national mobilization funneled an increasing stream of federal dollars westward it energized a dormant economy. Large businesses as well as small geared up for maximum production, stimulating the service industries and providing full employment. Westerners were determined to use this opportunity to diversify their economy, as they had been hoping to do for over half a century. Here was their chance to catch up with the older regions.

In the process, they won some battles and lost others. The structure of raw materials industries such as mining remained largely unchanged during the war. On the other hand, the extraordinary expansion of the shipbuilding and aircraft industries triggered expansion in many auxiliary manufactures throughout the West. It also resulted in the establishment of new western industries, such as aluminum, magnesium, and steel production, and in the advance of the petroleum production industry. And although the pace of western industrial growth was rapid, westerners avoided some of the worst despoliations of their fragile natural environment, which had marred mobilization during World War I.

The very real progress westerners made in diversifying economic life during the war years also had a profound psychological influence. The West emerged from the conflict with a new self-image, a new self-confidence that led its denizens to believe they could meet any challenge. If the West in 1945 still had not caught up economically with the older regions, the perception of many westerners was that now they were no longer colonials. Certainly such attitudes were reflected in the outpouring of plans for the postwar West that surfaced after 1944. The American Dream of unlimited opportunity in the West—muted during the Great Depression—was revitalized by World War II.

CHAPTER 2

The Western Mining
Industry at War

WORLD WAR II understandably
left its mark on the western mining industry. As the nation's prime storehouse for metals, the West occupied an important place in the national
mobilization program. Between 1939 and 1945 the United States had the
capacity for virtual self-sufficiency in mineral products needed in the war
effort. Yet during these years the nation became increasingly dependent
on foreign imports and by 1945 had abandoned any thought of self-
sufficiency. The war years thus saw the development of patterns that
were to form the model for the remainder of the century.

Westerners welcomed the new importance of their extractive industries, particularly after more than a decade of depression. Of course they
looked forward to immediate short-range profits, but beyond such gains
they viewed the war as a unique opportunity to further their long-range
goal of diversifying the economy and promoting industrialization. The
mining industry promised to be a means toward that end if westerners
could secure new processing and fabricating plants. Such plants would
limit the colonial relationship with the industrial East against which the
West had chafed restlessly for many years. Although the war brought the
hoped-for diversification, the change did not come primarily through
mining, as many westerners had expected.

Mobilization accelerated existing industry trends favoring big rather
than small mining interests. Technological innovations had precipitated
this preference long before 1940. A good example was the decline of
underground mining for copper in and around Butte, Montana, and the
consequent expansion of open-pit mining in Arizona, New Mexico, and
Utah. In addition, the most accessible mineral resources in the West had
already been exploited by 1940, so that greater efficiency was needed to

utilize more marginal deposits. That could usually be attained by large-scale, integrated operations. The availability of cheaper ores outside the United States led large corporations to import vast quantities of ores from around the world. Chile was a major source for copper, Mexico for lead and zinc, Peru for zinc, Bolivia for tin, and Spain for tungsten. Big business operations predominated in copper, lead, tin, and zinc production, in which multinational corporations controlled much of the smelting and refining, in addition to the mining.[1]

The interests of these large enterprises were important in the formation of federal mining policies, although those of the thousands of small miners in the West were not totally ignored. Central to the government's program was the Metals Reserve Corporation, a subsidiary of the Reconstruction Finance Corporation. Congress authorized the RFC on June 25, 1940, to acquire strategic and critical materials, and three days later chartered the MRC to carry out a comprehensive purchase and stockpiling program.

Charles Henderson, the Nevadan whom Roosevelt appointed as chairman of the MRC, explained that his agency had four major functions. One was to purchase strategic minerals at home and abroad for immediate use and for stockpiling. The agency spent more than $1 billion during the war performing this service. Second, the MRC was to build plants to process needed metals, such as the Basic Magnesium plant in Henderson, Nevada, near Las Vegas. A third purpose was to extend loans to miners to enable them to increase production, a program with special appeal to the tens of thousands of small miners in the West. The corporation was to make similar loans to mine processing operations.

But Henderson's primary emphasis was on purchasing metals from overseas. The MRC thus was very slow in developing domestic mineral production except where warranted by shortages, much to the disappointment of westerners. "The fundamental belief that our national interests are best served by utilizing the mineral resources of other countries while conserving our own," Henderson noted, "has perhaps been partly responsible for the slowness in developing our present mineral resources." He considered most domestic deposits to be of limited commercial value. They required intensive exploration, lacked the necessary processing facilities, and taxed an already strained transportation system.[2] Thus, most of the MRC's purchases were from foreign producers.

As a result, the large number of small miners in the West felt disadvantaged. The war was providing expanding markets for all kinds of minerals, but the MRC's ceiling prices and purchasing policies kept western miners from securing a lion's share of this new federal bonanza. Throughout the war years western miners and mining associations complained

19

about the MRC's import policy, its price levels, the ambiguities of federal policies and increasing bureaucracy, the labor shortages in the mines, the lack of access roads, and the seeming dominance of the large corporations in the industry. Most aggrieved were the gold miners, whom the WPB deprived of their livelihood when it ordered them to shut down their mines for the duration. More than ever, westerners felt like colonials, subject to the whims of distant bureaucrats in the nation's capital.

The war years therefore witnessed a very active and lively debate on the nature of national mining policy and the role of the mining industry in the West. Just what the relationship between multinational corporations and domestic producers should be became a major issue—forty years before it became a significant problem in many sectors of the American economy during the 1980s. Mining in the West was not self-contained but was related to other segments of the regional economy and to western desires for diversification. The dialogue thus involved questions far broader than whether to purchase the cheapest minerals available. Such issues touched on the nature of the western economy in a national context during the postwar era and on the West's status as a colonial area. Consequently, the advocates of western economic diversification mounted a strong effort in the Department of the Interior, in Congress, and elsewhere to safeguard regional interests. Their effort was not wholly successful, but they did secure some of their demands as the national mining policy crystallized.

Most small miners in the West were not as concerned with the broad dimensions of national policy as they were with their everyday problems. These covered a wide range, including a shortage of mine labor and what they perceived to be inadequate metal prices set by various federal agencies. These miners also complained about the morass of government policies that affected even the smallest mine and that added to their bewilderment. And underlying many of their concerns was the nagging feeling that the WPB, as well as the MRC was following policies that benefited the large mining corporations far more than the tens of thousands of small miners.

Throughout the West small-mine operators bemoaned the shortage of skilled and unskilled help. A typical case was that of Oscar Mills at the Nevada Scheelite Mine. Mills noted that many mines were near federal construction projects, which offered considerably higher wages. And since miners were not exempt from selective service, most younger men found little incentive to enter the industry. Even skilled miners sought jobs in other war-related industries, such as shipbuilding and aircraft manufacture, not only because of higher pay but also because of the possibilities for draft exemption. As Mills described the situation:

> Almost all of the United States employment agencies in and about the mining districts have orders for vast numbers of men. There is no possibility of their filling them all unless action is taken by the Government to see that each institution gets a quota based upon its needs and importance. . . . Now, I might add in there is a direct example, which is at Fallon, Nev. . . . There is a new airport going to be constructed. They are paying at the rate of $1 an hour for common labor and $1.50 for skilled labor. We were finally permitted after months of correspondence with the War Labor Board to pay . . . 85 cents to our miners. If the mine owner finds his pay is too low to attract the miner he must apply for relief to the War Labor Board, a long drawn-out procedure. This whole labor mess . . . tends to hurt the small miner.[3]

Western miners continuously complained about price levels set by the MRC or the Office of Price Administration (OPA). Mills produced vanadium and tungsten but felt that federal pricing policies deliberately discouraged small mines like his own. He charged that in November 1942 the MRC representative in Los Angeles announced that tungsten was plentiful and discouraged producers like himself. Then, on November 16, 1942, the MRC published what Mills termed a "socialistic" price schedule, and the corporation declared that any operation below certain determined levels was ineligible to bid on new contracts. At the same time the MRC issued a large contract to the U.S. Vanadium Corporation in Salt Lake City, which also had substantial processing facilities available.[4]

Other miners told similar tales of woe. Oscar Hogsett of Parker, Arizona, noted that whereas the MRC kept prices for minerals fairly steady, his production costs were constantly increasing. He charged that the price fixers in Washington were not considering the needs of small producers to make long-range plans and that the costs of small enterprises were higher than those of the large corporations. As Hogsett noted: "We are in a bad position in this country for manganese. . . . Manganese isn't like many other materials that run symmetrically. . . . It runs in and out, and when your high-grade streak runs out you have nothing but low-grade left. Then you have your development work to do to find your high-grade streak again. . . . If that price structure were more symmetrical . . . I believe I am safe in saying . . . they will double the amount of manganese shipped to the stock pile."[5]

Hundreds of such complaints were aptly summarized by Charles F. Willis, state secretary of the Arizona Small Mine Operators Association.

The Western Mining Industry at War

"Probably the foremost thing that has been brought out," said Willis, in discussing the many meetings of Arizona miners he had attended,

> has been the question of prices: First, the inadequacy of prices . . . ; second, the fact that a small mine necessarily has to have higher prices . . . ; Then the complications of the Washington plan on premiums, bonuses, and quotas . . . and all the tremendous red tape of routine and information that has to be filled out in order to get premium prices. . . . It is something the small fellow cannot do. He cannot submit the information and he cannot travel frequently to Washington. The price question is probably the greatest handicap to production that we have. If the price question were adequately answered, a lot of the other problems would disappear or at least be minimized.[6]

In commenting on the problems of Cliff Carpenter, a miner from Phoenix, Arizona, Willis pointed to what he considered to be the erroneous philosophy behind the government's price-fixing programs.

> The policies are drawn up by men who are industrialists. They know that when they build a factory to construct airplanes every factory they build is going to make airplanes. They know that every egg they lay is going to hatch. We know in mining that we have to lay 10 or more eggs to make 1 hatch. Therefore, if you are going to integrate your problems of mining . . . with your manufacturing facilities, you are going to have to lay a lot of eggs in order to get sufficient raw materials. Now, that is the fundamental philosophy that is lacking on the part of the policy makers in Washington . . . and the fundamental problem with the mining program.[7]

In addition to these frustrations, small-mine operators also chafed under a steadily expanding network of bureaucratic regulations, which introduced great uncertainty into their lives. Victor Hayek, secretary of the Mining Association of the Southwest in Los Angeles, voiced these feelings as he explained that his association had desperately tried to secure additional access roads to small operations. But he found it difficult merely to get data from the Public Roads Administration in Washington and was unable to receive a clear answer. "We are not seeking military information," he said, "but information as to what mining roads are being allocated or what specific mine-road projects have been approved, and where are those funds being used? I fear that this is not the type of information that should be withheld from the mining people of this district. . . . This is a very pertinent example of what we, as a mining association, are up against."[8]

The story of Charlie Brown reflects just how the maze of bureaucracy could stymie a small operation. Brown was the leading chrome producer in Placer County, California, but had to close his mine because it lacked an access road, one that had been provided for but not built. His account vividly reflects the problems small miners encountered with the federal bureaucracy.

Operating the largest chrome project in the Forest Hill district, Placer County, Calif., I wish to enter a complaint regarding the lack of aid we received from a number of different Federal agencies concerned with providing access roads to strategic mineral areas.

Our district qualified for such a road early in the summer of 1942, the forest supervisors at Nevada City, Calif., making a survey and recommending the expenditure of the sum of $10,000 for the grading and surfacing of the Finning Mill Road.

After several months there was no action, and winter was approaching. We called in the service of our Tri-County Chrome Association, which got busy with Washington and San Francisco authorities. Investigation showed there were so many agencies concerned in the expenditure of this small sum that the project was bogging down in red tape. The Tahoe National Forest office was concerned, also the forestry departments at Washington, their Salt Lake headquarters, and their San Francisco office. Then the Bureau of Mines in Washington and the Bureau's Salt Lake and San Francisco offices were concerned. But not one of all the officials of these agencies knew what had become of the matter. . . . There was more investigation, and finally one morning late in November a crew of men with borrowed county equipment came out to start the job. By noon that day, a snowstorm started; the equipment went back to town and nothing has been heard of the project since.

The red tape and delay which knocked us out of our winter road caused us to shut down for the winter and quit making deliveries of chromite.[9]

If Brown's odyssey was particularly frustrating, it was hardly unusual. The web of bureaucracy proved a real bane for most small western miners.

Right or wrong, these miners felt also that national mining policy was controlled by the large corporations in the industry. J. P. Hall, president of the Western Mining Council, pointed approvingly to an article by columnist Drew Pearson in October 1942, which he felt corroborated his own accusations. In a sensational piece Pearson charged that the WPB's Advisory Board on Mining was dominated by representatives of large eastern metals firms whose objective was to prevent the further growth of the mining industry in the West. Perhaps it was difficult to characterize the motivation of these men, but it was possible to identify their affiliations. They included Dr. John Johnston, who had been director of research for the U.S. Steel Corporation; Jay Jeffries from the General Electric Company, who had formerly been with the Aluminum Corporation of America; M. F. McConnell and Robert D. Sossman of the U.S. Steel Corporation; R. S. A. Dougherty, Charles M. Herty, and A. B. Kinzel of the Bethlehem Steel Company; James H. Critchell of the Union Carbide Corporation; and Clyde Williams, director of the Battelle Insti-

23

tute in Columbus, Ohio.[10] Westerners were obviously not well represented on this and most other advisory boards to federal agencies.

This was a sore point for most western miners and was openly voiced by such associations as the Western Mining Council. The council's statement to the Senate Committee on Small Business noted:

> We of the Western Mining Council are of the opinion that the main reason why small operators are not contributing more of their strategic and critical ores to the war effort can be determined right in Washington, D.C. . . .
> The lack of recognition of our western strategic and critical minerals is a disease of long standing—so long that it has affected every Federal and State mining department. Until the past year the United States Bureau of Mines has held to the theory that our domestic deposits should be conserved until we are forced to use them. This theory coupled with the "good neighbor" policy brought the exploration of our mineral resources practically to a complete stop.

And then the council charged that the federal minerals policy was dominated by the industry's large corporations. "These vast corporations, by means of key men on Donald Nelson's advisory board, actually control our mineral production and prevent thousands . . . of small owners from contributing to the war effort. If you cannot get by Nelson's advisory board you cannot mine."[11] If this was an exaggeration, nevertheless it accurately reflected the perception thousands of western miners had of themselves and of their place in the industry.

But of all the miners in the West it was the six thousand or more gold prospectors who suffered most after the War Production Board in 1942 ordered them to cease operation for the duration. Ostensibly the prime object of this directive was to conserve labor. The men in the WPB's Mining Division expected that gold miners would flock to more critical operations such as copper mining. Yet the WPB officials acted out of ignorance and with little sympathy for the West. A more realistic knowledge of gold mining would have alerted them to the fact that very few miners would take jobs involving other metals. And that was exactly what happened during the next four years. Meanwhile, the shutdown adversely affected thousands of miners in the region and decimated the small communities depending on them. The actual movement of a few hundred gold miners into other mining jobs hardly warranted the severe disruptions the WPB order caused.

The closing of the gold mines was gradual, beginning on July 29, 1941, when the OPM issued a directive limiting gold mining to conserve manpower and mining machinery. This order, P-56, excluded gold miners from eligibility for priorities to secure scarce materials. The directive caused hardships throughout the West but particularly in Alaska, where 799 of 855 gold mines were forced to close, putting 3,349 miners out of work.[12] So began the struggle over gold.

By the fall of 1941 OPM officials were convinced that they needed to take further restrictive action. At a meeting on November 25, 1941, Walter Gardner of the Federal Reserve Board and Shaw Livermore of the OPM argued for more limitations. They held additional discussions, and on March 12, 1942, Wilbur Nelson, chief of the Mining Division of the WPB (successor agency to the OPM) took their advice. He went to Reno, Nevada, to meet with western governors and congressmen to sound out opinion on the proposed closings. Speaking for his fellow westerners, Nevada Governor E. P. Carville strongly opposed such action.[13]

Westerners further expressed their displeasure at hearings of the Special Senate Committee on the Investigation of Silver in May 1942. Senator Pat McCarran of Nevada raised the question why the United States was exporting mining machinery overseas while denying it to domestic miners. In a letter to Wilbur Nelson he wrote: "I maintain that the object to be accomplished by those who propose shutting down the gold and silver mines will not be accomplished. The principal result would be the destruction of the moral and economic life of communities in the several states, without any beneficial results."[14] Time proved this to be an accurate assessment. But in 1942 McCarran had to fight hard for this point of view. That summer he met with William L. Batt, the new chief of the WPB Mining Division, but to little avail. Both the Army and the Navy departments were putting enormous pressure on the WPB to close the gold mines, and the WPB was already known to yield readily to the armed services.

By October 2, 1942, Donald Nelson, chairman of the WPB, had prepared an order calling for an end to gold production. On the following day Paul McNutt, chairman of the War Manpower Commission, and Wilbur Nelson met with McCarran in his office to tell him their decision. A day earlier Robert Patterson, the powerful undersecretary of war, had written to Batt: "I hope that prompt and effective action will be taken with regard to gold mining. I need not call your attention to the urgent need for more miners in the production of copper and other non-ferrous metals. . . . The longer the delay in shutting down gold mining, the further off will be the relief of the copper shortage. The matter has hung fire for some time, and I trust there will be no further delay."[15] A few days later Patterson was joined by James V. Forrestal, undersecretary of the navy. In their joint memo to Donald Nelson they were even more blunt and pushy. "The case of gold mining presents sharply the question whether we mean business or not," they said, "in doing everything possible to push war production." They estimated that two to three thousand hard-rock gold miners might transfer to the copper mines, an uneducated guess that did not materialize.[16]

Under such intense pressure Nelson yielded and on October 8 issued his famous Limitation Order L-208, formally closing all gold mines during the war. Perhaps it had more symbolic than real importance. Stopping gold production provided psychological assurance to the warlords in Washington that the nation was totally committed to the war effort. It was obviously done at the expense of westerners, but they were thousands of miles removed. The order came amidst an active debate between civilian and military leaders in Washington concerning maximum as well as minimum measures needed to make mobilization more effective. The line between essential and nonessential industries was not always clear, but the action appeared to signify American resolve for a full-scale effort.[17]

Understandably, westerners were furious about L-208. Legislatures in California, Nevada, South Dakota, and Alaska enacted resolutions condemning the action, even challenging the authority of the WPB to close down an entire industry. A group of thirty western U.S. senators petitioned the WPB on May 24, 1943, to rescind the order, but on June 15 the WPB denied their request.[18]

In operation, L-208 was totally ineffectual. At most 497 gold miners shifted to work in other mines. Wilbur Nelson of the WPB, who was appointed administrator of L-208, made detailed studies of its effects and formulated the results in official reports. In a memo to Howard I. Young of the WPB Nelson wrote of self-serving reports that other officials of that agency had made to claim the success of the program.

> In no place do any statistics refer to gold miners, but only to workers in gold mines. Those familiar with mine employment know that only about 60 per cent of the total workers at a mine are underground miners. . . . On the basis of my checks . . . it can readily be seen that instead of 1200 workers from gold mines going to copper . . . only between a third and a half of this number are actually working in such mines today. . . . 497 workers in gold mines probably were actually placed in metal mines and only a percentage of these workers were miners. . . . I believe that only between 3000 and 4000 tons of non-ferrous metals can be logically assumed as possible added production.[19]

The situation was neatly summed up by Edward H. Rott, deputy administrator of L-208 for the WPB. "The general effect of the Order has been to antagonize the individual, and the communities dependent on gold mining and caused large losses to the operators. . . . Many have lost their livelihood, relinquished leases, forfeited equity in equipment."[20] The order largely served as a symbolic test case for the broader federal policy of restricting nonessential industries.

The closing adversely affected the financial condition of some western states by reducing the severance taxes on gross mine production. Idaho, Montana, South Dakota, Utah, Arizona, New Mexico, and Alaska all suffered a significant loss of revenue. In Idaho, for example, the Homestake Mining Company had paid $1.2 million in such taxes during 1941. By 1943 this shrank to $98,929. Whatever symbolic significance the closing of the gold mines had in the heat of war—and even that was questionable—it had a decidedly negative effect on the West while having virtually none at all on its supposed prime goal—increasing the production of other metals.[21]

Not everyone in Washington was unsympathetic to the cause of the small miners, however, because many westerners and advocates of greater regional independence saw the war as an opportunity to lessen the dominance of big business in the mining industry. Among them Harold Ickes and his staff in the Department of the Interior were prominent, as well as New Deal liberals, Brandeisians, and antimonopolists. Yet this was not exclusively a liberal crusade. No less committed were Senator Pat McCarran of Nevada, a wide range of western political leaders in Congress and statehouses, and a substantial number of western business people. This was not so much a political as a regional issue that cut across political parties and ideologies.

Harold Ickes was clearly the most articulate and persistent proponent of western economic diversification, and he viewed the mining industry as one important means of attaining this goal. His aim was to increase domestic production of minerals, not only to bolster the economic fortunes of thousands of small mining enterprises but also to invigorate scores of communities. He hoped to lessen the region's dependence on eastern corporations and to increase its ability to shape its own destiny. In a letter to Senator Joseph O'Mahoney in 1942 he wrote:

> The West holds the answer to current problems of raw materials shortages which threaten the stability of great segments of industrial activity. . . . In the western States there are huge undeveloped resources of most of the very materials for lack of which the defense authorities are shutting off the supply of civilian industry. We have neglected our own resources and have been content to depend upon the output of other lands. Instead of developing the tungsten minerals of the Intermountain states, for example, we have sought tungsten in the remote parts of China. . . . The undeveloped mineral reserves of the West-

ern states constitute a challenge to a people who are rich beyond their dreams, but who have been led to believe that they are poor in the materials they need. . . . Most of the defense effort has been centered in the East . . . while the great mineral storehouse of the West remains almost untouched. . . . With few exceptions, mineral materials needed exist in ample amounts in the Rocky Mountains and neighboring states. There is a large force of unemployed men in those States. The knowledge of ways and means to make the minerals available is there, and railroads stand by to cooperate. . . . [A]dditional mineral development in the West provides the answer [to shortages].[22]

Ickes always viewed the West's minerals production within the broader context of economic development. Mineral resources and power were intimately related in this vision. "The Department's present program includes enough large scale development of our low-grade manganese ores . . . aluminum and magnesium . . . and low cost power." He was certain that new power projects would do a great deal to stimulate the processing of minerals that would otherwise be left untapped. And that would stimulate regional economic growth. "A wise and full development of the West is becoming increasingly clear to the Nation," he said with an optimism not universally shared. "The proper development of this region had been somewhat neglected, not by intent of the responsible agencies, not exactly by oversight, but by the policy of encouraging industrial plants to concentrate in the East. . . . If serious curtailments of our imports of minerals from overseas should occur, the rapid mineral and industrial development of the West would become a matter of life and death to us. We would find that the Battle of the West was as important as the Battle of the Atlantic."[23] Considering that he made these observations in 1941, he revealed much prescience.

In the exploitation of the region's minerals, Ickes took a decidedly long-range view. The West's economic future and its industrial expansion were more important than immediate defense needs. "The future of the West depends upon a greater diversification and a wider use of its resources," Ickes declared. That could be done "through the development of industries located close to the resources. No section of the Nation can prosper if it is treated as a colony; if its resources are pumped out of it and it is later left stranded. I believe that the West not only has many industrial opportunities, but has the right to insist that these opportunities be realized."[24]

In the early stages of the mobilization program Ickes had high hopes that it would stimulate western mines. "The immediate prospects favor a very considerable development of western mining and western power resources," he declared in 1941. "Certainly an all-out defense effort, which I personally feel we will make, would call forth a very great mining effort in the West, particularly in strategic minerals. . . . This great mining effort would involve low-grade ores and hitherto unused ores in many cases. . . . It could reasonably be expected to call forth, in turn, an increased fabricating and processing development as soon as it became clear to industrialists that the West insisted that it would no longer remain a raw-material hinterland for the East, and nothing else." Ickes felt that multipurpose power projects would do much to expand minerals industries.[25]

Mobilization promised to stimulate the whole western economy. "The defense activities have not yet been spread out through the West," Ickes noted.

> Presumably they will be spread out somewhat more in the future. Otherwise, there will be an even wider discrepancy between a more heavily industrialized East and a mining, agricultural-forest, or cattle West. This would be highly undesirable for the balanced economy of the Nation as the unbalanced economy of the South has been. . . . I believe that by taking thought now and working out a coordinated program for mining, industry, and agriculture in the Western States, the West will enter a new era of responsible progress. One of the reasons that I feel confident of this progress is that the Western States have, in recent years, been shaking loose a little from the control of some of the monopolizing interests which have had them firmly under a checkrein for so many years.[26]

In fact, Ickes not only placed minerals policy in the broader context of western economic development but also viewed it in an even wider philosophical framework as a means to preserve free enterprise in a democratic society. That meant that he was highly suspicious of big business, particularly monopolies and cartels. On the other hand, he had a decided sympathy for the underdog—in this case small business. Although originally a Bull Mooser, an admirer of Theodore Roosevelt's New Nationalism, Ickes was also a Jeffersonian at heart.

By January 1943 Ickes was becoming increasingly concerned about the further rapid growth of big business in mining and in other sectors of the economy. He decried the MRC's policy of relying primarily on imports rather than on domestic producers.

> Another battle we fight is to preserve free enterprise. We can clearly see the trend of most war contracts going to big business. War can be the final crushing blow to small business. It will take men of good will, hard intentions, and strong determination to protect and assure the future of America's small business. It will take ingenuity—economic, technologic, legislative, and administrative; it will take courage, guts, and more than lip service. More than all, it will take a burning conviction that the social and economic connotations of small business are an inseparable part of American life and of all democracy.[27]

29

The Western Mining Industry at War

Ickes emphasized that the crisis of the Great Depression through which Americans had just lived should serve as a grim reminder of the need to preserve the essentials of democracy.

> In this crisis of the Nation the people must cling to fundamentals. A depression reminded us that paper profits are not wealth; that a system exists for a people, and not a people for a system. In the thirties, to grapple with stark poverty in the midst of plenty, we reshaped some old concepts that stood between us and our wealth. Today the problem is much the same. The war reminds us that billion-dollar orders to billion-dollar corporations may fire too few cannon; that therefore no man's aid is too small to be spurned. Cannon and shell are made of the metals of our mineral ores, not of dollars and orders. . . . The fundamental fact and problem that we face is that both mineral resources and business talent lie idle. They must be brought together. In this aspect, small business, mineral ores and metals compose one problem. Small business is needed to get ores out of the ground and to fabricate metals. Without the metals of these ores small business cannot operate. Old concepts, threadbare business and financial habits and attitudes, ancient administrative procedures that block the way must be boldly reshaped or removed.[28]

Ickes decried the reliance on imports and urged the exploitation of low-grade ores in the West.

> The economics of mineral supplies . . . have been influenced by the operating structure of large industrial enterprises. This Nation, with its apparent unlimited wealth of minerals, in past years has crooned itself into thinking that it need only concern itself with the largest and richest ore deposits. Such ores were considered basic to our minerals industry. When we could no longer find them at home, we went abroad. . . . When war came, men now in Government and industry, who were trained in the peacetime business of getting minerals from bonanza ores thought that we could continue to import. "Oh" said they, quite naturally, "ample ships will be available." The Nazi submarine was Hitler's comment on that optimistic assumption.

Ickes urged more intensive exploration for low-grade domestic minerals.

> This has been done in Scandinavia. We must learn to use our sub-standard ores. . . . Monopoly freezes technology and prevents use of processes which could be used by small and medium sized operations. Opposition comes from the struggle of large corporations to maintain their dominant position at all costs. They wanted to develop only the processes they needed—not to develop processes for low-grade ores. And bankers trained to serve the needs of big business can be blind to the needs of small business. Today we must break the bottleneck occasioned by peacetime habits.[29]

From war, Ickes looked forward to the future of the western mining industry. "Should the small businessman go," he said, "we will all go. In fighting for him, we fight for all of us. Remember that in this fight the future will be molded more by what we do now than by what we plan for then. The plants that we build, the terms on which we build them,

30

the places where we put them, the persons to whom we give them—things like these are the mold that will determine the shape and structure of what is to be." He thought the best means to achieve these goals would be for the president to appoint a war minerals director to coordinate various federal policies affecting the mining industry. Obviously, he was thinking of himself for the position. He was also aware that Roosevelt disliked such centralized direction and that the president leaned more to Donald Nelson's view, which was to wait for the industry itself to shape the contours of the future.[30]

If he could play the key role in determining national minerals policy, Ickes resolved to put greater emphasis on the contributions of the small miners in the West and to restrict the emphasis on big business.

> We must do all we can . . . to assist our small operators to produce . . . but also to make certain that we will maintain a free competitive economy in which everyone, large and small, may have adequate opportunity in post-war America. . . . In the early stages of the defense and the war programs it appeared reasonable that the large enterprises, which had proven their capacity and ability to produce, should have been called on first. They had the materials, the resources, the know-how, and they were given large contracts to enable them to get under way with a minimum of delay. Today [1943], however, . . . it is paramount that we call into play every facility and enterprise that is available.[31]

Ickes was more eloquent than most, and his grasp of the big picture was outstanding, yet he was only one of a number of conservationists in the federal bureaucracy who were seeking greater prominence for the small western miners. Not all of them shared like ideologies. Some were nationalists like Ickes, whereas others were admirers of Brandeis and Wilson's New Freedom, favoring smallness and decentralization. But whatever their differences, they shared a vision of the West in which the war would bring the region greater economic independence. Moreover, they persisted in the Jeffersonian belief that small business should play a prominent role in the mining industry, not only for economic but also for social equality. Competition, rather than monopoly, was to characterize the postwar West. This Progressive vision was common in individuals as well as groups. Its spokesmen included some of those in Ickes's circle, such as Harry Slattery, Paul Raver, Harry Bashore, and Charles Eliot and Ralph Watkins of the National Resources Planning Board. To these men, mining policy was a key to achieving the broader goal of a more diversified western economy with a more egalitarian social structure.

Slattery was one of the most articulate proponents of small business. During the war he was administrator of the Rural Electrification Administration. He had become well known in the Theodore Roosevelt era as one of Gifford Pinchot's closest associates and one of the staunchest conservationists in public life. A skilled journalist, he had played a very active part in hounding Albert Fall and in revealing details about the Teapot Dome Scandal. Once a Bull Mooser like Ickes was ensconced in the Interior Department, Slattery found a congenial home there. In evaluating the national mining policy during the war Slattery waxed philosophical.

> Many years of public experience have given me a deep appreciation of the practically untouched resources of the West. One of the principal problems before the people of the United States today is to explore and determine the best methods of developing the natural resources—human as well as physical— to meet not only current defense needs but also to build a strong national economy. . . . One of the methods which have frequently been proposed . . . is the rational utilization of our natural resources through the development of small decentralized competitive enterprises designed to bring the strength of diversification to all parts of the country.

And then he brought his Brandeisian vision into full view. He wanted to espouse a theory he described as "The Greatness of Small Things." This was three decades before E. F. Schumacher, the British philosopher, wrote his paeans to smallness. "There is no doubt in my mind," said Slattery, "that numerous small decentralized plants will prove a great boon to the strength of our national economy." This could happen only if existing barriers to industrial development were removed. "Removal of these barriers . . . is not only a proper function of Government, but also the duty," Slattery concluded. As one example of the greatness of small things he cited the work of his own agency, the Rural Electrification Administration.[32]

Slattery reflected on the historical context of federal mining policies. "History repeats itself," he said, referring to his experience during World War I. "I was with Mr. Franklin K. Lane [secretary of the interior in the Wilson administration, 1913–20]. . . . I remember that the West brought the same arguments as you have here. I remember the War Minerals Board that grew out of those meetings and, under Secretary Lane's hammering with respect to the strategic minerals, the West did come into the picture, but not until quite late. It looks as if we are going through the same cycle." But Slattery hoped that a national stockpiling policy would become a reality. "Because modern mechanized warfare is an avaricious consumer of mineral products, our reserves must be so effectively developed, coordinated, and utilized that 'critical' shortages are impossible. The resources of the West must be tapped to meet these needs, and agriculture and industry must be so integrated as to guarantee the flow of essential supplies of all kinds. Decentralization of industry is an integral part of the program to achieve these objectives."[33]

Like Ickes, Slattery saw the expansion of public power as the key toward achieving decentralization of the mining industry and the western economy.

> The development of highly flexible and easily transportable electric power . . . have revolutionized the basic conditions of production. It is no longer essential to concentrate population in large urban centers for purposes of industrial production. For many years the economic and social desirability of decentralization has been recognized by great public leaders, among the first of which was . . . Justice Brandeis. . . . By providing assistance . . . the Government can break down many of the barriers now impeding the development of numerous decentralized enterprises in the West and create a strong economic society capable of raising and maintaining living standards. Such a development would make a substantial contribution to both the demands of our present all-out total defense program and to the long range economic stability of . . . the West. . . . It is clear that economic growth in this area is a matter of eliminating . . . barriers to the West, and if this had been done earlier it would unquestionably have been a more greatly developed country.

And then he concluded, in a familiar refrain of anticolonialists in the West, "You are never going to have a development of the resources in the West . . . until landlordism moves from other sections of the country and is controlled in your section."[34]

The crucial role of small miners in the hoped-for economic diversification of the West was also stressed by Paul Raver, administrator of the Bonneville Power Administration and one of the nation's leading advocates of public power. A major obstacle to western economic expansion, Raver believed, was

> the large amount of investment needed in a number of these mineral-using industries. . . . Among these other obstacles is first the concentration of output of some of these industries and their markets in the hands of a few corporations. I need not point out . . . the implications of such concentration to the freedom of enterprise and new industrial development. I do not mean to imply that these obstacles are completely blocking today all new channels of enterprise in the West. Many . . . feasible . . . opportunities . . . have not yet materialized. We certainly must question why they have been so long held back. For example, I am greatly puzzled why new electrolytic zinc capacity has not been added to the Pacific Northwest when it is obviously necessary and feasible on the basis of available concentrates and cheap power. Similarly, I am puzzled by the lack of explosives and munitions plants in the Western states in spite of the fact that the raw materials and the power are available.[35]

Like Ickes and other advocates of economic diversification, Raver urged greater government support of the small miners in the West. As he saw it, the mining industry was characterized by two major trends. "One of these has been the control by a few large industries of mineral deposits, such as bauxite, magnesite, and molybdenum. . . . The other has been the obvious tendency to treat the West as a colonial dependency of the United States, not only by industry, but unfortunately, to some extent by Government itself, as for example, in the I.C.C. freight structure." What was needed now in wartime was a much more intensive exploitation of western mineral resources.

> We could, of course, continue to rely upon eastern industries to use western minerals at the time and place determined by them. This, however, would leave many western mineral developments to arbitrary decisions governed by special interests. On the other hand, the most effective and large scale development of western minerals would unquestionably be secured through the development of industries in the western states using those deposits. Such a development would reduce the uneconomic effect of monopolistic restraints exercised by certain large corporations. . . . Such industrial development would go far toward emancipating the West from its colonial status.[36]

D. F. Hewett of the metals section in the U.S. Geological Survey further developed the argument that small miners would invigorate the whole western economy. In advocating more intensive utilization of western minerals, he placed the World War II era in historical perspective. Mining in the region, he believed, was in transition from an earlier epoch in which precious metals were exploited before agricultural development. But in the 1930s, by contrast, agricultural growth and expansion of electric power were balancing mineral development. This phase reflected a more balanced economy that provided a foundation for an expanded population, growth of new markets, and substantial industrial development. If only more electric power were to become available in western localities, the trend of exporting raw materials outside the region for fabrication would be arrested. Needed, therefore, was government assistance to mineral producers of the West and scientific guidance to enable these producers to exploit new discoveries.[37]

The theme that development of the West's mineral resources depended on the expansion of cheap power was enthusiastically supported by Harry W. Bashore, commissioner of the Bureau of Reclamation. "If the mineral resources of the West are to be brought into the service of the Nation," he said, expressing the conventional wisdom of the bureau that was planning the damming of much of the region, "low cost power must be available to every location where strategic materials are located. Such power is essential in extracting the minerals from the earth as well as in operating, fabricating, and serving industries, and for the population engaged in these activities." And then, plugging the programs of his own bureau, he noted that "reclamation has kept open the Nation's last frontier. It is providing the family-size farms which are the backbone of the country."[38]

Until abolished by Congress in 1943, the National Resources Planning Board was also an avowed advocate of the small miners of the West. Ralph Watkins, its associate director, was a highly respected economist who viewed the mining industry in the broader context of economic growth. Total self-sufficiency for the West was not desirable, he believed, because it would lower real income. Only about 2.5 percent of the western labor force was in mining, and certainly few new jobs would be created by expanding the industry. But such expansion could trigger a much more broadly based economic growth. Manufacturing offered far better prospects for diversification, and clearly the processing of minerals would lead to an increase of manufacturing. That, of course, depended on the availability of low-cost power, particularly for metallurgical industries.

Once these elements were in place Watkins foresaw the realization of the dream of economic diversification. When manufacturing was expanded, then "consumer industries would develop. Population growth in the West . . . promises to afford an economic market for a more varied industrial structure. The advantages of the region in climate and recreational facilities will attract a greater proportion of the total population as the average age of the American people increases and as income standards rise. Food processing, household equipment, furniture . . . may all experience a considerable expansion in coming decades." Watkins's predictions were remarkably accurate in light of subsequent events. As for wartime mining policy, he urged, "We must take the *broad* view and the *long* view . . . the development of *all* our resources, each in harmony with the other, to the end of maximum combined benefit to the people of the United States."[39]

The long view was not always as apparent in Congress, where representatives from western states tried strenuously to promote the interests of the small miners. One of the most outspoken advocates was Senator James E. Murray from Montana. As early as 1940 his lobbying of the Reconstruction Finance Corporation had led that agency to liberalize its lending policy for small mining enterprises. It was his persistent needling of the War Production Board that ultimately led it to authorize establishment of a milling plant for manganese in Butte. The constant pressure his Senate Committee on Small Business exerted on the WPB most likely resulted in a more sympathetic attitude toward the western mining industry. It was Murray's belief that extensive testimony before his committee persuaded the MRC to allow an increase in prices for selected metals and the establishment of a limited program of stockpiling. Although unable to prevent the closing of the gold mines, he did much to publicize the issue. He also persistently campaigned to limit imports and to place greater reliance on domestic sources. And his access to the president often led him to plead the domestic industry's case directly with Roosevelt.[40]

Nevertheless, Murray had no illusions. "Of course, this is a big country," he said. "The Western States have a very sparse representation . . . and it is often very difficult for us to get measures through which affect the particular interests of the West. There is somewhat of a hostility especially against mining." Yet he believed that the encouragement of small mining operations in the West had significance beyond the region. "This is sound national policy," he rationalized. "By this policy, we are preserving our American system of free enterprise in the mining industry. This is one policy . . . entitled to the unanimous approval of the American people."[41]

Murray was sometimes joined by Senator James G. Scrugham of Nevada, another active defender of the western minerals industry. Scrugham was most concerned with the lack of a coordinated national mining policy, since federal agencies such as the MRC, the WPB, and the OPA, to name only a few, made rules without much mutual consultation. "There is a lack of a co-ordinated over-all policy," he said. "Small operators are shunted from office to office . . . [amidst] helter-skelter activity and lack of policy." And he reiterated the concern about reliance on foreign ores.

> Our great quarrel with the W. P. B. Mineral Division is that they are prone to minimize the value of the small domestic deposits and place reliance on foreign production and importations. . . . The argument that is advanced is that we should not deplete these mineral deposits of our country, but should save them for future generations and should use the deposits of foreign countries. That would be all right, but no one knows at present what stupendous developments there will be in science and a metal that may be very valuable today might be of little use tomorrow. Who would have thought that the great production of Nevada today is not gold or silver, hardly copper, but a metal not heard of a few years ago—magnesium.[42]

Western congressmen also tried to present their case in the House. Representative Harry Welch of California noted: "The mining industry of the West and specifically as it applies to California, is at the crossroads of opportunity. . . . Now is the psychological time for you people to come into your own." His main concern was to boost the domestic stockpiling program through increased domestic production. And the war, he believed, provided an unusual opportunity for such action. "We are riding the crest of the wartime program. None of us wanted to break into business on a condition like that, but nevertheless it is here, and we will have to make the best of it. . . . If we people in California don't take advantage of the situation . . . we are going to find ourselves back in the same development effigy that we were in over a long period of time. . . . I want to see the West come into its own."[43]

Congressman Mike Mansfield from Montana expressed similar views. He also was primarily concerned with backing the federal government's stockpiling program, and he supported legislation toward that end. "I am very much interested in this matter of stock-piling assurances," he said. "The little fellow can't keep on taking the chances as he has been. He can't depend on a contract for 3 or 6 months, or even a year. After all, it takes quite a bit of time to get back the money he has invested, and I feel it is the duty of your Government to assure the small producer the necessary return."[44] That attitude prevailed among western members of Congress, who felt that they could not save the small miners if they left these producers to their own devices.

Many western corporation executives also felt that the mining industry was the key to further industrial diversification in the West. "We are Western men," declared William M. Jeffers, president of the Union Pacific Railroad.

> We . . . are intensely interested in the development of the West. . . . It has been a matter of great concern to us western men during the past year or two . . . to see so many industries located in the congested areas in the East. Naturally, population follows industry. We do not believe it is entirely fair to the West to see the labor of the West forced to leave their home States to find employment in these congested areas. We feel . . . that in . . . the national emergency if we are ever going to be recognized . . . now is the time to do it. . . . I firmly believe with respect to the deposits we have there—iron, coal, oil and gas, and other minerals—that if we can get started on their development, that will be permanent.[45]

Jeffers's perception was similar to that of other railroad men. B. W. Scandrett, vice-president of the Northern Pacific Railroad, noted, "The Northern Pacific, like every other railroad, is very naturally interested in doing anything it can in developing the mineral resources of this western territory." F. R. Newman, a vice-president of the Great Northern Railroad, concurred but had additional specific suggestions. "We work with researchers at various western state universities," he explained. "If they had behind them the prestige of a federal body to give broader consideration to . . . the usefulness and possibilities of various metals and minerals, I think it would be helpful and would make for the West as a whole a pretty good showing."[46]

But sentiments in the West differed from those in Washington, where myriad federal agencies were engaged in various aspects of mining with no coordination. Each agency had its own concerns, but their functions often overlapped. The War Production Board was a major player in the policy-making game. With hundreds of millions of dollars at its disposal, the Metals Reserve Company was also a power to be reckoned with, whereas the Office of Price Administration exerted a major influence as well. Trailing behind in influence were the Bureau of Mines and the U.S. Geological Survey in the Department of the Interior, the Bureau of Reclamation, the General Land Office, the National Park Service, the Forest Service, and a host of other agencies. From the welter of decisions made by the bureaucrats, a kind of patchwork quilt of federal mining policy emerged, although its directions were less than crystal clear. Not surprisingly, therefore, the western view of this federal policy was somewhat clouded.

Perhaps the War Production Board had the most difficult problems. In addition to allocating scarce minerals to industry through a complicated priority system, it also had to watch price levels in order to curb inflation. At the same time it had to balance foreign imports with domestic production, taking due consideration of the need to conserve the nation's mineral resources. But that was only half of its difficulties. The WPB also had to coordinate domestic policy with foreign economic policies. The good-neighbor policy toward Latin America required hefty imports of metals from that region in part because of political considerations. And although the WPB may not have been overly happy to buy much of Spain's output of tungsten, the president's policy of keeping Spain neutral in the war overrode strictly economic considerations. In addition, the WPB was extremely sensitive to the procurement demands of the armed forces, who had first priority in most policy deliberations. Donald Nelson, no wonder, was an extremely harried man. The variables he had to consider regarding a national mining policy were considerably more complex than those that were of primary concern to western miners.

But by 1943 the confusion in Washington over mining policies had become increasingly irritating to westerners, and Senator Murray took the initiative to seek clarification. In a letter to Roosevelt on February 19, he noted: "While our industries obviously must be curtailed to fit the raw material supply, at the same time the domestic raw material supply should be increased. . . . The tendency to withhold facilities for domestic strategic and critical mining expansion may not have been brought to your attention. I think a change in policy should be instituted." Roosevelt passed the letter on to Donald Nelson on March 11, 1943, and asked him to completely review the war metals program. The beleaguered Nelson called in R. S. Dean, assistant director of the U.S. Bureau of Mines, and Howard I. Young, chairman of the WPB's Minerals and Metals Advisory Committee. These men worked on a draft for a comprehensive policy statement, in consultation with Harold Ickes. On April 17, Nelson published the finished document under his own name.[47]

As the conductor of a cacophonic symphony, Nelson tried to conciliate various interest groups. "It is national policy," he declared, "to do full detailed production planning and to make actual investments now and in the near future . . . for certain metals and minerals. It is national policy to carry out exploration and determination of reasonably satisfactory sources of materials with full proving of reserves . . . for all critical metals and minerals through 1948."[48]

Beyond such generalities Nelson also stated some specific guidelines. "It is national policy to get the maximum possible output domestically and also to bring in as much as we can from overseas," he noted. If this sounded contradictory, it may have been because the statement reflected sharp divisions. "Contrasting views on this subject have been expressed," Nelson added in an understatement. "One view is that imports should be relied upon as much as possible in order to . . . conserve our own national resources. The other view is that domestic production should be increased to the maximum. My position is that these views are not mutually exclusive. . . . As I size up the risks involved in seeking all we can get versus something short of that, the risks are much less serious under a policy of seeking all we can get." Perhaps Nelson was less than frank in this regard because the WPB did not really encourage maximum minerals production in the West, but his statement brought the problem out into the open and henceforth made the WPB bureaucracy more conscious of the needs of domestic producers.

Nelson also announced that national policy would call for "the fullest possible use of small and marginal ore deposits," subject to certain limitations. These included the availability of labor and critically scarce materials and equipment. This was clearly a victory for Murray, Scrugham, Ickes, and those who had championed the cause of the smaller western mining operations. In addition, Nelson yielded to another demand of the westerners, noting, "It is national policy to build up stock piles of strategic and critical metals and minerals to insure us against unforseen [sic] developments." This had been a long-standing demand of westerners, and they were heartened to see its inclusion in a national mining policy declaration. Nelson also agreed that the mining industry should receive special treatment in equipment and labor allocation. Thus, although little was done in wartime concerning the structure of the industry or the role of the large corporations in it, many of the proposals made by the western miners were incorporated into public policy. Their crusade had not been in vain.[49]

With Nelson's announcement of guidelines for a national wartime mining policy, small miners in the West won acceptance of at least some of their demands. By their agitation throughout the war they had forced themselves on the consciousness of some of the eastern industrialists who dominated federal agencies. By 1943 the MRC and the OPA had made selective adjustments in price ceilings to benefit the small producers. And the WPB and the MRC now placed greater emphasis on domestic minerals production and adopted a policy of limited stockpiling. Low-interest loans for small mining enterprises became a reality after Maury Maverick became chairman of the Smaller War Plants Corporation. The WPB also gave small miners greater consideration in granting priorities for scarce materials.

All these measures reassured westerners. On the other hand, the structure of the industry did not change appreciably. Mobilization accentuated rather than diminished economic concentration. National policy continued to emphasize imports rather than domestic industry. Such concerns reflected broader foreign policy considerations as well as a desire to conserve domestic reserves. The mining industry thus did not contribute as much to economic diversification of the West as Ickes and the proponents of new processing facilities in the West had hoped. Nor did Ickes secure the centralization of federal mining policy in the Department of the Interior as he had planned. In particular, he was disappointed by the rejection of his proposal to initiate a national registration of all mineral claims.[50] Instead, federal mining policy continued to be a conglomeration of pragmatic programs administered by various federal agencies, without overall direction. This resulted less by accident than design, reflecting an inarticulate consensus of the various sectors of the industry, both large and small. And the war crystallized the realization that the United States was no longer self-sufficient as a minerals producer but was increasingly dependent on foreign imports. Perhaps that was the most important influence the war had in reshaping the western economy during these years. One era had ended, and another began.

CHAPTER 3

Wartime Industries
in the West:
Shipbuilding

I N T H E reshaping of the western economy during World War II the shipbuilding industry played a significant role. Although the infusion of federal money for shipbuilding was temporary and largely confined to the war years, it left long-lasting effects. Government investment, unlike that in World War I did not simply create a boom-and-bust phenomenon, so familiar to westerners. Instead, it triggered trends that helped to alter the economic structure of the West in the postwar era. It spurred a population increase, since many who came to work in the shipyards remained in the region, finding different types of employment after the war. Shipbuilding also spawned a wide range of related manufacturing industries. Although concentrated on the West Coast, it relied on thousands of subcontractors throughout the region. In addition, the shipyards stimulated many kinds of service establishments that proved significant for the economy, then and in later years. The vast sums the federal government poured into shipbuilding contributed to the growth of the military-industrial complex, an increasingly significant factor in the western economy. To some extent, shipbuilding also contributed to fostering new industries in the region, such as steel and electronics. In short, ship construction bolstered western economic growth in various ways during the war and for decades thereafter.

The wartime shipbuilding industry fostered many changes, of which the development of mass-production techniques was perhaps the most significant. Its influence was many sided. One result was a reorientation of management philosophy. In a craft-industry environment, corporate officers prided themselves on product knowledge. But in the sphere of mass production, managers were more concerned with their organizational skills and their ability to coordinate various production factors. Thorough knowledge of a particular industry became secondary.

In the Pacific Coast shipbuilding industry, the new entrepreneurs undertook a veritable revolution by developing assembly-line organization and prefabrication. This was bound to affect their workers. Skilled craftsmen were no longer vital to the new order; instead, unskilled or semiskilled people became the backbone of wartime shipbuilding. This in turn created new job opportunities for women and minorities, who had previously been largely excluded from the work force.

The development of mass production also affected perceptions of "just profits" as well as accounting standards. Before 1940 the principle of fair return on original cost or investment had been a widely used standard in many industries and public regulatory bodies. But with the increasing emphasis on managerial skill such a standard lost some of its relevance. Increasingly, the degree of management expertise, rather than the finished product, came to be used as a measure by which to apportion profits. Such changes were gradual, but they became a part of the postwar debate over fair profits in the shipbuilding industry.

Westerners played a crucial role in the national shipbuilding program, in both the quantity of ships produced and the striking innovations in ship manufacturing. Collectively, the Pacific Coast shipyards accounted for 52 percent of all vessels built during the war. For special categories, such as merchant ships, the percentages were even higher. Major ship construction centers grew in the Los Angeles and San Francisco Bay areas, in Portland, Oregon, in the Seattle-Vancouver region, and even in inland cities such as Denver. And each of these metropolitan regions had networks of subcontractors in other western states.

California was a focal point of West Coast ship construction. In addition to several older and smaller yards, S. D. Bechtel operated Calship in Los Angeles, one of the largest in the nation. Bechtel was head of one of the nation's biggest construction companies and had participated in the building of Boulder Dam. By 1941 he was applying his contracting skill to ships. But the San Francisco Bay was the center of wartime shipbuilding. It accounted for more than one-third of all the tonnage built in the war. Four major Kaiser yards in Richmond concentrated on producing Liberty ships and merchant vessels as well as "baby" aircraft carriers. In nearby Vallejo, the U.S. Navy's large Mare Island Yard built and repaired a wide range of naval vessels. Alameda boasted an established facility, the Moore Dry Dock Company, which worked on merchant ships as well as naval craft. South San Francisco boasted several smaller yards, and across the bay in Sausalito S. D. Bechtel built Marinship, one of the most efficient operations of its kind.[1]

The Pacific Northwest was another important site for ship construction during these years. Henry Kaiser's son Edgar built and managed Oregonship in Portland, which quickly established itself as the fastest yard in the United States. In the Portland-Vancouver area the Kaisers built vast new facilities such as the Swan Island Yard in Portland. Older companies, such as the Todd Shipyards and the Seattle-Tacoma Shipbuilding Company, concentrated more on the repair of naval vessels, including rebuilding some of the ships that survived the Japanese attack on Pearl Harbor.[2]

In the interior Denver became a significant center for the building of LSTs (landing craft) and barges. Its shipyards manufactured prefabricated parts for these vessels, which were then shipped by rail to the Mare Island Yard in Vallejo, California. There the ships were assembled, finished, and tested before undergoing formal launchings. It was an awesome sight to watch the long trains of the Union Pacific Railroad slowly wend their way over the Rocky Mountains to deliver these vessels. One of the first ships to make the trek was the SS *Carr*, which Cynthia Carr, the daughter of Colorado Governor John Carr, christened in Denver with snow brought from Pike's Peak. The ship was then transported to Vallejo where, after assembly, navy officials rechristened it the SS *Bentinck*, and sent it on its way in Pacific waters.[3]

The need for more ships did not really impress Americans until several months after the fall of France. By December 1940 President Roosevelt was alerting the nation about the need to bolster Great Britain. In a series of speeches he began to call for the increased production of ships in the United States. He noted: "The world situation requires that we develop a merchant marine capable of handling our commerce as foreign ships are withdrawn because of the war. . . . The Maritime Commission's construction programs . . . are therefore of special value."[4] In 1940 and 1941 German U-boats were exacting a frightful toll on Allied shipping in the North Atlantic, sinking about 450,000 tons monthly. That was about four times as fast as the ships could be replaced. The president first sought to bring his mobilization program to life after meeting with British Prime Minister Winston Churchill in December 1941, just after Pearl Harbor. He called on American shipyards to produce eight million tons in 1942 and ten million the following year, amounting to a tenfold increase in production.

Vice-Admiral H. L. Vickery, a member of the U.S. Maritime Commission, remembered those hectic times well. As he recalled in 1944, "In the early part of 1942, actually . . . in Christmas week . . . the President sent for me and told me he wanted to increase the troop-carrying capacity of our merchant fleet . . . because it was one of the things that he could see from the analysis of the fleet that we were going to be short of." As for meeting the president's production goals, Vickery had told Roosevelt, "We cannot make 9 million tons of ships, because I think all I can get is about 7 million tons." Vickery remembered, "That is all I could see in 1942, but I said, I will get 15 million tons in 1943 if you want it, and I immediately began to look around to see where I could find additional yards and additional yard managements." Meanwhile, the armed services were pressuring the president to raise production goals. On February 18, 1942, Army Chief of Staff George C. Marshall wrote Roosevelt that the demand for additional ships was more urgent than ever. The following day Admiral Emory C. Land, chairman of the U.S. Maritime Commission, went to see the president to ask him to raise that year's ship production goals again, from eighteen to twenty-four million tons. Roosevelt readily agreed. But when Land approached eastern shipbuilders with these figures they scoffed. There was absolutely no way, they told him, that they could speed up their schedules and even try to come near to such totals.[5]

This created a real dilemma. What could be done? Vickery and Land decided on two courses of action. "I came back from the meeting," Vickery said, "and immediately started issuing contracts." In addition, he and Land decided to go on a nationwide tour of shipyards. They planned to travel along the Atlantic Coast, to the South and the Gulf, and then up and down the Pacific Coast to assess the potential of existing facilities.[6]

Initially Vickery sent telegrams to shipyards around the nation on March 2, 1942, also asking them to submit bids for building new yards. In the West he approached the Six Companies, Inc., which had completed Boulder Dam. He was aware that these contractors had had little experience with shipbuilding but that they did have a reputation as miracle workers in the construction industry. When they had completed Boulder Dam in 1935 it was the largest such structure in the world. Between 1935 and 1941 they had also finished scores of military installations for the armed forces and were known to complete big projects efficiently and with dispatch. Among the Six Companies, those of Henry J. Kaiser and S. D. Bechtel were prominent. As Vickery noted: "We were not at that time buying shipbuilding brains. What we were buying was management brains. I knew the Bechtels and their people."[7]

Vickery received the first affirmative reply from S. D. Bechtel. Within a day Bechtel phoned to say that he would immediately begin to plan for an entire new shipbuilding operation in Sausalito, California. He thought it a good spot to build a yard because it was not a congested area. "We discussed very thoroughly the . . . labor situation over there," Vickery said. Bechtel vividly remembered the Maritime Commission's request: "We received a wire . . . [asking whether] we would operate another yard for the Maritime Commission. We were then sponsoring the operation of Calship on Terminal Island. [The] wire stated that the site of the yard should be a west coast port where our organization could operate to best advantage. . . . He connected that with a pretty strong appeal to us by stating that they were relying upon us to contribute our individual or-ganizations in order to build ships faster. . . . This wire was unsolicited. Frankly, it was a surprise to us." Between March 2 and 8 Bechtel made an estimate and with his staff worked out a complete proposal. By March 8 he was in Washington to present his plan to Vickery. The admiral gave him immediate verbal approval, and on March 12 the Maritime Com-mission issued a formal contract to Marinship, as the new company was to be called, to build at Sausalito. Within six months the yard was em-ploying eleven thousand men and women and was launching its first ships. Vickery, inspecting it in July, was tremendously impressed. At that time Bechtel told him: "A number of old-time ship-yards told us we were crazy to do it that way. I asked him what he thought of it. He said that is the only way we can do it because if you were to do it in the normal fashion you will still not be getting ships out, and they are the things we need."[8]

Meanwhile, in late February 1942 Vickery had begun his tour of ship-yards. He recalled that just before he left Washington the president had told him that he wanted "to increase the troop carrying capacity of our merchant fleet. . . . So, naturally, I looked to the older companies to build these ships. I had only three of the older companies who could undertake any of the work." And the older companies told Vickery that his demands were simply unrealistic. As he looked and listened he became convinced that traditional production methods just would not work. "Those people who have not had shipbuilding experience," he said a little while later, "have done a better job than the people who have had it. . . . If I had stopped to find out who had shipbuilding experience . . . I would not have gone to town with the Kaiser people, and it is not really shipbuilding we are doing on those ships. It is the manufacture of a standard-type ship. . . . It is a far cry from the normal shipbuilding pro-cedure. We are using inexperienced personnel and training them to do one particular job in a shipbuilding operation. Actually, they are not involved in the structural design of the ship." Mass-produced ships were coming out of the yards with revolutionary new designs, "all laid out on the principle that the material flows through the structural shops, and from the structural shops flows to the assembly plants, and from there on down to the shipways."[9]

Vickery was particularly impressed by the shipyards in the West. There he found attitudes quite different from those in the well-established yards of the East and the South. Instead of being wedded to age-old procedures, the western executives to whom Vickery spoke—men like the Bechtels and their partner John McCone, or like Henry J. Kaiser—were imaginative and daring and far more disposed to experiment with new techniques—and to think big.[10]

The Kaisers, Henry J. and his twenty-three-year-old son, Edgar, made an especially good impression on the admiral. In 1942 Henry Kaiser had only very limited experience in shipbuilding, having spent much of his career in road and dam construction. During his early career he had often taken his family along to the various construction sites, so that his sons early imbibed the entrepreneurial spirit and know-how of their father. Kaiser's limited interest in ships began in 1940 when he contracted with the Todd Shipyards in Seattle to repair two small cement carriers owned by his Permanente Cement Company. The impatient and restless Kaiser did not get along well at all with Todd and broke with them after two months. He then began to build ships himself for the British government at a Richmond, California, yard. With the direct help of British inspectors he started on a small scale, building an adaptation of a British tramp steamer. In an expanded version, Kaiser transformed this into the famed Liberty ship of World War II. Meanwhile, he installed his oldest son, Edgar, as manager of a new yard, Oregonship, in Portland.[11]

Just as the president was announcing higher goals for ship construction during the first half of 1942, the Kaisers were setting new records. In February Oregonship broke all previous schedules by building a ten-thousand-ton merchant ship in 71 days. Eastern builders had insisted that it would take a minimum of 360! Oregonship maintained its reputation as the fastest shipyard in the West—and the nation—and became the industry pacesetter. But the miracle at Portland was followed within a few days at Kaiser shipyard no. 3 in Richmond, California, which produced a vessel in just 80 days. Vickery was convinced. On February 20, 1942, he asked Edgar Kaiser to meet him while he was touring Mobile, Alabama. There they discussed increasing production in Seattle and Portland and expanding production in Vancouver to include twelve shipways. In addition, Vickery asked Kaiser to build an entirely new yard on Swan Island so that the Portland facilities would have thirty-one shipways. At the same time Vickery sent a telegram to Henry Kaiser instructing him to expand his Richmond yard from nine to twelve ways and in short order asked him to build a fourth yard in Richmond.[12]

During this period Vickery had virtual carte blanche from Roosevelt. Speaking of these hectic days just after Pearl Harbor, Vickery noted:

> We increased our production under directive of the President. When Mr. Churchill and the President were here they asked me if I could step up production. . . . I said "if I can get 8 million tons in 1942 it will be no problem in getting 10 million tons in 1943." He said, "can you do it?" I said, "I would like to ask three questions before I do it. In the first place, can I have enough steel to do it?" He said, "How much steel do you want?" I said, "I want this much steel plate a month. Secondly, can I select the managements and have these yards where I want them without interference from anybody?" The President said, "Did I ever interfere with you?" I said, "No, you never did." And he said, "I have no intention of doing so." The third thing I wanted was a 48-hour week on straight time.[13]

Vickery never regretted his decision on the Kaisers, and his respect for them did not flag. At war's end he noted:

> I would say of all the yards and of the management . . . the outstanding people are Edgar Kaiser and Clay Bedford [Henry Kaiser's manager at Richmond]. They are two of the ablest people I have been able to get to come into this program. . . . As far as the Kaiser production record goes I do not think there is any question about that. The record speaks for itself. They have the cheapest cost in man-hours, and the lowest total cost, dollar cost, and off on 11 ways they produce 17 ships per month. Richmond yards #2 and 3 together have produced more ships than any other yards in the country.

And when new yards were built in the East, such as those of the Rheem Company in Providence, Rhode Island, Vickery told them, "You better go out and take a look at those west coast yards . . . where various new techniques had been developed." As a result, some eastern yards now imitated many features pioneered in the West, such as greater spaces between the heads of ways and fabricating shops. Western shipbuilders were setting the pace.[14]

The management style of the newcomers to the shipbuilding industry differed sharply from that of established easterners. The latter included many trained in naval architecture or marine engineering, and workers on the job were usually skilled in the manifold operations needed to build a vessel. They were concerned with quality and individualized production and took enormous pride in shipbuilding as a profession. But the construction engineers—men like the Kaisers, the Bechtels, or John Mc-Cone—had a very different orientation. They viewed shipbuilding not as distinctive but as only one of hundreds of mass-production industries, one that had not kept up with new modes of production. To them ship-building was just another engineering problem in which thousands of operations had to be synchronized to turn out the final product. Building a ship was not a labor of love. It was a job that involved harnessing vast amounts of materials, hiring a largely unskilled labor force, and training workers to perform a single operation or several simple ones. Once the materials and workers had been gathered, then it was management's challenge to arrange work spaces and to regulate the flow of moving materials, coordinating thousands of operations and prefabricated parts as quickly as possible.[15] This was clearly mass production as opposed to a craft industry.

Ironically, mass production was the West's major contribution to ship-building, although the region was not industrialized. "In this type of shipbuilding," Vickery said, "shipbuilding experience has not been nec-essary, and those people who have not had shipbuilding experience have done a better job than the people who have had it." As one observer of the industry, Van R. Sill, aptly noted: "This was a 'natural' for contrac-tors . . . used to assembling huge quantities of heavy materials, hiring and training crews of skilled and unskilled workers, coordinating opera-tions for maximum speed and improvising new methods when old ones were inadequate. To them, building a ship was simply a matter of building another kind of structure."[16]

As they started out in the first months of 1942, the new shipbuilders tried to make use of those with experience in the industry. The Kaisers, for example, combed the Pacific Coast for men with prior expertise. Such individuals were few and far between, since shipbuilding in the West had largely disappeared after World War I. In fact, between 1920 and 1939 western shipyards did not construct a single merchant vessel, confining themselves to small-scale repair projects or to naval ships. Thus, the Kaisers considered themselves lucky to secure the services of Edward Hannay, Sr., who had been one of the Pacific Coast's master shipbuilders from 1917 to 1920. He appointed his son, Edward Hannay, Jr., as marine superintendent and rounded up a group of experienced individuals who had worked with him previously. Among them were sixteen experienced managers, who were soon joined by a much larger group from the Kaiser organization. Hannay was horrified when one of these ex–dam builders asked, "When do we pour the keel?"[17] That was the beginning of rivalry and mutual dissatisfaction.

Within a few months the experienced craftsmen became embroiled in bitter controversies with their new employers and left their yards, some-times voluntarily and sometimes with pink dismissal slips. The old-timers

required little or no skills, in contrast to the artisans of the prewar era. In his yards at Richmond, Portland, and Vancouver, Kaiser laid out his facilities to allow a continuous flow of production processes. He stored building materials in various locations around the yards, and workers then moved them to the shipways as needed. Each part of the fabrication shop specialized in only one operation. Parts were supplied by hundreds of subcontractors throughout the West, and most Kaiser workers performed some form of assembly. If particular parts were too heavy for women or older people to handle, management devised new automatic machines to perform such functions.[22]

The development of new production techniques was not always painless but was often the result of much trial and error. In 1942, for example, the Kaiser managers at Vancouver hoped to follow a procedure successfully pioneered at their Richmond yard. This involved placing completed deckhouses—each weighing about 210 tons—directly on ships in the process of assembly. But the Richmond operation specialized in Liberty ships, whereas the Vancouver yard concentrated on landing barges, troop transports, and small aircraft carriers. No one knew whether the Richmond technique could be adapted. On October 14, 1942, the Kaiser managers tried it in Vancouver, but the cranes holding the deckhouse dropped it some twenty feet into the waiting hull below, widely missing the mark.[23]

Western shipyards also attained speed by simplifying tasks and initiating training programs for inexperienced workers. Even Clay Bedford, the manager of the Kaiser yards in Richmond, had at the time of Pearl Harbor no knowledge about building ships, since his prior experience was in building contracting and dam construction. To meet his new challenge, early in 1942 Bedford made a trip to Detroit to visit the Ford Motor Company in the hope of finding new ideas.

> One of the things that impressed me the most was when I asked the personnel man how long it took him to train a man to take the position of one of the men on the assembly line. He said that ordinarily it takes two days, after which the new man is watched for a day or two to see that he understands his problem. I went away from there quite amazed. I thought, these fellows really have something. It if were only possible to train the new people that we have in two days, wouldn't that be grand? So we set up a specialization program on the same basis, so when making any certain section like a fore peak . . . or doing any of the single simple chores that are to be done on the ship, then that job was to be done by the same crew every day.[24]

Whether the quality of mass-produced ships was as good as that of handcrafted vessels was a question that invariably came up as the building program accelerated. In fact, that quality proved to be outstanding, but the newness of mass-production techniques raised questions among many, especially members of Congress. Legislators were particularly concerned about the safety of military personnel aboard troopships. Critics of the Roosevelt administration, particularly the Hearst press, also hoped to exploit safety problems as political issues. Except for a few isolated accidents, the safety record of Liberty ships was remarkable. But those few mishaps received extensive publicity. Still, the record of American shipbuilders in the war—especially the western yards—clearly indicated that the mass-produced vessels were in every way equal or superior to the products of American shipyards before 1940.[25]

Management and labor both took pride in their product. J. Lyell Wilson, assistant chief surveyor of the American Bureau of Shipping (which inspected all new ships and which included insurers as well as builders) declared that less than 2 to 3 percent of Liberty ships developed cracks and that almost all of these were insignificant. This judgment was reinforced by Willard Higgins, Jr., vice-president in charge of operations for A. H. Bull and Company, a large operator of these vessels for the Maritime Commission. Joseph Curran, president of the C.I.O.'s powerful National Maritime Union, which included most of the American seamen who crewed these vessels, was equally enthusiastic.

> Over 2000 Liberty ships have been constructed. From the reports of our membership, we are satisfied that these vessels, ugly duckling that they may be, cramped in quarters and with only the barest of facilities for the comfort of the crews, have been doing a marvelous job in the work for which they were built. . . . This is best proven by the tremendous amounts of raw material that have been carried to all the fronts under the most difficult circumstances of bombings, submarines, storms, black-outs, convoy difficulties, and all the rest. The percentage of loss through crack-up . . . is so small . . . against the percentage built . . . as to suggest that there might be some political significance in the stories by certain newspapers.

And he assessed the effect of such stories on the public. "We are deeply concerned over the implications of the stories carried in certain newspapers," he declared. "To the average reader it would appear that mass crack-ups of Liberty ships are occurring, while the facts are that only a handful have cracked up. None of the difficulties encountered by merchant shipping today . . . are told in these stories . . . nothing . . . of . . . terrific bombings . . . [or] whether the crack-ups have occurred when the vessels were loaded with cargo and travelling to the battle fronts."[26]

When construction defects did occur, they were influenced by a variety of factors, any one of which was usually difficult to isolate. Design could be a consideration but was not likely because Liberty ships were adapted from the North Sand type of British tramp freighter, which had been tried and tested for more than a decade before the war. More relevant were faulty materials, particularly the possible defects in steel plates. Although questions about metal weaknesses sometimes arose, such charges were difficult to prove. In any case, the Maritime Commission was loath to accuse the steel companies of wrongdoing. Enemy action, of course, was one of the intangible elements that added to the precariousness of ship operation in wartime.[27]

Newspaper reporters often charged that improper welding techniques were responsible for fissures, but investigations usually found such accusations unfounded. What contemporaries often did not realize was that historically most merchant ships built of steel tended to develop cracks or to have minor imperfections in construction that usually were not dangerous and were fixed easily. This was true even of ships that were riveted together, as most vessels were before 1940. During World War II when ships were assembled with prefabricated parts, builders used welding processes because they were so much faster and less expensive.

The major reasons for the cracks in merchant vessels were severe changes of temperature and the conditions under which most of the ships were forced to operate. Liberty ships often ran in convoys and were compelled to move at their top speed of twelve knots regardless of weather conditions. Even when seas were heavy and when it seemed desirable for their captains to slow down, these ships had to keep up with faster ones and to outrun enemy submarines. And severe changes in ocean temperature placed special stress on the hulls. It was not accidental that most problems occurred in the frigid waters of the North Pacific, on the run from Seattle to the Soviet port of Murmansk or to Alaska. And almost always the breaks occurred after the ships had unloaded their cargoes and were returning empty. Heavy cargoes evened out the stress on the fore and aft of the midsection. Without cargo, the ship's midsection underwent especially great strains.[28]

Such problems contributed to one of the most publicized accidents, involving the Liberty ship *John P. Gaines.* On November 23, 1943, the *Gaines* was returning empty from Murmansk in the icy waters of the North Pacific when it broke up off the coast of Canada. The vessel split into two parts, and ten sailors lost their lives. A survivor of the disaster, seaman Paul E. Tatman, vividly described his experience:

> I was on the 8 to 12 watch and at about 11 o'clock . . . there was an unusual cracking sound and the third mate went to investigate on the foredeck. He found nothing and so we turned in at 12 o'clock, and at 2:41—within 3 or 4 minutes from the time the cracking, grinding, tearing noise started—the ship

was completely in two. . . . We were encountering heavy swells so they could only release 12 to 14 men on deck at the time it broke in two—the rest were asleep. . . . So I hurriedly put on my clothes and by the time I got on deck they were launching the starboard lifeboats. . . . [N]one of the men had many clothes.

The officers decided that rather than abandon the ship to stay on board until it was definitely going to sink, so the first thing after the boats were launched the wind carried them away from the ship. One or two had not enough men— not full capacity—they could have handled many more men, but the men found it impossible to get in. In northern waters if you really get wet it seals your death sentence. When a ship breaks in two it tears down the radio wires, antenna, and things. We worked for 12 hours before it was possible to send out a message of any kind.[29]

Most of the ships that developed cracks on the high seas did not sink, however. The experience of the *Chief Washakie*, as described by Captain Charles C. Graham, was typical.

We were going from Adak to Dutch Harbor; in the forenoon it began blowing pretty heavy from the northeast. We were entirely empty with the exception of water ballast. . . . When it began blowing I ordered the revolutions cut down so as not to drive the ship into the sea and cause her to hammer, and about 10:22 I was in bed sleeping and something awakened me—a crash or some exceptional noise. I was called and told they thought the ship had cracked. So I immediately got up . . . and changed the course . . . and brought the ship into the wind and broadside. . . . It was snowing and blowing and we could not tell how far these cracks extended down the ship's side. . . . Two days later the repair ship "Heather" arrived and started making repairs. They welded the main deck plates across the ship . . . and we proceeded to Seattle.[30]

Such incidents invited enormous publicity and led to intensive investigations. The American Bureau of Shipping was one of the first to undertake an exhaustive inquiry. It reported in April 1943, on the case of the *Schenectady*, a vessel that split in two before it ever went to sea from Kaiser's Swan Island Yard. The bureau noted that a number of factors had contributed to the breakup, including improper welding, possibly the result of insufficient supervision of inexperienced workers. Poorly fitted subassemblies might have contributed as well. In any case, western shipbuilders made small changes in design to prevent a recurrence of such weaknesses. Moreover, they insisted on closer inspection of the steel plates, since weakness in steel was a possible contributor to cracking.[31]

In addition, the House Merchant Marine and Fisheries Committee appointed a subcommittee headed by Washington Congressman Henry "Scoop" Jackson to investigate the accidents. Jackson began an extensive inquiry in July 1943. He concluded that of one thousand Liberty ships built, only two revealed serious structural defects, and neither had been built by the Kaisers.[32]

Wartime Industries in the West: Shipbuilding

Senator Harry Truman was also drawn to the problem by virtue of his chairmanship of the Senate committee investigating the war program. Truman appointed Senator Warren Magnuson of Washington to chair a special subcommittee to inquire into ships that had cracked in the North Pacific, particularly those built by the Kaisers. Magnuson made a thorough inquiry and questioned scores of witnesses. On January 14, 1944, he reported that a total of fourteen vessels had developed some kind of fissures. Most of these cracks were so minor that crews repaired them while at sea. Others were corrected in port, but in no case was there any loss of life. In all instances the defects surfaced when ships were returning from Alaska without cargoes. Magnuson was especially concerned that no Liberty ship should be converted to a troop carrier unless its construction problems were fully identified and remedied. "I do not think that anyone," he said, "the Maritime Commission, the Army, the Navy, or anyone, would want to use these ships unless they know or feel that they are absolutely safe." Then, commenting on the unfavorable press when accidents occurred, he noted: "There has been some indication . . . that this might be due to faulty workmanship. I cannot come to that conclusion myself, because in the first place, the cracks and splits were sometimes in the hull—sometimes in the welding—and sometimes in the steel— and surely they all had a definite engineering pattern."[33]

Shipbuilders and ship operators largely concurred. Edgar Kaiser noted that Oregonship had built 322 Liberty ships by February 1, 1944. Of this number, only 14 showed minor defects, or about 4.1 percent. The average rate for all U.S. shipyards was about 3 percent, although the rates were higher for the Houston and Delta facilities. Kaiser noted that after he ordered a closer inspection of welding techniques and made slight changes in design none of his vessels had any more problems.[34]

Others in the industry amplified his views. William J. Bush, vice-president of the American President Lines, felt cold weather was a primary cause for cracks. Running a Liberty ship at full speed with only a light ballast in cold weather placed extraordinary strains on it, he believed. In peacetime such a situation was quite unlikely because the captain would reduce speed to ease friction on the vessels. H. Stubbs, a ship foreman at the Seattle-Tacoma Shipbuilding Company, explained that when a ship was empty it endured great strains on its midsection. Cold water has greater buoyancy than warm water and therefore increases pressure on the midsection. Clay Bedford, manager of the Kaiser yards in Richmond, which built 393 Liberty ships, pointed out with pride that only 26 had very minor fractures. He noted: "I don't think the fractures are limited to one single thing. I think they are a combination of design which had

55

not been refined to the ultimate, of materials which aren't as good as can be obtained under normal circumstances . . . and . . . temperature stresses occurring in operation where the ships are operating in comparatively unfamiliar locations."[35] That put it in a nutshell.

Reshaping the ship construction industry in the West had as profound an effect on workers and the labor movement as on the western economy. The transition from craft industry to mass production clearly changed the composition of workers in the industry. Unskilled or semiskilled workers proficient in a few simple tasks displaced skilled labor. Obviously the war was not solely responsible for this trend; technological innovations had accentuated it in many industries. But the war certainly accelerated the shift to unskilled labor in the West Coast shipbuilding industry of the 1940s. And that was bound to create new problems in the labor movement, particularly between the American Federation of Labor (A.F. of L.) and the Congress of Industrial Organizations (C.I.O.), representing craft and unskilled workers respectively. The fact that the hundreds of thousands of new shipyard workers who were hired after 1941 cared little for one union or another clouded the issue. Most considered their war jobs to be temporary and had few loyalties to shipbuilding as a craft or as an industry.[36]

In 1940, during the early stages of mobilization, the A.F. of L. dominated union organization in the industry—as it did throughout the war. After World War I the shipbuilding industry had shrunk to insignificant proportions on the West Coast, employing no more than a few thousand people. Most of them were members of the Boilermaker's Union (A.F. of L.). An exception were the workers at the Moore Dry Dock Company in Alameda, which had agreements with the C.I.O. Machinists Union. Most shipbuilders were like the Kaisers, who liked the A.F. of L. because the union helped in recruiting new labor. And the A.F. of L.'s Metals Trades Department also outlawed jurisdictional strikes, dedicated itself to maximum production, and opposed the closed shop.[37]

Moreover, some of the A.F. of L. labor leaders on the West Coast had links to the administration dating back to World War I. At that time Franklin D. Roosevelt was assistant secretary of the navy in charge of shipbuilding activities and labor relations in U.S. Navy yards. In 1917–18 he was bothered by the absence of a standard wage policy and of industrywide guidelines. One of the western labor leaders who worked with Roosevelt, was John Frey, in 1940 the president of the A.F. of L. Metal Trades Union. "As a result of the President's vivid and clear recollections of what occurred during the First World War in the field of shipbuilding," he recalled in 1943, "and I might say that I was in some contact with him during that period . . . I was aware that he wished to avoid confusion throughout the industry . . . and the lack of common policy which occurred during the First World War."[38]

With that experience clearly in mind Roosevelt created the Shipbuilding Labor Stabilization Committee in October 1940. Within three months the committee had worked out an agreement for uniform wage scales in the shipbuilding industry. It divided the nation into four zones: the Pacific Coast, the Gulf, the Great Lakes, and the Atlantic Seaboard. Within each zone labor standards were to be the same to avoid the raiding for scarce labor that had arisen in 1917–18. In early February 1941 the American Shipbuilding Council, a trade association, called a conference of all interested parties to San Francisco to work out specific details. Attending were representatives from shipyard management and from the A.F. of L., Admiral Julius A. Furer of the Navy Department, and Daniel Ring of the Maritime Commission. Their recommendations were discussed further in Washington with national leaders of the various interests, after which the group reconvened in San Francisco. There they agreed on a uniform wage scale for the Pacific Coast of $1.12 an hour for mechanics. This policy became a model for stabilization agreements in the other zones. Under terms set by the president, however, unions had to ratify the agreement. On April 19, 1941, Roosevelt appealed to workers to support the pact, and they responded positively by an overwhelming vote. Among employers only the Bethlehem Steel Company refused to abide by the new policy because it was one of the few nonunion yards in the West. But the A.F. of L. appealed the issue to the National Labor Mediation Board, which advised Bethlehem to sign what was now beginning to be called the Master Agreement. Under such pressure Bethlehem complied, although a few Pacific Coast yards continued to hold out.[39]

Some shipyard workers, however, were opposed to any industrywide pacts and in March 1941—defying the A.F. of L. leadership—went on strike. The San Francisco Machinists took the lead in the walkout, egged on by the militant leader of the West Coast Longshoremen, Harry Bridges, a reputed Communist. At the time the Soviet Union was still allied with Adolf Hitler—until the German invasion of Russia in June 1941.[40]

The Master Agreement clearly did much to stabilize wage rates in the West, but it also gave the A.F. of L. a decided advantage in organizing the more than four hundred thousand workers who were to flock to the shipyards during the next three years. As newcomers came to the Pacific Coast yards their employers were obliged, under the Master Agreement, to require them to join the A.F. of L. as a condition of employment. By

1944, therefore, the A.F. of L. had enrolled more than 350,000 shipyard workers in the West. Only 18,000 joined the C.I.O. and its affiliates. Not surprisingly, the C.I.O. leaders became increasingly restive as they saw slipping from their grasp a golden opportunity to organize hundreds of thousands of potential union members. Although it was clear that strikes would disrupt production, the C.I.O. was also prompted by self-interest. The A.F. of L. Metal Trades Union sensed trouble as early as January 1942 and called a conference of all labor representatives to ease tensions. But neither that meeting in San Francisco nor others held later that year improved the bad feelings. By October 1942 the C.I.O. was ready for action, encouraged partly by the administration's attitude. President Roosevelt had decided somewhat coyly not to become directly involved in this interunion dispute and expressed his belief that the National Labor Relations Board should handle the controversy. Several members of the board were openly sympathetic to the C.I.O., which explains why that union began raiding the shipyards to increase its membership and why it instituted formal action with the federal agency.[41]

In October 1942 the C.I.O. brought a formal complaint against the Kaiser yards in Portland for signing the Master Agreement. Admiral Land and the Maritime Commission were horrified because they had hoped to avoid any disruption of production schedules. But leaders of the C.I.O. and their friends on the National Labor Relations Board were determined to proceed. Although on a national level President Philip Murray agreed to a nonraiding policy, C.I.O. leaders in the West were loath to make such promises. And in 1943 the board began to hold hearings on the case, ultimately deciding that the Master Agreement was invalid. Under this ruling every shipyard would need to hold special elections to allow workers to decide whom they wished to represent them for purposes of collective bargaining. Most workers really cared little one way or another, but the decision threatened to upset the much-sought-after stability in West Coast labor-management relations. Arrangements for such elections were expected to take from six to twelve months. The Maritime Commission, the employers, and the A.F. of L. were aghast.[42]

During this dilemma Frey called a meeting of the A.F. of L.'s high command in California, Washington, and Oregon. On April 21, 1943, they met in Portland and decided to lay the issue before Congress and the president. Frey also talked with James F. Byrnes, director of the Office of Economic Stabilization. But Roosevelt deftly passed the buck and delegated Attorney General Francis Biddle to render a decision. Biddle reported back to the president that his authority to settle the controversy was limited, since the Wagner Act gave the National Labor

Relations Board primary responsibility. Under these circumstances the A.F. of L. leaders looked to Congress. In their resolution the labor representatives noted:

> The present members of the National Labor Relations Board are engaged in a national disservice. Their policy as now being applied is retarding instead of stimulating production for war purposes. . . . Their present policy is stimulating discord and dissension among workmen. They are encouraging a condition of civil war between labor organizations. Their policy has become nationally harmful, destructive, and . . . contrary to common sense.[43]

Both the Judiciary and the Appropriations committees of the House conducted investigations of the shipbuilding labor jurisdictional dispute in the West. They concluded that the practice of allowing contractors to sign agreements with unions before large numbers of workers were actually hired was unwise. As congressional hearings aired the issue in 1943 the West Coast shipyards began to wind down their operations. Congress took no formal action, and in 1945 the issue became moot as the shipyards terminated vast numbers of wartime employees. Still, the dispute clearly reflected the changing structure of the shipbuilding industry in the West.[44]

This reshaping left its imprint not only on the organizations representing workers but also on the very composition of the labor force itself. With wartime conscription and the mushrooming of thousands of new industrial establishments, the industry found itself chronically short of workers. Estimates in 1942 indicated that the western shipyards would need at least four hundred thousand new people, not even counting additional numbers required because of turnover. If production quotas were to be met, this problem required imaginative approaches.

The solution of most shipyard operators was to turn to a segment of the labor pool previously largely ignored, namely minorities and women. Henry Kaiser was among the pioneers, adopting nondiscriminatory hiring policies with generous fringe benefits for all his workers. Advertising in newspapers throughout the nation, he promised not only high wages but medical care and decent housing as well. So enterprising was Kaiser that he began hiring blacks in New York City for his Oregon yards in December 1942, transporting them in special trains across the continent. He also understood the importance of morale. On their arrival, he spoke to them at mass meetings about his production goals and about his policies for equal opportunity. Other shipbuilders were not as flamboyant, but also loosened discriminatory practices. The Moore Dry Dock Company in Alameda hired thousands of blacks from the rural South who could not bend rigid discriminatory practices in their native region. More than twenty different racial and ethnic groups were represented in the work force at Moore, which was representative of the heterogeneity in western shipyards.[45]

The A.F. of L. did not welcome these newcomers and in many cases refused them membership. When it did admit them—as in the case of blacks and women—it organized auxiliary locals without full voting rights. The Boilermakers were particularly notorious, demanding full dues but denying voting rights or office-holding privileges. Nor could black workers chose delegates to the national convention or air their grievances except through white male officials in other locals.[46]

These blatantly discriminatory policies did not go unchallenged. At the Kaiser yard in Portland in the summer of 1943, several hundred black workers refused to pay their union dues under such circumstances. The Kaiser management had no alternative but to dismiss them under its agreement with the union. Thereupon, the fired employees filed a complaint with the Fair Employment Practices Committee. That agency gave them a hearing and then ordered their reinstatement. Edgar Kaiser was willing, but the Boilermakers' Union objected. At that stage the aggrieved individuals appealed the case all the way to the California Supreme Court. In *Marinship v. James* that tribunal ordered the union to admit them to full membership. The labor organization continued to be recalcitrant in the face of this 1945 decision, but beginning with the 1944 annual convention, the Boilermakers gradually began a retreat from their hard-line discrimination policy by allowing black auxiliary locals voting privileges at conventions and a choice in the selection of their business agents.[47]

Black workers at Calship in Los Angeles also bridled at rank discrimination. That shipyard employed about five thousand blacks, most of them from the South. Walter Edward Williams, chairman of the Shipyard Workers Committee for Equal Participation, Auxiliary of Local 92, International Brotherhood of Boilermakers, explained in June 1943:

> I am chairman of the shipyard workers committee for equal participation, a committee of workers employed at the California Shipbuilding Corporation, the Western Pipe and Steel Shipbuilding Company, and the Consolidated Shipbuilding Company. . . . The grievance that we present involves discrimination practiced by the Boilermaker's Local #92 executives against the Negro employees of the three shipyards mentioned. . . . They have a policy of refusing to admit Negroes into their organization. . . . All of the workers in their jurisdiction—regardless of race . . . are admitted into their union with full membership privileges, that is, with the exception of the Negro workers. . . . There are approximately between 4000 and 5000 Negroes in the Boilermakers auxiliary. The committee contends that such a policy is demoralizing, that it impedes production, and that it serves to disunite the workers in the yard rather than to unite them, and we feel that through integration of Negroes into the Boilermakers union this problem can naturally be abolished.

Wartime Industries in the West: Shipbuilding

In their formal petition the black workers also noted that they were "only too willing to give their all, even their lives, in order to insure victory to America and to the Allied Nations; but the burden in this regard becomes almost unendurable when intentional and systematic plots and conspiracies are entered into which undermine this desire." And Williams warned that although the blacks were patient, "they do not intend to pay dues into that organization very much longer. They say they are paying for Jim Crowism, and that is something we are fighting against."[48]

One of the members of Auxiliary #92, Fred Jones, demonstrated the ridiculous nature of the discrimination, noting: "We have been forced into a Jim Crow outfit. It is much against our will. Thus, the union [uses] Hitler tactics." When Jones had originally applied for shipyard work, and admittance to the union, he had claimed to be a Hindu—whereupon the Boilermakers admitted him to full membership. Later, when he told officials that he was a Negro, they immediately changed his status and consigned him to the auxiliary![49]

Nor could management and labor ignore extension of equal rights for women. By 1942 women were beginning to enter West Coast shipyards, and two years later they constituted about 20 percent of the total work force. Of the workers at the Richmond yards, 23 percent in 1943 were women; Oregonship counted 31 percent by the end of the war. West Coast shipbuilders like Henry Kaiser found that women could be trained more rapidly in installing electrical connections, for example, than could men. But the Boilermakers resisted the admission of women and assigned them, like blacks, to auxiliary locals.[50]

Women faced special problems as full-time industrial workers, since they were also expected to take care of their homes and children. Mary Michener of the C.I.O. described inadequate child care facilities. In March 1943 14,200 women were working in southern California shipyards and 10,000 more were needed. Yet there were few child care facilities. She complained that it took more than nine months of bureaucratic red tape to process applications for federal funds under the Lanham Act to expand child care. She explained that applicants had to begin with the Federal Works Agency, then have applications sent to a field office of the Office of Education in the Federal Security Agency, which in turn would forward them to the Washington office of the Federal Works Agency. This office then sent the papers to the Office of Defense Health and Welfare Services in the Federal Security Agency, which forwarded them to the Project Review Board of the Federal Works Agency, which ultimately sent them to the Office of the President for approval. But the estimated 213,000 children in the Los Angeles area could not wait; they needed care if their mothers went off to work.

61

Wartime Industries in the West: Shipbuilding

The Kaiser shipyards were in the forefront of child care services. Almost from the start of his operations Kaiser provided day nurseries in his yards, first at Richmond and then at Portland. Mothers paid only fifty cents per day. The Maritime Commission reimbursed Kaiser for expenses but gave him a free hand in construction and operation. In view of the slow pace of the federal bureaucracy, private enterprise was more effective in this vital function.[51]

At times even minor inconveniences could loom large and result in absenteeism for women. Dirty laundry was a case in point. Mildred Gionninni, the international representative of the Laundryworkers International Union, A.F. of L., explained:

> I might say I made a very thorough investigation of the Oregon yard under the supervision of . . . Mr. Kaiser as to absentee causes among women. We found that better than 38 per cent of the excuses given for absenteeism of women in the shipyards was because they had no way of getting their laundry done, no other way than staying at home and doing it. If we cannot maintain laundry service here with 15,300 houses in Vanport [which] has no facilities for laundry . . . you are going to have more absenteeism. . . . In . . . the Pullman Company where thousands of troops move through the city every day the laundry is stacked up 10 sacks high, and for 3 or 4 weeks it will be in these laundries. Our laundry workers . . . are working 12 to 14 hours a day. . . . Some of these shipyard workers are forced to pay as high as $18 a pair for coveralls to get along with because they cannot get them out of the laundries where they are stacked up waiting to be done. . . . Even though it is a menial job it has to be done for the health and welfare of this community. . . . Oregon, Washington, and Alaska are the only States in the Union that have been declared essential manpower in the laundry industry.[52]

The war thus had a lasting influence on shipyard labor in the West. It accelerated the shift from skilled to unskilled workers, which was consequently reflected in the rise of industrial unions like the C.I.O. The conflict also diversified the labor force, catapulting a larger number of minorities and women into the labor pool. Although shipbuilding declined after 1945, both the people who had been associated with it and the western economy continued to feel its effect in succeeding years.

The economic restructuring that was accelerated by the war affected most aspects of the nation's economic life, including perceptions of reasonable profits and related accounting standards. Under pressure of the emergency, Congress decreed that business people should be compensated not only for the goods they produced but also for the services they rendered. Such a practice was unfamiliar to the older generation, however, whose conception of profit had been formed three or four decades earlier. They viewed profits as returns on original capital investment, the entrepreneur's reward for establishing a successful venture. But by the

Wartime Industries in the West: Shipbuilding

1930s managers, rather than entrepreneurs, had become the dominant figures in the industrial world. In 1941 it had been hardly a decade since Adolf Berle and Gardiner C. Means had published their classic study *The Modern Corporation and Private Property*. In that famous book they underscored the significant divorce between ownership and management that had taken place in large business in the preceding ten years or so. The concept that managerial skill should be compensated as fully as entrepreneurial innovation was still in the process of being accepted. World War II, however, gave this change a decided impetus.[53]

In addition, political hostilities compounded the issue of just wartime profits. Opponents of the Roosevelt administration and of the New Deal had been relatively silent during the crisis. Once victory had been attained, they vented their hatred not only against the national leadership but also against the contractors—like the Kaisers—who had had close ties to the administration. Between 1945 and 1947 various congressional committees held hearings on wartime profits and in particular cast aspersions on Kaiser and his supposed profits of more than 600 percent on his original investment. Obviously, the precise profit earned was directly related to the accounting procedures used. Whether the loans taken up by Kaiser or the stockholder's equity were to be counted as part of his investment was one of the questionable issues. Moreover, what value was to be placed on the managerial skills of builders like Kaiser? Admiral Land well expressed the official view when he said that essentially Kaiser received fees for selling services rather than earning profits.

Since war pressures were no longer extant in 1946, hindsight suddenly endowed critics with supposed wisdom. Typical was Congressman Roy C. Woodruff on the House Ways and Means Committee who wrote rather recklessly to his colleague, Otis Bland of Virginia, on September 23, 1946: "War profiteering on the part of New Deal sacred cows has cost the American people billions of dollars. Many of these billions have been illegally and contrary to law paid to these New Deal sacred cows . . . [like] Henry Kaiser. I sincerely hope your committee will properly and exhaustively explore the whole Kaiser group and other war profiteering conditions in the Maritime Commission." As Henry Kaiser noted, with some sarcasm, "I recall quite vividly that it was important at one time to win the war [and] that ships were necessary to win the war."[54]

War experiences accelerated changing perceptions of just profits. The nation was entering a postindustrial, technologically oriented, mass-production and service economy in which managerial skills and the purveyance of information were frequently important elements of economic change. Although such were to be more visible in the 1950s and 1960s, they were already in place at the conclusion of the war and perceived by sensitive observers. Thus, Marvin J. Coles, the legal counsel of the House Merchant Marine and Fisheries Committee, noted in 1946:

> The determination which the Committee must make is whether the amounts they [shipbuilders] received as fees and profits were reasonable and proper, or unreasonable and unconscionable. There is no accurate formula or rule to measure this, nor any precise dividing line as to what constitutes reasonableness or . . . profiteering in the unpleasant sense of that word. In most cases the operator of the shipyard had no money of his own invested in the physical plant. The procedure used was for the Maritime Commission to make two contracts. The first . . . [a facilities contract] provided that the company would build a yard at the expense of the Government. The second . . . would provide that the contractor would construct ships in that yard.[55]

The chairman of the Maritime Commission, Admiral Land, observed the new industrial order with even greater clarity.

> There was the requirement of shipbuilding brains, including not only ordinary labor, but also white collar labor, technical, engineering and skilled and unskilled labor. . . . Reconversion of industry to war production was under way [1941]. There was a bottleneck in brains and know-how much more serious than any other difficulty. To bring private capital into such a transitory undertaking was wholly impossible. The reliance had to be placed principally upon the furnishing of capital funds by the Government. . . . The capital requirements for the emergency shipbuilding program are of two kinds; namely current working capital, principally to meet payrolls, and capital for plant investment.

And then he put his finger on the function of western shipbuilders.

> It is not the capital of the shipbuilder which has been brought into the service of the Government . . . but, rather, the management skill and organization. . . . That shipbuilding profits are properly to be measured by output rather than by capital invested is recognized by Congress both in the Merchant Marine [1936] and Vinson-Trammel [1938] Acts which set limits at 10 per cent upon the shipbuilder's profit, based not upon his capital, but upon his output. . . . I point to it merely as showing the utter absurdity of attempting to relate the shipbuilder's profit to his invested capital under the conditions which had to be met to make our shipbuilding program possible.[56]

Henry Kaiser himself also perceived his functions quite accurately. "We provided the organization," he said, "the major portion of the operating capital, the brains—and I hope that brains is not yet a thing that is without value in our country—the brains and the production. The Government provided the facilities." That summed it up neatly. Nevertheless, many members of Congress were still preoccupied with measuring his profits on the basis of invested capital.[57]

The issue was further muddied by controversy over accounting standards. In the heat of war, concern for careful accounting techniques did not always have the highest priority with government auditors. Moreover, rivalries between various federal agencies were quite common during the war years. The auditors in the office of the comptroller general and those in the Maritime Commission fought their own special wars between 1941 and 1945. When in July 1946 Comptroller General Lindsay Warren appeared before the Senate Special Committee Investigating the National Defense Program to testify on war procurement programs, he blasted the policies of the Maritime Commission. He charged that their actions had led to excess profits, particularly in cost-plus contracts, and had given virtually unlimited powers to procurement agencies, including the right to renegotiate contracts without approval from the General Accounting Office. In its frenzied efforts to secure maximum ship construction, the Maritime Commission often did not set up well-organized audit systems for its contractors even when some—like Kaiser—pleaded with them to do so for their guidance. On the other hand, when Kaiser and his son went to see Lindsay Warren to ask him to establish more systematic accounting procedures for them, the comptroller general likewise refused because he did not want to rely on statistics produced by auditors of the Maritime Commission whom he distrusted.[58] The feud between the comptroller general and the Maritime Commission therefore left contractors caught in the middle, more vulnerable to potential critics.

Certainly the Maritime Commission's accounting procedures were not beyond reproach. W. L. Slattery, its new director of finance for operations in 1946, made a report on wartime practices in which he identified certain weaknesses. Between 1941 and 1945 the commission was desperately short of skilled auditors. It often operated with insufficient financial information because of the lack of experienced personnel. In many phases its accounting practices were not closely coordinated with auditing procedures. Accounts dealing with the agency's properties were particularly unclear. And the commission did not collect sufficient information from contractors concerning the removal of property and supplies. Such weaknesses were inflated by postwar critics.[59] Yet they were virtually inevitable under wartime conditions and the extraordinary expansion of federal shipbuilding activities. Under the circumstances it was remarkable that the Maritime Commission performed as well as it did.

A precise determination of wartime profits in the shipbuilding industry is difficult because estimates depend directly on variables used to determine profitability. What seems reasonably certain is that profit incentives were very successful. From February 1939 to February 1944 the Maritime Commission supervised the construction of 2,950 ships exceeding thirty million tons. Major shipbuilders like the Kaisers were well rewarded, but not excessively, for their contributions. Reviewing his wartime service, Admiral Land showed his grasp of the big picture.

> Of course it might be argued that all of this management skill which has built our ships should have been available to the Government on some other basis than appealing to the profit motive. . . . The United States of America has undertaken to fight the war without abandoning the basis of its economy. . . . We obtained the capital for prosecution of the war by taxes or by borrowing. . . . We obtained the industrial manpower by paying the highest wages of all history. We are continuing to follow the national policy of obtaining managerial skill . . . by the process of profit and loss.[60]

That was a masterly summary by a man who saw the problems in the broad context of national policy and who did not share the more parochial views of subsequent critics. The reshaping of the economy prompted by the war changed not only the industrial structure of the West but also perceptions of the nature of economic growth.

The war affected the reindustrialization of the West in many ways, and some of these were starkly reflected in the region's shipbuilding industry. It stimulated new management philosophies, the adoption of mass-production techniques, an expanded and diversified composition of the labor force, and changing perceptions of profitability. Certainly shipbuilding was one of those industries that shrank significantly after the war. But many individuals who were closely involved with the industry utilized their experiences in other fields in succeeding years, very much like Henry Kaiser who became involved in the housing, aluminum, steel, and automobile industries. The war was one of the progenitors of a new era in the nation's economic growth.

CHAPTER 4

The Western
Aircraft Industry

I N M A N Y different ways the war had an enormous effect on the reshaping of the aircraft industry in the West. It brought extensive expansion, new methods of production, and significant changes in the labor force. But perhaps its most lasting influence in the postwar era was the creation of a research and development establishment, which changed the nature of the industry and strengthened the military-industrial complex that was to play a central role in the economy during the next four decades.

By 1945 the aircraft industry was firmly established as one of the new ingredients in the more diversified economy of the West that emerged from the mobilization crisis. Airplane manufacturers had greatly expanded existing plants while operating scores of new facilities built by the federal government. As in shipbuilding, the desperate need to increase the quantity produced led industry leaders to transform what had been a craft industry into a mass-production industry. That led to fundamental changes in the labor force. Skilled craftsmen were now no longer as much in demand as unskilled or semiskilled workers who had to perform only a single operation, or perhaps several simple ones. And again, labor shortages opened up jobs for women which had previously been restricted to males. Unlike the shipbuilders, however, the aircraft companies did not hire blacks or Mexican-Americans in significant numbers. And the emerging research laboratories established by the airplane companies now hired a new breed of employee, those with special skills as scientists, engineers, and technicians. To an unprecedented degree, the industry now focused on research and development. That also led to a closer relationship with the army, the navy, and the air force, particularly since team research now displaced individual tinkerers.

The Western Aircraft Industry

When World War II broke out in Europe, American air power was in a woeful state. The air force, attached to the army and the navy, numbered fewer than one thousand worthy planes, and most of those were antiquated and not very serviceable. General George C. Marshall recalled in 1945, "The air force consisted of a few partially equipped squadrons serving Continental United States, Panama, Hawaii, and the Philippines; their planes were obsolescent and could hardly have survived a single day of modern aerial combat." In 1940 the combined expenditures of the Army Air Corps and the Bureau of Aeronautics were a mere $157.6 million—or 8.7 percent of total army and navy appropriations. That amounted to about 1.75 percent of the federal budget that year.

America's military leaders and also the politicians were slow to recognize the inadequacy of the nation's air defenses. It was not until after the fall of France that a majority of Americans slowly started to realize the seriousness of the world situation, and the need for national rearmament. As the French armies collapsed, on May 16, 1940, President Roosevelt galvanized the nation by calling for the construction of fifty thousand planes in the ensuing year. At the time, such figures seemed utterly fantastic to many Americans and wholly outside the realm of possibility. But the president was serious and ordered the Defense Plant Corporation to build new aircraft plants to be operated by private corporations. In addition, existing manufacturers were asked to expand their facilities and their production schedules. Roosevelt directed the Reconstruction Finance Corporation to grant them extensive loans for such purposes, usually with three options. A company could acquire the plant it was operating at cost after a period of five years. Or the company would be offered generous depreciation allowances for five years if it owned the facility. And corporation officials could also let the plant revert to the federal government if they so chose.[1]

Although the Roosevelt administration favored dispersal of manufacturing plants as a safeguard against possible enemy air attacks, in practice most major producers were clustered in various urban areas on the East Coast, in the Middle West, and on the West Coast. Southern California, with San Diego and Los Angeles, became a major hub of the industry, along with Seattle, Wichita, and Tulsa. However, maximum production in the aircraft industry was achieved only through a vast subcontracting network involving thousands of small businesses throughout the West. Most states west of the Mississippi had some form of enterprise that was involved in the manufacture of aircraft components or parts. Smaller cities such as Tucson or Cheyenne served as assembly or testing areas. But the Pacific Coast was clearly one of the great centers of production. The

The Western Aircraft Industry

Detroit automobile companies supplied the engines, but the westerners fabricated fusilages and other necessary parts. Between January 1, 1942, and April 1, 1945, the companies on the Pacific Coast produced more than 46 percent of the national total, or 125,823 of the 273,528 aircraft built during that period. Every day they turned out 138 planes—one every eleven minutes. It was a staggering performance![2]

San Diego quickly became one of the frantic new wartime boomtowns. Three major manufacturers had operations there. Ryan Aeronautics had begun manufactures on a small scale during World War I, but now greatly expanded. Consolidated-Vultee became another giant, building the B-24 Liberator bomber, the PBY Catalina flying boat, the B-32 bomber, and the famed Lockheed P-38 Lightning fighter. Between January 1, 1941, and June 30, 1945, it produced a record 30,782 aircraft and had as many as 101,624 employees. Consolidated Aircraft also had its headquarters in San Diego and produced a variety of models for other manufacturers.[3]

Not far to the north, Los Angeles boasted several major producers. Prominent was Douglas Aircraft, which constructed a wide range of models. As Donald Douglas noted in 1941: "We are manufacturing civilian and Army transports of two and four engine types . . . a fighter bomber for the British, and our Army. We are getting ready to manufacture the four-engine Consolidated bomber in Tulsa in connection with Henry Ford. We are getting ready to manufacture the four-engine Boeing [B-17] at Long Beach as a joint venture with the Lockheed Company and the Boeing Company, and we are also building dive bombers at El Segundo." Douglas agreed that perhaps there was an overconcentration of manufacturers in Los Angeles, but he emphasized the need to secure maximum production as quickly as possible. It would have slowed mobilization considerably, he believed, to move entire plants inland and to search for needed labor. "It is a rather large job," he said, "for instance, in our case to go and start a new plant of quite a size in a town like Tulsa, Oklahoma. We don't know much about local conditions there. We are certainly aware of the fact that there is not much labor available of the type that we need."[4]

In addition to Douglas, the other major companies in the Los Angeles area were Lockheed, North American Aviation, and Northrop. Hughes Aircraft in Culver City remained rather small, with no more than two thousand employees, because air force officers disliked and distrusted Howard Hughes. Lockheed was the giant of the group, with more than ninety thousand on its payroll. Its plant in Santa Monica was one of the nation's largest. It also built huge facilities in Long Beach and Burbank, with satellites in Santa Barbara, Bakersfield, and Fresno. North American

Aviation built more than forty thousand planes during the war and was known for the B-25 Mitchell bomber, the widely used AT-6 combat trainer, and the P-51 Mustang fighter. Northrop prided itself on having the largest experimental research and design program in the industry. Although the company built 25,068 engine nacelles for B-17s and 44,832 engine cowls and manufactured night fighters and flying boats, research was a major concern. As John K. Northrop explained: "The company was formed with the declared intention of adding to the long record of the group of engineers and scientists employed in the development and production of outstanding aircraft and aerodynamic improvements. We formed in 1939 and designed the all-wing plane, and high efficiency gas turbines. We pioneered with corrosion free methods of welding magnesium, and development of magnesium planes. . . . We also perfected launching methods for missiles before we knew how the Germans did it."[5]

In Seattle, the Boeing Company undertook significant expansion. More than most aircraft manufacturers, Boeing engaged in extensive subcontracting, building an intricate network throughout the West. One of its major contributions, of course, was the B-17 bomber, designed and modified for the European theater. That aircraft became the workhorse of the army air force, with Boeing and its subsidiaries building more than thirty thousand. In fact, California manufacturers built B-17s under Boeing's direction, since more of them were needed than the Seattle company could supply. But perhaps Boeing's greatest contribution was the B-29 Superfortress, designed in a crash program for the Pacific area. Since the range of the B-17 was only up to one thousand miles, a long-distance plane was needed to attack the Japanese homeland. Boeing engineers provided the answer with the B-29 on which they worked frantically for four years after 1940, with volume production centered in the firm's vast Wichita facility. The Seattle plant concentrated on further experimental designs for the model and built large plants in Seattle and nearby Renton for high-volume output. Boeing also built another large factory to concentrate on B-17s at Wichita, integrating eight new feeder plants with these expanded operations.[6]

Howard Hughes was somewhat bitter about being frozen out of high-volume airplane production during the war. Nevertheless, he took pride in his more limited contribution. "During the war my aircraft division in California manufactured a good deal of material," he reflected in 1947. "One of the principal contributions was the flexible feed chute, which was used in practically all of the B-17 bombers and saved the lives of many of the waist gunners. It was a very substantial contribution. In addition, on the coast I manufactured some 6000 wing panels which were used in the Vultee trainer, and over 3000 fusilages."[7]

The western airplane industry's leaders undertook their rapid expansion—and the reshaping of their industrial complexes—in a variety of ways. Creative financing played a part in enlarging their plants. They did invest some of their own capital, but the bulk of the new investment came from the federal government. Mere expansion would not necessarily have resulted in increased production, however. Westerners proved themselves particularly adept in subcontracting with the thousands of smaller firms throughout the region. Consequently, the aircraft industry invigorated not only the economy of southern California but also that of scores of localities from Kansas to the Pacific Coast.

Another method used by the manufacturers to boost production was the establishment of modification centers. These were *ad hoc* facilities that adapted production models off the assembly line for particular theaters of war or special missions, without impeding production processes at the major plants. The volume of output was also increased by cooperative and pooling arrangements between the largest companies in the industry. Many of these agreements would have been illegal under antitrust laws in peacetime, but such coordination greatly facilitated common goals in wartime. And the job could not have succeeded had it not been for ingenuity up and down the line in the development of new production processes to speed output.

Imaginative financing quickened the expansion program. Most of the western aircraft manufacturers invested their own funds in enlarging their main plants. When private banks were unwilling or unable to provide the necessary capital, the Defense Plant Corporation granted extensive loans. In many instances the DPC built entire new factories for the private firms to operate. Some were constructed by private contractors and other by the Army Corps of Engineers. The DPC would usually lease such facilities to the aircraft companies or charge the companies nominal fees to have them as operators. The flexibility of such financing served the industry well and achieved the government's goal of securing maximum production.[8]

The western manufacturers found these combinations eminently workable. As Donald Douglas told Harry Truman in 1942:

In the main, I would say that Government is paying for . . . the expansion program [but] all of the companies . . . have also spent their own money. Our policy at Douglas has been like this: All expansions at our parent plant at Santa Monica we pay for from our own capital. That goes also for El Segundo. Our Long Beach plant, which is the emergency plant, was built entirely of government funds. . . . That was built under the emergency plant facilities affair, wherein the banks loaned a holding company the money to build the plant; then the Government, in turn, contracted with that holding company to pay off that plant in 60 monthly installments. The plant we are building in Tulsa is a Government owned plant. The Corps of Engineers are building that [and it] will be leased to the Douglas Company for us to construct bombers at that site.[9]

The experience of North American Aviation was very similar. As T. H. Kindelberger, its president, explained: "We have expanded double the size of our plant in Inglewood, and we paid for that out of our own capital entirely. The plant in Dallas is a DPC plant . . . and is leased to us and we operate it. We designed the plant and all its equipment . . . and saw the whole thing through for a fee of $1. The same thing was done in Kansas City."[10]

The unprecedented production goals could not have been reached without extensive subcontracting, which the manufacturers had begun by 1941. Even those who were reasonably self-contained depended on thousands of subsidiary manufacturers throughout the West. As Robert Monroe, director of purchasing at North American Aviation, explained: "We are subletting contracts on various kinds of work to many concerns in this vicinity [but] less so than other companies since our plant is self-contained. . . . We have approximately . . . 860 different companies that we patronize." In Seattle, the Boeing Company, more than most firms in its field, relied on subcontractors. It built an intricate network of thousands of small shops in the Pacific Northwest in addition to large feeder plants in Washington state, including those in Aberdeen, Bellingham, Hoquiam, Everett, Chehalis, South Tacoma, and Tacoma. The company developed a similar pattern in Kansas after it built its large Wichita factory for B-29s. And some companies, like Douglas, used the device deliberately. Donald Douglas noted: "We always have . . . [been] using . . . small manufacturers. . . . The policy of the Douglas Company from the time it started here, when it had rather insufficient capital was that, rather than try to be completely equipped itself, it went out and helped develop small shops in the Los Angeles area."[11]

Newly created modification centers also did much to accelerate the flow of planes to the armed forces. Throughout the war, by the time a plane was off the drawing board, or even the assembly line, the demands of combat required substantial changes. That was true, for example, of B-17s, which by 1942 were found to have insufficient armament. Moreover, the aircraft were to be operated under very different climatic conditions, from North Africa to the Aleutians. To send them back to the factories in which they had originally been fabricated would have resulted in serious disruption of the entire production process. Thus, early on most of the major manufacturers built modification facilities to outfit airplanes for special missions or to make substantial changes. Consolidated-Vultee built such centers in Tucson and Fort Worth to serve the main plant in San Diego. The Boeing Company was pressured by the War Department in March 1942 when the army ordered it to modify two hundred B-24 bombers that Boeing had built as trainers but that the army now wanted for combat duty in the Pacific. Army air force officers demanded much heavier armaments on the craft as well as an extended flying range. Boeing had no facilities at which to accomplish this difficult task. But, with great ingenuity, company officials lined up the planes on four Kansas airstrips, which only recently had been farmland. During a two-week period six thousand Boeing workers braved blizzard conditions and freezing temperatures in those open fields to modify the planes to air force specifications. It was a herculean task, but the Boeing work force performed on schedule. At the same time the air force began to establish fourteen modification centers under their own jurisdiction, in addition to those operated by the manufacturers, to undertake the continual changes that the demands of war required.[12]

T. H. Kindelberger, the president of North American Aviation, in 1942 reflected on his not uncommon experience.

> As an example we are building a bomber which had a certain armament. That armament was decided upon 2½ years ago [1939], when the War Department specifications were prepared. It was found that the armament was inadequate . . . as a result of the experience of the war. Therefore, it became necessary to quadruple the amount of defensive armament that is put on the airplane. In doing so, naturally, the weight of the airplane was greatly increased. . . . There have been things of radio, new discoveries in the ways of bombsights and miscellaneous other things which it is difficult to discuss publicly. The net result is that we have had . . . a continuous stream of changes . . . interrupting the flow.[13]

Wartime exigencies led the major aircraft producers on the Pacific Coast to pioneer new forms of cooperation, which set the standards for the industry nationwide. They not only formulated standardized policies governing job classification, wages, and labor relations but also exchanged airplane designs, and aided each other with supplies of spare parts. At times the manufacturers even shared trade secrets, which they had jealously guarded before 1941.

The mechanism that facilitated such industry collaboration was the Aircraft War Production Council, formed by six major western manufacturers in February 1942: Douglas, Consolidated-Vultee, Lockheed, North

American, Northrop, and Ryan. The council evolved from informal meetings held by the southern California executives every two weeks at Donald Douglas's Santa Monica plant. The members discussed common problems they were facing, which during the latter months of 1941 concerned labor issues, materials shortages, and subcontracting. The men who managed these companies and who came to the meetings knew each other well. Harry Woodhead would usually represent Consolidated-Vultee, Donald Douglas spoke for his company, Robert E. Gross for Lockheed, J. H. Kindelberger for North American Aviation, LaMotte Cohn for Northrop, and T. Claude Ryan for Ryan Aeronautics. Courtland Gross of Vega and Richard Millar of Vultee were also usually present. Howard Hughes was not a member of the "club." In March 1943 the council added Boeing to its ranks. The group rotated the presidency and vice-presidency every three months.[14]

So effective was the interchange of information in the West—on matters such as joint research by Douglas and Boeing on the aerodynamics of wings, fuselages, and tails—that the War Production Board urged a similar organization in the East. Consequently the eastern aircraft producers in April 1943 created a similar group and joined with the westerners to form the National Aircraft War Production Council. One estimate of its effectiveness was the exchange of more than eighteen thousand technical reports by manufacturers, which used the council's elaborate index card system to facilitate the interchange. Boeing's special expertise on the use of plastics thus became available nationwide; Northrop's unique heliarc welding process for magnesium and stainless steel became known to all who wanted to make use of it.[15]

Whether in design or parts, such pooling of skills and knowledge did much to boost production goals. Northrop designed the P-61 Black Widow fighter but lacked experience with tricycle landing gears for such a fast and heavy plane. But its neighbor, North American Aviation, came to the rescue and sent over detailed plans for a gear similar to one it had designed for the Mitchell bomber. On the other hand, North American had virtually no experience in building braking flaps for dive bombers such as the A-36 Mustangs. But Vultee had manufactured such flaps and sent over the necessary blueprints to North American—greatly speeding up production schedules there. As William Peters, executive manager of the National Aircraft War Production Council, said in 1945: "Pooled engineering built quality into all of our airplanes. It saved time and built them faster . . . but the most important factor was quality." The Big Seven on the Pacific Coast increased their production more than tenfold after 1940, in part because of such innovative cooperative techniques.[16]

The Western Aircraft Industry

An urgent need for maximum production led aircraft executives to innovations in manufacturing techniques. Essentially, they transformed what had been a craft industry before 1940 into a mass-production industry. Before the war airplane construction had been in the hands of highly trained, experienced, individualistic craftsmen who lovingly fashioned the various parts for a particular plane over a period of many months. The needs of war revolutionized airplane manufacturing, however. Manufacturers redefined operations so that a large number of unskilled workers could perform just a few simple tasks. Management and industrial engineers redesigned the entire production process to encompass thousands of relatively uncomplicated operations, somewhat on the model of the automobile industry. Standardization and the interchangeability of parts were important components of this reindustrialization. The different parts of landing gears, for example, were not manufactured by a single plant but by a dozen factories throughout the United States, each of whom machined the elements in identical fashion. Such retooling permitted greater simplicity and speed. Thus, aircraft manufacturers who had devoted twelve thousand hours to a pho-template process before 1940 now redesigned the functions to be accomplished in just forty-eight hours through a myriad of simultaneous operations. A drilling job that had taken two hours and thirty-six minutes before 1940 now could be performed in thirty seconds. Similarly, airplane design before the war had been in the hands of only a few people. Now, industrial engineers broke the process down into thousands of small functions, each of which could be dealt with by relatively unskilled persons working in thousands of different locations.[17]

Once the separate parts were manufactured, unskilled workers could assemble them without great difficulty. They could bring subassemblies together in major assembly areas to fabricate a few big, finished sections of a plane, composed of perhaps as many as 100,000 different pieces. One observer estimated that a Convair B-24 required 49,000 fabricated parts, 53,000 pieces purchased from subcontractors, 85,000 nuts and bolts, 400,000 rivets, and certainly as many as 587,000 separate items.[18]

Mass production, therefore, was not a challenge for production as much as it was for management ingenuity. It provided an intellectual rather than a material challenge. And the brilliant success of the aircraft industry in the West during World War II was not merely a production miracle but a triumph of management and operational skills. That lesson—that the reshaping of industry was as much a problem for brains as for brawn—was one of the lessons of the wartime industrial experience.

As might be expected, the reshaping of the industry also brought an equivalent reshaping of its labor force, which now became increasingly diversified as management shifted performance of production processes from skilled to unskilled individuals. That led employers to reclassify job routines to reflect the changing modes of aircraft production. But as the work force became more heterogeneous, management responsibilities broadened considerably. Now employers had to be concerned with problems of housing, health, child care, and general well-being. This resulted in a major reorientation of business attitudes, one that was to have major significance in the postwar era with its growing awareness of the social responsibilities of large corporations.

Western airplane plants increased their work force almost fifteenfold in wartime. In 1940 West Coast aircraft plants employed 36,848 persons, choosing one of five applicants; in 1945 they had 474,198 on their payrolls. In view of an annual turnover of 100 percent, however, the companies had to train about one million people, since two out of three could not endure the job pressures for more than a year. In addition, Selective Service took some of the best workers, although the conscription of aircraft workers was deliberately gradual to avoid disruption of production. Most companies negotiated directly with individual draft boards on specific cases. In fact, the Douglas Company created a special selective service group in its personnel department to undertake this task. One of its leadmen, during a thirty-month period, had twenty-nine transactions with his draft board. The personnel department carried on a running battle with his draft board in an effort to keep him as long as possible.[19]

Given this drain, the companies simply had to widen the pool of workers from which they hired. As one supervisor in the personnel department at Douglas noted: "We used to test people for two or three days before we hired them. . . . We tested them for their intelligence, their manipulative dexterity, their mechanical aptitude, their temperament. . . . We wound up by rejecting four applicants out of five. Now—we feel them, if they're warm, we hire them." During the war Douglas hired twelve thousand disabled persons, most of whom performed very well. Convair and Lockheed employed children. The former hired hundreds of San Diego schoolgirls who labored in a special building in Balboa Park where vocational education teachers supervised their work on thirty-five hundred subassemblies weekly and on as many as forty thousand sheet metal details. Lockheed drew on students in at least forty high schools in the Los Angeles area. At least four thousand boys worked for them half days and on Saturdays.[20]

Most of the aircraft plants were resolutely opposed to hiring blacks. The manager of industrial relations for Consolidated-Vultee wrote the Los

Angeles Council of the National Negro Congress in August 1940: "I regret to say that it is not the policy of this company to employ people other than that of the Caucasian race. Consequently we are not in a position to offer your people employment at this time." The president of North American Aviation echoed these sentiments in 1941 when he said: "Regardless of their training as aircraft workers we will not employ Negroes in the North American plant. It is against company policy." Robert Weaver, the distinguished black economist, told a congressional committee in July 1941: "There were exactly four Negro production workers in the aircraft industry in southern California a month ago. . . . In the Los Angeles area . . . several thousand trainees could have been recruited and that population has been completely untapped to date." The situation did not change significantly during the war years in the aircraft plants, in contrast to the shipyards. In Seattle, the Boeing Company, despite official denials of discrimination, did not hire blacks throughout the period, except to fill janitorial positions. Nor were many Mexican Americans welcome in the airplane factories of the Pacific Coast.[21]

Thus, women became the major new source of workers. By 1943 various estimates indicated that more than 40 percent of the labor force in California aircraft industries was female. In addition to the time they spent in the factories, most women employees continued to be homemakers and to care for children and so had more responsibilities than men. The accumulation of such pressures accounted for the very high rate of turnover among women in Pacific Coast airplane plants.

The problems for women aircraft workers ranged from housing, shopping, and child care to transportation. George Barton of the Consolidated-Vultee Company explained that landlords were loath to rent rooms to single women. In 1941 he was hoping that his company and Ryan Aeronautics could jointly build dormitories to provide at least minimal room and board for women. In housing projects, such as Loma Vista in San Diego, sometimes as many as eight people slept in a single room in shifts around the clock. Yet this housing project had no shopping of any kind until 1943. And then it provided one Safeway store to serve sixteen thousand. As Homer Kerr of the Civic Committee of the Loma Linda Housing Project explained: "It often takes as much as an hour for the shopper to go through one of the 5 cashier's lines. This is the only commercial facility on the project." And child care facilities were very limited. The Los Angeles Area Committee of the Aircraft War Production Council did establish some child care centers with federal aid—largely funds from the Lanham Act—but these were too few and far between to meet the surging demand.[22]

77

The Western Aircraft Industry

The employment of large numbers of women accelerated the simplification of production processes and added to the momentum for reshaping the western aircraft industry. To accommodate women, the southern California plants established four-hour shifts. As management found that women were concerned about working on high or elevated work stations, they moved production to platforms or to floor space. New women workers, especially those working on subassemblies in a rigid jig, at times had problems reaching inaccessible areas within planes. To overcome this difficulty, industrial engineers developed trunnion-type jigs with swivel arrangements that rotated the work while the employee stood still. Instead of the worker maneuvering to reach the assembly, the assembly parts rotated to reach the worker.

Another example of production modification occurred at Convair, which assigned one of its women employees to a mill equipped with a moving table on which parts were held firm by a crank-operated clamp. The woman found it difficult to fasten the clamp, since her grasp was not firm enough to tighten it. Falling back on her ingenuity, she used a mallet to tighten the hand-operated crank. But the industrial engineers in the plant came up with a better way. They developed an automatic pneumatic clamp requiring no more than the touch of a button. Power tools such as wrenches, screwdrivers, drills, and rivet squeezers became common during wartime, not only speeding up operations but also allowing for use by inexperienced workers.[23]

In four short years both employers and employees did much to reshape the aircraft industry. What had been a craft industry became a mass-production enterprise. That led to the gradual diversification of the work force, particularly through the entrance of a significant number of women. Such a change also promoted alteration of work processes, as simplification and standardization led to greater efficiency and speed. The entire transformation of the industry, bringing with it new problems in housing, transportation, and health and child care for workers, caused a slow reorientation of management attitudes toward corporate responsibilities.

As no other event before it, the war dramatized the importance of research and development in aircraft production. Those in the industry did not immediately recognize that this was a crucial element in the reshaping of airplane manufacture. Rather, this perception evolved gradually during the war years. By 1945 most executives of the large aircraft companies had crystallized research and development as the essential element in their competitive stance. At the beginning of mobilization, however, such a vision was less clearly defined, as the tribulations of Howard Hughes well indicate.

The Western Aircraft Industry

A visionary and a dreamer, Hughes teamed with Henry J. Kaiser to build a large airplane—larger than had ever been attempted—to serve as a troop carrier. The idea of developing a giant air freighter had come to Henry J. Kaiser early in 1942 when German submarines were wreaking havoc with Allied shipping in the Atlantic. A man accustomed to great problems, Kaiser envisaged a fleet of large planes that would carry not only soldiers but also their equipment throughout the world. According to Glenn Odekirk, superintendent of Hughes Aircraft Company and later the designer and builder of the craft, he and Kaiser were talking about the rapid sinking of Kaiser's ships by the Germans when Kaiser said, "Well, I guess I'll have to put wings on my boat." That was the germ of the idea for what was to become the Spruce Goose.[24]

Kaiser had no experience building airplanes but was convinced he could revolutionize the industry as he was already transforming shipbuilding. That made him anathema to virtually every other executive in the industry. And despite his enthusiasm he was to learn that he could not buck the establishment, including not only the leaders of the major companies but highly placed military chiefs in Washington, D.C., as well.

Kaiser began to broach his idea publicly in a speech in Portland, Oregon, on July 19, 1942. Within a week he went to see Donald Douglas in Los Angeles to get his reaction to the project. "I asked if he was interested," said Kaiser. "Donald Douglas exhibited a great interest, so much so that he sent at least a dozen men to our shipyards and prepared in his own plant an area lay-out, and also analyzed our curve costs of the ships and found that our curve costs . . . [were] almost identical to his. He was tremendously enthusiastic and captivated by the program." But Douglas wanted to think about it some more and suggested Kaiser consult with Glenn Martin, who already had a federal contract to build the Mars *Flying Boat*, an experimental troop carrier not quite as large as what Kaiser had in mind. Kaiser did not know Martin, so Douglas agreed to make an appointment for him at Martin's Baltimore plant. Since Kaiser lacked experience with airplanes, he hoped to enlist the major manufacturers in his project. At first he hoped that all of them would pool their efforts and perhaps build the plane in one of his shipyards. "We were tremendously short of steel," he recalled, "and we were becoming idle. . . . So the thought was that we could take these facilities and use them." He also presented this idea in testimony before the Truman Committee. He told the committee on July 30, 1942, "If . . . we could be thrilled and stirred and all join in together and make a real project out of a large air-cargo ship, that . . . would be very wonderful for a solution of the problem." Kaiser seemed somewhat naive because at the same time his plan for building one hundred small aircraft carriers was arousing only coolness from the White House and outright opposition from the Navy Department, although later his idea proved itself.[25]

As could have been expected, Kaiser's plan did not sit well at all with Glenn Martin. He saw Kaiser as an archrival in building a large cargo plane and thus expressed only marginal interest, hoping instead that the army and the navy would order his Mars Flying Boat once his prototype had been perfected. Martin recalled that after he saw Kaiser on July 29, 1942, he phoned Douglas to talk about the proposition. Douglas said that he too was unwilling to join a consortium to build the Kaiser plane and that Kaiser was persona non grata with the chiefs of the military services. Nevertheless, an advisory committee of aircraft manufacturers to the War Production Board agreed to make a formal consideration of Kaiser's proposal. That group met on August 24, 1942, in Donald Douglas's office in Los Angeles and allowed Kaiser to state his case. They kept him and his staff of twelve engineers waiting in an anteroom for six hours before allowing them to make their proposal. In the hearing they consistently pressed him for specific details, whereas he was prepared to discuss only general objectives. When the proceedings were completed, they rejected his plan outright. Glenn Martin declared: "We were not at all concerned about Kaiser being in the aircraft business. We were concerned about being able to do his suggestions and our own." And they were certainly not ready to challenge the army and navy procurement officers to whom Kaiser was anathema.[26]

Kaiser anticipated problems with the leading men in the airplane industry and three days before his meeting at Douglas contacted the black sheep of the industry, Howard Hughes. One of the nation's leading and most glamorous pilots, Hughes was also one of the industry's pioneers in research and development. He had broken many speed records with planes he himself had designed and piloted. The most spectacular was his transcontinental flight in 1935, which set new nonstop speed records. Although somewhat unorthodox and disliked by military men, who considered him a playboy, Hughes had a very solid reputation in the industry. As Glenn Martin said of him in 1945: "Howard Hughes . . . was considered probably one of the most able cockpit engineers in the country. . . . There never has been any suspicion on Howard Hughes' company as to their integrity or what they could try to do, and Howard himself, would put forth his best effort." Hughes had also been recommended to Kaiser by Jesse Jones, who had been acquainted with Hughes's father in Texas and who had known Hughes since he was a small boy. "Whatever you do, Henry," said Jones to Kaiser, "do not interfere with Howard. He is thorough and he is a genius."[27]

The Western Aircraft Industry

Kaiser went to see Hughes, who was not feeling well, in a San Francisco hotel room on August 21, 1942, to broach his plan for the cargo plane. Hughes was mainly interested in research, design, and development. He hoped to innovate with new types of aircraft and was not much interested in production. But he agreed to build a prototype with Kaiser. On October 7, 1942, they signed a formal agreement establishing a corporation. Hughes was in charge of research and development, whereas Kaiser would attend to actual production. After delicate negotiations the War Production Board, on November 18, 1942, issued a contract to the new Kaiser-Hughes Corporation to build three models of the cargo plane, granting $18 million from the Defense Plant Corporation.[28]

By now army and navy officials were furious at what they considered to be a direct threat to their authority. The assistant secretary of war for air, Robert Lovett, bluntly noted that the Joint Chiefs of Staff jealously guarded what they considered to be their exclusive right to determine the design and manufacture of all military airplanes. Research and development was to be performed by private manufacturers under their direction. To them Kaiser and Hughes were interlopers without much standing and, perhaps worst, were unorthodox and unpredictable. Lovett relayed the strong objections of the Joint Chiefs to the Kaiser-Hughes proposal. The War Department closed ranks up and down the line. Undersecretary of War Robert P. Patterson wrote to Donald Nelson as early as July 30, 1942, when the plan was still in the discussion stage:

> The report on cargo aircraft . . . was sent to me by the Joint Chiefs of Staff for comment. I received this morning the following reply marked "secret" from the Joint Chiefs of Staff: "The Joint Chiefs of Staff have considered very carefully the reports submitted to Mr. Nelson on cargo aircraft. Our views are since the maximum production of combat planes is essential to our war effort, none of the existing facilities for the production of these planes should be diverted to the production of cargo aircraft. It is very evident that any large increase in cargo-plane production can be accomplished only if the production of combat planes is reduced. . . . We also feel very strongly that the requirements of the Armed Forces of the U.S. and the U.N. for transports in connection with military operations are of such importance that control of the use of transport aircraft should, without question, remain vested in the Armed Services."

To these strong views Secretary of War Henry L. Stimson added his own endorsement. In a letter to Nelson on August 10, 1942, drafted by Lovett, he declared that the army had absolutely no need for a flying boat. And the army's Aircraft Production Board, an advisory panel, continually urged abandonment of the project.[29]

Clearly, Kaiser and Hughes were the outcasts of the airplane industry's establishment. Military officials sought to maintain their primacy in research and development, and their major contractors were loath to challenge their authority. Moreover, as Kaiser correctly surmised, many industry leaders were somewhat unnerved by the prospects of competing with someone as unorthodox as he. From the start, the project had a dubious future.

But as an aviation enthusiast, Hughes was excited about the research possibilities of the cargo plane and for the next five years worked intensively on the project. Most of the work was performed at his small California plant in Culver City, about twenty-seven miles from the coast. As Hughes noted:

> I designed every nut and bolt that went into this airplane. I carried out the design to a greater degree than any other man that I know in the business. I worked anywhere from 18 to 20 hours a day on this project for between 6 months and one year and this, coupled with . . . other work I did during the war, resulted in me being so completely broken down physically that I was sent away for a total of 7 months for a rest after the war. I do not know how anybody could have worked harder than I did. . . . I am frequently accused of going too far and not delegating enough of the work to other people. . . . I am by nature a perfectionist and I seem to have trouble in allowing anything to go through in half-perfect condition. So if I made a mistake it was in working too hard and in doing too much of it with my own two hands.[30]

But the work proceeded much more slowly than anticipated. The wingspan of the plane was 320 feet, and the body was more than 200 feet in length. This eight-engine craft was three times as large as any other plane then in existence. Hughes was enormously impressed by the scientific knowledge he gained while working on the project. He tried to explain his discoveries in lay terms.

> A good deal has been learned already . . . about the design and building of big airplanes. For example, it has long been considered that the bigger the airplane is, the more efficient it is. . . . It should cost less to operate per mile and it would carry a larger load at a higher speed, and over greater distance. We have discovered . . . that is not the fact. . . . There is apparently a point beyond which size will not be all right. The skin area [of the fuselage] becomes more efficient as it is larger. The skin area, which determines the drag, goes up as the square of the size; whereas the volume, which determines the cargo or passengers it can carry, the volume goes up as the cube. You can see that the cube will exceed the square and therefore the carrying capacity will be greater in relation to drag as size goes up. But, on the other hand, we have discovered that wing design is quite different, and as the wing becomes larger, it weighs more per square foot than a smaller wing. Now, a point is reached apparently, where the loss in wing efficiency . . . exceed the gain in body efficiency, and where the two lines cross, apparently, it is not desirable to build a bigger ship. . . . Furthermore, this ship for the first time has exceeded the size where a man can manually . . . operate the flight controls.[31]

But no matter what scientific value the project had, key figures in the armed forces disliked Hughes even more than Kaiser. Hughes felt that one of his chief detractors was Major General Oliver P. Echols, assistant chief of air staff, who was also requisitions officer for the air force. Allegedly Echols had told one of Hughes's assistants, Noah Dietrich, about his personal dislike of Hughes, with whom he swore not to deal under any circumstance. His antagonism had originated in 1935 when Hughes had set his record for nonstop transcontinental flight. At that time Echols made arrangements for Hughes to fly to Wright Field in Ohio—a major air force center—but Hughes never came. On another occasion air force officials asked permission to examine a photoreconnaissance plane he was building. Hughes consented, but when Echols sent two men for the purpose, Hughes allowed only one of them to see it, amidst an aura of secrecy.[32]

And Hughes did not exactly endear himself to other air force officials. At one time General Hap Arnold, then the chief of the army air corps, came to California to inspect one of Hughes's experimental aircraft, a two-engine fighter. Hughes remembered:

> Of course I would not have gone to this extent had I known him, but I left orders that no one was being permitted in this plant. . . . Now General Arnold came to the . . . factory and they would not let him in. And you can imagine that caused an explosion the like of which you have never heard, and that also did not enhance the feeling of the Army officers towards me and my company. The Army . . . liked to have their fingers in everything. . . . That left me in a position where the Army did not want to touch me with a 10-foot pole and that is why I had so much trouble.

Hughes also wondered whether the army resented his status as a Hollywood celebrity and expected him to share Hollywood glamor—and actresses. "I did not entertain and extend the hospitality and cordiality to these officers," Hughes said, "that they received from the representatives of the other companies . . . [and] they considered me to be stuck up. They considered that I was too good for them, that I sat out in my bailiwick in Hollywood, I did not come to Wright Field to, let us say, kowtow to them there, and when they came to Hollywood, I ignored them."[33]

Between 1942 and 1944 opponents of the cargo plane project united and in February 1944 pressured Donald Nelson to cancel the WPB's contract. The progress of the war now made the project unnecessary, except for its research and development contributions. Hughes felt, however, that the scientific value of the plane warranted the continuation of government support.

> At the time when pressure was brought to cancel this project, and when approximately thirteen and a half million dollars had been spent, I came to Washington and did my best to persuade the people involved that this project should go on. Because I felt for a small, comparatively small expense to the government we could finish and fly the biggest airplane in the world, and that the infor-

mation derived therefrom would be of great value. I thought such value would exceed the additional expenditure, when you weighed it in terms of what this Government was paying for aeronautical research at the NACA laboratory and other places. I felt that the gain from the standpoint of information and research to be derived from completing this airplane would be greater than the additional expenditures to the Government. . . . Well, there was a lot of doubt in the minds of the people here. . . . So I had said that my company was willing to take a fixed-price contract. . . . So I finally accepted a contract which provided for an over-all expenditure of only $18,000,000 on the part of the Government. . . . I accepted the proposal . . . indicating that my company would lose $2 millions. Since then [1947] I've lost $7.2 millions.[34]

After cancellation of the project, Hughes used his own funds to complete the plane. As he said, "I believe in the future of aviation in this country and I think this plane is a step forward." Then, on November 2, 1947, Hughes himself took the controls of the giant carrier and took it off for a test flight of eleven seconds.[35] He proved his point that the plane could fly. Above all, this experimental model did contribute to the development of large aircraft.

During the war years Hughes was also involved with the development of a photoreconnaissance plane for the armed forces. He persisted with this project despite initial disappointments. His first contact with air force officers, and his first disappointment, was in 1940 when he submitted a design for a fast, two-engine bomber that was based on the one he had used to set his transcontinental record in 1935. After Hughes submitted his bid, the air force officers made him wait for four months while they solicited a proposal for a similar plane from the Lockheed Corporation. In this period, Hughes claimed, his best engineers who had worked on the design left him to join Lockheed. Hughes felt that the Lockheed team incorporated some of his best ideas into its model. When Lockheed finally submitted its plans, the army accepted them while rejecting Hughes's. This plane was to become one of the most famous built in World War II, the Lockheed P-38.[36]

This experience convinced Hughes to emphasize secrecy on his next project—a fast, light plane suitable for either photoreconnaissance or fighter service and initially dubbed the F-11. Hughes said: "I have reasons to think that there was something vague when the Army would not buy that airplane. However, I just went back to my shell . . . and . . . felt Lockheed got the two-engine idea from some of my engineers. I felt I had gotten rough treatment, so . . . I decided to design and build from the ground up with my own money an entirely new airplane which would be so sensational in its performance that the Army would have to accept it. I designed and built that airplane under closed doors." General Arnold was impressed by the plane's potential and ordered an experimental model.[37]

Since Hughes was such a perfectionist and was oriented to research and development rather than production, he was unable to ready this plane for service while the war was in progress. And after the war, air force officers under Arnold were still reluctant to deal with Hughes. In addition, political partisans soon joined these officers in lambasting this particular project, which was colored by political controversy because of the involvement of Elliott Roosevelt, one of the president's sons.

During the war Elliott Roosevelt had served as a colonel in the air force, specializing in photoreconnaissance. He flew dozens of missions in Europe and North Africa, but in July 1943 Assistant Secretary of War Robert Lovett called him back to the United States and assigned him to the air force purchasing program. In fact, Lovett placed him in charge of buying photoreconnaissance aircraft.[38] It was in that capacity that Roosevelt came into contact with Hughes Aircraft. General Arnold sent Roosevelt on a tour of various airplane manufacturers in California where on August 9, 1943, he arrived in Los Angeles. Roosevelt visited Douglas, Lockheed, Consolidated-Vultee—and Hughes. While in California the different companies wined and dined him and his staff, as was the custom. In fact, John Meyer, Hughes's public relations representative, paid for the group's hotel bill while they were in California and arranged for them to stay in a house Hughes owned, although they were unaware of it at the time. A month later Roosevelt, who was not famous for his good judgment, stayed at the Hughes corporate suite in the Waldorf-Astoria Hotel in New York City, and a year later he borrowed $1,000 from Meyer. None of these actions were illegal, but they reflected dubious judgment. Roosevelt knew Meyer through his new wife, Faye Emerson, an actress who had been acquainted with Meyer when he was a press agent at Warner Brothers Studios in 1941. Nevertheless, Roosevelt opened himself to attack when on August 20, 1943, he recommended to General Arnold that the army purchase the Hughes plane, to be delivered within six months. Arnold was pleased with Roosevelt's report and on October 12 accepted it. At the same time he reassigned Roosevelt to the active war zones and ended his connection with the F-11.[39]

Despite Roosevelt's recommendation, other air force officers obstructed production of the F-11. The air force's material division studied plans for the plane in the next eleven months. Then they required modifications that Hughes felt were virtually impossible to meet. Officers of the air force's Material Command also disliked the plane and suggested innumerable changes. An air force review panel, Roosevelt said, recommended against the plane because it would be made out of wood rather than metal, although Hughes had difficulty securing WPB priorities for such scarce materials. The intense personal dislike of Hughes by some air force officers also surfaced. Roosevelt later charged, although it would be difficult to prove, that Major General Echols, director of the air force's matériel and purchasing program, was partial to the older, established aircraft manufacturers. Be that as it may, in 1945 Echols was chosen by the manufacturers as president of the Manufacturers Aircraft Association, the industry's main trade group. Such revolving doors were to become rather typical of the emerging military-industrial complex in the United States. Roosevelt also felt that some of the antagonism toward Hughes was due to his longtime friendship with Faye Emerson. In 1943 Hughes had paid the hotel bills for their honeymoon as a wedding present for Roosevelt and his wife.[40] Research and development in the airplane industry obviously took strange turns.

All these details surfaced soon after the end of the war when Republicans returned to Congress with majorities and when some of the more rabid anti–New Dealers hoped to embarrass the dead president. Stalwart partisans like Senator Owen Brewster of Maine, Senator Homer Ferguson of Michigan, and freshman Senator Joseph McCarthy of Wisconsin utilized the Truman Committee in 1947 to inquire into the Hughes project. Their investigatory tactics foreshadowed the infamous McCarthy hearings just a few years later. The proceedings embarrassed Elliott Roosevelt, who already had made good copy for journalists through the years. And they thoroughly embittered Howard Hughes, who soon became known as an eccentric and a recluse. His prime object had been to further research and development, not only of the giant cargo plane but also of highly advanced bombers and photoreconnaissance planes to help the war effort and to further aviation. Circumstances combined to prevent him from making his fullest contribution.[41]

But if Hughes lost many of his battles, he did not wholly lose the war in terms of his broad objectives. Later years and the consequent development of aeronautics—such as the development of large aircraft—testified to his vision during World War II. The experiences of western aircraft manufacturers during these years shifted their attention to the importance of research and development and to the creation of a sophisticated science-technological complex that would characterize the industry in the next several decades. Henceforth, research and development would be the cutting edge of America's air power.

By 1945 the leading aircraft executives were cognizant of the importance of research and development. Those in the West were particularly concerned about maintaining the plants and the research facilities they had developed during the war. And they were aware that they could not accomplish this without substantial federal aid. W. E. Beall, executive vice-president of the Boeing Company, voiced these concerns, emphasizing the need to maintain large parent plants. "A community economy has been built up around these plants, and thousands of workers, many owning their own homes, have established themselves near them. . . . The people of the west coast would probably elect not to change location." If industry were removed to remote areas, it would slow production. Beall emphasized that his industry could not survive unless it received orders allowing it to maintain research and development activities and staff. That was much more important now than in the prewar era because higher-performance aircraft required greater expenditures, more complex designs, larger numbers of workers, and more sophisticated facilities. He pointed out that whereas it had taken 150,000 man-hours of engineering to complete the first B-17 to fly between 150 and 250 MPH, it required 1.5 million man-hours of engineering to develop the B-29 bomber to fly at 350 MPH, if research and development, testing, and analysis were included.[42]

Beall cited the enormous strides in technology made by the aircraft manufacturers during the war. If 1941 was indexed at 100 to chart the time spent on research and development at Boeing, the figure increased to 212 in 1942, 470 in 1943, and 840 in 1944. Looking back just a decade, Beall recalled: "I can remember the time when the structural analysis of any given plane amounted to a book one inch thick. Now, you couldn't pile a B-29 analysis on this table without collapsing it." He described how in 1934 the Y 18–9A-2 two-engine bomber prototype required 40,000 engineering man-hours; the 299 in 1940 took 138,000; and the XB-29 needed 1.3 million. That was just the beginning. Boeing devoted 433,000 engineering man-hours to the B-29 before the first flight; the company added another 6,133,000 to secure the first production model. By the time the plane actually began rolling off the assembly lines, Boeing had invested 7,566,000 engineering man-hours in the course of four years, from design to first flight. Between 1920 and 1940, Beall noted, the aircraft industry had engaged in very little research and development. Instead, the armed forces had simply kept many of the old Liberty engines left over from World War I. That, Beall warned, should not be repeated.[43]

Beall also noted that the increased complexity of planes required more research and development. The Boeing 299 had 18,000 parts; the B-17 had more than 48,000; and the B-29 contained one million parts without counting bolts and rivets. "Basic research," he declared, "if it requires facilities that no aircraft manufacturer can afford . . . if it applies to all airplanes in general, and is really basic, then it should be done by the Government. . . . Otherwise, it should be done by the industry." Beall urged government programs to support basic research as well as applied research, product development, and procurement. He also hoped universities would engage in basic aeronautical research that industry could utilize. All these goals could be achieved through federally sponsored production programs to maintain aircraft manufacturing plants. That was the road, Beall felt, to giving the United States the lead in aeronautics.[44]

To a considerable extent Donald Douglas agreed with this position. In 1945 he expressed his hope that the aircraft industry would not be dismantled. Of the industry performance in World War II he noted: "It was an epic of production we may never again be permitted to duplicate [but] modern weapons have made geography of minor importance in national defense. This Nation must find its security for the future not so much in aircraft plants moved a few hundred miles inland or buried underground, but rather in the possession of a most modern and invincible striking force." To accomplish that, the nation needed continued research and development. "This Nation, cannot, like a giant ostrich, hide its plants beneath the island sands," he declared. "We cannot trust the destiny of our future generations to the safety of a Maginot Line, in fortification or plants. World War II is full of monuments to that type of defense psychology—the French Maginot Line, the German Siegfried Line, Britain's Singapore—none of them could withstand modern weapons of attack. I do not believe that the removal of our aircraft plants inland is itself the answer to the problems and dangers of the next war."[45]

Instead, Douglas emphasized, research and development would be America's first line of defense. "Constant, intelligent technological research and development will provide a more dependable and elastic defense from sudden attack than mere removal of aircraft plants from their present locations." But that could be accomplished only with government support. He himself hoped to purchase, at bargain prices, government properties built during the war. "America cannot trade or auction its way into reconversion by making profits on its war surpluses. New jobs, new products, new opportunities must be created if we are to have prosperity and progress in our industry." With a prescient look into the future his vice-president for engineering, Arthur R. Raymond, predicted, "The atomic bomb has revolutionized our ideas of strategic bombing, but it is not a weapon that can be employed for all purposes and has heretofore not outmoded . . . planes." Raymond suggested the creation of a government agency, similar to the Office of Scientific Research and Development, to promote basic research in aeronautics.[46]

The idea that research and development provided a key to national security was also stressed by Harry Woodhead, president of Consolidated-Vultee. He believed that by 1945 any area in the United States would be vulnerable to enemy attack, and thus he urged retention of aircraft factories on the Pacific Coast. But these plants needed extensive government support.

A new field of technology has appeared on the horizon, which includes jet propulsion, supersonic aircraft, radio-controlled missiles, and atomic energy. We recommend intensive research in all of these new fields in order that this Nation may lead the world technologically. At the same time we recommend that we keep our feet on the ground and continue the development and manufacture of aircraft in the trends that have proven their validity. . . . We wish to emphasize the importance not only of research and development, but also of manufacturing in production. It is only in this way that the aircraft industry can be kept in a fully integrated position with process planners. . . . To confine aircraft development in peacetime to experimental projects only would be analagous to setting up a football team and paying attention only to the quarterback. . . . A football team is effective only to the extent that it learns to operate as a unit, and this comes from experience. The same is true to an even greater extent in aircraft manufacturing.[47]

Other industry leaders echoed these sentiments. J. H. Kindelberger, president of North American Aviation, emphasized the crucial role he assigned to research and development and to the maintenance of a strong airplane manufacturing industry through government support. John K. Northrop, president of Northrop Aviation, recalled that the lack of government support of research before 1941 had seriously hampered his company's war production program. Alluding to Northrop's enormous success especially with the P-51 Mustang fighter, he noted that the company had built a seaplane for the British in 1940 but that much of the necessary research and development had preceded that order by several years. Its development was "the organized expression of a vast body of accumulated technical knowledge, weighed and evaluated by skilled minds." Northrop took pride in the fact that his company's research and development program was the largest in the industry. But if it had not been for the British orders in 1939 and 1940, the company would not have survived. "The refusal of U.S. procurement agencies to provide funds for R7E would have ruined Northrop's efforts." He cited his experiences primarily to emphasize how important he considered government support for research and development in the postwar world.

Although basic research could be performed by government agencies, he hoped research and development would be mainly in the hands of private industry.[48]

By 1945 westerners had done much to reshape the aircraft industry, transforming it from a small-scale craft into a large-scale manufacture. This they did by using innovative financing, by adopting creative new production techniques, and by realigning the labor force. They also developed creative new means of management as they built what had been relatively small entrepreneurial craft enterprises into large-scale bureaucratic organizations geared to mass production. But perhaps the most significant wartime contribution was the newfound role of research and development in the production process. Its importance was not lost on the postwar generation, who made the aircraft and missile industry a major foundation for western economic growth in succeeding decades.

CHAPTER 5

New Basic Industries
for the West:
Aluminum

THE EXTRAORDINARY expansion
of the airplane and shipbuilding industries in the West during the war
triggered the creation of new basic manufactures such as aluminum. Before 1941 the demand for light metals in the region was negligible. But
during the years between 1940 and 1945 the needs for aluminum seemed
insatiable. The West profited from the crisis as both private producers
and the federal government sought to boost production in the shortest
possible time. Increased output required considerable development of
the metals industries in the region, *ipso facto* lessening the West's colonial
dependence on the East. The war thus not only led to the establishment
of new industries such as aluminum but also laid the foundations for the
postwar economy.

As the Roosevelt administration embarked on a rather slow and lum-
bering mobilization effort in 1939, it became painfully aware that the
situation in aluminum was precarious, since the one company in the field
enjoyed an absolute monopoly. The Temporary National Economic Committee, which Roosevelt had appointed to study economic concentration
in 1937, was just beginning to report its findings when World War II
broke out in Europe. Concerning aluminum, it noted that the Aluminum
Company of America (Alcoa) completely dominated the industry.[1] In 1940,
therefore, the federal government found itself totally dependent on the
sole private supplier of aluminum, now desperately needed for large-scale
aircraft production. This placed the Roosevelt administration in a vulnerable position. On the one hand, the country needed vast quantities
of aluminum; on the other, critics of the Aluminum Company of America
maintained that wartime conditions provided an excellent opportunity to

break the company's monopoly. The federal government could provide direct competition not only by building its own plants but also by financing new private operators in the industry. Moreover, such federal intervention could do much to further economic diversification in the West. To a considerable extent, Roosevelt followed this policy suggested by the critics, but he balanced it carefully so as not to antagonize Alcoa. The administration did little to undermine the company's dominant position in the industry but stimulated an extensive expansion of aluminum production by building a dozen new plants, half of which were located in the West. By the end of the war the federal government had provided the region with the basis of an aluminum industry where, before 1940, there had been none.

Alcoa had developed its monopoly over a period spanning more than three decades. Although its basic patents had long expired by 1940, the corporation managed to keep its primacy by dominating every aspect of the production process. Through a myriad of contracts it gained control over major sources of bauxite—the raw material needed for aluminum production—both in Arkansas and Dutch Guiana. Over the years it also acquired excellent low-cost power sites, so necessary for efficient production. Moreover, since 1888 the Mellons of Pittsburgh had held a significant stake in Alcoa and had utilized the family's financial resources to sustain the company's position. That dominance became even more solid in the 1930s when markets for aluminum shrank drastically and when even a monopolistic producer like Alcoa operated at considerably less than capacity. Nevertheless, Alcoa emerged from the Great Depression with its monopoly position unimpaired.[2]

With the inauguration of the New Deal's antitrust campaign in the late 1930s under Assistant Attorney General Thurman Arnold, Alcoa became a prime target for prosecution, charged with violation of the Sherman Anti-Trust Act. In 1937 the Department of Justice initiated proceedings to dissolve the company, contending that it exercized absolute control in the industry, that it controlled prices and reaped unreasonable profits, and that, in fact, it limited the use of aluminum in the United States. Alcoa, in turn, declared that it was not a monopoly because its customers could readily find substitutes for aluminum. Initial court proceedings began in the District Court for the Southern District of New York, where arguments raged over the next four years. The deliberations resulted in the longest trial on record, ending only on March 12, 1941, and producing fifty-eight thousand pages of transcript. In his decision, Judge Francis Caffey rejected the government's position. After due deliberation, the

Justice Department filed a petition on September 14, 1942, for an appeal to the United States Supreme Court.[3]

But by this time the United States was involved in war, and the major concern of federal agencies like the War Production Board and the Metals Reserve Corporation was to boost aluminum production rather than to prosecute Alcoa. Nor did Congress have much enthusiasm for breaking up Alcoa. On June 9, 1944, it enacted a special law to confer jurisdiction on a special appeals court composed of three senior judges from the federal circuit court of appeals in New York to hear the case. In January 1945 the Justice Department lamely proceeded with its action, claiming it would not affect maximum war production. The special court handed down its decision on March 12, 1945. Although finding Alcoa to be a monopoly, the justices declared that economic changes generated by the war, especially the new federally built aluminum plants, lessened Alcoa's control. Consequently, the court refused to recommend Alcoa's dissolution. "Dissolution is not a penalty, but a remedy," the judges noted. "If the industry will not need it for its protection it will be a disservice to break up an aggregate which has for so long demonstrated its efficiency." The court left it to the Surplus Property Board to dispose of federally owned surplus aluminum plants, with an eye to further discourage Alcoa's monopoly, and instructed the District Court for the Southern District of New York to decide in the future whether dissolution would be necessary. In short, increased competition in the industry due to wartime mobilization, although it did not significantly lessen Alcoa's dominant role in the 1940s, persuaded the federal courts to abandon efforts to dissolve the company.[4]

But the slow progress of the federal court suit against the company between 1937 and 1945 did not dampen the ardor of Alcoa's critics. Westerners especially welcomed new aluminum plants in their region as a unique opportunity to diversify the economy. They rallied behind Secretary of the Interior Harold L. Ickes, Senators Harry S. Truman and James E. Murray, the administrator of the Bonneville Power facilities, Paul Raver, and the congressional delegations from the Pacific Northwest, all of whom consistently battled to break Alcoa's hold. By the war's end they had made significant progress.

Ickes was among the most vociferous critics of Alcoa. "I have been interested in aluminum development for some time," he noted in 1941, "both as a member of an informal committee of the Cabinet on aluminum and magnesium and as the officer responsible for much of the national water power development." His concerns began to mount late in 1940 when Alcoa showed itself unable to meet burgeoning defense needs. The company insisted it could handle all demands and issued a press release on November 28, 1940, assuring Americans that it could meet all of the nation's civilian as well as military requirements.[5]

Ickes was one of the company's doubters, however, and was loath to make additional federal power available to it lest he strengthen Alcoa's monopolistic position. On February 4, 1941, the Office of Production Management requested 65,000 kilowatts of power for Alcoa from Bonneville, the large federal power project in the Pacific Northwest. This was in addition to the 162,500 kilowatts Bonneville had already agreed to sell to Alcoa. At this point Ickes used stalling tactics. A week later he brought up the OPM's request before the informal cabinet committee on aluminum and urged that the federal agency make a more accurate estimate of aluminum requirements. In particular, he urged greater competition in the industry. If that could not be achieved through new private investment, Ickes declared, then he favored the building of new plants by the federal government.[6]

In ensuing months Ickes continued his attempt to foster competition in the aluminum industry. He recoiled from the prospect of allocating at least 80 percent of Bonneville's current capacity to Alcoa. Instead, he was hoping to provide such energy to new competitors. His refusal to allocate power from federal dams under his jurisdiction did prompt the OPM to negotiate contracts with a newcomer, the Reynolds Metals Company. But in March and April 1941 the OPM requested another 85,000 kilowatts for Alcoa from the Bonneville dams, and that led Ickes to advocate additional government-built plants to expand production. By this time the nation had been gripped by a severe aluminum shortage that was hampering aircraft production. This prompted the fiery secretary to charge that Alcoa's management was characterized by "either incompetence or self-interest, both of which are dangerous." He believed that Alcoa was deliberately restricting its output so that it would not be left with excessive productive capacity when hostilities ended.[7]

Above all, Ickes viewed the expansion of aluminum plants as a major step in diversifying the western economy.

> The Government is assuming almost all of the risk inherent in our rapidly expanding aluminum production. It is guaranteeing the market. It will take everything anybody can produce. It is putting up, at its own expense, huge generating facilities which it will have on its hands at the end of the emergency unless the Nation continues to expand as I, apparently unlike the Aluminum Company hope that it will. . . . There is an obligation on the part of the Government not to take a fool's risk with the people's money. I do not believe that we should invest all this money for national defense purposes and end up either

New Basic Industries for the West: Aluminum

by treating the Pacific Northwest as a colony or by making a Christmas present of all of our expensive facilities to the Aluminum Company.[8]

His primary goal was to foster more aluminum production plants as well as processing plants in the Pacific Northwest where power was cheap. "It should be pointed out," he noted, "that, although it is both desirable and necessary that aluminum reduction plants be located in the Northwest near available sources of public power, this location would place a heavy burden upon the Nation unless fabricating plants were also located in that region." He decried the unnecessarily high price of aluminum, noting that the cost was partly due to the cumbersome transportation of bauxite ore from Arkansas back and forth across the country. "At the present time, alumina produced from bauxite is shipped from Mobile and East St. Louis to the Northwest," he explained. "It is there reduced to pig aluminum; the pig aluminum is then transported to fabricating plants in the East; the fabricated metal is then sent back in huge quantities to the Pacific Coast—and even to the Northwest itself—for airplane manufacture. The shuttle system is obviously expensive. More important, it adds a terrific burden to our critically overladen transportation system." Ickes concluded, "It seems to me to be essential that prompt action be taken to locate sufficient of these plants in the Northwest . . . thereby avoiding these long cross hauls." But he warned, "A concentration of aluminum manufacturing plants in the Northwest would be disastrous for that region unless there is assurance that the aluminum companies will not consider themselves as transient aliens, but will plan to stay in that area and locate fabricating plants there."[9]

Ickes viewed the aluminum shortage within the broader context of western economic growth. It was part and parcel of larger issues "in the defense program of the whole area west of the Mississippi. I believe that it has been somewhat neglected, not by the intent of the responsible agencies, not exactly by oversight, but by the policy of allowing existing companies to concentrate in the East if they so desire. . . . Instead of moving plants out West, some eastern companies have bought up heavy machinery in the Middle West and have shipped it East." The shortage of aluminum in the spring of 1941 thus presented an unusual opportunity for the government to lessen Alcoa's monopolistic hold on the industry, Ickes firmly believed.

I do not think it desirable that we . . . should . . . further aid . . . monopoly. Monopoly may be even more dangerous in dangerous times than it is in normal times. Our whole defense effort becomes dependent upon the skill, resourcefulness, and devotion to the public welfare of a few individuals who own and control the monopoly. . . . We will have lost a great deal of ground if our present plans are so devised that the reduction plants that the Government is now building can be bought by only one big and wealthy company. . . . If the aluminum plants established by the Defense Plant Corporation are few, and of such gigantic size, it will be impossible for average men or corporations either to stay in or go into the aluminum business at the end of the emergency. . . . Large units might well mean the end of the development of the light-metal industry in the Northwest.[10]

Ickes's views were reiterated by Assistant Attorney General Thurman Arnold, who was arguing the government's case against Alcoa, and by Senator Joseph C. O'Mahoney of Wyoming, who was concluding the extensive antitrust investigation of the Temporary National Economic Committee. And Ickes's frustrations were shared by his subordinates, particularly Paul Raver, chief of the Bonneville Power Administration. "During the latter part of May," Raver recalled, "the officials of the Office of Production Management asked the Department of the Interior for a statement of the amount of power available . . . under the supervision of the Department . . . from the Bonneville and Grand Coulee Dams. . . . The OPM stressed the need for speed on this, and we went to work, thinking that speed was essential, and that we would be in a position to proceed quickly." Raver stated that within two days his staff had made the necessary estimates and that he had been ready to sign a contract with the Defense Plant Corporation to inaugurate aluminum production. He and his associates flew to Washington, D.C., on June 5, 1941, where they met with Roger Cortesi and Clarence H. Jones, representing the OPM.[11]

Then disillusionment set in. The OPM officials indicated that they expected no more than a single large plant to boost aluminum production. "This would have meant," Raver complained,

> that we would have had in the Northwest two large aluminum plants, one of which is now in operation at Vancouver [by Alcoa] . . . and another of similar size. We protested against having this additional block of aluminum concentrated in one plant. We had a number of reasons for protesting. We felt that from an operating view, certainly Bonneville could provide this capacity much more efficiently and at less cost . . . if this load was distributed over our transmission system instead of being concentrated at one spot. We recommended that the power load be divided up into at least three aluminum plants instead of concentrating it in one.

Unlike the men in the OPM, who sought only an immediate increase in aluminum production for war, Raver hoped to further the economic diversification of the Northwest.

> Under the Bonneville Act, from the regional point of view, it was better to decentralize this large industry rather than to concentrate it at one point, to

give a better balance to the economy of the region. . . . The monopolistic implications of the single-plant location also struck us rather forcibly. It was apparent . . . that the Government would have to have so vast a plant operated and managed by the Aluminum Company of America since only that company, according to these OPM officials, had the requisite skill and managerial ability to run a plant of that size. Moreover, after the war emergency is over and production for defense is curtailed the Government plant or plants will presumably stand idle unless private concerns take them over and run them. In other words, the Government plants will be real war babies after this emergency, unless they are now designed and planned . . . in such a way as to enable private capital to take them over and continue to operate them after the war emergency is over. . . . From a monopolistic point of view . . . it seems to me that if we have several plants out here, operated by independent operators, we have a much better chance of those plants continuing in operation after the emergency is over than we do if the entire operation is under the control of the present monopoly. . . . If they control the entire aluminum production in the Northwest it will be their choice when this emergency is over, as to what plants will continue in operation, and the Government, not having developed any other operators, will be at their mercy in that decision. . . . I don't want this to be a Muscle Shoals after this war is over.[12]

To Raver's dismay, the differing views concerning the expansion of aluminum production in the region led to an initial deadlock that impeded the mobilization program. OPM officials like Cortesi and Jones simply ignored Raver's pleas. After a period of silence Raver wrote to William L. Batt, the OPM's aluminum specialist, urging a plant in Tacoma with a thirty-million-pound production potential, as well as others at Cascade Locks and Spokane or Grand Coulee with twice that capacity. During the next weeks OPM officials were silent, however. Then, on July 2, 1941, the OPM informed Ickes that it was planning to build a major facility at Cascade Locks capable of producing ninety-seven million pounds annually and another in Spokane, but nothing at Tacoma, the only location to which Bonneville could provide additional power. Raver was exasperated. "We want to see the Northwest come into its own, with a balanced economy," he declared, "which can rest largely upon the light-metal industries, providing some attention is given here by responsible Government officials to making out of this defense effort a development that will fit the regional economy after the defense effort is over."[13]

Senator Truman, displaying his customary bluntness, strongly reinforced Raver's protests. Truman openly charged Alcoa with abetting the OPM's delays in accelerating new aluminum production so that it could monopolize the power available from the Bonneville system. In his estimation the aluminum shortage had become the major bottleneck in the president's program to build fifty thousand planes that year. "Aluminum constitutes between 54 and 80 percent of the weight of airplanes," Truman stated, "including the motors, and a much greater percentage when you exclude the motors." Alcoa's executives had clearly underestimated the demand for aluminum in 1941. In that year they produced thirty-one million pounds, yet by May it was clear that needs would exceed fifty-one million pounds. Alcoa's reluctance to expand production was perhaps a reflection of depression psychology, emphasizing limited demand. But Senator Truman personalized the blame and placed it squarely on Alcoa's chairman, Arthur V. Davis. Truman declared that Davis was "following a policy of being half asleep, instead of waking up to the situation as it is." Such a condemnation echoed in part Thurman Arnold's indictment of Alcoa in the Justice Department suit against the company. Arnold charged Alcoa with restricting production, a judgment with which Senator Joseph C. O'Mahoney concurred after the Temporary National Economic Committee studied the problem. To convinced antimonopolists, the aluminum situation in 1941 was a striking example of their dire warnings about the consequences of monopoly.[14]

Potential competitors to Alcoa were also critical of its performance, and among these Richard S. Reynolds was prominent. Testifying in May 1941 Reynolds recalled that a year earlier, just after the fall of France to the Germans, he had gone to Washington, D.C., to warn Arthur V. Davis of impending aluminum shortages. Reynolds had also consulted with Senator Lister Hill of Alabama, a member of the Senate Military Affairs Committee, who had made special studies of light metals. Hill urged Reynolds to implore Davis to boost production before it was too late. "I thought he should inform our Government of the true situation in France," Reynolds remembered. "I urged him to ask for Government funds sufficient to enable his company to produce 1,000,000,000 pounds of aluminum with full protection to his company." But Davis felt that Reynolds was unduly alarmed and discounted predictions of possible shortages. "In his opinion, there was ample aluminum, and . . . there would be no shortage," Reynolds said. "I reported the results of this conference back to Senator Hill who quickly turned and said, 'Old Fellow, what are you willing to do for your country?' I said, 'Senator, that is putting me on the spot. But we have 18 plants that are not mortgaged, and I will certainly recommend to our board that we mortgage these plants to secure funds for the production of aluminum . . . to quickly increase production.'"

Hill quickly set wheels in motion. "He immediately phoned Mr. [Emil] Schram, chairman of the Reconstruction Finance Corporation, and asked that he see me," Reynolds recalled. "The loan was tentatively approved within 30 days and was finally closed in August, 1940. . . . The total loan was fixed at $15,800,000 with which we expected to produce from sixty to eighty million pounds of aluminum ingot per year. . . . We are building two plants, one at Lister, Alabama and the other at Longview, Washington. . . . In my opinion, at least 10 standby aluminum plants should be built at different locations."[15]

Alcoa's executives defended themselves against charges that they were impeding the mobilization program. I. W. Wilson, vice-president for production, argued as early as 1940, at the antitrust trial, that his company could supply any and all of the nation's aluminum needs, this despite the fact that Germany's aluminum production capacity in 1940 was three times that of the United States. To put the accusations of its critics to rest, on November 28, 1940, Alcoa issued a press release to announce publicly that it was not aware of any aluminum shortage and that, in any case, it was prepared to supply all requirements. That statement proved embarrassingly wrong within three months when a critical aluminum shortage impeded aircraft production. However, during the early stages of the mobilization program procurement agencies did often make inaccurate projections. Both the Army and the Navy departments changed their estimates frequently, sometimes on a weekly basis, thus making it difficult indeed for suppliers like Alcoa to plan precisely.[16]

Wilson attempted to clear Alcoa's name. Responding to critics like Ickes, he noted: "Alcoa has done everything within its power to . . . building up our defenses. . . . As late as April 3, 1939 Congress had only authorized the Navy to build 3000 planes, and the Army 6000. Such a program required no expansion of production facilities." Yet late in 1938 the company did expand, spending $200 million, doubling its work force to twenty-five thousand, and also doubling the previous year's production. With injured pride Wilson asserted that many of the accusations were

> based on the assumption that it is the function of a private industrial corporation . . . to estimate not only what it will produce to meet the defense needs of the United States, but also to set itself up as an authority for what those needs are. Under this assumption we should not only have been able to tell how much aluminum will be required . . . to build the number of airplanes needed to defend the democracies, but to forecast how many of these planes will be needed. . . . We have not presumed to tell Congress, the Army, or the Navy how many planes are needed for defense.[17]

George R. Gibbons, vice-president of Alcoa, reinforced Wilson's position. In attempting to explain the company's predicament he noted a lack of data.

> For example . . . a Boeing B-19 requires so much aluminum, and as a rule we know what the propellers amount to in weight, what the engine forgings and engine castings . . . and if someone will tell us how many B-19s they want we

99

can figure it up. We may be a little more expert in converting square footage and weights of propellers into pounds than some of the Government people . . . but we haven't the slightest idea of how many planes are wanted, what size planes are wanted, or anything until someone says, "We want so many planes of such and such type" and we say "Give us a bill of material" . . . and convert it into pounds of aluminum. . . . We haven't the slightest conception of what is wanted until he tells us what sort of plane is wanted, and how many are wanted.[18]

The new mobilization agencies that Roosevelt created in 1940 and 1941 also shrugged off blame for the aluminum shortage. William L. Batt, deputy director of the Division of Production in the OPM, explained how the war preparation program appeared to a harried and somewhat inexperienced bureaucrat like himself. In May 1941 he said:

We came down here about June of last year and found a production capacity of about 30,000,000 pounds a month. It was impossible to get detailed estimates from the services as to how much aluminum they would require for aircraft manufacturing for a variety of reasons. In the first place their program had expanded overnight at a tremendous rate, many of the designs were still on the drawing board, bills of materials weren't available, and so the Defense Commission had to estimate as well as it could. . . . In this May, actually, instead of the military requirements being 25,000,000 pounds a month, the requirements . . . are about 50,000,000 pounds. If that was a poor estimate [it was] because this was a new industry.[19]

By the spring of 1941 it was clear that army and navy procurement officers, and to some extent Alcoa's chief executives and OPM mobilization officials, had seriously underestimated the demand for aluminum. In December 1940 and January 1941 major aircraft manufacturers like Northrop and Glenn Martin curtailed production because of inadequate aluminum supplies. The shortages might well have been averted. In the summer of 1940 congressional delegations from the Pacific Northwest had appealed to the Council of National Defense's advisory commission to build aluminum plants in their region. On July 13 and 14, 1940, they met in the Washington, D.C., office of Oregon Senator Carl Holman, with his senior colleague Senator Charles McNary presiding. There they urged representatives of the Council for National Defense, William L. Batt and Gano Dunn, to build new aluminum plants in Washington and Oregon. Still influenced by a depression psychology and by an eastern orientation, Batt and Dunn downplayed the predictions of an aluminum shortage. The chairman of the council, Edward R. Stettinius, was equally smug and, as events revealed, equally wrong.[20] It was no wonder, therefore, that Senator Truman, in a thorough investigation of the aluminum shortage in May and June 1941, made a scathing indictment of Alcoa and OPM officials. Thoroughly chastened, they now hastened to accelerate the program and on June 26, 1941, announced that they would recommend the construction of eight new plants.[21]

Roosevelt himself took a direct interest in stimulating greater competition in the aluminum industry and expanding it in the West. "Whenever I heard from him in this vein I knew that some meddler had been talking to him," wrote Jesse Jones a few years later, referring to his archrival Harold Ickes. Roosevelt was constantly reminded of Alcoa's monopoly by Ickes. For example, Alcoa wanted to build only one large plant in the state of Washington, which would fit nicely into its own national network of facilities. But Ickes and Raver were successful in forcing the Defense Plant Corporation to further decentralize plants to contribute to the economic diversification of the West in the postwar era. Thus, beginning in 1941 the DPC built six new aluminum plants in the region, including those in Los Angeles, Spokane, Cascade Locks, and Vancouver, Washington, all operated by Alcoa. Reynolds Metals managed the DPC facility at Longview, Washington, while the Olin Corporation ran a smaller one in Tacoma. By 1943 these operations were producing, but not fabricating, about one-third of all the aluminum in the United States. Within four years, therefore, the federal government had endowed the West with an aluminum industry that brought significant diversification to the regional economy.[22]

Meanwhile, in the midst of the aluminum shortage in the spring of 1941, the OPM was exploring new processes to solve its dilemma. One of these was to utilize the alunite process that westerners strenuously lobbied for. This involved the manufacture of alunite clays—found mainly in Utah and other western states—instead of bauxite. Over several decades some scientists had proposed this alternative. In 1910 the U.S. Bureau of Mines had located extensive alunite deposits in Piute County, Utah, near the town of Marysvale. In a special report of 1932 the bureau noted that there were more than one million tons of alumina in that area, enough to supply the nation's needs for twenty years. During the Great Depression such news was hardly welcomed. But with the aluminum shortage of 1941, boosters argued that alunite could provide the solution to the nation's problem.[23]

The alunite interests began lobbying in earnest in 1940. In the forefront was Utah's congressional delegation, which hoped to secure federal aid for the exploitation of that state's alunite reserves. In July 1940 Senator Abe Murdock and S. P. Dodds, a member of the Democratic National Committee, met with William L. Batt, the OPM's aluminum specialist. They sought federal funding to expand a small alunite processing plant at Marysvale. Although the Reynolds Metals Company had offered to buy the product of this small facility, Senator Murdock hoped to expand its output. Murdock also went to the White House to press his request with the chief executive. Roosevelt encouraged him, and thus Murdock introduced an amendment to the Department of the Interior appropriation bill for 1941 authorizing $85,000 for work on alunite by the Bureau of Mines. In addition, the Senate Appropriations Committee approved another $415,000 for scientific investigations into aluminum ores.[24]

Meanwhile, Murdock gained another ally. On June 15, 1941, Secretary Ickes told Harry Truman that he firmly believed aluminum could be produced more cheaply from alunite than from bauxite. To a considerable extent, his passionate desire to lessen Alcoa's monopoly position clouded his judgment. "I have urged that a full sized commercial operation of this [alunite] process be financed by the Government." There "was enough to keep a 60,000,000 pound plant running for over 10 years," he proclaimed enthusiastically. "That is in Utah. We don't know how much there is in Washington."[25]

Alcoa officials were not as sanguine about the commercial feasibility of using alunite. George R. Gibbons felt that perhaps one day alunite might be practical, but not in 1940.

> There are two conditions relating to the use of alunite which I hope some day will be overcome. One is that the alumina made from the alunite is not a pure material under any process that has thus far been commercially used. . . . I haven't the slightest doubt that the scientists will lick that problem like they do all of them. The cost of aluminum from alunite is quite a little in excess— I would think it might be 50, perhaps 100 per-cent, greater, maybe more than that—of alumina produced from bauxite. . . . But there has never been any real commercial alunite venture.[26]

Such views influenced OPM officials, who displayed little enthusiasm for the alunite process. Ickes first suggested the program in April 1941 but received no positive response. When he had still heard nothing by July, he informed the Utah delegation that he would take the matter up directly with the president. That got results; within a week Arthur Bunker of the OPM informed Ickes that the agency would consider the process. Bunker instructed the Olin Corporation, which was operating a processing plant in Tacoma, to utilize alumina produced at Marysvale.[27]

Slowly, the bureaucratic wheels began to turn. In July 1941 the National Academy of Sciences issued a report on its investigation of the alunite process. Although it considered the process feasible, the academy's scientists wondered whether the quantity of ores available in Utah warranted construction of a large government plant such as Ickes was advocating. Meanwhile, Senator Truman was attributing OPM's reluctance to endorse alunite to Alcoa's influence in seeking to preserve its monopoly. And Senator Murdock visited Batt of the OPM in August to renew his demands for adoption of the alunite process. Within a few days the OPM bowed to the inevitable and joined the Bureau of Mines and the U.S. Geological Survey in recommending the grant of federal funds to the Kalunite Corporation of Salt Lake City (a subsidiary of the Olin Corporation) to build a new plant in Marysvale.[28] Batt informed Murdock on August 18, 1941, that the OPM had instructed the Reconstruction Finance Corporation to provide $5 million for a processing plant to convert one hundred tons of alunite daily, with the alumina it produced to be sent to the Olin fabricating facility in Tacoma. The planned capacity for this operation made it a pilot project. Further negotiations between the OPM and the company led to the construction of a $3-million plant at Marysvale by the Kalunite Corporation.[29] Although completed in 1943, it was unable to attain commercial production levels during the war. The processing facility in Salt Lake City received twelve thousand tons of ore from Marysvale, but the result of all its activity was only six hundred tons of aluminum. In short, wartime experience indicated that the alunite process was not very feasible commercially in the 1940s.[30]

Alternatives other than alunite also occupied the minds of the OPM officials. In their frenzied search for aluminum during the mobilization crisis they turned to still another potential source: the Aluminum Company of Canada (Alcan). At the urging of the War Department, in May 1940 Jesse Jones of the RFC began to investigate the possibilities of tapping Alcan's huge facility at Shipshaw in the Canadian province of Quebec. Alcan was a wholly separate and distinct corporate entity with no legal connections to Alcoa, its American cousin. On the other hand, its chairman, Edward K. Davis, was the brother of Arthur K. Davis, Alcoa's chief executive. Given the critical shortage of aluminum in 1941, the near desperation of federal officials was understandable as they sought to utilize any and all means of increasing aluminum production. But the contracts they signed for the Shipshaw project became one of the most controversial mobilization issues to arise in wartime and directly affected the economic diversification of the West.

Alcan had sought to expand its production at the Shipsaw site as early as 1928. In an effort to establish Canada's largest aluminum production facility, the company began expanding electric power installations on the lower Saguenay River during the 1930s, although the depression slowed the project. Then, in 1939 the British government requested significant increases in production as war broke out in Europe. The following year it lent $55 million to Alcan so that the company could boost its output to

435,000,000 pounds annually, a more than fourfold increase over its pre-war capacity. By 1941 both the Australian and the U.S. governments had invested another $117 million in Shipshaw, increasing its annual output to 1.1 billion pounds.[31]

As the aluminum shortage worsened during the first half of 1941 Jesse Jones searched for new sources regardless of the cost. Consequently, in April 1941 he instructed the Metals Reserve Corporation, a subsidiary of the RFC, to advance Alcan $93 million on future aluminum deliveries. Of this amount, $68.5 million was an interest-free loan. The rest was to be paid off by deducting five cents per pound from the aluminum Alcan delivered to the United States. In addition, the Metals Reserve Corporation established a line of credit for Alcan amounting to $34,250,000, to be made available as deliveries came in. Alcan pledged to provide 1,370,000,000 pounds in 1942, at a price of fifteen cents per pound (somewhat above prevailing market prices) on 1,096,000,000 pounds for direct American use and seventeen cents per pound on the remainder, which was destined for lend-lease. At the same time the Canadian government freed Alcan from most income and excess-profits taxes and also permitted it an accelerated depreciation for the new facilities. All in all, Alcan secured an exceptionally favorable deal, much better than what American producers were able to obtain at the time.[32]

But the implications of these contracts went beyond the enormous profits insured for Alcan. Since the summer of 1940 congressional delegations from the Pacific Northwest had tried in vain to persuade the RFC and the OPM to undertake large-scale expansion of aluminum production in their region. The OPM ignored their entreaties and left them deeply disappointed.[33] Ostensibly, securing additional aluminum quickly from an old, experienced operation appealed more to Batt and his OPM colleagues than did taking risks with newly established plants in the West. In part, however, the decision reflected a preference of easterners for eastern facilities and a certain disinclination to expand industrial production in the West.

The Shipshaw contracts portended new problems for westerners. In essence, the U.S. government was financing a vast expansion of Canadian production that would certainly hamper the growth of the aluminum industry in the Northwest during the postwar era. Moreover, the United States had absolutely no control over Shipshaw. To make the situation even more galling to westerners, in 1944 the Metals Reserve Corporation was expanding Shipshaw at the very same time that the War Production Board was curtailing domestic production and construction of similar projects in the United States allegedly because of severe shortages of strategic materials and power generators. In fact, during 1944 the War Production Board canceled four million kilowatt hours of electric power to be produced at Grand Coulee and Shasta dams because of such shortages. For similar reasons the agency suspended the development of more than one million horsepower in western dam projects that Congress had authorized. Western states felt keenly that their postwar industrial expansion was closely bound to the availability of low-cost electricity. The Shipshaw project, to them, undermined the very vitals of western economic growth.[34]

Although the OPM did not keep the Shipshaw contracts an absolute secret in 1941—as Harold Ickes charged in 1943—it did maintain a low profile concerning the project. During the summer of 1941 the agency issued a laconic press release about the contracts. Amidst the hustle and bustle of the intensified mobilization the news slipped by most members of Congress and most administration officials. Even the president himself, who in 1941 had given his blessing to the deal by approving a memorandum that Jesse Jones had submitted to him, could not remember the situation clearly two years later. By that time the aluminum problem had changed radically. Instead of a critical shortage, American manufacturers now produced more than was needed. Unfortunately, they achieved their production peaks at just about the same time that aluminum deliveries from Canada were also reaching their maximum levels.[35] Thus, American producers faced the anomaly of increasingly stiff Canadian competition financed primarily by their own government.

As might be expected, by 1943 a loud protest arose in the United States as Canadian aluminum poured in. Two congressional committees began extensive investigations of Shipshaw. And Harold Ickes became the most vehement administration critic as he led his followers into the fray. Congressional delegations from the Pacific Northwest vociferously charged that Shipshaw was undermining their region's present and future economic health. Meanwhile, Alcan's major American competitors charged that Shipshaw represented U.S. government favoritism for a foreign company. OPM officials were exceedingly vulnerable to attack. In the midst of an aluminum glut in 1943, they were hard put to defend their actions of 1941, taken in the very different context of an aluminum shortage.

Ickes felt that Shipshaw was directly impeding his plans for economic diversification of the West. Moreover, he felt that if he had only been more closely consulted by OPM officials in 1941 he could have forestalled the contracts by increasing aluminum production in the West. He could have increased the power output of Grand Coulee and Bonneville dams, which would have made the importation of Canadian aluminum unnecessary. And he was even more infuriated in 1943 and 1944 when the WPB, in keeping with prior contractual commitments, signed additional agreements with Alcan's Shipshaw facility. With biting sarcasm Ickes noted in 1943, "The impression apparently intended to be left . . . was that the Shipshaw contract was necessary to provide aluminum for the war." To him, nothing was further from the truth. In fact, he intimated that OPM officials were motivated by a bias against the West, virtually all of them having been executives of large eastern-based corporations. Ickes insisted that available power in the West during 1941 had been more than adequate but that the OPM simply had not wanted to utilize it. "I think that this deal was a mistake in judgment from beginning to end," he declared. "We must recognize that these Government plants can become an important factor in our postwar economic stability. . . . They must be kept in production. . . . That is why I question the soundness of the latest Shipshaw contract. I look to the Government's aluminum reduction plants in the Northwest as a source of abundant low-cost raw material for small business engaged in the independent fabrication of metal."[36]

Ickes elaborated his position. "I have no quarrel with the purchase of . . . aluminum . . . prior to 1943 . . . based upon the existing power facilities in Canada. I agree that we should have bought aluminum wherever possible at that time. But I see no reason why it was necessary to make a deal that would build a power plant for the Canadian Aluminum Company to compete with American power and aluminum facilities." He pointed an accusing finger at the OPM. "OPM had figures on domestic power possibilities prior to the Shipshaw contract. These showed that the Northwest power facilities could provide all the power that was obtained at Shipshaw. . . . Notwithstanding the knowledge that this power was available, the Shipshaw contracts were made." Ickes noted that his motivation was simple. "My long-standing interest in aluminum is the result of the tremendous power program that we had planned for the Northwest. This area, with its abundant low-cost power, is destined to be one of the world's centers of light metal production." At some length he analyzed the OPM's decision to favor Canada. Dismissing the claims of OPM officials who were concerned by the lack of bauxite resources in the West, the labor shortage on the West Coast, and the submarine menace in the Atlantic that made it difficult to ship bauxite from East to West, he argued: "It would have been possible to develop in this country hydro power capacity in the Northwest to have produced during 1942–1944 as much aluminum as was delivered by Canada." Moreover, Shipshaw only strengthened Alcoa's monopoly in the United States.

As a result of the policies that I have discussed . . . [we] promoted and strengthen that monopoly and its Canadian twin. There has been a neglect of our own power resources and of the use of our own Government plants to the fullest extent possible. . . . I see no excuse for keeping partly idle the Government plants in the Northwest while we go ahead and take deliveries of Canadian aluminum. Secondly, I urge that we view these Government owned plants . . . to be disposed of for the purpose of strengthening post-war employment and the national defense. . . . I think that the Government must deliberately use its aluminum plants for the purpose of assisting another responsible producer or two to enter the aluminum industry. . . . Never again should this country be placed in the position of having to rely largely upon one company for so vital a war material as aluminum. Monopoly can be even more dangerous in dangerous times than in normal times. . . . But the Government must lend some reasonable assistance if producers are to enter the industry. The problem of securing raw materials will be difficult. The development of market will take time.[37]

Ickes's views were reinforced by Paul Raver, administrator of the Bonneville Power Administration. "Starting in 1940 and throughout the period of the national emergency the record is clear," he said, "that the Bonneville Power Authority was not only willing, and anxious to expand power supply facilities and service for aluminum production in the Northwest . . . [but] was constantly urging higher priorities for generators . . . and additional loads. Our principal difficulty was that we were not informed on any over-all program." Then he leveled charges against the OPM and its successor, the WPB. "While the Bonneville Power Administration was thus pressing for a unified and rapid development of Northwest power facilities at . . . Bonneville and Grand Coulee Dams. . . the war agencies were thinking of these projects as only incidental sources of power supply." This was largely, Raver believed, because the OPM felt that the Northwest was too far removed from bauxite sources in Arkansas.

No serious consideration apparently was given to a rapid and integrated development of the aluminum industry in the Pacific Northwest. From our point of view the Bonneville Power Administration was denied the opportunity of making effective a program in keeping with the urgent need for the expansion of the aluminum and other war industries. The fact is . . . Shipshaw . . . worked and will continue to work, to the extreme disadvantage of the Northwest. I therefore feel keenly that from the lessons of the Shipshaw story the Congress should turn in the post-war period toward the problem of disposing of our Government owned aluminum plants with one conviction: we have helped others more than necessary, and now let us adopt new policies deliberately to make the utmost use of the aluminum plants we have built here for the benefit of our own workers and businessmen.[38]

Raver considered Shipshaw directly harmful to the western aluminum industry.

Based largely on Shipshaw, the Canadian company now has an aluminum capacity of 1,000,000,000 pounds. This makes it larger than the Aluminum Company of America. The favorable financial terms given the Canadian company should help it produce at lower cost than American plants. Its investment cost has been paid by our Government. . . . The Government and private plants in the Pacific Northwest ordinarily might have looked toward Asia during the postwar reconstruction period for large aluminum markets. Canadian aluminum can easily prevent this by taking over these markets. In this sense our Government policy may have destroyed some of the investment in Government plants. The process already has begun due to curtailment of output begun by the War Production Board in 1944. If Shipshaw had not been built, new producers would have greater interest in government surplus aluminum plants.

And Raver decried what he viewed as federal favoritism toward Alcoa. "It is essential from the point of view of our national economy to expand peacetime operation of these plants for both peacetime and war use. Government plants are too large for private operators to operate successfully."[39]

As the champion of small business in the West, Senator James E. Murray also became increasingly concerned about Shipshaw's influence. "We believe . . . the role which small and independent business can play in a competitive economy . . . to be substantial if we are to enjoy a healthy economic future. We seek . . . to remove the barriers to free enterprise," he declared. For that reason, "we are concerned about Shipshaw, not so much as an event which has taken place, but what its bearing might be on the future."[40]

Congressional delegations from the Pacific Northwest were appalled at the continuation of the Shipshaw contracts. "I want to know why we have to go outside the United States to get aluminum and leave plants idle," said Oregon Senator Guy Cordon. In fact, he led a group of legislators from the Pacific Northwest to the War Production Board in 1944 to demand the reopening of government aluminum plants in Troutdale, Oregon, and in Spokane, Washington, which the WPB had ordered closed with growing piles of aluminum. Representative Hugh De Lacey of Washington spoke for the entire Washington delegation when he noted: "We don't even object to Canada getting some help. But for the life of me I can't see why Alcoa . . . should get help that we believe our industry . . . in our part of the country can well be given."[41] Representative John M. Coffee of Washington was more explicit.

The people and the natural resources of the Pacific Northwest have made a monumental contribution to the production and fabrication of the light metals products. . . . What is to become of this great new industry in the Northwest? . . . It was no easy battle for us to convince the Federal Government in the early days of the war, that we should be given an opportunity to play a large part in the light metals production program. . . . As one member of Congress who was happy to play an active role . . . in breaking down the opposition of those Federal officials charged with responsibility for the production of aluminum, I am frankly apprehensive when it comes to reposing too much responsibility in the hands of those same officials in determining what shall be the future course of light metals production in the Pacific Northwest.[42]

Senator Wayne Morse of Oregon added more pungently, "My own personal judgment is that the record of the Office of Production Management and War Production Board in regard to the handling of aluminum during the war just stinks with inefficiency and mismanagement . . . [and] they have contributed to building up a great monopoly which . . . is the enemy of sound private enterprise in this country."[43] Congressman Homer Angell of Washington added, "We on the West Coast . . . are most interested in seeing that we utilize and develop our own power and make some aluminum here in this country rather than at Shipshaw."[44]

The politicians from the Pacific Northwest clearly understood the issue as it affected western economic expansion. As Congressman Coffee said in 1944: "We look forward to a permanent emancipation from the colonial economy status in which we have been held, in part, by the inability of our local industrialists to secure a place for themselves in the sun in competition with corporate monopolistic industries concentrated in the East. . . . We are also alert to the post-war commercial potentialities offered by the market for fabricated goods made from aluminum . . . offered by the consumer requirements of the populations across the stretches of the Pacific, ranging from Siberia to India." As for administration policy, Coffee commented: "The recent Shipshaw contract is nothing more than a move that will freeze out the low-cost Pacific Northwest plants for post-war operation, and thus deny employment opportunities to returning veterans and unemployed war workers. . . . We are going to be faced with a competitive situation which menaces aluminum development in the Pacific Northwest."[45]

Washington's Senator Warren Magnuson was similarly worried about the effect of Alcoa's monopoly on the region. "Here are two aluminum plants," he said, "one in Oregon and one in Washington—managed by Alcoa. . . . Now Alcoa can forget about these two plants [in view of Shipshaw] . . . and continue any plants it wants to throughout the country, and as long as it has the 5 year contract no independent company can go ahead and operate these plants."[46] Competition in the industry, therefore, would be severely restricted.

Congressman Charles R. Savage of Washington was particularly critical of Alcoa's labor policies, which he felt had impeded production in the company's West Coast plants. "Labor problems in the production of aluminum in the Pacific Northwest . . . have evidently been handled not very effectively by either the Federal war agencies concerned or by the Aluminum Company of America," he said. "The result has been the false charge of labor shortage given as a reason for curtailment of aluminum production in Oregon and Washington during part of 1944. . . . The weak handling of the labor situation has been partly responsible for the alleged need to buy more Canadian aluminum under the new Shipshaw contract. There is no sign now that proper measures will be taken to correct the aluminum labor situation in the Northwest." Savage concluded: "It is too dangerous to reply upon one company for so vital a war material. Alcoa's policies have not always been in the public interest. Government policy should correct this situation now that we have the opportunity through disposal of the Government-owned plants."[47]

Perhaps the best summary of regional views was made by Representative Hugh De Lacey.

> The things which we possibly object to more than any other are three. First, whether every effort was made to develop our power facilities in the Northwest; second, who in the world imagined the scheme for locating aluminum plants, many of them in the most uneconomical locations possible; and, lastly, this latest [1945] contract. . . . We would like to recommend . . . three steps: First, that an aluminum administrator be set up upon whom we could rest the responsibility for all phases of the program. Second, we recommend the cancellation of the Shipshaw contract. Third, we ought to get into the DPC plant at the earliest moment private operators other than Alcoa, to make it possible for them to learn the whole process and to begin to acquire the facilities which we hope the Government can dispose of later.[48]

Alcoa's major new competitor was similarly concerned about the influence of the Shipshaw contracts on the western aluminum industry. In a letter to Senator Tom Stewart, Richard S. Reynolds noted, "Our Government grossly discriminates against Reynolds Metals Company in favor of a foreign corporation beyond the reaching of our tax, renegotiation, and anti-trust legislation." Alcan, he complained, secured higher prices from the federal government, obtained interest-free loans, and was not required to put up security to guarantee deliveries. By contrast, the WPB charged Reynolds 4 percent interest on loans to build new aluminum production facilities and, in addition, required Reynolds to mortgage all of its assets as security. And whereas the Shipshaw contracts did not require Alcan to repay any of its loans if the federal government no longer needed the aluminum for which it had contracted, Reynolds was to repay all of its loans at 4 percent interest irrespective of whether the government bought its output. "The Canadian contracts clearly indicate crass favoritism to a foreign operator at huge expense to our Government," Reynolds declared. "Had Reynolds Metals Company received the same terms as the Aluminum Company of Canada, it would have received $19,000,000 as escalator payments. . . . Reynolds Metals Company cannot be expected to incur further risks to provide employment and salvage value for the Government-owned plants unless it is assured that the Government is prepared to make some fair-minded adjustment to the operation of this discrimination . . . and . . . unless it is assured ₁ . . terms . . . as favorable as those granted to its competitors."[49]

The men largely responsible for the Shipshaw contracts constructed elaborate defenses for their actions. The group included the OPM deputy director of production, William L. Batt; his assistant, William L. Clayton; the OPM's specialist on power, Gano Dunn; and Arthur Bunker, who was in charge of the OPM and WPB's Aluminum Division. Above all, these men emphasized the crisis atmosphere that had pervaded most federal agencies at the beginning of the mobilization program and the serious shortages of aluminum at the time. Moreover, they noted, in 1941 the United States and Canada were just embarking on closer relationships for common wartime ventures in which cost was a lesser consideration than maximum production. In 1945, when the Allies were assured of victory, the situation had changed dramatically, and a very different mood had enveloped the nation's capital.

Early in 1941, the nation suddenly found itself severely short of aluminum, Batt explained, directly slowing vital aircraft production. Much of the blame for the shortfall he placed on the armed forces, particularly the army, which had been exceedingly complacent throughout 1940 and had simply misjudged the amount of aluminum that would be needed for increased production. "We needed vast quantities of aluminum," Batt recalled in 1945, "and we needed it desperately soon. We were buying time then and any step and every step that would produce aluminum quickly, was believed to be amply justified." Moreover, on March 1, 1941, Roosevelt announced his intention to expand aircraft production to a level that made all previous production goals obsolete. The shortfall was at least two hundred million pounds, and Batt noted, "The question was, where could we get it?"[50]

111

New Basic Industries for the West: Aluminum

At the same time, Roosevelt was fashioning closer ties to Canada. In mid-April he met with Canadian Prime Minister Mackenzie King at Hyde Park. There they signed the Hyde Park Agreement on April 20, 1941, to facilitate closer cooperation between the two countries in a wide range of activities affecting their national security. Within this context Batt and his associates looked to Canada for aluminum. A Canada connection would also bypass the problems he was having with Harold Ickes concerning the additional power needed for Alcoa from Bonneville and other federal dams. Ickes, it will be recalled, was loath to allot energy to expand Alcoa's production because he was seeking to stimulate competition in the industry. Batt's major concern, however, was to secure maximum production of aluminum rather than to cope with the structure of monopoly. Given the hectic crisis atmosphere in Washington during the spring of 1941, Batt saw additional Canadian production as an enormous boon to the president's airplane program. "Since the demands of the aluminum program could not be satisfied in the time required in the United States," he said, "it followed naturally from the mandate given us at Hyde Park that we should seek the necessary aluminum in Canada." Between January 1 and May 1, 1941, the president had raised aluminum requirements fourfold. Thus, on May 2 the Metals Reserve Corporation, acting for the OPM, signed the first Shipshaw contract with Alcan for one hundred million pounds annually. That amount was doubled in an additional contract signed on July 15. And, as already noted, the terms of these agreements were rather favorable to the Canadians.[51]

Batt himself was not too pleased with these arrangements. But the choice was between the long-term expansion of power output in the Pacific Northwest and the immediate delivery of Canadian aluminum for planes and weapons. "I have to remind the committee again," Batt declared in 1945, "that these were extraordinarily hectic days . . . and we were well nigh desperate." Still, he relayed his doubts about the provisions of the Shipshaw contract to his associate, William L. Clayton, who had similar reservations. "We share your dislike for that particular part of the proposal which runs into 1945," Batt wrote him in early June 1941.

However, there is one basic consideration which motivates our judgment, and that is that by this contract we shall get additional aluminum in 1942 and 1943. The 30,000 metric tons additional to that already provided for 1942 will bring 1,500 heavy four-motored bombers, and the 45,000 tons for 1943, 2,100 four-motored bombers. These will be the most important elements in our aircraft program and the time of delivery is so vital that the cost is a secondary conclusion. Aluminum at almost any price in 1942 is, therefore, in our judgment justified, and our strong recommendation is that you make the best possible deal that you can.[52]

New Basic Industries for the West: Aluminum

Right or wrong, that was the prevailing attitude among the power brokers in Washington. Batt's deputy chief at the OPM, A. I. Henderson, similarly defended the agency's policy in a letter to William Knudsen, head of the OPM, on April 30, 1941.

"Dear Will," he wrote, in the course of our telephone conversation on Monday you asked me to give you an outline of the aluminum situation to show why it was desirable to buy aluminum from the Aluminum Company of Canada. The most recent estimate . . . shows requirements of about 1,600,000,000 pounds per annum at peak rates. . . . Capacity which is in existence . . . is estimated at 800 million pounds per annum. . . . It will be difficult to make use of the power at Boulder Dam . . . as the amounts available are not sufficient to justify the erection of new plants. . . . This leaves a minimum of about 420,000 kilowatts to be obtained from Bonneville-Grand Coulee. . . . It is important that we obtain an increased supply of aluminum at an early date. Under the proposed arrangement with the Aluminum Company of Canada we can obtain a substantial amount of aluminum during the next 12 months. There does not seem to be any other way in which such large amounts of aluminum can be obtained promptly.[53]

That the situation in 1941 had been critical was also stressed by William L. Clayton, assistant secretary of state and deputy loan administrator, who had handled the negotiations with the Canadians. Clayton recalled that the idea of turning to Canada came from him and other associates at the OPM early in 1941. He began his negotiations with Edward Davis, president of Alcan, on April 25, 1941. The American team included Jesse Jones, Clayton, and Clayton's assistant, Simon Strauss. The Canadians were represented by Davis, R. E. Powell, an Alcan executive, and E. G. McDowell, an Alcan director. The Canadians drove a hard bargain, and as Clayton noted, "We made the best deal we could."[54]

American negotiators took great pride in what they considered to be a real achievement. Jones announced the contract at a press conference on May 16, 1941. Senator Truman told Batt: "You ought to get all the aluminum you can. . . . Our main purpose was to get aluminum." Within this context Jones personally handed letters explaining the contract—along with a few words of personal amplification—to Roosevelt. The chief executive considered it and wrote "O.K., I approve" on Jones's memo. In later years, when the contracts came under criticism, Roosevelt professed not to remember his action. On April 19, 1943, he sent a memo to Jones in which he noted: "Please let me have a copy of the Shipshaw Dam contract with the Aluminum Company [of Canada]. Honestly, I do not remember specifically approving the contract—but I may be wrong."[55]

The Shipshaw contracts were the products of wartime necessity, hind-

113

sight notwithstanding. In 1941 and 1942 the need for aluminum was urgent, with chronic shortages due largely to the wrong estimates of the War Department and of industry leaders at the beginning of the mobilization program. Moreover, officials in newly established government mobilization agencies such as the OPM and the MRC were inexperienced and not at all well versed in the vagaries of readying the nation's economy for war production. At the same time, military and domestic pressures on them were enormous. Few could foretell that the contracts with Canada might pose problems for the domestic industry and for the West. But in 1944 maximum production was no longer the priority it had been three years earlier. And the progress of the war relieved apprehensions that had driven federal officials during the incipient stages of the mobilization program. Moreover, the president's monthly changes of mind about production goals in 1941 had made life miserable for the bureaucrats who served him. Thus, both the critics as well as the defenders of Shipshaw made many valid points, but the context of their appraisals changed greatly over time.

Although the Shipshaw agreement continued to be controversial after 1945, it could not be undone, and public attention shifted to the larger problem of the disposal of government-owned aluminum plants in the West in the postwar era. That point was well made by Paul Raver in 1945, who said, "I therefore feel keenly that from the lessons of the Shipshaw story the Congress should turn . . . toward the problem of disposing of our Government-owned aluminum plants with one conviction: We have helped others more than was necessary, and now let us adopt new policies deliberately to make the utmost use of the aluminum plants we have built here for the benefit of our own workers and businessmen."[56]

Such were the sentiments of many who were concerned about the reshaping of the western aluminum industry in the closing months of the war. Indeed, by 1944 aluminum production was peaking and actually exceeded demand. As the WPB ordered decreases in production and the closing of some of the DPC plants in the Pacific Northwest it brought the question of restructuring into the mainstream of public policy. The nature of this restructuring was of particular significance to westerners, who viewed disposal as a unique opportunity to bring about the long-desired diversification of their region's economy. It also presented a unique opportunity to break Alcoa's monopoly. And some business interests saw disposal as a good time to expand West Coast trade with the Orient and Pacific rim. By the end of 1944 public discussion concerning the disposal of government plants intensified.

The absence of coherent disposal policies on the part of the adminis-

Senator Harry S. Truman conducting public hearings of the Senate Special
Committee to Investigate Defense Expenditures during World War II.
Office of War Information. Courtesy of the Harry S. Truman Library.

Senator Harry S. Truman inspecting military facilities in
Utah, 1943. Courtesy of the Harry S. Truman Library.

Champion of small business: Senator
James E. Murray of Montana in
the 1940s.
Courtesy of the Mansfield Library,
University of Montana.

Maury Maverick, chairman of the Smaller War Plants Corporation, in his office, 1944.
Courtesy of the Barker Texas History Center, The University of Texas at Austin.

Western critic of big business: Thurman Arnold.
Courtesy of the American Heritage Center, University of Wyoming.

Senator Joseph C. O'Mahoney of Wyoming: antitrust advocate from the West.
Courtesy of the American Heritage Center, University of Wyoming.

Maury Maverick inspecting aircraft production at the North American Aviation Company in Los Angeles, 1944.
Courtesy of the Barker Texas History Center, The University of Texas at Austin.

Architects of western economic growth: Secretary of the Interior Harold L.
Ickes and Undersecretary Abe Fortas, January 20, 1945. Left to right: Mrs.
Fortas, Fortas, Mrs. Ickes, Ickes.
Courtesy of the Franklin D. Roosevelt Library.

Harry S. Truman (front row, second from left) and Harold L. Ickes (front row, second from right), 1945.
Photo by Abbie Rowe, National Park Service. Courtesy of the Harry S. Truman Library.

Copper mining in World War II. Treatment center for Santa Rita mines in
Hurley, New Mexico.
Courtesy of the E. R. Harrington Collection, Special Collections Department,
General Library, The University of New Mexico.

First tanker launched by Marinship, the SS *Escambia*, in Sausalito, California, hits the water on April 25, 1943.
Courtesy of the Franklin D. Roosevelt Library.

Assembling prefabricated ships at the Kaiser Shipbuilding Company in Richmond, California, during World War II.
Courtesy of The Bancroft Library.

Starting a ship's hull at the Kaiser Shipbuilding Company in Richmond, California, in wartime.
Courtesy of The Bancroft Library.

The new labor force in the West: women workers at the Kaiser shipyards in Richmond, California.
Courtesy of The Bancroft Library.

"This is how to do it, Henry." Henry J. Kaiser (right) and his "boss," Admiral H. L. Vickery of the U.S. Maritime Commission.
Courtesy of The Bancroft Library.

Henry J. Kaiser (right) surveys shipbuilding activities in San Francisco Bay Area.
Courtesy of The Bancroft Library.

President Franklin D. Roosevelt watching the launching of the merchant ship *Joseph N. Teale*, built in ten days by the Oregonship Company in Portland, September 23, 1942.
Courtesy of the Franklin D. Roosevelt Library.

President Franklin D. Roosevelt addressing workers at the Bremerton, Washington, U.S. Naval Shipyard, September 22, 1942. In rear, Vice-Admiral C. S. Freeman and the president's aide, Rear Admiral Ross McIntire.
Courtesy of the Franklin D. Roosevelt Library.

Woman at the lathe: Consolidated Aircraft Company, California, October 1942. Courtesy of the Franklin D. Roosevelt Library.

The overhead conveyor line at North American Aviation's plant in Inglewood, California, manufacturing B-25 bombers.
Courtesy of the Franklin D. Roosevelt Library.

Mechanics working on engines of C-47 transport planes at the Douglas Aircraft Company in Long Beach, California, in wartime.
Courtesy of the Franklin D. Roosevelt Library.

Women at work with men at the Douglas Aircraft Company in Long Beach, California, on A-20 attack bombers.
Courtesy of the Franklin D. Roosevelt Library.

President Franklin D. Roosevelt inspecting the assembly line at the Boeing Aircraft Company in Seattle, Washington, on September 20, 1942. Courtesy of the Franklin D. Roosevelt Library.

President Franklin D. Roosevelt gets a firsthand look at the bomber assembly line of the Douglas Aircraft Company in Long Beach, California, on September 25, 1942.
Courtesy of the Franklin D. Roosevelt Library.

Model sketch of the Kaiser-Hughes transport plane the Spruce Goose.
Courtesy of the Franklin D. Roosevelt Library.

Building the Spruce Goose at the Hughes Aircraft Company during World
War II. Courtesy of the Franklin D. Roosevelt Library.

Steel in the West: Henry J. Kaiser inspects the construction
of his new plant at Fontana, California, July 2, 1942.
Courtesy of The Bancroft Library.

Pumping oil near Venice, California, during World War II.
Courtesy of the E. R. Harrington Collection, Special Collections Department, General Library, The University of New Mexico.

Bess (Mrs. Henry J.) Kaiser at dedication of the first blast furnace of the
Kaiser Steel Company at Fontana, California, December, 1942.
Courtesy of The Bancroft Library.

The Kaiser Steel Company facilities at Fontana, California, upon completion. Courtesy of The Bancroft Library.

Advocating western economic independence: Maury Maverick, chairman of the Smaller War Plants Corporation, delivering the message.
Courtesy of the Barker Texas History Center, The University of Texas at Austin.

Senator Harry S. Truman presiding over hearing of Senate Special Committee to Investigate Defense Expenditures, 1943. Jesse Jones (behind Truman) waiting to testify.
Courtesy of the Harry S. Truman Library.

World War II battleground over conservation: Jackson Hole, Wyoming.
Courtesy of the American Heritage Center, University of Wyoming.

Cyclotron of the Lawrence Radiation Laboratory at the University of
California, Berkeley, during the World War II era.
Courtesy of The Bancroft Library.

Advocate of western economic independence:
Senator Pat McCarran of Nevada.
Courtesy of the Nevada State Historical
Society.

War industry in the desert: Basic Magnesium Plant near Las Vegas, Nevada, in
World War II. Courtesy of the Nevada State Historical Society.

tration encouraged such discussion. Roosevelt loved to stimulate created competition among his subordinates, and so members of his staff often spoke with forked tongues. Harold Ickes and his supporters continued to urge an end to Alcoa's monopoly. Attorney General Tom Clark focused on the need to develop a unified policy before taking specific action. Maury Maverick and his cohorts at the SWPC advocated a program of disposal of aluminum plants to benefit small business, particularly in the West. Meanwhile, western state governors and legislatures rallied behind Maverick with enthusiasm. In Congress small business advocates such as Senators Murray and O'Mahoney followed suit but kept their options open. Western business groups were divided on the issue. Some favored expansion of aluminum production to augment Pacific trade, whereas others hoped for improved competitive positions in domestic markets. Organized labor shared the hopes of business leaders.[57]

Attorney General Tom Clark made a special report on the aluminum industry in September 1945. Although he dealt with the industry on a national level, much of his discussion pertained primarily to the West. Of the twelve new ingot plants built during World War II, seven were located in the West, where none had existed before 1939. Clark's primary concern was Alcoa's monopoly position. He noted that though wartime pressures had brought a sevenfold increase in aluminum production and the entrance of some competitors, in 1945 Alcoa continued to hold a preeminent position in the industry. This was despite the fact that the DPC owned one-half of all the nation's productive capacity. Alcoa operated 90 percent of all production plants and 75 percent of all fabrication facilities. Consequently Clark recommended that Alcoa be dissolved and split into competing companies, a suggestion reminiscent of the dissolution of the Standard Oil Company ordered by the United States Supreme Court in 1911. Clark's recommendation followed closely on the heels of the U.S. District Court decision of March 12, 1945, which had found Alcoa to be, in fact, a monopoly. Clark urged the Surplus Property Board to encourage competitors to enter the industry, which would also achieve the postwar objectives of achieving full employment and full production. And as far as the West was concerned, Clark noted: "Many DPC plants were built originally to be operated as part of Alcoa's system, not to be the basis of competition. Consequently, neither their location nor their size make it possible to realize the benefits of integration. . . . The Pacific Northwest ingot plants . . . need a West Coast alumina plant because the rail haul from the midwest is too costly for postwar operation."[58]

These views were widely lauded by champions of small business like Maury Maverick who hoped to carry Clark's recommendations even further. They hoped that the disposal of federal plants would result not only in the breakup of monopoly but also in a more positive federal policy of direct support for small business. Speaking in 1945, Maverick amplified his dream. "Cheap production of materials by unrestricted manufacture, not dominated by cartels and monopolies, will lead to widespread use of finished products. This will mean in America that tens of thousands of little companies could fabricate such materials into peacetime products." Maverick did not favor a rapid disposal policy, however. Instead, he urged the federal government to embark on "leasing . . . for periods of from 2 to 10 years . . . [so that] then they would be able to ascertain the true value of the property. . . . Speeches against monopoly will not gain our objectives. We must break monopolies if we are to remain a free enterprise economy and a constitutional democracy."[59]

Many of Maverick's views were shared by Senator Murray. "It has already been made sufficiently clear," he declared, "that the greatest expansion of the light metals business in the immediate post-war period can come only through the cooperation of aluminum and magnesium metal suppliers with small fabricators and sales units spread throughout the country. It is the development of such independent business firms that we seek to foster." And he went on to reiterate his philosophy. "It has been the genius of America that we have faced every great crisis with our courage. As we look ahead to the day of victory, we know that that day will bring with it great crises in our industrial life. The American wartime economy with its $90,000,000,000 of annual Government expenditures and its vast organization of industrial plants and equipment must be remolded into an economy dedicated to the pursuits of peace." And he stressed the need for effective restructuring. Speaking of the surplus disposal policy, he said: "When this matter was up before Congress, the idea was advanced that in the disposal of these plants the Government should get the fullest value for themselves. That proposal was rejected by Congress when we were studying the Surplus Property Disposal Act and it was specifically stated as the policy there that we were not to try to get the fullest, the last dollar out of these plants, but were to work out a program whereby we were going to reconvert to civilian production with the idea of bringing about a quick reconversion."[60] O'Mahoney seconded these views, also urging the U.S. Bureau of Mines to create experimental plants to produce aluminum from alumina clays in Wyoming and Oregon to stimulate small producers in that region.[61]

Western business interests were of different minds about the disposal of federal aluminum plants in the region, but most looked forward to greater economic diversification. One of the most farsighted was Henry

J. Kaiser, who envisioned vast new markets for aluminum in the postwar West. Speculating about the future in 1945, he described five major segments of these expected markets, "most of which cannot be discussed because of their essentially confidential nature in time of war. However, it is possible to say, from work which I have undertaken for both the Army and the Navy, that magnesium and aluminum will be more extensively employed than ever before in the manufacture of aircraft and aircraft accessories . . . and in motors." He saw a second segment in the construction of naval combat vessels. He remembered that before 1941 few people considered it feasible to build whole ships out of aluminum, but by 1941 he was considering building an aluminum destroyer capable of traveling sixty knots. Skeptical minds in the navy had deferred that project, however. A third market segment would be the building of new merchant ships. Aluminum and magnesium superstructures, Kaiser believed, had many advantages (such as weight) over those made of more traditional materials such as steel. Another segment of the market would develop in the construction of new ship terminal facilities, he predicted. With accurate foresight he envisaged the increased use of containers, which he felt would revolutionize shipping in the future. Aluminum containers, he was sure, would "reduce the high cost of loading and unloading, storing, and freight." He added, "At present terminal costs are roughly equal to one-half of the total cost of waterborne traffic." Those costs could be reduced greatly, Kaiser believed, if freight was shipped in "special demountable containers [that could] be transferred from trucks to railroad cars, to ships, and from ships back again to railroad cars and trucks with a minimum of handling."[62]

In addition, Kaiser expected aluminum to be increasingly used in a fifth market segment—the manufacture of trucks and buses. "The lightness of the metals will save fuel and permit an increase in size and speed," he predicted, with great acumen. At the time Kaiser was using his own fleet of trailer trucks to haul cement for the Permanente Corporation up and down the Pacific Coast for testing purposes. His experience by 1945 indicated that hauling costs could be significantly reduced by using trucks built of light metals. He related how his engineers had made "experimental models of truck bodies and buses and . . . detailed preparations for the post-war manufacture." They had constructed a Peterbilt truck with two Trailmobile magnesium units at the Permanente plant that effected significant savings in operation when compared to steel units. "Truly," Kaiser declared, "a new era has been opened in highway transportation."

Kaiser's views on the displacement of steel by aluminum obviously did not endear him to major steel producers, who were already suspicious of his unorthodox ideas. But Kaiser was unperturbed. "We will have prosperity," he said, "when we produce more at a lower cost and at higher wages. That will create the prosperity and the production requirements [that] can not even be conceived at this time, if only we as Americans measure up to the full possibility."

Concerning the immediate problem of the disposal of federal aluminum plants, particularly those in the West, Kaiser had specific recommendations. "The American people by their own energies and efforts created the weapons, plants, and the facilities which are now being used by the armed forces to fight this war. All that remains of these facilities is the property of the American people." Consequently, he urged a clearer and more explicit statement of federal disposal policy. "Plans should be worked out now which can be executed as soon as the plants are no longer needed for war purposes." The prime objective in plant disposal should be full employment. "I believe they should be operated by American industry on either lease or purchase basis," Kaiser said, "which will be equitable for the established private enterprises which have investments in comparable plants and at the same time stimulate and encourage competition. Instead of merely closing these federal plants the government should [give] everyone in business a fair opportunity to operate them."

The absence of clear-cut federal disposal policies in 1945 disturbed Kaiser. He argued that such were essential to guide private industries and thus to maintain economic stability. He criticized the Surplus Property Act of 1944 as overly complicated and cumbersome, and he pleaded for simplification. He deplored as well the prevailing multiplicity of federal policies and the overlapping functions of many wartime agencies. "Government should speak with one voice," he said. "There should be an earnest endeavor to avoid duplications of authority or conflicts in administration and interpretation." As he viewed the morass of regulations in force, he mirrored the frustrations of many business people who were unsure of the main elements of public policy. Such confusion was impeding the needed industry restructuring. "Most important of all, these policies should be formulated and made known at the earliest possible moment." Reflecting the increased attacks on himself by members of Congress, he urged that private investors in surplus government plants not be subjected to severe criticisms. "If industry is to be cursed with the criticism that it is directly or indirectly enjoying Government subsidy by utilizing these plants . . . the entire impetus of our increased productivity would be lost. . . . I purposely believe that there is only one way of saving America and that is to provide employment."

New Basic Industries for the West: Aluminum

Summarizing his views on the disposition of government aluminum plants, Kaiser expressed his philosophy for the reshaping of industry. "The American people, 130,000,000 strong . . . now own these facilities. Congress is unqualifiedly their agent. Industry's function is to operate these plants so efficiently and effectively that employment will be assured and essential investment encouraged. . . . All we need, to move forward, is the announcement of the policies as to the disposition and utilization of this vast productive force on which our future depends."[63]

Not all business leaders shared Kaiser's views. O. J. Gallagher, president of the Columbia Metals Company, a small fabricating concern in Salem, Oregon, recalled that a group of businessmen in the Pacific Northwest had organized his company in 1941 to develop the light metals industry under the aegis of the DPC. "I believe that Government plants should be rendered into the hands of private industry, but that the national welfare demands that orderliness . . . not be sacrificed. . . . At the end of the war we will have had a War Production Board for upward of 5 years, for the purpose of controlling, marshalling, and directing the forces of industry. The obvious impact on our economy has been such as to make it inconceivable to me that we will not have a peace production board, with adequate controls, for some period after the war." He hoped to secure an interest in one of the aluminum plants in the Pacific Northwest, either at Troutdale, Jones Mills, or Spokane. But he warned that private enterprise could not succeed without some government aid.[64]

Many western business people expected aluminum plants to promote the diversification of the region's economy and the expansion of their markets in the Orient. James A. Ford, the managing secretary of the Spokane Chamber of Commerce, spoke about his hopes for the light metals industry in the Northwest. "There is a big airplane industry on the West Coast to be served with aluminum and magnesium. Further, the entire West is headed for its greatest growth and development. It has emerged from a colonial economy, and I am sure that . . . Congress would [not] consider for a moment throwing the West back." Moreover, he reflected the optimism of many westerners about the potentials of Far Eastern markets. "In addition to the markets that will be offered in western United States, which is now emerging as a great industrial empire, the markets in the Orient and Siberia will offer almost unlimited opportunities. . . . This Nation will face West to what we call the Far East following this war, where the teeming millions . . . live. . . . Where could these light metal plants be better situated to meet the demands in the post-war era than in the Pacific Northwest?" Ford believed that if Alcoa or Reynolds Metals bought the largest surplus plants, thousands of

119

small businesses would benefit. With considerable foresight he predicted, "Our industrial machine must meet the competition of state-owned monopolies that will come at us from across the water and government cartels will come at us from other directions." Summarizing the hopes of many business leaders in the Pacific Northwest, he told visiting members of Congress: "We cannot conceive that our government, having forced upon us . . . a tremendous and rapid industrial development, will throw the Pacific Northwest back into a colonial status to a country of agriculture, lumber, and fisheries, and bring about an even greater industrial concentration than already exists in the East. . . . We are not asking you to drive industry West, [but] do not drive it out of the West."[65]

The lure of the Orient was also on the mind of W.D.B. Dodson, the Washington, D.C., representative of the Portland Chamber of Commerce.

> We urge a strong West Coast economic front. In the past, the West Coast has been held a weak back door to the Nation. If there ever was given an effective example of the mistake in pursuing such a policy, we have it in the present war. . . . Practically all of the essentials for this Oriental war have to be shipped across the continent. . . . Another aspect . . . is . . . should the Oriental market prove heavy . . . our position would be made vastly stronger if we could produce a heavy percentage of our oriental exports on the west coast. . . . In considering plans for the future light metals industry . . . we hope that . . . the Pacific seaboard [will be recognized] as the logical area for heavy development [in addition to] "all of the territory west of the Rocky Mountains [that] can be reached most advantageously by aluminum plants in our area."[66]

Representatives of other business associations had similar perspectives. One of these was D. W. Walters, managing engineer of the Inland Empire Industrial Research, an organization established by a group of business people in the Pacific Northwest to expand private enterprise. He advocated the transfer of government aluminum plants to big corporations, since he believed that these corporations, in turn, would stimulate many small fabricating enterprises. Then, "the Pacific Northwest will be in a strong position to become one of the light metals centers of the world. Low cost aluminum, low cost electric energy, and the presence of skilled light-metals workers should provide a sound foundation for a great new western industry after the war."[67]

Many labor leaders shared such aspirations for the reshaping of the West. Elmer E. Walker of the International Association of Machinists (A.F. of L.) was enthusiastic about expanding the light metals industry in the Northwest. In fact, the union worked closely with the futurist, Buckminster Fuller, in developing innovative and unconventional mass housing units in which aluminum was a major element. Walker's reasoning was close to Kaiser's. He interpreted the Surplus Property Act of 1944 as encouraging competition, discouraging monopoly, and providing full employment. These goals could be achieved only through large-scale expansion of the national economy, and the light metals industries were a key component of such growth in the West. Walker insisted, however, that labor representatives have a voice in postwar planning.[68]

N. A. Zonarich, the international representative of the United Steel-workers of America (C. I. O.), was even more outspoken. Expansion of the aluminum industry should be undertaken by industrial councils on which business and labor had equal representation. "The country needs a big aluminum industry to provide jobs," he declared. He set as his goal an annual production of no less than 1.6 billion pounds of aluminum. "We believe that the post-war enterprise of the American people will result in a sharply rising demand for aluminum." His estimate was about one-half the maximum wartime production by full operation of all former DPC plants. That would also undercut Alcoa's monopoly in the industry. "We look forward to possible future expansion in an increasingly prosperous post-war America . . . [in which] DPC plants and equipment be made available only on a lease basis. The basic operator should be obliged to assure a high level of employment . . . [so] the enormous public invest-ment of some $600 millions will not be wasted." Summarizing his position, he declared, "Our stated goal visualizes the complete retention and the further development of the Northwestern aluminum industry."[69]

A detailed analysis of the complex process by which the government disposed of its aluminum plants is beyond the scope of this study, but it can be noted that this disposal process resulted in some restructuring of the industry. It transformed a monopolistic industry into one more akin to oligopoly. Although Alcoa maintained an important position in the decade after 1945, it met new competitors, such as Reynolds Metals and Kaiser Aluminum, who captured over one-half of the market. Surplus disposal also contributed to the diversification of the western economy. The West retained most of the government aluminum plants built during the war, which were now operated by the industry's corporate giants. Government disposal thus achieved somewhat more and somewhat less than what the various economic interests had advocated. Although it changed the prewar status quo, it did not seriously challenge Alcoa's primacy. Instead, it provided a pragmatic compromise in which each of the affected economic interests received something, but less than what they had expected. The war thus stimulated the restructuring and the significant expansion of the aluminum industry in the West, helping to lay a foundation for economic growth and affluence in the region for the next two decades.

121

CHAPTER 6

Sinews of War: Magnesium, Steel, and Oil

AS AMERICANS mobilized their economy for war they became aware that magnesium, steel, and oil had become essential sinews of mechanized combat to an unprecedented degree. And, unlike its role in World War I, the West's part in World War II was essential, since the region provided these essentials. In 1917 armed conflict was largely centralized in Europe and drew primarily on the energies of the eastern half of the United States. But the situation between 1941 and 1945 was very different. Now the United States was heavily engaged in the Pacific area, and the American West suddenly assumed a new importance as a staging and supply region for the nation's military effort. In a sense, the West symbolized the highly mechanized warfare that was characteristic by midcentury. Magnesium came to be an essential ingredient not only for the almost three hundred thousand planes that composed America's air force but also for the fire bombs used against Japan. Similarly, as the West became heavily involved in shipbuilding—supplying one-half of the nation's expanding merchant fleet—demands for steel became greater than ever. Involvement in the Pacific also required more petroleum supplies than before, now that a mammoth air force required vast quantities of aviation fuel and petroleum products. The changing requirements of warfare, therefore, impinged on the West's economic structure, requiring significant reshaping.

After Pearl Harbor the demand for magnesium intensified. In peacetime magnesium had a variety of limited uses in chemical manufactures. During the Great Depression markets for magnesium were extremely limited. In fact, only one major producer operated in the United States, the Dow Chemical Company, which in 1939 produced 7 million pounds, twice as much as it had sold earlier in the decade. Wartime pressures led to enormous increases in the use of magnesium, however, and by 1943 national production reached 368 million pounds. Given the sense of urgency, the DPC under the prodding of Jesse Jones saw no alternative but for the federal government itself to build new plants and to supervise production. Much of that expansion took place in the West because it had the needed raw materials and also the kind of plant sites suitable for fabrication.[1]

Among the western states, Nevada offered several advantages. Southeastern Nevada contained extensive magnesite deposits, which provided one of the basic ingredients for magnesium products. The area also had cheap electric power, available from the recently completed Boulder Dam. Moreover, it was a remote, inland location secure from possible enemy air attack. The small town of Las Vegas was on the main line of the Atchison, Topeka and Santa Fe Railroad to Los Angeles, thus providing reasonable access to transportation. The carrier had first come to the sleepy little hamlet in 1884 and over the years had maintained shops and servicing facilities there. Since about one-half of the nation's airplane fusilages were being manufactured in southern California, the proximity of Las Vegas to the Pacific Coast was another advantage. In addition, the town was well situated with respect to major ordnance depots throughout the West, including some right in Nevada.[2] For almost a century Las Vegas had been an isolated desert outpost. In the changed technological context of 1941, however, it could boast many advantages for certain types of industrial production. Even so, such desirable attributes in themselves were insufficient to attract new wartime plants, for political machinations were also required.

In the decade before World War II the presence of brusite and magnesite deposits in the Paradise Mountains of Nye County, Nevada, had attracted some small-scale exploitation. The Basic Refractories Company of Cleveland had begun to manufacture granular magnesite refractories used to line steel furnaces. In 1936 it acquired selected leases on magnesite ore deposits. At the same time the British and the Canadian governments expressed interest in the area, as they were considering expansion of magnesium production in Canada. By January 1941, the negotiations for these Nevada mines had collapsed. Nevertheless, officials of the Basic Refractories Company approached a British firm, Magnesium Elektron, about possible collaboration in Nye County. They also notified the Iron and Steel Branch of the OPM that they hoped to expand their magnesium production. While their request for government aid was pending, on April 3, 1941, Basic Refractories officials signed an agreement with Magnesium Elektron to produce forty million pounds of magnesium annually through a newly formed company named Basic Magnesium (BM).[3]

At the OPM the magnesium magnates found a receptive ear. Acting Chairman Sidney Hillman was particularly favorable. In a letter to Undersecretary of War Robert P. Patterson on April 22, 1941, he expressed special concern about Dow Chemical Company's virtual monopoly in the industry. Like others in the Roosevelt administration, he hoped to lure new companies into this field and to make it more competitive. He also spoke with representatives of other chemical companies about increasing magnesium output. By May 1941 he and Patterson had decided that in a proposed program of eighty-nine million pounds for that year, Basic Magnesium could play a role by supplying twelve million pounds. To work out the myriad of details, Patterson delegated Major J. C. Hall to meet with Howard Eels, an executive of Basic Refractories, on May 17, 1941, at Wright Field in Ohio. After four days of discussion Eels left to survey possible sites in Nevada. BM now made a formal request to the DPC for subsidies and loans to launch the new venture.[4]

Yet Nevada might not have secured a new plant had it not been for the strenuous efforts of its political leaders, particularly Senator Pat McCarran. Local officials in Las Vegas and in Clark County had for some years hoped to attract industry to their community, without much success. Now they viewed the mobilization program as an unusual opportunity. Representatives of the Las Vegas Chamber of Commerce such as W. W. Hopper, Clark County officials such as S. M. Pickett, and their colleagues spoke to army officers in Nevada and succeeded in establishing a joint commission to work out details concerning land purchases, housing facilities, and schools for the proposed BM plant, expected to employ fourteen thousand persons, twice the population of Las Vegas. Once they had organized, they contacted Senator McCarran. He, in turn, began to make the rounds of federal agencies in Washington during April and May 1941. In particular, he frequented the War Department and the OPM, buttonholing their officials "toward the end of securing for Nevada a share in the defense program looking toward the production of strategic minerals."[5]

McCarran too saw the magnesium venture as an unusual opportunity. It provided, he said, "promise of increased industrial activity for our state." With some pride he noted that whereas representatives from California had also lobbied for a major magnesium plant in their state, his intensive activity had landed it for Nevada. In early June 1941, he had played his trump card by going directly to the president. Roosevelt spoke with him briefly at the White House to hear his proposal, which McCarran then formalized in a letter to the chief executive on June 14, 1941. All the elements of a successful political coup were in place, and McCarran gloated over the results. "Together with your suggestion that these ore deposits be utilized in connection with the recommendations of the OPM for increased magnesium production I am glad to be able to advise you," Roosevelt wrote McCarran, "that a project for producing 33,000,000 pounds of magnesium annually has already been approved by the Materiel Division, U.S. Army Air Corps. . . . The new plants will be located at Gabbs, Mead, and Las Vegas, all in the State of Nevada." The happy combination of locational advantages and political orchestration bore fruit, as the president instructed Jesse Jones to authorize construction of the world's largest magnesium plant in Henderson, Nevada, just ten miles southeast of Las Vegas.[6]

During the second half of 1941 the administration moved the magnesium production program into high gear. In July 1941 the DPC requested BM to produce 112 million pounds annually, which was considerably more than earlier estimates. Instead of seeking a lease agreement with BM, the DPC now offered it a contract to manage the new plant, which would be wholly owned by the federal government. As Undersecretary of War Robert P. Patterson wrote on July 19, 1941, "It is recommended that an agreement be negotiated between the War Department, the DPC, and Refractories for a project of a capacity of 112,000,000 pounds to cost $63,820,663." On August 13, 1941, BM signed its contract with the DPC to design as well as to manage plants for producing magnesium at Henderson. BM was to receive a fee of 0.5 percent of construction costs to supervise the building of the new facilities. It was also entitled to receive royalties amounting to 2 percent of sales, or no less than half a cent per pound. The DPC could sell the plant after three years if it chose to do so, but BM received first option for purchase. If the DPC sold the facility to other parties, BM would be entitled to a $1-million royalty on ores and would be protected against competition should the new owners choose to enter the refractories business.[7]

Construction of the plant took about one year. When it was near completion, Jesse Jones of the DPC announced on October 26, 1942, that the Anaconda Mining Company had acquired 52.5 percent of the Eels interest in BM and would have a strong hand in management. Meanwhile, the DPC purchased ore-bearing lands from BM in nearby Gabbs. The total cost of the plant exceeded $140 million, making it one of the DPC's largest wartime investments. During 1942 and 1943 it employed more than fourteen thousand persons, who lived in the newly built town of Henderson (named after a prominent senator from Nevada who was chairman of the RFC). The venture gave an enormous boost to the entire Nevada economy but was particularly important to stimulating growth in the southern portion of the state and in the small town of Las Vegas.[8]

McCarran always felt a personal attachment to BM and its role in stimulating the diversification of Nevada's economy. When he visited the site in November 1941, he noted with evident satisfaction: "For the first time we have something which is bringing wealth into Nevada instead of taking it out. Every ton of ore which is taken from a mine depletes our wealth. Every ton of concrete poured here adds to our prosperity." To him, the BM plant was "the greatest thing ever to happen to this state."[9]

Back in Washington, Jesse Jones also took great pride in BM's achievements. As he recalled after the war:

> After a poor start . . . we employed Anaconda Copper Co. to operate the BM plant, which we built in the desert heat that sometimes soared to 120°. The plant was in production in September, 1942, within a year of breaking ground, and was finally completed in April, 1943. Before it was shut down in December, 1944 because of a surplus stockpile—and a need for its labor in shipbuilding yards—it had produced one-fourth of all the magnesium made by various processes during the war. In one year, 1943, this one plant provided 39 per cent of the nation's magnesium production.[10]

BM obviously did the job!

BM's record was particularly notable when compared to that of other, less successful ventures. The RFC also made loans to Henry Kaiser to produce magnesium in a new plant that the DPC financed for him in Los Altos, California, just south of San Francisco. Jesse Jones, who greatly disliked Kaiser, remembered that when Kaiser heard about the WPB's intention to sponsor a magnesium plant in California, he "came to Washington to see us. The private capital he proposed to put up to go into magnesium manufacturing was only $100,000—the stock of the Permanente Metals Corporation which he had organized. He wanted to borrow a good many millions. He employed Thomas G. Corcoran, a White House favorite of the Roosevelt days and a former attorney in the legal division of the RFC to help him wangle the loan. Mr. Kaiser knew nothing about manufacturing magnesium so I was a little skeptical." Kaiser experimented with a European process developed by F. J. Hansgirg, a Hungarian engineer. He hired Hansgirg to build and operate this plant, which he constructed with a $28-million loan from the RFC. Although the facility produced magnesium, its manufacturing cost was almost twice as great as at BM—thirty cents per pound compared to sixteen cents per pound at Dow and eighteen to twenty cents at BM. The Metals Reserve Corporation bought the magnesium from Kaiser only during periods of short-age in 1942 and 1943. As magnesium production increased by 1944 the MRC ordered the Kaiser operation closed. "By comparison with others," Jones noted with some venom, "Mr. Kaiser was no great shakes of a success in magnesium." On the other hand, the plant provided much needed magnesium at critical times, as the counsel of the Truman Committee, Hugh Fulton, noted after a closer investigation of the venture.[11]

In view of the growing stockpile of magnesium late in 1944, the WPB began gradually reducing output and closing some of the major facilities in the West. On April 4, 1944, Philip Wilson, director of the WPB's Aluminum and Magnesium Division, instructed F. O. Case, the general manager of BM, to reduce his operation from ten to six units. By September, Sam Husbands, chairman of the DPC, had sent Case further instructions to wind down operation and to prepare for total shutdown by December 15, 1944. Westerners viewed this order with great dismay, for it dimmed their dreams of economic diversification.[12]

This dismay was transformed into strong protests, particularly by Senator Pat McCarran, BM's guardian angel. He, like many westerners, believed that the closing of BM was a conspiracy of eastern industrialists, ensconced in various echelons of the WPB, to restrict economic expansion in the West. McCarran was not about to give in without a fight, and he mobilized his forces. A master of public relations, he succeeded in securing congressional approval of a newly created Senate Committee on the Centralization of Heavy Industry. That committee, in some ways a descendant of the prewar Temporary National Economic Committee, was to hold extensive hearings throughout 1944 on industrial centralization in the East and on the slow growth of industry in the West. But McCarran also devoted considerable time to delving into the WPB's closing of the BM plant and to the possibilities of keeping the facility in operation.[13]

During the course of these hearings administration officials patiently explained the essentially valid reasons that had led them to close the giant Nevada plant. Sam Husbands, chairman of the DPC, Charles E. Wilson, vice-chairman of the WPB, and Philip Wilson and Arthur Bunker of the WPB's Aluminum and Magnesium Division, among others, spoke about their decision. Clearly, the growing national surplus of magnesium and the higher cost of producing it in the newer western plants were two considerations. In addition, they argued somewhat less persuasively for a need to save petroleum. Moreover, they claimed that labor was desperately needed in West Coast shipyards and that closing the BM plant would ease that problem. They also discussed relieving pressures on the region's transportation system, particularly by eliminating the hauling of peat from Canada to Nevada for the production of magnesium. Taken together, these varied considerations made a potent defense.[14]

But McCarran attacked their assumptions. He had serious doubts whether closing the BM plant would result in substantial savings of money, energy, and labor. Ironically, he found a close ally in Harold Ickes, although the two were usually at loggerheads and were just then embroiled in a bitter dispute over western grazing lands. But Ickes, like McCarran, was passionately devoted to economic diversification for the West and favored the conversion of the BM plant to alternate uses, rather than its closing. McCarran introduced a letter that Ickes had written him in which Ickes strongly opposed the WPB action and stated that it could not be justified as a fuel-saving measure. McCarran also wondered whether the termination of fifteen thousand employees would do much to relieve the labor shortage in Los Angeles because at the time that city had a critical lack of housing. Rather, McCarran smelled an eastern conspiracy. "They are using the War Production Board as an agent, as leverage for the monopolistic move," he declared, echoing similar charges by Nevada Governor E. P. Carville. Moreover, the advisory engineer of the Los Angeles Department of Water and Power, E. F. Scattergood, wrote McCarran that southern California had plenty of power and needed no additional sources. "We certainly do not want to encourage any curtailment of war industries either at Las Vegas or any other part of the Pacific Southwest," he declared. "My interest in this . . . " McCarran noted, "is that no discrimination shall be made against the West. . . . [It] will cripple the economic conditions in the State, will be a blow at Western industries, and it will only serve to favor some particular individual or . . . outfit."[15]

The closing of the BM plant raised questions about its immediate future. Like many westerners, McCarran hoped that the DPC would sell it to private interests who might diversify Nevada's economy. To that end he requested a series of technical papers from BM's staff in 1944 concerning possible uses of the facility. These reports considered manufactures of various chemicals and related products marketable in a peacetime economy. But the engineers who prepared these studies felt that the magnesium industry would first have to develop new markets. From such a perspective, the immediate postwar era presented great uncertainties. DPC officials agreed with this assessment, although they felt that eventually the development of new products made from magnesium might make peacetime operation feasible.[16]

Throughout 1944 and 1945 proponents of western economic diversification made additional proposals for salvaging BM. One of the most cogent came from Maury Maverick, a persistent advocate of small business. Maverick suggested that the actual cost of the plant could be reduced by eliminating excess cost during the war; then that cost could be further reduced by write-offs for the salvage of unneeded equipment; finally the plant could be offered for sale by the DPC, not for dollars but for whatever portion of the facility a private operator might want to use. According to Maverick's plan, the DPC would sell to whatever bidder could utilize the largest portion of the plant, and the DPC would require that bidder to amortize the proportion of the adjusted cost by the proportion of plant facilities used. In essence, Maverick was advocating a total write-off in a bookkeeping transaction.[17]

But officials in Washington had other priorities, among which cost efficiency was high. Jesse Jones, generally inclined to favor big business, well represented their view.

> It is my conviction that every plant that can be used in the production of something useful in our economy should be saved. But, as I have said, many Government war plants and projects will not be capable of competing in private industry. Those that can be used should be fitted into our economy. . . . The others will be chargeable to the cost of the war, and the salvage will not be great. . . . If there ever was a question which must be settled in the national interest it is the future utilization of this vast new industrial empire.

Then Jones touched on the light metals industries.

> In those industries where Government facilities approximate or exceed those in private hands the solutions will be more difficult. We could very easily destroy private investment in some industries, but certainly we should not, and will not. In some instances Government must continue to have a hand in business. It must make investments and take risks where private capital cannot afford to. . . . No formula can be evolved for disposing of these properties that will fit the many different kinds and sizes.

Jones was quite specific about magnesium.

> Private industry will own only about 8 per cent of the total production of the country at the end of the war. The Government has invested approximately $430,000,000 in plants for its manufacture. . . . Obviously, the Government will be in a position to smother private industry in the manufacture of magnesium and also to dominate the aluminum industry because Government alone will have more than enough capacity to supply the entire needs for aluminum.

Although Jones leaned toward big business, it would be inaccurate to call him an advocate.

> It would not be in the best interest of the country if all our Government plants got into the hands of big business and thereby increased monopolistic tendencies. We should not permit the war further to concentrate our economy in big units. The country is better off with smaller units, even if not always so effi-

129

ciently. . . . Certainly, wherever possible, local people living in the sections where plants are operated should have every encouragement and opportunity to buy and operate the plants and equipment when they can furnish capable management and an appropriate amount of equity capital.[18]

Of course, these had traditionally been the problems of many small business entrepreneurs.

Although the West was unable to retain the magnesium plants the government had built in wartime, it benefited from their presence. These facilities brought a surge of population that contributed to the later development of communities such as Las Vegas. The plants also did much to whet the desire of westerners for more rapid economic diversification, which was, under favorable circumstances, quite feasible in the region, as industrial experiences between 1941 and 1945 indicated. The West had met the challenge of supplying magnesium in a time of crisis, and that realization instilled a new sense of confidence in westerners, even if they did lose much of the industry in the immediate postwar era. They may have lost the battle, but they won the war.

The war had a more lasting influence on the steel industry of the West than on magnesium production. Before 1940 the region was almost entirely dependent on the East for steel. Essentially, only one large integrated steelmaking facility operated west of the Mississippi River, the Colorado Fuel and Iron Company in Pueblo, Colorado. Even that enterprise was financed and controlled by eastern capital, and had been since the 1890s. The dominance of eastern steel interests in the West was further institutionalized and perpetuated by the basing point system of the railroads. Under this method of tabulating discriminatory railroad rates—sanctioned by the Interstate Commerce Commission between 1890 and 1947—westerners had to buy steel f.o.b. Pittsburgh, Pennsylvania, irrespective of where it was actually manufactured. That proved to be a major deterrent to the growth of local industries and was often cited by westerners as a chief reason for their colonial subservience to the East.[19]

But the war brought dramatic changes. Whereas the West had contributed only 2.5 percent of the national steel output in 1940, it doubled its capacity by 1945. Certainly this growth did not end western dependency on eastern steel, but it helped to ease the chronic reliance on the East. The total ingot capacity of eleven western states more than doubled. In fact, in 1945 the West had ingot capacity to produce an amount greater than all the steel it had consumed five years earlier. On the other hand, eastern financial interests controlled many of the steel manufacture and fabrication facilities in the West. And many of the rolling mills established during the war years were not directly adaptable to peacetime uses. Created primarily to supply western shipyards, they were geared largely to the manufacture of structural shapes and plates. Nevertheless, despite such qualifications, the expansion of the western steel industry during wartime was notable, fostered by the gradual removal of discriminatory freight rates by the Interstate Commerce Commission after 1943.[20]

Unlike in the East, steel manufacturers in the West were not clustered. In addition to the Colorado Fuel and Iron Company, several small fabricators were scattered along the Pacific Coast. In 1922 the Columbia Steel Corporation purchased iron ore properties in Utah and two years later built a blast furnace in Ironton, near Provo. The U.S. Steel Corporation bought this enterprise and on the eve of World War II was operating a partially integrated steel manufacture and fabrication plant there. A few small mills also existed in port cities such as Los Angeles, San Francisco, and Seattle. The Columbia Steel Corporation and the Bethlehem Steel Corporation had facilities in Los Angeles and San Francisco, whereas the Bethlehem Steel Corporation and the Northwest Steel Rolling Mills supplied Seattle. Most of these enterprises had installed their equipment before 1926, however, and by 1940 lagged far behind the state of the art in steelmaking.[21]

The reindustrialization of the western steel industry did not proceed easily. The older, well-established eastern steelmakers strongly opposed expansion in the West. Various motives underlay their reluctance. Most of these steelmakers were still obsessed with depression psychology and feared shrinking markets once the war emergency passed. They had just lived through a decade of overproduction and falling prices, an experience that left deep scars. Moreover, the Senate investigation of munitions makers, conducted by Senator Gerald P. Nye in 1934, had charged that ammunition and steelmakers were "merchants of death" who had allegedly brought the United States into World War I in a ruthless search for profits. A few years later steel executives were still smarting from these accusations and were somewhat loath to become involved in this new mobilization program. Of course, they were also wedded to the status quo in which they enjoyed a dominant position in an oligopolistic industry. These feelings had regional implications, for the eastern manufacturers were determined to maintain their dominance and looked askance at efforts to develop potential western competition. The reshaping of the western steel industry thus was to be a painful process, with established interests often fighting tooth and nail against expansion.[22]

In the West, local business people had tried unsuccessfully for years to establish a steel industry. The Pacific Northwest had especially high hopes. As George Watkins Evans, a consulting engineer, noted in August 1941, "In the State of Washington, we have iron ores . . . a considerable area of coking coal . . . [and] water transportation." As early as 1902 a report by Solon Shedd for the Washington Geological Survey evaluated the quality of iron ores in the Pacific Northwest and suggested that production costs there would not be higher than in Pittsburgh or Gary, Indiana. On the eve of war Raymond M. Miller, a senior industrial engineer for the Bonneville Power Administration, similarly felt that prospects for a steel industry in Washington were excellent but that federal and state aid was necessary to promote it. His views were seconded by E. L. Davis, president of the Washington Nickel Mining and Alloy Company, who declared that only a lack of capital prevented steel manufactures in his state. What local boosters often ignored was that western population and markets were perhaps not yet large enough to sustain big ventures.[23]

When the Roosevelt administration attempted to boost steel production in June 1940, just after the fall of France, it met direct opposition from industry leaders. Irving Olds, chairman of the board of the U.S. Steel Corporation, openly declared in September that the industry could handle all contingencies that mobilization might bring. Similarly, Ernest Weir, president of the National Steel Corporation, noted with great confidence at about the same time that his industry could supply all defense needs without problems.[24]

Such myopia of the executives was reinforced by official government reports—which they or their representatives often crafted. In January 1941 the chief engineer of the Council of National Defense Advisory Commission, Gano Dunn, issued a comprehensive study of the steelmaking capacity in the United States. Dunn was a former Alcoa executive and had served as a paid consultant to U.S. Steel. Not surprisingly, he reflected the assumptions as well as the fears of the established companies. In his report Dunn predicted (inaccurately, as it turned out) that there would be no steel shortages but that surpluses were more likely. He erroneously estimated that the nation's steel requirements in 1941 would be seventy-five million tons, leaving an excess of ten million tons of productive capacity. For 1942 he predicted a likely overproduction of about two million tons. Underlying his report was a great reluctance to change the status quo.[25]

But by the spring of 1941 the administration was finally shifting its mobilization program into high gear, particularly after Congress approved the Lend-Lease Act in March. By that time government economists were predicting a need for 120 million tons of steel in 1942. Even so, in May

Sinews of War: Magnesium, Steel, and Oil

1941 Irving Olds once again reiterated his belief that existing facilities were more than adequate and that great caution should accompany any plans to expand production. In view of conflicting estimates Gano Dunn made another inquiry into steel capacity, but this time he predicted a shortage. Allegedly this conclusion incurred the wrath of industry executives, who forced him into early retirement! But in this second report, published on May 28, 1941, Dunn now also urged the expansion of steel-making facilities.[26] To avert possible shortages and to stimulate some expansion in the industry, on June 4, 1941, Jesse Jones of the Reconstruction Finance Corporation offered to furnish capital to finance new steel ventures. That still left the question open as to where the new plants were to be built.[27]

Increasing public discussion of the need for more steel in the spring of 1941 aroused the hopes of westerners. Utah's congressional delegation became particularly active in lobbying for further development of the modest U.S. Steel Corporation plant near Provo. On April 12, 1941, Governor Herbert Maw and U.S. Senator Abe Murdock went to see President Roosevelt to brief him on the current steel situation. Roosevelt noted that Utah could certainly make a contribution to ending the steel shortage on the Pacific Coast if it could accommodate an $8-million pig iron plant and a $3-million steel mill to produce one thousand tons daily.[28] Meanwhile, the Utahns were also carrying on discussions with the dynamic West Coast shipbuilder Henry J. Kaiser. As he was increasing production at his shipyards he found himself continually hampered by steel shortages. Kaiser complained that eastern steel manufacturers were not supplying him with all he needed and that theirs was a deliberate attempt to stifle western enterprises, especially those of unorthodox newcomers like himself.[29]

Kaiser's frustrations with the old-line steel companies was so great that he now considered directly embarking on steel manufacturing himself. Together with Senator Murdock, who enjoyed access to the White House, he visited Roosevelt during the last week of April 1941 to propose federally supported expansion of the steel industry in the West. Kaiser's plan envisaged a pig iron plant in Mt. Pleasant, Utah, with $150 million furnished by the DPC, a steel mill in the Bonneville Dam area for the Pacific Northwest, and another steel mill in southern California. Roosevelt inquired whether Utah had enough coal for such operations, leading Murdock to conclude that he was being advised by individuals leary of western steel expansion.[30]

Murdock's suspicions were not entirely unfounded. W. A. Hauck, the principal steel consultant of the OPM, opposed further development of steel manufactures in the West. And his views were representative of those held by executives of the established steel companies in the East, many of whose employees were already ensconced in the OPM and other mobilization agencies. In April 1941 Hauck made an inspection trip to the Pacific Coast and consequently announced that Kaiser's proposed expansion program was overly ambitious. Slight increases in steel production might be warranted, Hauck noted, but these could readily be secured through simple expansion of existing facilities. He thought that it might be well to construct two one-hundred-ton blast furnaces and twelve one-hundred-ton open-hearth furnaces in Provo, Pueblo, and Los Angeles. But he emphasized, "In no event should any blast furnace be established on the West Coast by any new companies until there is positive assurance that there are adequate reserves of suitable iron ore and coking coal available and accessible for their successful operations." At Hauck's recommendation the OPM rejected the Kaiser plan on May 23, 1941, and announced that only companies already active in the steel industry would be allowed to expand.[31] Clearly, Kaiser was not very popular, in either steel industry or government circles.

Within a few weeks the OPM acted on Hauck's recommendations and solicited proposals from the old-line steel companies. Among those submitting bids was the Columbia Steel Corporation of Provo, and after several months of negotiations the OPM agreed to provide it with $35 million for a pig iron plant with a capacity of 750,000 tons yearly. By February 1942 the DPC had advanced $126 million for new installations in Provo. The area was favorably located for iron ore and coal and enjoyed easy access to rail transportation. In addition, it had some proximity to the Pacific Coast, where the shipbuilding industry was using ever increasing quantities of steel. Under the agreement that the DPC made with the U.S. Steel Corporation—the parent company of the Columbia Steel Corporation—U.S. Steel would build this major new plant without fee and then would manage it. The government provided the financing of the facilities but let U.S. Steel operate them under generous terms. In August 1943 the U.S. Steel Corporation formed the Geneva Steel Works to consolidate operations in Provo and selected Walter Mathesius, a prominent steel executive, as president. When fully completed in 1944, the Geneva Steel Works encompassed three 1,100-ton blast furnaces, nine 225-ton open-hearth furnaces, 252 by-product ovens, and a structural steel plate mill. With forty-two hundred employees, it instantly became the largest integrated steel manufacture facility in the West, processing almost one million tons of iron ore under federal auspices.[32]

Meanwhile, Henry Kaiser redoubled his efforts. After the OPM rejected his comprehensive proposal for expanding the steel industry in the West, he licked his wounds. But immediately after Pearl Harbor he tried again. This time he applied to the RFC for a loan of $150 million to establish a new steelmaking plant in California. Jesse Jones was hardly thrilled, sharing with eastern steel executives and bankers a negative view of Kaiser. As Jones cryptically described his dealings with Kaiser:

> When Mr. Kaiser heard the government wanted a steel plant built near the Pacific Coast, he went to see Sam Husbands, President of the Defense Plant Corporation, and proposed to build and own the plant himself, if the Reconstruction Finance Corporation would lend him the money, taking a mortgage on the plant, and an assignment of shipbuilding fees from three of his shipyards. Sam agreed and Kaiser built the steel mill. He capitalized his Fontana Steel company for $100,000 and borrowed the balance of the money, for construction and operating capital, something more than $111,000,000 from the Reconstruction Finance Corporation. . . . Ship plates and structurals were Fontana's only products. Mr. Kaiser was smart to invest his ship fees in plants, because if he had not done so, probably 90 per cent of them would have been taken from him in excess profits taxes.[33]

The contract did not allow Kaiser to build a fully integrated steel mill, but one intended primarily to supply his shipyard needs. And although Kaiser pleaded for a location near the coast, where water transportation would allow him a better competitive situation than if he had to rely on more expensive rail carriers, Jones and Husbands forced him to build at Fontana. This site was about fifty miles inland and was ostensibly more secure than Terminal Island or Port Hueneme on the Pacific, which had been Kaiser's preferences.[34]

Despite these obstacles, Kaiser turned his enthusiasm and entrepreneurial skill toward the construction of what was to become another major steel production facility for the West. His staff began designing the new mill immediately after he secured his loan. In just nine months, on December 30, 1942, he placed the first blast furnace into operation. With his customary foresight, Kaiser viewed this enterprise as more than a wartime expedient. He hoped that eventually his plant would attract new steel-consuming industries to southern California and that it would trigger the long-desired economic growth and diversification of the West.[35] As he wrote to columnist Walter Lippmann in 1944: "We see a greater America out there. And across the Pacific we think we can make out the shape of a new continent rising from a long sleep."[36]

After the war Kaiser secured additional loans from the RFC to install expanded processing facilities, but his opponents continued to place obstacles in his path. The RFC refused to renegotiate or reduce the large loan it had made to him. And the eastern steel companies virtually declared war on him, blatantly refusing to supply him with steel for his automobile manufacturing. And the approval by the Interstate Commerce Commission in April 1947 of a 31 percent reduction in railroad rates from the Geneva Steel Works in Utah to the Pacific Coast enabled the U.S. Steel Corporation to undercut Kaiser even in California. Only the extraordinary growth and expanded markets of the West in the postwar decade sustained Kaiser's steel manufacture plant.

But in wartime Kaiser's Fontana operation made a substantial contribution to the metamorphosis of the western steel industry. In 1940 the West had produced 700,000 tons of steel and consumed 2.5 million tons. By 1951 western steel production totaled 3.6 million tons, and the region consumed 6 million tons. During the decade after 1942 the Fontana Works contributed one-third, and in some years more, of the total steel produced west of the Mississippi River.[37] Certainly wartime exigencies played an important part in bringing about this enormous growth of western steel. But some credit was also due Kaiser himself, whose vision exceeded that of most of his contemporaries.

Like the steel industry, petroleum production in the West was profoundly affected by the war mobilization program. If the changes were not quite as sweeping, that was because the petroleum industry was already mature on the eve of World War II. The war brought about notable changes in the transportation of western oil to the population centers of the nation, particularly with the development of pipelines. Wartime experience did not change the basic structure of the industry, but it ended the self-sufficiency the United States had enjoyed. By 1945 it was clear that the West could no longer supply all of the country's needed petroleum, and henceforth reliance on foreign imports became more pronounced each year. Concomitantly, the war intensified the search for oil in North America. Frantic but futile exploration of Alaska between 1941 and 1945 presaged patterns of petroleum exploration evident during the remainder of the twentieth century.[38]

Between the two world wars the western petroleum industry had devoted much of its effort to limiting overproduction in the hope of stabilizing oil prices. That had been a prime goal of producers large and small during the 1920s. But their problems were grievously aggravated by the Great Depression, which mired the entire western industry in utter chaos. In 1931 crude oil was selling for ten cents per barrel, far below production costs. The New Deal did much to stabilize conditions, first with the Oil Code framed by the National Recovery Administration between 1933 and 1935 and then with the Interstate Oil Compact and the Connally "Hot Oil" Act in 1935. The outbreak of World War II in Europe dramatically changed conditions. Instead of insufficient markets, oil producers now found a growing oil shortage in the world as the federal government urged them to meet higher production goals.[39]

The growing petroleum shortage after 1939 was due to various factors. Obviously, the demands of the British and French war machines were one influence. German submarines in the North Atlantic restricted the flow of foreign oil to England and were also affecting patterns of oil transportation in the United States. They not only interfered with oil shipments from California to the northeastern United States via the Panama Canal but also limited shipments from Gulf Coast ports in the Southwest. Such disruptions began to affect easterners by the fall of 1940 as they experienced serious fuel oil and gasoline shortages. The situation was also worsened by Roosevelt's decision to lend fifty American tankers to the British, which reduced the East Coast's petroleum supply by about 250,000 barrels daily. Existing rail and truck lines could not make up the shortfall for the large cities of the East Coast and Middle West. Few large pipelines were in operation that could link the Texas and Oklahoma oil regions to the East, or to California. The war would revolutionize the transportation of oil from West to East. Instead of placing prime reliance on tankers, railway cars, and motor carriers, Americans increasingly turned to pipelines. It took the first great energy crisis of 1940 to shock them into a greater awareness of their vulnerability.[40]

As the petroleum shortage worsened during 1941 Roosevelt decided to increase government supervision of the industry, primarily to bring about greater coordination. Instead of creating an entirely new agency, the chief executive entrusted the task to Harold Ickes, his secretary of the interior. In May 1941 Roosevelt appointed him petroleum coordinator for national defense, a position that expanded Ickes's powers.[41]

With his accustomed vigor, Ickes lost little time in seeking to alleviate the oil shortage. One of his first actions was an attempt to stop U.S. oil exports to Japan in June 1941. That effort infuriated Secretary of State Cordell Hull, who felt that Ickes was interfering with his department and who successfully challenged his authority. Ickes had better luck, however, inducing petroleum distributors to make greater use of railway tank cars. They were reluctant at first because the cost of shipping oil by rail was ten times as high as transporting by water. Moreover, terminal facilities were geared to ships rather than to railroads. But Ickes provided them with various incentives, including the suspension of the antitrust laws that previously had prevented them from pooling reserves or shipments. This brought an immediate increase of 142,000 barrels daily to the East Coast. Also, since the general mobilization program was making it difficult for the railroads to secure new tank cars or trucks, Ickes began to campaign for the building of new pipelines by the federal government. Throughout 1941 he encountered stiff opposition not only from the major railroads but also from an array of local interests. But as the emergency worsened during 1941 Ickes prevailed. In the following year he obtained a congressional appropriation for the building of the Big Inch pipeline from East Texas to New York, which greatly helped to resolve the transportation problem.[42]

After Pearl Harbor the president expanded Ickes's powers, appointing him petroleum administrator for war. He now enjoyed broad jurisdiction over petroleum production, distribution, refining, and transportation. During the war years Ickes frequently intervened with the WPB on behalf of western oil producers so that they could secure scarce oil exploration equipment. To boost production, he encouraged wildcatting and stripper wells by offering subsidies and other financial inducements. One of his most successful programs was the increased refining of 100-octane aviation gasoline. Ickes encouraged a crash effort to build sorely needed refining facilities for aviation fuel, largely financed with federal funds. Instead of acting unilaterally, he developed an extensive network of industry advisory committees in the five major districts of the Petroleum Administration for War. These committees also made specific plans for the construction or remodeling of facilities in their areas, utilizing generous government purchasing contracts issued by the RFC.[43]

At the same time, Ickes expanded more conventional practices such as stricter conservation and increased research by the U.S. Bureau of Mines to improve recovery of petroleum products. On various occasions he also intervened with the Office of Price Administration to secure higher prices for oil producers and distributors. His efforts did much to boost oil production. The industry increased its output from 1,353,214,000 barrels in 1940 to 1,713,655,000 barrels in 1945. During World War II the West was able to supply virtually all of the nation's needed petroleum. Ickes realized, however, that the war years brought an end to petroleum self-sufficiency for the United States and that henceforth the nation would become increasingly dependent on imports from South America and the Middle East. He thus attempted to increase the flow of foreign oil, largely through the formation of the Petroleum Reserves Corporation, a government entity that was to exploit oil resources in the Middle East. Congress balked at such direct action, although American companies took over the corporation's functions. Even though foreign oil imports in 1945 were less than 5 percent, Ickes was more farsighted than many of his contemporaries in realizing that imports were destined to play a larger role in the nation's energy future.[44] No longer would the West serve as the sole source of petroleum for America.

It was, in fact, a growing awareness of the nation's energy vulnerability that led military officials to eye Alaska's petroleum potential. Beginning in 1942, the War Department embarked on what became known as the Canol Project, to exploit Alaskan oil. Unfortunately, the War Department's ignorance of the history, geography, and geology of the area selected for prospecting made this one of the most expensive failures of the war mobilization program. Its implications for the future, however, were significant.[45]

The idea of utilizing the resources of Alaska and the Yukon was first suggested to the War Department in 1941 by Dr. Vilhjalmur Stefansson, a world-famous Arctic explorer. As a special adviser to the War Department, he alerted government officials to the desirability of a supply route from the Pacific states north to Alaska by way of Canada. Stefansson thought that either a highway or a railroad could provide a vital transportation link. His suggestion greatly influenced Lieutenant General Brehon B. Somervell, the army's chief of supply. Somervell knew very little about Alaska but became enthused about the concept. A railroad might be too ambitious for a wartime project, he reasoned, but a highway would certainly be feasible. Thus was born the Alcan Highway Project. Somervell lobbied mightily for it, and Congress appropriated more than $60 million as a start, authorizing the U.S. Army of Corps of Engineers to undertake the construction. In addition to tapping Alaska's oil resources, the new road promised to ease supply problems of U.S. military units in the territory and to facilitate the shuttling of American aircraft bound for the Soviet Union under the lend-lease program.[46]

Regrettably Somervell and his staff knew little about conditions in Alaska, nor did they try very hard to inform themselves. The general's major adviser on petroleum was James A. Graham, a geologist who had been dean of the College of Engineering at the University of Kentucky. Graham casually discussed Canol with various individuals in the War Department but made no formal study. In April 1942 he asked Major General Arthur H. Carter, at the time the chief of the Fiscal Division of the Services of Supply, to get in touch with the Standard Oil Company of New Jersey, which operated a small producing and refining facility at Norman Wells, Alaska, through its subsidiary, the Imperial Oil Company, Limited. On April 29, 1942, Carter met with representatives of the company in Washington, D.C., where they attempted to dampen his enthusiasm. They wondered whether production of oil in the area could reach even an insignificant quantity, such as three hundred barrels daily. But

General St. Clair Streett, who was present at the meeting, was ebullient about the plan, feeling that it would be a godsend to have supplies of high-octane aviation gasoline near the Alcan Highway where the army was building new airfields. Company officials were more pessimistic. R. V. Le Sueur, vice-president of the Imperial Oil Company, wrote to General Carter on May 2, 1942, that his plan to build an oil pipeline south from Alaska along the length of the highway for hundreds of miles across mountains and other difficult terrain was utterly unrealistic. Cargo planes, he argued, would be much cheaper. Meanwhile, other company officials were meeting with Major General T. M. Robins, deputy chief of the Army Engineers, to tell him that they did not want to be involved in the project. Robins himself believed that barges could supply needed fuel for Alaska quite effectively through inland routes and that the cost would be only one-tenth that of the projected pipeline.[47]

Despite such doubts, Somervell persisted. In early May Graham wrote a memorandum to Somervell in which he urged two objectives for the project. One goal was to drill more wells in the Norman field to increase production. The other was to build a four-inch pipeline from Norman to White Horse, which would complement the Alcan Highway then under construction. The pipeline would be 550 miles long, extending over country as yet unmapped and unsurveyed. It would also cross two mountain ranges. Anyone who would have seriously studied the feasibility of this part of the project would have become faint hearted. But not General Somervell. He was so excited about Graham's memo that he approved it the same day he received it. And on the next morning he instructed the chief of engineers to begin construction.[48]

Somervell's unrealistic optimism about oil reserves near Norman and the pipeline were fueled by some very realistic strategic considerations. Air force officials feared the Japanese threat to Alaska and the possibility that disruption of American shipping in the North Pacific could interfere with the operation of U.S. forces in the area. Whether the navy could supply needed quantities of gasoline along the Pacific Coast in 1942 was problematical. Yet the defense of Alaska was primarily in the hands of the air force. Clearly, a local supply of petroleum, especially aviation gasoline, would be highly desirable.

But in making his hasty decision Somervell ignored well-informed advisers. He neglected Stefansson and did not bother to inform Ickes, who as petroleum administrator for war was the major figure in the government's oil program. He even failed to consult the WPB and his own Army Corps of Engineers, who were assigned to build the pipeline. Nor did

Somervell consider the extraordinary cost of the project or the scarcity of machinery and construction equipment.

Under Somervell's reckless leadership the army hired the Standard Oil Company of California as technical consultant and authorized it to operate the refinery and the pipeline. The company was as dubious about the project as most other critics. J. L. Hanna, a Standard official, on June 4, 1942, wrote Secretary of War Henry L. Stimson that the pipeline could not be built in the short time Somervell envisaged. Moreover, the amount of high-octane gasoline that could be produced was at best minimal. A much better and cheaper alternative, he suggested, would be for Somervell to build inexpensive storage facilities at Norman.[49]

When Ickes accidentally heard about the project he was furious. Ever one to protect his turf, he wrote to Stimson on June 3, 1942, to protest his exclusion from the Canol Project. Considering the difficulties involved, he questioned the entire scheme. As for getting aviation gasoline to Alaska, he proposed an alternate plan. If petroleum could be brought up the Alaska coast by ship to Skagway and placed in storage facilities there, then a short pipeline could provide more than the three thousand barrels a day proposed for the refinery.[50]

The War Department closed ranks. Undersecretary of War Robert P. Patterson replied that his department was committed to the Canol Project and was determined to complete it. Ickes was not easily put down, however. He sent another protest to Stimson on June 22, 1942. To mollify him, Stimson responded that his suggestion for a short distribution pipeline might be practical, and he invited Ickes to send a consultant to Alaska for a feasibility study. Ickes agreed and sent Glen F. Ruby, former chief geologist of the Hudson's Bay Company, who was very familiar with the area and its petroleum resources. Ruby filed his report with Stimson on November 29, 1942. He concluded that neither a pipeline nor a refinery was justifiable in the area, although further exploration for oil in the region was certainly warranted.[51]

But Stimson, Patterson, and army officials were determined to proceed. The War Department's budget of May 6, 1942, contained $25 million appropriated for Canol. By February 1943 cost estimates had risen to $95 million! That alarmed the Bureau of the Budget, which sent its own investigator to Alaska. He reported that a minimum of $119,080,000 would be needed to complete construction. This was an exorbitant sum, he stressed, in the light of benefits to be obtained. Consequently, he urged abandoning the difficult pipeline project from Norman to White Horse and also the refinery at Norman. Officials of the Standard Oil Company of California endorsed this recommendation and were backed by renewed protests from Ickes. Still, Patterson stood firm. In a letter to Ickes on July 27, 1943, he echoed a familiar refrain of military officials accused of profligate spending, "Military necessity requires that the Canol Project be completed as rapidly as possible." Abandonment would result in the immediate loss of the $50 million already spent.[52]

Meanwhile, officials at the WPB heard about Canol only casually, late in 1942. They were horrified. When Fred Searls, Jr., director of the Facilities Bureau, first got wind of Canol, he noted: "The entire program will subtract from, rather than add to, the war effort. . . . The WPB stopped hundreds of useful . . . civilian projects to save material, only to have it used for a huge and useless program in Alaska." In March 1943, Chairman Donald Nelson of the WPB sent his own consultant to Alaska. This technical expert, H. LeRoy Whitney, reported, "It is both our right and our duty to insist that the present wastage of scarce materials and equipment be immediately stopped."[53]

By the fall of 1943 the chorus of critics was becoming too loud to be ignored. In September 1943, Senator Harry Truman had heard enough complaints to appoint a subcommittee of his Committee to Investigate Defense Expenditures to look into the Canol Project. The group held hearings in the Yukon and reported back that the project was indefensible. That prompted War Mobilization Director James F. Byrnes in October 1943 to ask the Joint Chiefs of Staff to review the program. Aware that military leaders would stick together, Somervell prepared a memorandum for them in which he advocated continuation of Canol. On October 26, 1943, the Joint Chiefs gave him full support, arguing that the venture was necessary for the war effort. In truth, they spent very little time on it.[54]

Such truculence persuaded Truman to take on the military establishment. On November 22, 1943, the full Truman Committee began to hold hearings on Canol. A few weeks later Truman invited Secretary of War Stimson, Secretary of the Navy Knox, and Secretary of the Interior Ickes, as well as Donald Nelson of the WPB, to testify about the enterprise. In a meeting held on December 9, 1943, Ickes, Knox, and Nelson agreed to the abandonment of Canol, which would save $30 million as yet unspent. But Stimson stood by his generals and insisted on continuing, which would require another $28,650,000. His undersecretary, Robert P. Patterson, described Canol in glowing terms. With considerable imagination and hyperbole he noted, "The War Department is proud of Canol." Moreover, it was "a bold undertaking. The results so far have surpassed our hopes. We are confident that even greater success lies ahead."[55]

This purple prose covered up the fact that only inconsequential amounts of oil had been retrieved by December 1943 and that the three-thousand-barrel-a-day pipeline was not to be completed until the middle of 1944. Meanwhile, in 1944 the Joint Chiefs of Staff ordered a reduction of American military forces in Alaska, eliminating even the lame argument of national security for the completion of Canol. Under intense questioning, Somervell was forced to admit to Truman late in 1943 that had he realized the problems and difficulties of the project he probably would not have approved it.[56]

On January 8, 1944, the Truman Committee issued a highly critical report on the Canol Project. It concluded that Somervell had rushed into the venture without adequate information concerning either the logistical problems involved or the enormous cost.

> The committee is definitely of the opinion that the Canol Project should not have been undertaken, and that it should have been abandoned when the difficulties were called to the attention of the War Department. Projects of this character ought to be undertaken only at the direction and with the approval of the Petroleum Administrator for War. However, this project was undertaken by the War Department and has been so largely completed that only a small amount, proportionately, could be saved by abandoning it now. The committee therefore believes that the decision as to whether it should be abandoned now should be made by the War Department.

Since the committee made no specific recommendation on the completion of Canol, the army requested another $16.4 million for operation and maintenance expenses in 1945. And the Joint Chiefs continued to insist throughout 1945 and 1946 that the continuation of Canol was necessary for unspecified military reasons. When the committee reviewed the project in 1946, it noted that the first crude oil had come through the pipeline to White Horse on April 16, 1944. The army closed the refinery on April 5, 1945. The total production was 23,417 barrels of aviation gasoline, 31,370 barrels of regular gasoline, and 256,358 barrels of diesel fuel. One seagoing tanker of average size could have delivered the entire output of Canol in three months, at a small fraction of the cost.[57]

Despite stonewalling by the military chiefs, Canol was in many ways one of the major fiascos of the World War II mobilization program. By 1946 Admiral Ernest J. King, chairman of the Joint Chiefs of Staff, agreed that the pipeline and refinery at White Horse had no military value. It should be noted that the navy had not supported Canol from the beginning.[58] Meanwhile, the army tried to sell the equipment. But Alaska and the Yukon were not known as congested areas in the 1940s, and few buyers appeared. Eventually the army sold the refinery to the Imperial

Oil Company for $1 million and auctioned off the pipeline as junk for $700,000.[59] The ultimate sufferer was the American taxpayer, since the total cost of Canol was $134 million, excluding the labor of four thousand troops and twelve thousand civilians. A rough estimate of a total of $200 million in expenses for Canol would not be unrealistic.[60]

Canol was not without its lessons. It was clearly one of the army's worst boondoggles of World War II and made no contribution to augmenting the nation's petroleum supplies. From a long-range perspective, perhaps Canol focused attention on Alaska as a major petroleum reserve. Undoubtedly such a focus could have been secured at much lesser cost. But the project illustrated the increasing power of the military establishment over civilian agencies and indicated that henceforth military officials would play a more prominent role in reshaping the West's economy.

Given the nature of wars in the twentieth century, perhaps such military influence was not surprising, particularly because magnesium, steel, and oil had become so vital. The contributions of the West to the increased production of these commodities were considerable. In the process, the war induced changes that affected the structure of the western economy to a limited extent. It brought significant expansion in the production of magnesium, steel, and petroleum, and also far-reaching changes in transportation patterns. The result was to contribute to the diversification of the western economy, about which so many westerners had dreamed for decades before 1940. The war did not end such dreams, of course, but rather opened new vistas for the future. By 1945 westerners were actively engaged in planning for a still brighter future.

CHAPTER 7

World War II
and the Western
Environment

WORLD WAR II ushered in a period of intensive reshaping of the American economy in which the utilization of the West's natural resources played an important role. To the industrial East the function of the West appeared as it had for more than half a century—to serve as a storehouse of vital raw materials to feed the factories of the Northeast and Middle West. But westerners had resented this colonial status for years. They viewed the mobilization program as a unique opportunity to emancipate themselves from the shackles of colonialism and to establish their own manufacturing facilities and thus a more diversified economy. To a considerable extent the exploitation of the West's raw materials during wartime was characterized by these differing visions of the West's functions and its future. The East expected the region to continue as an underdeveloped economy, whereas the West looked forward to a new era of economic independence.

The western view was conditioned by a realization the the plenitude of natural resources so characteristic of the nineteenth century was limited. The Great Depression had already made Americans painfully aware of their limitations, including the vulnerability of their resources. The era of self-sufficiency was about to end, and henceforth greater conservation, as well as increasing dependency on foreign imports of raw materials, was at hand. The extravagance and wastefulness that had been so common in the nineteenth century had no place in the increasingly conservation-minded West during wartime. World War II contributed to this growing awareness of a limited environment as much as did the Great Depression.

Few grasped the broader dimensions of these changes better than Secretary of the Interior Harold Ickes. He saw more clearly than most that the issue of industrialization in the West was directly tied to the process of national mobilization. These problems were related to conversion from peace to war and reconversion from war to peace. The path was often beset by cultural lags, as many individuals and institutions were often loath to change either their outlooks or their policies formed in earlier years. Ickes lamented this situation as early as 1941, noting particularly the backward attitude of eastern industrialists who were reluctant to support—or were even opposed to—economic diversification in the West.

> For many years this Nation had been deluded with the idea that it was practically self-sufficient, that its industrial processes were the world's best, and that its supplies were practically inexhaustible. A painful hangover resulted from that spree. We woke up to find out that we did not have enough . . . to do the job. . . . We discovered so far as our natural resources were concerned we had been doing everything in the easy way. We had . . . been skimming the cream, and the cream ran out. . . . We had constructed our whole economy on our fat.[1]

But Ickes believed he had the solution to the problem. "We have so far advanced conservation that nearly every individual on this continent may improve his lot if only we have the will to make our gains serve the logical purpose—the advancement of human welfare. . . . The advent of hydroelectricity [is] so developed that it can revolutionize heavy industry, and accompanied by equally developed supporting facilities mainly to introduce a new generation to an historical occurrence." Ickes felt that no agency was more qualified to accomplish the task than his Department of the Interior. But he lamented the opposition to rapid economic conversion, which he saw all about him. He noted in 1942:

> It was with this process of conversion that the Department of the Interior was chiefly concerned. I cannot with candor assert that we have been successful. Our proposals for the complete utilization of certain domestic minerals, for example, did not meet with wholehearted welcome. In some instances temporary expedients seemed to be preferred by some groups to imaginative, full-scale adoption of novel, though proven methods. . . . The inertia of the old way, the weight of industrial tradition, the following of the established pattern, frequently induced heavy industries to postpone technical innovations. In my opinion, this was a postponement of the inevitable.[2]

Instead of maximum exploitation of western resources by eastern industrialists, Ickes advocated a more balanced economic development for the region. In essence, he urged the West to conserve its natural resources and to expand its manufacturing facilities, undertaking fabrication of such resources rather than sending them East for processing. This would give the West greater control over its destiny. "We would determine the location and volume of the ores and the bases of plastics that are amenable to processing or manufacturing by means of electricity," he wrote. "We would forestall or ameliorate the pollution of streams, safeguard the soil against erosion, protect wildlife, and develop recreational areas. Considered as a transition from war to peace, conservation unitized on a great scale, is especially timely. . . . By committing ourselves to the development of all the resources of a region we preclude those conflicts that result from a commitment to half measures." He continued, "There are vast areas throughout all of the West in which great potentials would be realized by similar coordination."[3]

Ickes saw the wartime mobilization program as an extraordinary opportunity to reshape the western economy. In 1942 he reflected: "In our biggest job, that of mobilizing the Nation's natural resources for war, we have been tested for agility in improvising new tactics on the field as new challenges arose and old ones changed, for economic performance, and for resistance to that wartime itch for overcentralized authority. The secondary job is to maintain a reduced conservation program." By 1944 Ickes had turned his thoughts to the reconversion from war to peace, which he felt offered as great an opportunity to advance his ideas of regional coordinated development as did wartime mobilization. Speaking of the vast new reservoir of electric energy created during the war, he noted in 1944: "Our job soon will be to turn this vast block of power from war to peace. Is is a herculean job but I think that we can master it by shifting from war to its nearest equivalent in the field of conservation, namely regional development. The program must embrace entire areas, usually the basins of great rivers and their tributaries, it must provide for full and unified development of all the resources within the region." Then he itemized his vision. "We would provide for irrigation at the upper reaches of a river, for deep-water navigation and for flood control. . . . We would impound water for municipal supply, generate hydroelectric power, and transmit it for use in factories and homes on farms."[4]

Ickes was aware that the intensive use of the West's natural resources during wartime could impede his long-range program. As he wrote to F. C. Walcott, president of the American Wildlife Institute:

For some time I have been concerned with the conflict that is almost inevitable in the wartime use of our resources. As a result of the unavoidable necessities involved in war production, it is only too likely that some of the ideal practices for which we have all worked will have to be laid aside. My own position is that we should insist on the wise use of resources as far as possible, but I recognize that our demands of war must be met. I would not like to see conservationists misunderstand this situation. . . . I think what may be called for is some kind of Federal Board of Conservation Protection.

That was a proposal the president was unwilling to support.[5]

Ickes's views were amplified by one of his chief aides, Paul Raver, the administrator of the Bonneville Power Administration. The department assumed, Raver noted in 1941, "that the West is not only building for the war, but for its future and that of the nation." Also referring to his own experience in the Pacific Northwest, he emphasized that every electrochemical industry established there was started not merely to exploit natural resources but to provide processing facilities and to create a more balanced and integrated economy. The management of natural resources in wartime should be oriented not only to the winning of the conflict but also to the long-range industrial development of the region.[6]

But the perception of the West as a purveyor of raw materials to the East did not fade quickly, particularly in the East. There representatives of established industries assumed that the colonial relationship would continue. Self-interest impelled them to protect the status quo. And their power was considerable. Executives from large corporations dominated many wartime federal agencies, especially the War Production Board, which became a chief antagonist of the Ickes program.

Such diverging views on the West's future were reflected in the expansion of the region's electric power program, a key to the success of the entire mobilization effort. Electricity was needed for the vast new airplane and shipbuilding facilities on the Pacific Coast. Although Boulder Dam had been completed in 1935, Bonneville Dam was still under construction in 1941. Thus, the extent to which the Bonneville projects should be expanded and just what their role should be in the economic diversification of the West were disputed by Ickes and the WPB. As early as January 1941 the Bonneville Power Administration recommended a speedup in the installation of its generating units if it was to supply the rapidly burgeoning war industries. Moreover, the agency was planning vastly increased power output by 1945 because private utilities—still smarting from the depression—were loath to undertake any expansion of their own. But the completion of Grand Coulee Dam required the shifting of generators from other projects, since such turbines were in short supply. Nevertheless, the WPB refused to give clearance to the BPA for additional needed equipment, despite loud protests from Raver and Ickes.[7]

The WPB continued to refuse some of the requests the BPA made for scarce materials that would enable it to undertake large-scale expansion of power production. Raver complained that the WPB considered only immediate short-range wartime needs, and he urged the board to have an appreciation of the long-range requirements of the Pacific Coast for economic diversification. To accomplish this latter goal, he felt that BPA power should be made available especially to industries, like aluminum production, that could best develop regional resources. These should be developed in conjunction with fabricating facilities instead of relying on eastern firms. Although emphasizing that much of the industrial development of the Pacific Northwest should be by private enterprise, Raver urged that government laboratories conduct the research necessary to develop new processes. Directly alluding to Alcoa's monopoly in the aluminum industry, he urged regulation of existing industries that sought to restrict competition by newcomers.[8]

But wartime pressures forced the WPB to foster expansion of BPA facilities. By 1943 Bonneville's dams were producing twice as much electricity as in the preceding year. In fact, between 1941 and 1945 the BPA increased its power output by a whopping 400 percent, of which 90 percent was consumed by the new war industries up and down the Pacific Coast. The capacity of new facilities installed during the war years was more than the total available capacity in 1940. In the Southwest, war industries were receiving from Boulder Dam 50 percent of the power they required. The giant Basic Magnesium plant in Las Vegas consumed fully one-fourth of Boulder Dam's output. If the seventeen western states are considered as a region, the Bureau of Reclamation was able to increase power production by 500,000 kilowatt hours in thirty-one plants in twelve western states. Later critics of the bureau's policies usually ignored its accomplishment during World War II in supplying much needed electricity during the war emergency. Without the electricity, aircraft and shipbuilding industries would have been severely hampered.[9]

Like the Bonneville Power Administration, the Bureau of Reclamation had its share of troubles with the WPB. The bureau was vitally concerned, for example, with increasing food production in the West. Part of its program entailed encouraging farmers to shift from less essential crops to those that were critically needed, such as beans and potatoes. But the execution of such a policy required machinery to expand farm acreage through irrigation. On October 20, 1943, the WPB issued an order to stop the bureau from acquiring such equipment, thus preventing the bureau from carrying out its conversion program, except for five small projects. Only after the bureau made a special appeal to the Facility Review Committee of the WPB was permission granted for limited allocation of needed irrigation equipment.[10]

World War II and the Western Environment

Most of the bureau's peacetime activities were placed on hold during the war. Shortages of materials and labor and the urgency of the war mobilization program precluded large-scale irrigation and reclamation development unless directly related to war goals. The maximum production of food was one such endeavor. But the bureau's staff devoted a great deal of time to making detailed, specific plans for thousands of postwar irrigation and reclamation projects. Their hope was that they could play a major role in alleviating mass unemployment as veterans and war workers streamed back into the civilian labor force. In such a scenario the bureau's staff saw a crucial role for themselves on both a national and regional scale.

By 1945 one of Ickes's dreams had come true. The extraordinary expansion of power facilities in the West during the war had created a foundation for more extended and diversified economic growth. Beginning in 1943 the Bureau of Reclamation complied with the president's request to create postwar programs. It made an inventory of 236 irrigation projects for the future, expected to provide employment for more than a million veterans. To secure community support the BPA created a Northwestern States Development Association. Composed of the governors of Idaho, Oregon, Washington, Montana, and Wyoming, the group hoped to foster more balanced economic development of the five-state area and to prepare plans for specific projects. The Bureau of Reclamation incorporated many of these proposals into its own program in 1945 when it identified 415 needed irrigation projects in seventeen western states, expected to create as many as two hundred thousand new farms. That, the bureau hoped, would generate new purchasing power in the West and would spawn service industries as well as small businesses. Just two days before his death, Roosevelt enthusiastically endorsed this program. [11]

The chief executive fully embraced the reclamation ethic. In a letter to Chairman John R. Murdock of the House Committee on Irrigation and Reclamation, dated April 10, 1945, the president noted:

As I stated in my message to the Congress of January 13, 1944, demobilization starts long before the war ends, add it is essential that programs of assistance to veterans be authorized and adequately prepared now. One such program . . . is . . . the work of the Bureau of Reclamation. I have frequently spoken with pride of the accomplishments . . . in western Reclamation projects. The great . . . projects will . . . be golden opportunities for returning veterans. Such projects constitute great increases in national wealth and income. They also offer splendid opportunities for secure and abundant livelihood to men and women, willing to engage in the arduous, though stimulating, tasks of pioneering these latest frontiers. I commend and urge your favorable consideration of Federal Reclamation projects as an important opportunity for returning veterans.

A program to facilitate settlement of returning veterans on farms can be of great value in assisting them in returning them to civilian life. It can also be of great value in the reconversion of our national economy to fully prosperous peacetime basis. . . . The purchasing power created by reclamation projects is a stimulus to industry and commerce, thus promoting full employment. [12]

Electric power was only one of the Pacific Northwest's regional resources contributing to the war effort and consequent diversification. The region's fisheries were also mobilized. The extraordinary demand for increased food production did much to stimulate markets for Pacific Coast and Alaskan fishermen. But their efforts were beset by serious obstacles, including a lack of boats, nets, and other needed equipment as well as a severe shortage of labor. More than one-fourth of professional fishermen served in the armed forces, and most of them had been captains or officers on fishing vessels. Moreover, the navy commandeered a large portion of the Pacific fishing fleet and virtually monopolized the supply of navigational instruments, nets, and fishing gear. At the same time, Japanese military operations in the North Pacific restricted American fishing there and forced the evacuation of the Pribilof Islands. Just as the need for fish became more pressing, production problems loomed more ominously. [13]

In the first year after Pearl Harbor the Fisheries and Wildlife Service in the Department of the Interior valiantly attempted to cope with many of these problems, but not with great success. It began a public relations program designed to persuade American consumers to eat previously unpopular varieties of fish, such as carp. The service's scientists also experimented with new canning techniques that would conserve tin and explored alternate methods of fish processing that would not require scarce metals. Yet, as the American armed forces around the world increased their consumption of fish, available supplies failed to keep up with new demands. In 1941 the total catch of the western fisheries was five billion pounds; a year later, after the U.S. Navy requisitioned seven hundred fishing boats, production dropped by 20 percent. In some localities the armed forces appropriated more than one-half of the fishing fleet, usually the fastest and most modern boats. Most seriously affected were the Alaskan fishermen, who lost almost all their vessels. [14]

As the anguished cries of concerned fishermen reached Ickes during the first half of 1942 he attempted to persuade the president to grant him additional powers over the fisheries. Roosevelt appeared reluctant, but as the situation worsened he finally relented. On July 21, 1942, he ap-

151

pointed Ickes coordinator of fisheries. In that capacity Ickes secured war-time powers delegated by the president that allowed him to regulate virtually every aspect of the fishing industry, as conditions warranted.[15]

Nor was Ickes loath to use his new authority. He immediately set about securing new fishing boats. Contacting the War Food Administration, he secured their support before the WPB for priorities for scarce materials needed to construct fishing vessels. In this manner he added two hundred new fishing boats to the fleet within a year. In addition, he effected the return of almost half the ships the U.S. Navy had requisitioned. Since military operations in the North Pacific prevented full-scale fishing there, he ordered intensified operations in the South Pacific. To alleviate labor shortages, Ickes secured draft deferments with Selective Service boards for fishermen who appeared indispensible. His plant to use Italian prisoners of war in the industry was unsuccessful, however, because of their need for protective custody and because of their lack of enthusiasm.[16]

Ickes was also a firebrand in obtaining new equipment for the fisheries. During 1943 and 1944 he used his authority to secure priorities from the WPB for steel, copper, and needed machinery. By acting as a direct advocate for the entire industry he cut through red tape and provided necessary nets, cord and twine, and fishing gear. Until Ickes intervened, the military needs for camouflage netting had absorbed almost all of the nation's production.[17]

As coordinator, Ickes exercised increasing control over the operations of fish canneries in Alaska and the West. He centralized operations in the most efficient salmon canneries in Alaska and ordered the less efficient ones to close. This conserved a diminishing labor force. In his order of 1943 Ickes closed forty-three of the smaller operations and concentrated all canning in the seventy-seven remaining plants, eliminating the need for about five thousand workers. Ickes used a complex process of negotiation to accomplish these measures. He met with groups of fishermen and cannery operators, discussed the various options open to them, and gradually developed the regulations, which he issued through elaborate consultation. In 1943 the centralization plan worked very well. The industry exceeded its production totals of the previous year, but with far less equipment and five thousand fewer workers. In fact, the scheme was so effective that late in 1943 the operators of eleven canneries in Seattle petitioned Ickes to extend it to their area. That done, the sardine fishing industry leaders in California petitioned Ickes for a similar plan. The federal government had requisitioned more than one-half of California's sardine pack for the armed forces and for lend-lease programs. Ickes held mass meetings of fishermen, boat owners, and cannery operators in California to work out the details. The highly complicated program rigidly allocated fishing and canning operations according to government requirements—with the suspension of antitrust laws that would have prohibited collusion.[18]

Through the centralization of powers affecting virtually every aspect of the fishing industry, Ickes did the job. Despite smaller fishing fleets, fewer workers, shortages of equipment, and the closing of canneries, the annual production of the western fisheries slowly increased during the war years, with annual catches exceeding five billion pounds. Alaska provided herring, halibut, and salmon, whereas the California fisheries were a main source of sardines and tuna. Precise statistics vary, but all together the western fisheries produced about one-half of the nation's needed fish during World War II.[19]

If the West was a chief source of food from the ocean floors, it was also a chief purveyor of meat, both here and abroad. As prices rose steadily with growing demand, western cattle growers became increasingly restive over federal restrictions. In many ways these conflicts had been developing since the passage of the Taylor Grazing Act of 1934, although the Department of the Interior had not begun to implement that measure fully until after 1940. But the act set the stage for increasingly acrimonious confrontations between the Grazing Service in the department and many western cattlemen. In addition, as the General Land Office withdrew fifteen million acres of land from the public domain for use as military installations, the public range available to cattle growers shrank accordingly. Tempted by higher prices and increased demand after two decades of hardships, the cattle growers vented their mounting frustration.

Their principal spokesman in Congress was Senator Pat McCarran, a tough and implacable advocate. Already critical of federal grazing policies during the New Deal era, he used wartime conditions to bring about significant changes. As early as 1939 the Nevada State Cattlemen's Association had mounted an attack on the secretary's policy of issuing only temporary grazing permits. They desired long-term or ten-year permits and took Ickes to court. In the Nevada state courts they secured favorable decisions, but in 1941 the U.S. Supreme Court reversed the state court decisions and reaffirmed the secretary's right to issue only short-term grazing licenses.[20]

That action galvanized McCarran. By 1940 he had secured a place on the U.S. Senate Committee on Public Lands, and for the next six years he used this body as a springboard. With a Senate resolution calling for a comprehensive investigation of the public lands, McCarran became Ickes's chief antagonist over grazing, holding hearings throughout the

West that provided a forum for discontented cattlemen, to the exclusion of most others.[21]

Nevada, of course, had a vested interest in public grazing policies. The state had more federally owned acreage within its borders than any other. Few industries thrived in its arid domain, but livestock was one of the exceptions. Moreover, Nevada's isolation and distance from the nation's capital led Nevadans to regard the federal government as an absentee landlord. Many honestly believed that they too should have a voice in the management and disposal of the public domain. Five of the largest grazing districts in the nation were located in Nevada. McCarran contended that individuals who used the public lands should have a role in determining the level of fees they paid. On the eve of war, western cattle growers had not yet adjusted to the new demands of the Taylor Grazing Act. Before 1934 the federal government had had a policy of free and open ranges for everyone—a policy it had followed for more than a century. Such old habits were hard to break in just a year or two. And personal animosities entered into the controversies as well. McCarran cared little for the New Deal liberals Ickes had on his staff, whereas the secretary was seeking greater centralized control over natural resources and less autonomy for local groups.[22]

By 1941, therefore, the stage was set for a confrontation over grazing policies. McCarran had various goals. He hoped to reduce grazing fees, and he planned to restrict the growth of the Grazing Service. Instead, he wanted to increase the influence of local and state interests over federal grazing policies. In addition, he made a concerted effort to diminish the federal power to withdraw public lands from private use. At the same time he advocated a wide range of federal aid programs to assist livestock producers, including weed control, predator eradication, and disease prevention. More than any other U.S. Senator, McCarran was Mr. Cattleman—representing the interests of the western cattle growers and their state associations. In stubbornness, determination, forcefulness, and persistence, he matched the Old Curmudgeon (Ickes) in the Interior Department.[23]

The battle began in 1941 when Ickes announced he would raise grazing fees. During the depression years, rates had been very low, no more than five cents per animal monthly. Obviously, the department was trying to help cattlemen through difficult times. But with the improvement of economic conditions after 1940 federal officials felt that some increases were warranted. After surveying the western ranges in 1941 the Grazing Service concluded that a tripling of fees was extremely reasonable. This was still less than what states and private individuals were charging for grazing privileges, and much below the rates charged by the U.S. Forest Service. Meanwhile, the Grazing Service was seeking to carve out a small bureaucratic empire for itself, expanding staff and administrative services steadily each year after 1940 and asking Congress for increased appropriations.[24]

McCarran vigorously opposed the proposed fee increase. At his subcommittee hearings on the issue held throughout the West in 1941 and 1942 cattlemen raised howls of protest. Ickes realized that he had stirred a hornet's nest. At a time when he was hoping for increased meat production he was loath to antagonize westerners. Thus, he ordered the Grazing Service to withdraw its proposal. In many other ways the federal government was already subsidizing the industry, and grazing fees were really only a small part of the total package.[25]

But in 1944 Ickes appointed a new director for the Grazing Service. A former employee of the U.S. Forest Service, Clarence L. Forsling was aware of the higher fees that agency had imposed for years and promptly announced his intention of tripling existing rates. He first made his recommendation to the National Advisory Council of the Grazing Service, which had been created by the Taylor Grazing Act and was composed of cattle growers. As soon as he made his suggestions most members voiced strong objections. At the same time they deluged their representatives in Congress with telegrams and letters. That had its effect, as McCarran sprang into action. On December 16, 1944, he introduced a Senate resolution that noted: "It is the sense of the Committee on Public Lands . . . that no increase in grazing fees should be imposed until the Committee . . . has had an opportunity to make a full and complete study of the subject."[26]

Back in Nevada the legislature was shouting loud hurrahs and egging McCarran on. In February 1945 the state assembly enacted a resolution criticizing the Grazing Service. It urged Congress to repeal the Taylor Grazing Act unless the Grazing Service should "show a proper disposition to conform with and carry out the said assurances and promises in connection with their administration of the Taylor Grazing Act." Nevadans did not so much object to higher fees as to the basis on which these were calculated. They wanted charges to be based on the costs of administration, whereas the service sought to base them on the estimated value of the range. What seemed reasonable to stock producers was obviously not reasonable to Ickes and his staff.[27]

Unfortunately, since 1934 the Interior Department had been seriously underestimating the administrative costs related to the execution of the Taylor Grazing Act. At its inception Ickes had publicly stated that no new agency would be needed to carry out its provisions. He believed, at the time, that the General Land Office and the Geological Survey could easily apply the act for less than $150,000 annually. That proved to be totally unrealistic and raised false expectations. In 1936 Ickes created a Division of Grazing in his department. That was expanded under the Government Reorganization Act of 1939 as the Grazing Service—and was perceived as an expansion of New Deal bureaucracy.[28] By 1941 many western cattle growers were becoming increasingly dismayed by the rapid growth of the new bureaucracy administering the Taylor Grazing Act, with its mushrooming costs of millions of dollars annually. One critic wondered whether Interior Department officials had deliberately underestimated the cost of administering grazing regulations to appease economy-minded easterners in Congress.

As he had done three years earlier, in 1944 McCarran again used the Committee on Public Lands to block the suggested increase in grazing fees. First, he extracted a promise from a chastized Forsling not to raise fees until the committee finished its investigation of the increase. Then McCarran took his subcommittee back on the road, to every western locality where cattlemen wanted a forum to voice their discontent. In addition, McCarran mobilized senators from other western states and orchestrated the question into a national issue. Poor Forsling got more than he bargained for.[29]

In fact, the House Appropriations Committee now took note of the controversy. Its members were becoming concerned over the steadily growing budgets of the Grazing Service. Since prices for livestock were so much higher than a decade earlier, the committee believed that an increase of grazing fees was certainly justified. But it undertook an extensive study of the Grazing Service and concluded in 1945 that the service should do more to pay its own way. This could be done by increasing grazing charges. If the service failed to do that, the Appropriations Committee would reduce its annual budget. Such action placed the service in an untenable position. Whereas the House Appropriations Committee was seeking to force the service to increase its fees, the Senate Committee on Public Lands warned of dire consequences if the service did so. In this predicament Forsling did nothing. That infuriated the House Appropriations Committee, which in March 1946 decided on drastic cuts for the service. As Representative Jed Johnson of the committee noted:

> They went out and practically turned [the public range] over to the big cowman and the big sheepman of the West. . . . It is common knowledge that they have been running the Grazing Service. They did not choose to assess

grazing fees that were anywhere comparable to the fees the other people pay. . . . They have made a joke out of the Grazing Service. . . . Why, they even put them on the payroll.[30]

The scenario now took on the dimension of a comic opera. Many who had attacked the service suddenly became its defenders. Representative W. K. Granger from Utah felt that the committee's action reflected bitterness toward Ickes and was a personal attack on him. Congressman Berkeley Bunker of Nevada confessed that many westerners really liked the Grazing Service, despite their hostile rhetoric. Congressman Frank A. Barrett of Wyoming urged generous appropriations for the service, although he had lambasted it for years. Congressman Robert F. Rockwell of Colorado praised the Grazing Service for being so responsive to local users.[31]

Nevertheless, McCarran's campaign against the Grazing Service continued. The Nevadan particularly disliked Forsling, whom he blamed for his poor relations with the House Appropriations Committee. Although the Senate Appropriations Committee tripled the amount recommended in the House, McCarran prevailed in the conference committee, which reduced appropriations for 1946 to $550,000. That required the dismissal of 110 employees and achieved McCarran's objective of making the service more dependent on local interests than on the central administration in Washington, D.C. In addition, the National Park Service and the Forest Service could not help but be intimidated by this show of power. Meanwhile, McCarran supported President Truman's Reorganization Plan #3 under which, on July 6, 1946, the Grazing Service merged with the General Land Office.[32]

Like many westerners, McCarran had become increasingly concerned about the rapid growth of the Grazing Service bureaucracy. In the decade after 1934 the service's budget had increased more than tenfold. Many of its functions overlapped with those of the Forest Service and the General Land Office. Under a succession of directors the Grazing Service had also become involved in intensive bureaucratic infighting, encouraged by Harold Ickes, who was eager to extend his empire. That did not win the service friends in other federal agencies and in Congress.

By the end of World War II McCarran had largely succeeded in making federal grazing policies more responsible to user demands. When Julius A. Krug succeeded Ickes as secretary of the interior in March 1946 he appointed McCarran's protégé, Rex L. Nicholson, to survey industry attitudes toward grazing fees. At the time Nicholson was himself in the livestock business. He reported that most people in the industry were not opposed to increased fees, if the rise was modest. That view was supported by the National Advisory Council of the Grazing Service. In September 1946 it advocated higher charges if Congress also made amendments to the Taylor Grazing Act. Meanwhile, in 1947 the House Appropriations Committee succeeded in further cutting the service's budget, effectively crippling its operations. Essentially, Congress was accepting the principle for which the cattlemen's associations had fought, namely that grazing fees should be based on administration cost rather than on the value of the land.[33]

McCarran represented a view popular in the nineteenth century, that the public domain should be transferred to private interests. Despite his success in abolishing the Grazing Service, however, McCarran did not necessarily represent a majority of westerners. The consensus that was emerging during the New Deal favored the management, rather than the distribution, of federally owned resources. Although World War II provided some opportunities for further transfers of public properties, the experience effectively crystallized and institutionalized a national commitment to greater managerial efficiency in the operation of the public domain. Perhaps that goal was not always achieved, either then or in succeeding years, but it provided guidelines for the next generation and was a significant aspect of the broader effort to reshape the economy of the West.

Like the Grazing Service, the National Park Service found that wartime conditions created new pressures to relax conservation practices designed to protect the environment. Ickes had predicted such a trend at the onset of the mobilization program. Visitation to national parks declined drastically after 1942 with gasoline rationing, conscription, and war industries. Nor did the administration place a high priority on the National Park Service. During the war it moved the NPS offices from the nation's capital to Chicago to make room for war agencies. And it cut the staff from 4,510 in 1942 to 1,974 in 1943 and to 1,577 in 1945. Congress also reduced the NPS budget from $9.3 million in 1941 to $4.7 million in 1945. Some of the problems the national parks experienced during the war years could be traced directly to this shrinkage. The staff lamented spruce budworm epidemics in the Rocky Mountain area, bark beetles in Utah's Bryce Canyon, white pine blister rust at Yosemite, and cactus necrosis at Arizona's Saguaro National Monument, all of which could have been prevented.[34]

Where it could, the NPS turned its energies to aiding the war effort directly. It issued special permits to the army and the navy, for example, for the use of its facilities. During 1942 it made 403 such permits, including one at Mount Rainier National Park, where the army trained troops for mountain warfare. In Nevada it turned over the Boulder Dam National Recreation Area to the Defense Plant Corporation to establish new airports and to provide water for the Basic Magnesium plant. Many national parks were used by the armed forces as rest camps. The navy took over the Ahwahnee Hotel in Yosemite as a convalescent hospital. As the United States prepared for the invasion of North Africa the army used desert areas in Arizona and California for special warfare training. The desert warfare training units at Joshua Tree National Monument so damaged the natural environment that in 1942 army officers chose alternate sites for future use. To prepare men for Arctic warfare, the NPS made Mount McKinley National Park in Alaska available as a testing ground for clothing and equipment suitable for frigid climes.[35]

With great reluctance NPS officials allowed the removal of needed resources from selected areas. When, early in 1942, the Basic Magnesium plant in Las Vegas was in desperate need of salt, required for manufacturing magnesium, the NPS opened Death Valley National Monument because it was the closest source. During 1942 Basic Magnesium extracted fifteen million tons of salt there, but the constant entreaties of the NPS led it to look elsewhere in succeeding years. As NPS director Newton Drury ruefully noted, "It will be many decades before nature can gradually soften the scars and restore the picturesque salt pinnacles that were destroyed by these operations."[36]

Under wartime pressures the NPS grudgingly opened the Olympic National Park in Washington during 1943 to allow the cutting of Sitka spruce, allegedly needed for aircraft production. In later years that decision was severely criticized, but at the time Drury felt that, in view of a severe shortage of spruce, he had few options. He thus yielded to the demands of the WPB, which was not overly sympathetic to conservation anyway. Responding to the pleas of private lumber operators in the area, the WPB ordered the cutting of four million board feet in the Queets Corridor of the park. Yet vast amounts of spruce were available in nearby British Columbia and in Alaska on U.S. Forest Service lands. Moreover, by 1944 aluminum production was so high that the Army canceled most of its orders for wooden planes. In 1944, therefore, the WPB withdrew its order, after Ickes himself wrote a strong protest letter to Donald Nelson, chairman of the agency.[37]

Other wartime agencies were similarly insensitive to the national parks. In 1942 the Metals Reserve Corporation yielded to the demands of army and navy contractors and allowed them to remove 130,000 tons of sand and gravel from Rialto Beach in Olympic National Park. More painful to environmentalists was that agency's order to allow the mining of tungsten within Yosemite National Park, despite vehement protests from Drury and NPS officials. The mine operators found only small quantities there, and after they had extracted fifty-five tons Ickes revoked the permit he had issued. The NPS took an equally strong stand against the demands of cattlemen in California who in the midst of a drought in 1944 sought the opening of California's national parks for grazing. Range conditions in the state at the time were only 50 percent of normal. The NPS had learned lessons of political warfare, however. It created an advisory commission on California grazing composed almost entirely of conservationists. It included representatives of the Sierra Club, the California Conservation Council, the Western Federation of Outdoor Clubs, and the U.S. Forest Service. Somewhat predictably, this group unanimously recommended against opening up national parks to cattle grazing. Although cattle associations prevailed on Congressman Clair Engle of California to sponsor a bill allowing cattle grazing, nothing came of the bill, as it failed to secure congressional support.[38]

One of the most insensitive requests of the WPB was its demand for the scrapping of historical statues and cannon. In 1943 the agency ordered a survey to be made of nonferrous metals contained in historical objects. The NPS had 985 tons of such relics under its jurisdiction, most of them in the West. Director Drury took a very strong stand against such requisitions. "The National Park Service took care to point out," he wrote in 1943, "that these historic objects and memorials are part of our national heritage which should be preserved inviolate." In view of this reaction the WPB beat a partial retreat and pledged not to destroy any cannon antedating 1865. Still, the action did cause considerable damage. Perhaps the most glaring tragedy was the destruction of the famous U.S. Navy battleship *Oregon,* which in 1899 had made the long and historic ninety-nine-day voyage from the Atlantic to the Pacific around Cape Horn. Its feat had provided a big boost for those who, like Theodore Roosevelt, were advocating the construction of the Panama Canal. The navy had retired the old ship in 1925 and had given it to the state of Oregon, which made it into a very popular historic site. In the rush of patriotism immediately after Pearl Harbor, state officials donated the vessel to the WPB's scrap drive. The great *Oregon* was quickly demolished, although the amount of metal derived from its scrapping was insignificant. One of Washington's congressmen, Homer Angell, noted in the aftermath that the ship's destruction was totally unnecessary, and he introduced bills in Congress to prevent the recurrence of similar mindless cannibalism of historic objects.[39]

Wartime pressures on the national parks also resulted in the controversy over Jackson Hole National Monument in Wyoming. In Jackson Hole, private interests had been contending with the federal government for ownership of the scenic area for several decades before World War II. As early as 1923 Horace Albright, director of the National Park Service, made plans to create a national recreation area at Jackson Hole. Three years later he secured the support of John D. Rockefeller, who invested in private properties in the area that he expected eventually to donate to the federal government. During the Great Depression, however, Congress, Rockefeller, and conservation groups were not inclined to change the status quo.⁴⁰

But by 1942 Rockefeller was becoming somewhat impatient and hoped for action in establishing federal jurisdiction. In a letter to Harold Ickes he noted that if "the Federal Government is not interested in the acquisition . . . it will be my thought to make some other disposition of it or, failing in that, to sell it on the open market to any satisfactory buyers." Ickes supported Rockefeller's design and now urged the president to bypass Congress and declare Jackson Hole a national monument by executive order under the Antiquities Act of 1906. On March 16, 1943, Roosevelt followed his advice.⁴¹

The president's action set off a furor in Congress. Many there saw it as an infringement on congressional authority over national parks. In addition, western livestock associations and the Wyoming delegation were incensed, since they believed that the land should be developed by private interests and should be available for grazing, business ventures, and tax revenues for local governments. In May and June 1944, Congressman William Barrett of Wyoming held extensive hearings on the dispute under the auspices of the House Committee on Public Lands, which recommended the abolition of the monument. Congress enacted legislation to accomplish that in December 1944. President Roosevelt, preoccupied with the Yalta Conference, used a pocket veto to kill the measure. The issue continued to smolder, however, and the Wyoming delegation successfully limited appropriations for Jackson Hole in 1945 and 1946. Meanwhile, tourism waxed there between 1947 and 1950, and local opposition waned accordingly. In 1950 President Truman included Jackson Hole in Grand Teton National Park. At the same time he yielded to many demands of the Wyoming delegation, including provisions for special grazing and hunting rights, maintenance of existing private properties, and federal compensation for localities in lieu of taxes.⁴²

The Jackson Hole controversy was an example of changing land use patterns in the West. The most pronounced was the shift from distribution of public lands to management of the public domain. Such a change had been taking place for decades, of course, but it was accentuated by the war. It was also due to changing perceptions of the West and of the limitations now visible in the West's natural environment, which once had appeared almost limitless. And the change was a reflection of increasing urbanization and affluence in the United States, which were turning tourism in the West into a booming industry. The war thus did much to crystallize as well as institutionalize a growing awareness of the need for improved management of the West's environmental heritage.

In many ways Jackson Hole's problems were only a reflection of much broader issues of disposal and management that surfaced during World War II. The conflict clearly placed special pressures on the public domain. Beginning in 1941 President Roosevelt by Executive Order #9146 authorized the secretary of the interior to withdraw all public lands that might be needed for the mobilization effort. In the course of the next four years Ickes withdrew approximately 16 million acres for military purposes and another 70.8 million for minerals development. These lands were used for bombing ranges, combat training areas, storage depots, airfields, and a wide range of facilities, including the Manhattan Project in Los Alamos, New Mexico. Officials in the General Land Office were seriously concerned about these withdrawals because they were hoping to maintain what public lands there were for returning war veterans. As Commissioner of the GLO Fred W. Johnson noted in 1945: "Never before in history had the public lands under the General Land Office been called upon to provide such an abundant supply of natural resources for military purposes as in the period of World War II. . . . More than 16 million acres of the public domain were made available as sites for camps, gunnery ranges, aviation bombing fields, tank training areas, and other combat training uses." The problem seemed especially acute in sparsely settled parts of the West, such as Alaska, because the GLO hoped to avoid the boom-bust syndrome that had afflicted so many western towns in the past. In many ways GLO officials and members of Congress were still affected by nineteenth-century preconceptions in their belief that sizable numbers of World War II veterans would want to embark on homesteading after the war. That seemed highly unlikely in the 1940s, particularly since so few good farmlands were left in the public domain. But symbolically the idea of distributing land to veterans was still significant. As it had done after every war in which it had engaged, the United States government in 1944 provided legal preference for veterans who wanted to venture into homesteading.[43]

During the war the GLO shifted its emphasis from land distribution to improved management of the public domain. As Lee Muck, executive assistant to Ickes, commented in 1942:

A soundly conceived land and resource program is an essential part of public works expenditures designed to stimulate a high level of employment and production. A substantial part of such a program will be largely self-liquidating through the establishment of a maximum degree of production and increased returns from the resources under management. The future is unpredictable, but it seems clear that the value of land and its resources will continue to increase and that the maintenance of a high level of production is essential to the future of the Nation. Consequently, the formulation of land improvement programs . . . is a major responsibility of management organizations, and the successful prosecution thereof is definitely in the public interest.[44]

Throughout the war Ickes attempted to improve the efficiency of federal land administration, usually by extending his own powers of centralization. He was particularly eager to create a uniform system for recording mining claims, a proposal that made much sense. But he encountered bitter opposition from industry leaders, who were loath to see him with further powers over their activities. He also advocated an inventory of remaining federal lands by the Department of the Interior. But other federal agencies successfully obstructed him. From their perspective, Ickes was merely seeking to extend his influence over their own operations. Still, the intense utilization of resources during the war focused attention on the need for greater efficiency in the administration of the public domain.

Even if some of Ickes's recommendations were not accepted, he stimulated a greater consciousness of the public land problems. In an unheralded but significant action, Congress in 1946 abolished the GLO, which for more than one hundred years had distributed, managed, and mismanaged the public lands. Congress integrated its functions into a new agency with a significant title to illustrate the end of an era and a great change in public land policy—the Bureau of Land Management. This action also dramatized an obvious fact, namely that arable lands in the public domain were no longer available for distribution. Henceforth, the federal government would emphasize not land distribution but effective management. As Lee Muck, in 1944 the director of the Division of Land Utilization, wrote, "The challenge involved in reconversion places[s] a responsibility upon the land and resource management agencies of the Department to provide a more fully coordinated and integrated management program by virtue of which the public lands and resources will be so administered as to insure the greatest possible returns to society in the years ahead." The war heralded a new era.[45]

World War II and the Western Environment

Some of the most important lands were those containing minerals needed in the mobilization effort, such as metals and petroleum. Rapid exploitation between 1941 and 1945 crystallized a trend that had been developing for some decades, namely the decreasing self-sufficiency of the United States. Although the nation had been able to supply all of its needed raw materials from its beginnings, by 1945 the age of self-sufficiency had clearly passed. Henceforth the country would become increasingly dependent on foreign sources.

Ickes was prescient in grasping this new stage in American environmental history. As he wrote in 1944: "We were still searching the earth for the minerals that were needed in ever increasing quantities to equip our own fighting forces. . . . While we were searching for these minerals . . . we were spending them with wanton prodigality. . . . The drain on our national assets had been staggering. Only nine of the major minerals remain in our known domestic reserves. . . . Our known usable reserves of 22 essential minerals have dwindled." He warned that the future would not be as kind to the United States as the past. "The past had not taught us how severely we can be penalized for a lack of metals," he said. "We have always had time between the threat of war and actual war to get the materials which we lacked . . . but we cannot henceforth count on any appreciable lapse of [such] time. . . . We should stockpile . . . we should import and intensify exploration." And then he added some sage advice. "All that I can set down by way of a formal conclusion is that the situation with respect to many of the minerals upon which our very manner of living depends is such as to give the United States of America real national concern. If we do not remedy that situation we will most certainly and indisputably wish we had."[46]

To increase the production of critical materials, both the Bureau of Mines and the U.S. Geological Survey expanded their exploration programs. They intensified the search for known metals and now looked also for new and previously unexploited materials. They developed new processes for extracting minerals from low-grade ores and for developing synthetic materials to take the place of unavailable resources.[47]

By 1942 the Bureau of Mines was in full swing, searching for a wide range of metals including chromium, manganese, mercury, tungsten, and bauxite. Some metals were found where they had not been sought out before. Central Idaho yielded mercury; Nevada and Idaho had reserves of tungsten; southeastern California surprisingly contained manganese, as did South Dakota and western Arizona. No western steel industry could have been built without at least some access to these alloys. New iron ore deposits were discovered by the bureau's engineers in Arizona, California, Oregon, New Mexico, and Utah. Vast supplies of zinc were uncovered near Leadville, Colorado, lesser quantities of vanadium in Wyoming, and molybdenum in Montana and Arizona. The West was still America's minerals storehouse! But the search for needed materials transcended vital metals. In California the bureau's staff found sands, previously imported from Belgium, that were suitable for industrial uses, such as for refractories. Ceramic talc, insignificant before World War II, was now secured domestically for radio insulators. And when the war cut off imports of magnetite brick from Austria and Greece—used in steel furnaces—the bureau found domestic volcanic rock that served as a substitute.[48]

In part the enormous demand for minerals was met by the development of new methods to exploit low-grade ores. As early as 1941 the Bureau of Mines developed laboratory processes to increase the yield of manganese, magnesium, copper, and iron. Government scientists also established pilot projects to extract gasoline from coal. Such techniques had been developed in Germany in 1913, and during World War II they contributed a significant share of the fuel used by Hitler's armies. "There is no mystery about how to make synthetic gasoline," Ickes commented in 1945. At his behest Congress in 1945 enacted the Synthetic Liquid Fuels Act, which with an appropriation of $30 million established a five-year program for research and demonstration plants. The bureau set up one plant in Grand Forks, North Dakota, and oil shale facilities in Laramie, Wyoming, and Rifle, Colorado.[49]

Ickes became somewhat depressed by the exhaustion of resources in the United States, although he did not give up hope. He believed that if westerners undertook more intensive exploration, more research and development, improved extractive processes, and greater regional development, the situation might improve. He had great hopes that the Outer Continental Shelf could rescue the United States from its predicament. "If we discount the obvious fact it is uninhabited and uninhabitable, the Continental Shelf ranks with the lands we acquired by the Louisiana Purchase, or by the opening of the West, or by the purchase of Alaska. And the exploration of this vast underwater area will be an important historical event." To him, it was America's next frontier.[50]

As for regional development, Ickes asserted that it was

not a new theory of conservation, but rather an improved technique for developing, using, and conserving our resources by the usual means—but doing it better, cheaper, faster, and to better purpose. It is the kind of logical next step in conservation that mass production was in production. . . . We would continue to build dams, power plants, reservoirs, irrigation facilities, and other adjuncts of conservation. We would improve navigation, advance the propagation of fish and wildlife, and create and preserve recreational facilities. We would provide for flood control and for the alleviation of stream pollution. . . . We would draw into one plan all . . . that a large region would need to develop and conserve its resources . . . and we would design these unified projects to be operated as a single conservation-and-development program for the benefit of an entire region.[51]

Like Ickes, many westerners realized by the end of the war that mobilization had placed great strains on the region's natural resources. Although environmental protection efforts were far more effective between 1941 and 1945 than during World War I, four years of warfare took their toll. Resource utilization spurred by mobilization did accelerate the production of electric power, but it also intensified utilization of the public lands, ended American self-sufficiency in metal and oil, and depleted the fisheries. Diminishing natural resources focused attention on the need for economic diversification. The goal of Westerners now was to create industries that would allow them to fabricate resources rather than to send them East for processing. Moreover, the war unexpectedly spawned new industries in aerospace, nuclear energy, scientific research, and electronics development, which promised to hasten the long-desired economic diversification. Many of these hopes were reflected in an intensive movement for postwar planning. The American Dream for a postwar world, particularly as it concerned the West, was actively being fashioned even before the conflict ended.

CHAPTER 8

Visions of the Future: Westerners in Washington

THROUGHOUT the war most people who lived and worked in the trans-Mississippi West were dimly aware that the mobilization program was bringing significant changes to the region. The underdeveloped and depression-wracked colonial economy, based largely on the export of the region's raw materials, was rapidly being augmented by new manufacturing and service industries and by the creation of a new network of scientific and technologically oriented research and production facilities. This more dynamic and diversified economy came to be a pacesetter for the nation in ensuing years, bringing a new self-image for the West. Such far-reaching changes triggered a lively debate over the future of the West. Many in the region realized that the war provided them with a unique opportunity to reshape the West's destiny, to throw off the shackles of subserviency to the older sections. Some westerners dreamed big dreams; other dreamed small. But whatever the scope of their expectations for the future, they had a vision of an economy significantly reshaped by the war. And if they did not all agree on the best ways to achieve their dreams, nevertheless the excitement generated by the new opportunities stimulated an extensive debate over what the West was to become.

That debate raged in the public as well as in the private sector. In Washington it echoed in the halls of government both in the executive branch and in Congress. In executive departments several individuals and agencies were directly concerned with the reshaping of the western economy, notably the National Resources Planning Board. But its activities were jealously eyed by Harold Ickes and his associates in the Department of the Interior, who felt strongly that they—and they alone— were the rightful planners of the West's economic future. Within the department the Bureau of Reclamation hoped to play a significant role in redirecting the West's economic life. Meanwhile, a lively debate was swirling on Capitol Hill about reconversion and the shape of postwar America. Westerners took an active part in seeking to direct the economic reconstruction of their region and to carve out a new niche for it within the national economy.

Although many of the proposals made were far ranging, they tended to focus on a few key issues. Few disputed the commonly held goals of diversifying the western economy and of lessening the West's dependence on the older regions. But the selection of means to achieve these goals was a more troublesome question. Those in Washington, in particular, tended to favor well-defined planning efforts executed by centralized administrative policies emanating from the nation's capital. In the states and cities, however, and in the private sector, individuals and groups favored a more flexible approach, one that envisaged the reshaping of the West primarily by private enterprise. Whether the region should be developed by centralized or by decentralized planning, therefore, came to be a lively issue.

The planners of the postwar West were also bedeviled by a problem with which they had already wrestled—if somewhat inconclusively— during the New Deal. Should the West be developed by big business, by corporate America, or should expansion be undertaken by small business enterprises? Was the West to follow in the footsteps of the East and allow large corporations to shape its new economy? Or did the postwar era provide a unique opportunity, another chance, to create a more highly diversified economic and social structure characterized by small entrepreneurs in business, agriculture, and science? This was clearly part of a broader American problem, one that Theodore Roosevelt, Woodrow Wilson, Louis Brandeis, and Franklin D. Roosevelt had struggled with in a previous generation. It had special relevance to the West in 1945, however, because the region presented new opportunities for varying strategies of economic development. The West that emerged during the two decades after 1945, then, came out of the myriad of plans formulated in the heat of war and represented a combination of government as well as private efforts.

Even while American forces were still fighting around the globe westerners were realizing that their colonial dependence on the East was being lessened by the flood of wartime contracts that were forcing the rapid diversification of many areas in the region. "We have sniffed our destiny," declared California's governor, Earl Warren, in 1944. "We people out here in the West have our noses high in the air. . . . Anyone who has had the opportunity to travel and consult with Western business, finance, and industrial leaders during the past year has been heartened by the atmosphere of expectancy, faith, and determination which is everywhere encountered. Never before have there been quite so many people possessed of faith in our future or quite so intent on giving voice to the conviction that we have our foot in the door of an era of dream realization." That summarized the prevailing mood with practicality and eloquence. And, mirroring the feelings of the Pacific Coast sales executives whom he was addressing, he alluded to the recent wartime experiences that had given birth to his optimistic forecast. "Any summarization of the manner in which California and the West have been able to marshal resources, manpower, and initiative in the support of the war effort leads to the perfectly logical conclusion that we possess the essentials for tremendous peace time development."[1] Clearly, the war-induced economic mobilization of the West had inspired a new sense of self-confidence and had led westerners to shed the gloom and pessimism that had been endemic throughout the Great Depression.

In Washington the National Resources Planning Board became an early proponent of this mood. Initially it had favored centralized planning for the West because of the conventional wisdom that the frontier supposedly had closed and that in a closed society more rigorous planning was necessary. But by 1940 it shifted its energies to postwar planning. In November President Roosevelt sent a directive to the board—on which his uncle, Frederick Delano, was prominent—asking it to undertake comprehensive postwar planning studies. Accordingly, to coordinate such work the board created a special Post-war Agenda Section in the director's office under Luther Gulick, a specialist in public administration. A prime motive in creating this unit was the hope that perhaps the nation could avoid the serious hardships it had faced in postwar readjustments after World War I. Those difficult years between 1919 and 1921 had been marked by total absence of national planning for the transition from war to peace. The mistakes of that era could hopefully be avoided, with planning to begin even before this new war was concluded.

As one of the federal government's major planning agencies between 1939 and 1943, the NRPB embarked on numerous studies of possible postwar readjustment policies, some of them directly relevant to the West. To a considerable extent the NRPB and its staff during these years were impressed by current conventional wisdom in economic thought as represented by the theories of the British economist John Maynard Keynes. Professor Alvin Hansen of Harvard University, perhaps the leading disciple of Keynes in the United States, was an influential consultant

169

to the board and shaped much of its thinking. He also authored one of the board's early publications, *After the War*, in which he popularized Keynes's ideas. Focusing on the need for full employment, Hansen argues that the federal government should take an active role in creating a post-war economy characterized by full employment and affluence. The means to create such a more prosperous society were at hand through the federal government's pump-priming powers and deficit spending, which could fuel vast public works projects. The implications of these views for the West were obvious. Government-sponsored highway construction and especially dam-building and reclamation programs could provide jobs for millions of returning service men and women and war workers.[2]

A second theme in the NRPB publications dealing with the West concerned a fear of concentrated economic power and monopoly. That was a prime focus of two of the NRPB's assistant directors: Myron Watkins, a respected economist, and Thomas C. Blaisdell, a political scientist. Both were still under the impress of the massive Temporary National Economic Committee study of American industry, conducted between 1937 and 1941, which decried economic concentration in the American economy and urged a more prominent place for small business. That theme too was particularly relevant to the West, home to very few major corporations.

A third theme pervading NRPB planning for the postwar West concentrated on the regional character of the national economy and the geographic and economic structure inherent in the location of industries. This interested not only Watkins—who had been an economics professor at the University of Pittsburgh before joining the NRPB—but also some of his colleagues from the university department whom he brought along to Washington, most notably Glenn McLaughlin and Wilbert G. Fritz. McLaughlin was a specialist in location theory and gathered others about him with similar interests, such as E. M. Hoover, a staff member who served as NRPB director of research.[3]

Given the perspectives of these researchers, it was not surprising that the agency's studies emphasized regional economic specialization, the desirability of industrial decentralization, and the assistance of government policies for the attainment of full employment. These issues were prominent in at least four major publications on the future on the West that the NRPB published before its demise in October 1943. The staff focused on three subdivisions of the West: the Pacific Northwest, the Pacific Southwest, and the Rocky Mountain area. In addition, the board prepared a comprehensive analysis of industrial location and national economy that bore directly on the future of western economic growth.

Visions of the Future: Westerners in Washington

As Chairman Frederick Delano noted, "These studies are primarily concerned with a review of the various factors which influence plant location decisions, and which therefore are shaping the geographical pattern of American industry." Delano hoped that the board's reports would aid policy makers in arriving at decisions on the disposal of federally owned war plants and on their conversion to peacetime uses. He also anticipated that regional, state, and local planning commissions and private businesses could make use of the board's findings in adjusting their policies from war to peace. In this manner the NRPB hoped to shape the pattern of postwar economic growth in the West.[4]

In their study of the Pacific Northwest (Washington, Oregon, Idaho, and Montana), McLaughlin and his staff concentrated on familiar themes. A return to peace, they noted, should rest on a diversified economic base. That could be attained by national planning for the region, a comprehensive program to govern the disposal of federally owned war plants, and foreign policies that would stimulate the Far Eastern trade of the Pacific states. The report called for an extensive survey and inventory of the region's resources and industries and envisaged a more stable economic base in the years ahead. It urged a greater balance in the regional economy, more emphasis on conservation of renewable resources, and a lessening of waste. Finally, the authors advocated positive government policies to maintain full employment, which they expected would sustain expanding markets and consumer purchasing power.[5]

The report on the Pacific Southwest (California, Arizona, Utah, and Nevada) predicted a bright future. "As a result of wartime economic expansion," it noted, "a new economic frontier is being opened for exploration in the Pacific Southwest. Development of more electric power and of new plants for the refining of ores and production of metals . . . is broadening the region's economic base and increasing the possibilities of many kinds of manufacturing heretofore lacking in the regional economy. The Far Western states have prospects of becoming one of the major light-metal producing areas of the world." The study also waxed optimistic on the future increase of foreign trade. "The war production program not only has given a new impetus to the Nation's manufacturing industries; it is creating opportunities for a more diversified industrial development during and after the war, an adjustment long needed in the Pacific Southwest. It's [sic] rapid growth and strategic position in relation to the Orient have made the region increasingly prominent in the life and economy of the nation." The report predicted a difficult transition from war to peace for the area. It advocated planning by federal agencies but also by civic organizations and private businesses. It urged new fabricating and assembly plants, expansion of the electrochemical industries, federal aid to aircraft manufacturers, and an extensive public works program. The NRPB staff envisioned the expansion of service- and consumer-oriented firms as well. But in contrast to the agency's national vision, their view of the Southwest included a decline in small business enterprises in the postwar era.[6]

The report on the Rocky Mountain area (Colorado, New Mexico, and Wyoming) was more cautious. In view of the great emphasis here on mining and natural resource industries, the agency did not expect as much diversification as on the Pacific Coast. But it urged a greater effort by government as well as by private industry to establish fabricating plants for the processing of the region's raw materials so that less of its natural wealth would be directly exported out of the area. The NRPB also supported revision of the discriminatory freight rates that had retarded the Rocky Mountain area's economic development in the prewar years. Since the region had fewer wartime manufacturing plants than other parts of the United States, the authors expected the transition from war to peace to be less painful than in more highly industrial sections.[7]

Although the studies made by the NRPB varied with each of the subregions covered, they did contain certain similar assumptions about the postwar period. Recognizing the opportunities provided by the war for reshaping the economies, the authors assumed that the federal government would play a prominent role in that restructuring and in assuring full employment. In their projections they accorded a much larger responsibility to government than what was to occur. They assumed that the western economy would be much more diversified than it had been before 1940, and in that assumption later developments were to prove them right. Despite the effort to consider the function of small business in American life, when surplus government war plants were transferred to private operators it was the large corporations who were the prime beneficiaries. The NRPB researchers were also accurate in predicting that the West would become more involved in trade with the Orient. But they were less successful in appraising the direction of that trade. Their expectation was that the United States would have a favorable trade balance. Instead, the United States developed an increasingly negative trade balance, as Far Eastern imports into the West increasingly outstripped American exports to Asia.

By the middle of 1943 increased opposition to the NRPB was taking shape in Congress and elsewhere. Anti–New Deal members of the House and Senate as well as important spokespersons for the business community combined in the attack, concerned about the type of centralized government planning that the NRPB had been advocating. Hostility to the board had been growing in the House Appropriations Committee for some time after 1939. Finally, in 1943 the House simply refused to make any further appropriations for the agency, purportedly because it was duplicating the work of other federal entities. The Senate Appropriations Committee members fought to a deadlock, and the issue went to the floor of the Senate. There, after six hours of acrimonious debate, the NRPB's opponents won another victory, as the Senate also refused to allot funds for further operations. One of the most bitter critics was Senator Robert A. Taft of Ohio, who questioned the NRPB philosophy. "The first is the theory of unlimited public spending," he said, enumerating his objections, particularly to Keynesian doctrines. "A policy of deficit spending is implicit in the measures which the Board proposes and in its attitude toward the spending of government money. In the second place, the Board's plans are based on unlimited government interference in and regulation of all business activity, plus a very large amount of government regulation in what is now private industry."[8]

With the abolition of the NRPB in October 1943 the focus of planning for the West in the executive branch shifted to Harold Ickes and the Department of the Interior. Behind the scenes Ickes must have been delighted about the NRPB's demise because now he could relish his role as the administration's chief spokesman and planner for the West. A decade earlier—at the very beginning of the New Deal—he had served as chairman of the National Resources Committee, predecessor of the NRPB. When President Roosevelt transformed that committee into the NRPB in 1934, Ickes violently objected, showing his profound disappointment. Although he refrained from public criticism of the NRPB, neither did he give any public support or endorsement to its recommendations. He viewed it as a rival, and Ickes was not one to suffer rivals gladly. As he noted in his diary about Roosevelt's action: "I hit the ceiling when I learned of this plan. In the first place, I don't believe in establishing any more independent agencies; in the second place, I think planning should be attached to the Interior Department." Meanwhile, he used what occasions did arise to try to undermine the NRPB's influence. Late in 1938, for example, he wrote to the president that he believed planning to be essential for the defense effort just beginning and that the Interior Department's studies, especially on power, would be of the utmost importance to any mobilization effort.[9]

After 1943, therefore, Ickes and his associates became more active than ever in developing plans for their vision of the West's future. As early as 1941 Ickes specified some of his hopes for the region. "The development of the whole area west of the Mississippi . . . had been somewhat neglected," he said, "not by intent of the responsible agencies, not exactly by oversight, but by the policy of encouraging industrial plants to concentrate in the East. . . . The importance of the industrial development of the West is far greater than the immediate defense needs. It is a matter of special concern to the Department." After staking out his turf, Ickes then outlined his ideas about the future of the West. That future, he said, "depends upon a greater diversification and a wider use of its resources through the development of industries located close to the resources. No section of the Nation can prosper if it is treated like a colony; if its resources are pumped out of it and it is later left stranded. I believe that the West not only has many industrial opportunities, but has the right to insist that these opportunities be utilized."[10]

To achieve greater independence the West had to diversify. That might be done by "increased fabricating and processing development as soon as it became clear to industrialists that the West insisted that it would no longer remain a raw-material hinterland for the East, and nothing else." Similarly, he felt that the "great electric power resources in the West . . . could aid its growth, its industrialization, its increase in wealth." Ever mindful of the influence of the Interior Department, Ickes believed that multipurpose projects under its auspices—like the Tennessee Valley Authority—provided the best road to economic independence. By becoming involved in irrigation, rural electrification, flood control, navigation, and recreational facilities development, his agency could provide opportunities for the vast growth of population in the West. Moreover, he argued that his department possessed the scientific expertise needed for the reshaping of the region. If given the opportunity, his department could accomplish much more than it had before 1941. Ickes noted that some senators had recently complained about an unrecognized monopoly of information about the West exercised by a few large corporations that had confidential data concerning the estimated value of western raw materials. The Department of the Interior, however, was the most important depository of such information, he argued, and was ready to place its expertise at the public's disposal.[11]

Ickes believed that the future of the West lay in comprehensive planning under the aegis of his department. "I believe that by taking thought now [1941] and by working out a coordinated program for mining, industry, and agriculture in the Western states, the West will enter a new era of responsible progress. One of the reasons that I feel confident of this progress is that the Western states have, in recent years been shaking loose a little from the control of some of the monopolizing interests which have had them firmly under a checkrein for so many years. . . . There can be no successful, coordinated development of the West simply through a brief mining boom, or a brief power boom," he declared. The coordinated plan he proposed included establishing new aluminum processing plants, developing public power, and taking antimonopoly action against corporations seeking exclusive control of western raw materials. He was aware of the need for low-cost capital for western economic growth and urged both government and private bankers to provide cheap credit. "I do not believe in the Government doing things for people which they can do themselves," Ickes said. "But I believe strongly in the Government taking down the hurdles and barriers so that people can do things for themselves. In Lincoln's time this meant taking down the barriers to the settlement of land. In later days it has meant making water available for farmers who could not live without it. . . . In the industrial age it means also making power available." Ickes expressed his hopes for the West's future. "As the natural depository of so many raw materials and the physical resources to develop them [the West] has enough to make itself a far more industrialized section than it is now," he said. His aim was to "help in a new type of development of the West. Perhaps the most hopeful part of the prospect, however, is the fact that the West is not inclined to let itself be stopped forever by obstacles, if it can see a way of overcoming them."[12]

By 1943 Ickes and his assistants had prepared a specific program for developing the seventeen western states. The attack on western colonialism was to be spearheaded by the Bureau of Reclamation, which identified hundreds of specific projects involving navigation improvement, irrigation, and the development of public power. Ickes estimated that such construction would employ at least 500,000 war veterans and would open up settlement on new farms for another 165,000 returning service men and women and war workers. "Our job soon will be to turn . . . from war to its nearest economic equivalent . . . namely, regional development . . . at its boldest. The program must embrace entire areas." And he discussed his intended policies in some detail. "We would provide for irrigation, for deep-water navigation . . . and for flood control. . . . We would impound water for municipal supply, generate hydroelectric power and transmit it for use in factories and homes and on farms. We would determine the location and the volume of the ores and the bases of plastics that are amenable to processing or manufacture by means of electricity, and improve the means of processing them. We would forestall or ameliorate the pollution of streams, safeguard the soil against erosion, protect wildlife, and develop recreational areas." Thousands of business people and organization leaders wondered whether there was any place for private enterprise in the West of Harold Ickes.[13]

Ickes left few open ends. "We have also shaped our program," he declared, "by devising a large-scale work program to reemploy returning service men and demobilized war workers. But, in addition, we have sought to provide settlement opportunities in the West and Alaska. We have carried on research that will give settlers a better chance than their predecessors to succeed on the public lands."

Once Congress had abolished the NRPB, Ickes felt that the time had come to institutionalize his image as the major planner for the West's economic growth. By 1945 he was quite freely advocating the administration of that function by a single individual, namely himself. "Whether administration should be in the hands of a single administrator or a board is not so much a matter of principle as it is of practicality," he wrote. "I cannot concur in the disposition that some people have to set up so-called independent boards that can go their own way in criss-cross fashion without any effective control by a principal executive. . . . As our Government is constituted today it seems to me that these administrations should clear to the President through the Secretary of the Interior. The Department has had more experience than any other in this type of administration. . . . I do not happen to believe in administration by a debating society." Oddly enough, his chief opponent in the Senate, Pat McCarran, who was at loggerheads with Ickes over grazing and minerals policies, shared Ickes's views on this issue. In fact, McCarran introduced a series of bills to establish a Department of Conservation that would provide Ickes with the broad powers he desired. Both men had an autocratic streak, and perhaps it was recognition of this personal quality that led most members of Congress to withhold their support from such a measure.[14]

Within the Department of the Interior the Bonneville Power Administration was seeking to carry out some of the programs in the Pacific Northwest that Ickes hoped to extend to the entire region west of the Mississippi River. Its administrator, Paul Raver, was a Bull Moose progressive who saw himself as carrying on the traditions of Gifford Pinchot, Theodore Roosevelt's fiery chief of the Forest Service and one of the nation's leading conservationists. Raver's policies had strong support not only from Ickes but also from the top brass in the department including Abe Fortas, deputy secretary of the department, John C. Page, director of the Bureau of Reclamation, and Walter Goldschmidt, director of the Division of Power.

Raver was a persuasive spokesman for the group. As early as 1941 he noted, "The west is not only building for the war, but for its future, and that of the Nation." Every electroindustry being established as a result of mobilization, he declared, should fit into a broader pattern of industrial development for the region, which desperately needed new and complete processing facilities to turn the resources of the Pacific Northwest into consumer goods. Like many westerners, Raver believed that the War Production Board, staffed largely by employees of large eastern corporations, was seeking to impede western economic growth. Instead, he advocated the use of Bonneville power to diversify the economy of the Northwest. That could be done by various means, which he outlined in detail. Bonneville's power should be sold only to industries that promised to develop regional resources. The agency would give preference to fabricating plants as one means of attracting them. Although the main burden for developing this future West should fall on private enterprise, Raver noted, government still had important functions, including researching new processes, particularly to entice small businesses. Raver was not concerned with encouraging monopolistic enterprises but rather with stimulating industrial decentralization. The Interior Department hoped to locate new plants only where they could contribute to a more balanced economy and where the likelihood of their operation in the postwar era was great.[15]

By 1943 the Bureau of Reclamation had worked out rather grandiose plans for the reshaping of the West or, as critics termed it, for the damming of the region. Page had developed an inventory of 236 specific irrigation projects for western states, which he estimated would provide employment for at least 1,250,000 veterans. He estimated that his program would generate at least $1.2 billion in purchasing power and would result in the creation of 135,000 new farms. Such development, he expected, would stimulate manufactures throughout the United States and would integrate western industry, agriculture, and multipurpose projects offering cheap power.[16]

Goldschmidt was more blunt. He felt that in the West of the future, "the problem of how to cope with abundance will beset our economy all along the line." To maintain this momentum he was virtually advocating that the Department of the Interior become a major employment agent for the West, a proposal that alarmed private business entrepreneurs.[17]

In fact, the Bureau of Reclamation kept expanding its planned programs as the war progressed. By 1945 Commissioner Harry Bashore identified 415 specific irrigation projects in seventeen western states designed to create two hundred thousand new farms. He was now thinking of hundreds of thousands of new jobs, vast employment opportunities, and

177

genuine diversification of the western economy. Just two days before his death Roosevelt endorsed this vision of what was essentially an enlarged New Deal for the West. In a letter to Representative John R. Murdock, chairman of the House Committee on Irrigation and Reclamation, Roosevelt wrote: "It is essential that programs of assistance to veterans be authorized and adequately prepared now. One such program . . . is . . . through the work of the Bureau of Reclamation. I have frequently spoken with pride of the accomplishments of this administration in western reclamation projects. . . . Such projects constitute great increases in national wealth and income. They also offer splendid opportunities for secure and abundant livelihood to men and women willing to engage in the arduous, though stimulating, tasks of pioneering these latest frontiers." The American Dream of the West was still alive and well. The president went on to urge congressional approval of federal reclamation programs expected to cost $5 billion (in 1940 dollars). When completed, the projects were expected to bring another eleven million acres under irrigation and to double the federal production of power in the western states.[18]

Commissioner Bashore waxed enthusiastic about the West that would emerge from his agency's program. "For 43 years the Bureau of Reclamation has been working on programs for developing the land and water resources of the West," he declared in 1945. "The value of those developments has been effectively demonstrated during the war. The need for continuing and expanding such developments has also been demonstrated. At present there are about 2½ million more people living in the 11 Far Western states than there were before the war. They will want jobs . . . opportunities . . . trades and professions. An increase in the basic irrigated agriculture of this area will therefore be necessary to support and sustain the growth and the continuing industrial expansion of these states. It is to meet this challenge and to open up a new frontier of opportunity in the West that the Bureau of Reclamation presents its post-war program."[19]

Remaining in the bureau's vision of the future West was a Jeffersonian bias, a hope that small business, rather than large, would play a significant role in reshaping the economy in the nation's most underdeveloped region. That perception was not stressed in most national programs for postwar reconstruction, such as the influential report made for the president by Bernard Baruch and John Hancock. But the cause of small business was taken up by one of its most ardent champions in the administration, Maury Maverick, chairman of the Smaller War Plants

Corporation. Soon after assuming his position early in 1944 he conducted a campaign to bring this view before the public.[20]

Maverick testified before various congressional committees. His message was usually the same, namely that Congress should adopt long-range plans to ensure the small business tradition in America, and especially in the West. The means were readily at hand, he argued forcefully before the House Committee on Post-War Economic Problems in the spring of 1944. They included a gradual rather than a sudden contract termination policy, the disposal of surplus federal property to benefit small rather than big business, and the resumption of civilian production. In particular, he urged greater tax benefits for small business. These could include depreciation allowances to induce new investments, and limited taxation only of investment income. He also argued for a much wider dissemination of patents and for government insurance for small business loans made by private banks—not unlike the FHA program in the housing industry. If that proposal was unacceptable to Congress, Maverick declared, perhaps creating a federal industrial development bank for small business would accomplish the goal.[21]

In a major address to the Commonwealth Club of California in San Francisco a month later, Maverick reiterated these proposals with a more direct focus on the West. He urged westerners to "keep fighting" for greater economic independence, especially for an end to discriminatory railroad freight rates. "Demand that discriminatory freight rates be abolished!" he shouted. With considerable foresight he predicted, "Then, with a super highway and air travel system you can trade on an even basis with the East." The war had brought the West to a crossroads in the reshaping of its economy, he believed. He warned against the crushing of small business by "great industries which have sprung up in the West. Prepare now in order to fit them into the peacetime economy, in which small business will be vigorous, strong, and healthy." Maverick knew how to get his audience on their feet. "You must all get together," he said. "I mean the states of Washington, Oregon, and California, British Columbia and Alaska, and also Baja California. . . . Your economy has revolutionized itself in two years. The waves of the Pacific may have lashed against your shores, but population and new industry have stormed into your lands, like tropical tidal waves. It has been the greatest peaceful industrial and human revolution of any people in the entire history of the world," he declared with his customary ebullience, and some exaggeration. "Following this war must come another revolution. You can call it 'reconversion' if you want. . . . Because we converted to total war we had the economic revolution known as a war economy. Changing back will be a revolutionary process." And, he concluded, "I would have you take all the essential ingredients of civilized society and build a balanced economy—because I know that too much big business, or little business without any big business, will make everybody broke."[22]

From San Francisco Maverick went up and down the Pacific Coast to preach his gospel. In Los Angeles he spoke of the relation of government to the reshaping of the West. "It is nonsense to say that constructive public improvements are harmful to free enterprise," he noted. "Already there are those who are proclaiming that we must let free enterprise carry the entire load of reconversion from war to peace. This can't be done. . . . Private enterprise and public improvements go hand in hand." But he hoped that at least five hundred thousand new small businesses would be established after the war, since many new ideas and technologies came from small rather than from large enterprises.[23]

In his address in Portland, Oregon, Maverick stressed the psychological dimension in planning the West's future. "Confidence in the future," he declared, "is a powerful stimulant in creating effective demand. Assurance of employment creates confidence." With public works planned by the state of Oregon, by the Bonneville Power Administration, and by the city of Portland, he felt sure that the Pacific Northwest could look forward to a bright future.[24]

But it was in Seattle that Maverick unveiled his comprehensive plan for the postwar development of the Pacific states and the West. That plan was later formulated in a written report issued by the Smaller War Plants Corporation. It was prepared with the advice of chambers of commerce in Seattle, Portland, San Francisco, and Los Angeles and of business associations such as the California State Chamber of Commerce and the Builders of the West. All believed in 1944 that postwar adjustment would be difficult. But Maverick noted, "The existence of large, unsatisfied demands for a great variety of consumers' and producers' goods . . . mean big markets within the West itself." He felt that these demands would sustain confidence and a high level of business activity and would lead to much needed diversification of the western economy. That could be further facilitated by expanding transportation systems. "Mass production may not have been economically justified within the region before the war," Maverick noted. "Today, it is." He proposed a series of superhighways from east to west and north to south, in addition to what he hoped would become a superairport system. "As a region the West Coast needs more transportation of all kinds to prosper and get into the markets of the United States. To meet this situation highways and airports must be built on a great scale, and as part of a super-system for the whole country. There must be competition in transportation as in little business."[25]

Maverick also felt that the war had enormously increased the significance of the West in international trade because of its strategic location. He foresaw more trade with the Soviet Union, Latin America, Australia and New Zealand, and, of course, China and the Orient. "With the proper industrial conversion of the West," he said, "overseas ship and plane transportation will carry a volume of five, ten, or fifteen times as great as ever before." Transportation development would also provide employment for as many as two million people. "It will save the West and strengthen our nation's economy. It will join together all parts of the nation and be of tremendous strategic, military value." The cost of such a system he estimated at $10 billion. With three east-to-west highways and six from north to south, he advocated at least one airport at each of eighteen key intersections of the road system. With a comprehensive system of internal transportation, the West would be in a prime position to garner a substantial portion of the nation's international trade and to move to the forefront of American economic penetration in the Pacific area and in the Western hemisphere.[26]

Maverick's plans were as prophetic as they were thorough. The broad contours of his proposals, and the degree of government intervention that they required, aroused opposition from those who feared greater centralization of government—and expansion of New Deal ideology. And yet in the 1950s Republican administrations implemented an extensive interstate highway system and expanded the nation's airports, largely with federal expenditures. The economic diversification of the West that Maverick envisaged was also attained within a decade. But his hope that such a development would be promoted by small rather than big business was not fulfilled, as the tendency toward industrial concentration continued in the succeeding decade with few signs that the majority of Americans were concerned about the process, except for occasional lip service and Jeffersonian rhetoric.

That inveterate foe of monopoly, Assistant Attorney General Thurman Arnold, also articulated his vision of the West's economic future. As he saw it, "the problem . . . is as between unorganized business of the West and organized business of the East. . . . It is already apparent . . . that you have . . . a sort of colonial system which has been developed by the East in the West. The colonies have got to support the mother country. It is a perfectly natural development. The mother country does not like to see competing industries develop in the colonies which would interfere with the dividends and the financial structure of the East." He agreed with Senator Joseph C. O'Mahoney that "in the West we are confronted by a sort of double headed monster of absentee landlordism of fiscal power in New York and the absentee landlordism of bureaucracy in Washington. . . . The West is not the only colony of the industrial world . . . [and] as long as you do not have the free exchange between the West and the East, so long as you prevent the West from building up industries at the source of supply, you are going to have protective tariffs." Arnold believed that the problem could not be solved by general legislation but by the encouragement of private enterprise. He proposed the abandonment of discriminatory freight rates, a vigorous antitrust policy to encourage competition, a greater emphasis on the role of small business, and the promotion of small farmers.

> The great Eastern corporations who have the money to develop the country will do it only insofar as it obviously pays them, and each enterprise which they develop locally will be looked upon as a colony to be exploited by the mother corporation. The only solution in my opinion, therefore, is to encourage independent capital, local so far as is possible, in order that competitive American enterprise may gamble, lose, or win after the manner in which the country as a whole has developed. . . . Big Business in the East . . . has a number of devices by which it can stifle the industries in the Rocky Mountain region. In some cases the action is direct which consists substantially in knocking infant industries in the head as fast as they are born. In other cases they buy out from under the little man his essential raw materials in a local area and leave his stranded. . . . The West should be developed competitively by small local business so far as capital is available.[27]

While the NRPB, Ickes, Maverick, and Arnold were unveiling their particular visions of the West's future, westerners in Congress were also engaged in formulating postwar blueprints for the region. Although scores of individuals were involved in the House and the Senate, three prominent senators provided visible leadership. They included James E. Murray from Montana, a powerful New Dealer who wielded great influence as chairman of the Senate's Special Committee on Small Business. The second senator, more muted during the war years than he had been in the heyday of the New Deal, was Wyoming's Senator Joseph C. O'Mahoney, who served on the Senate Special Committee on Post-War Economic Policy and Planning and chaired its western subcommittee. The third member of the West's Big Three was Senator Pat McCarran of Nevada, who took it upon himself to unify the western states and to act as their spokesman. To further that end he chaired a Senate Special Committee to Investigate Industrial Centralization, which gave him a forum for his views. Together, these three men kept the issue of western economic development before the Congress and the public and substantially contributed to the region's industrial reorganization.

Senator Murray was perhaps the most persistent and quietly influential member of the trio. As a fervent advocate for small business in the economic development of the West, he hoped to increase its role in the postwar years. His main platform was the Senate Small Business Committee, which in 1944 was shifting its attention from wartime contracts to plans for the economic diversification of the West in the future. During 1944 and 1945 the committee held extensive hearings on the issue throughout the West. Resulting in the publication of more than seventy volumes of testimony, these hearings attracted a broad spectrum of interest groups who laid out their particular visions of the economic future of the area.[28] In urging regional diversification Murray said: "I do not imply support for any narrow, sectional outlook upon the post-war development of the West. It is not a matter of the West against the East, or vice-versa. It is rather that the future prosperity of the country as a whole, can no longer be built upon the denial to any great region of its normal and healthy economic development. The war has forever put an end to the practice of using any section of the country merely as a source of cheap labor and raw materials for the benefit of some other section."[29]

Murray spread his gospel by making speeches from coast to coast. "The establishment of a prosperous and secure small business economy in the large industrial area west of the Rockies can be obtained only by the development of those vast areas rich in raw materials and resources," he said, "reaching from the Pacific Ocean to the eastern foothills of the Rocky Mountains. . . . I want to make it clear that I believe that we still have a great empire to develop." But in the past the East had restrained western growth. "The West has been held back in the past through restrictive railroad rate policies and through other methods, which we must now try to overcome to give the West its opportunity, and permit it to expand and develop. . . . With the splendid leadership that the West Coast has given us we should develop the wonderful resources and provide for an expanding economy."[30]

In a speech in Seattle Murray bemoaned the many barriers the prewar West had encountered. "We know . . . the barriers which have impeded western progress in the past. We know of the construction of freight rates, the difficulty of obtaining venture capital, the paucity of technology, the lack of access to patents, and the dangers of monopoly. All these have held us back."[31] But he turned to the future with confidence. He had high "aspirations in developing the great markets which are the West's by location and by destiny. We know that the great West, when fully developed, will support millions of people in addition to those now here, on a standard of living unparalleled in the world. With you, we look out across the Pacific Ocean and northward to Alaska where lie tomorrow's markets. . . . The development of that market will be a new epoch. We stand now on its threshold."[32]

The prospects of the Pacific rim intrigued Murray, as it did other westerners. "It is to these Western states that we must look for the largest part of the industrial and business expansion which will take place in the post-war period. Our Eastern states will for a long period face a Europe of dubious economic prospects, whereas our Western states, facing the great potentialities of the Pacific, offer possibilities of tremendous growth and industrial expansion. With the ending of the war, the seaboard States of the West will face a continent where one-half of the people of the world live—the half that will offer us the greatest economic possibilities in our history."[33]

Murray did more than talk, however, for he was one of the chief architects of reconversion legislation. In 1942 he gained a seat on the Senate Military Affairs Committee. That body also created a War Contracts subcommittee that Murray chaired, with Harry Truman of Missouri and Chapman Revercomb of West Virginia as members. Murray's hope was that he could prepare a bill that would provide for the fast settlement of canceled federal war contracts, particularly for small business people. Moreover, he desired to provide quick financing for manufacturers facing termination. Above all, equitable treatment required uniform procedures for all federal agencies rather than the great diversity that was causing many hardships. The consequent Murray-George Bill contained these features in addition to a Murray-Taft (Robert) amendment providing for the SWPC to aid small businesses in termination settlement. Roosevelt signed the act on July 1, 1944, which also created an Office of Contract Settlement to administer the law. In the next two years it supervised the termination of 315,000 contracts worth $54 billion, thus avoiding the thousands of lawsuits that had plagued the federal government after World War I.[34]

Murray also shepherded legislation for the disposal of federal surplus property. With Senators Robert Taft and Tom Stewart, he sponsored bills to allow the SWPC to acquire surplus plants for resale to small businesses, thereby aiding the industrially underdeveloped West. The *Wall Street Journal* vehemently accused Murray of advocating crass sectionalism. He failed to achieve all of his objectives but succeeded in establishing a Surplus Property Board in the Office of War Mobilization. His hopes were dashed because by late 1946 almost three-fourths of the dollar value of surplus plants had been acquired by the nation's 250 largest corporations. "The program of disposal," Murray stated sadly, "appears to have increased the level of industrial concentration." In addition to this handiwork, Murray was one of the principal architects of the Employment Act of 1946 and the prime sponsor of the Missouri Valley Authority.[35]

Not quite as energetic as Murray, O'Mahoney served a symbolic role in wartime as a link between the antimonopoly sentiment of the New Deal and the federal policies toward business between 1941 and 1945. O'Mahoney had been chairman of the Temporary National Economic Committee from 1937 to 1941, which spearheaded Roosevelt's antimonopoly campaign in Congress. O'Mahoney continued to espouse his antimonopoly views, if less vehemently than Ickes, Maverick, Murray, or McCarran. As chairman of the subcommittee of the Senate Committee on Post-War Planning in 1943, O'Mahoney conducted extensive hearings throughout the West to determine grass-roots sentiment about the West's future. "The Government has taken the lead in transforming our economy in order that we should be able to meet the totalitarian dictators and mobilize all of our resources," O'Mahoney declared. "We have transformed the United States from a peace-loving economy to one of the mightiest economies that ever existed. Since we were able to adjust ourselves to the war economy . . . there is no reason to believe that we cannot do the job in reverse, although it may be a much more difficult task." O'Mahoney estimated that in 1943 there were already at least 160 organizations involved in postwar planning. Thus, he noted, the main question was "how are we going to coordinate the desires and the activities of commerce, industry, agriculture, and labor, and what can be done . . . by Government . . . to stimulate peacetime activity and provide full employment?"[36]

That question was answered in no uncertain terms by the tough, pugnacious, and uncompromising advocate of western economic diversification, Pat McCarran. His solution was to seek economic decentralization in the United States, with the West playing a more important part in manufacturing than in the prewar years. That objective could be secured by converting government-owned war plants in the West to peacetime uses under private auspices.

McCarran's interest in industrialization grew out of his wartime experiences. He had been active since 1939 in securing government contracts for his native state. It was largely due to his influence that Roosevelt in 1941 agreed to locate Basic Magnesium near Las Vegas. McCarran had also had a hand in attracting to Nevada important military installations, such as Nellis Air Force Base and Fallon Air Force Base, and in expanding

the large Naval Ordnance Depot at Hawthorne. McCarran was not parochial, however, and soon took it upon himself to speak out about the
potentials of the whole western economy. During the war years he regularly called senators from seventeen western states to meetings in his
Washington office to discuss issues of common interest, whether these
related to land, water, mining, or other aspects of regional development.
His interest in western economic growth was also demonstrated in his
championship of air transport in the United States. One of the sponsors
of the Civil Aeronautics Act of 1938, he continued to be a chief spokesman
for the airline industry in Congress.[37]

By 1943 McCarran's interest in the economic future of the West and
in postwar planning had become more pronounced. One example of that
concern was his sponsorship of the Special Committee to Investigate Industrial Centralization. As he recalled in 1944, he had visualized the
conditions that would follow the war.

> In 11 Eastern states there was a concentration of industry with exceedingly
> augmented appropriations of Federal money in new construction and devel-
> opment of industry. . . . If those industries would start up in private business
> immediately after the cessation of the European phase of this war . . . and the
> West was still engaged in the war effort . . . then there was bound to be a
> disposal of those plants that have been constructed with federal funds . . . at
> probably 10 cents on the dollar of cost of construction. If that were to follow,
> and the West was still engaged in war production . . . with war conditions
> intensified in the West and lightened in the East, then our Western industries
> would be immediately set back in our economy for half a century or
> more. . . . That being true we wrote a letter to some 50 of our [Senate] col-
> leagues. . . . 150 members of the House and about 40 members of the Senate
> met and appointed a committee with 7 Senators and 7 Congressmen to study
> the question.[38]

In the ensuing eighteen months the committee held extensive hearings
and did much to give shape to the problems of economic concentration
in the West. Although McCarran had a reputation as a political conservative, his effort was really part of the strong antimonopoly movement
in the West during the war, spearheaded by such liberals as Thurman
Arnold, Maury Maverick, James Murray, and others concerned about the
colonial dependence of the West.

McCarran felt that if the nation was to achieve balanced economic
growth in the years ahead, Americans needed to recognize the regional
character of their economic life. "While Western resources lie idle and
undeveloped," he said, "intensification of manufacturing in the East cannot and will not help the West. On the other hand, increased manufacturing in a few of our states where industry is already excessively

186

concentrated, without attention to adequate purchasing power of the people of the rest of the Nation cannot but bring an economic crisis to the industrial States as well as the rest of the States in a very short time." To McCarran, his position was not one of sectionalism but of realism. He considered the creation of new jobs and new economic opportunities to be the nation's top postwar economic problem. A fuller development of the West, he believed, offered a partial solution to this national problem, by creating increased employment and expanded markets.[39]

McCarran placed the issue in a broad context. Since the early days of settlement, he argued, the word *West* had symbolized opportunity for Americans. "Westward, always westward, has run the historic course of this country," he exclaimed. "Once on that westward tide of our destiny, the time has come to scrap the old and dated notions of the West. . . . Half the world's people are before us in the Pacific. The richest, the most populated and the least developed areas of the world invite our industry, our commerce, and the fruits of our civilization and culture. The West today is the land of empire, of opportunity, of destiny. Today, more than ever, the West is plain every day American for 'opportunity.' "[40]

McCarran left his imprint on the committee's work. Most of its hearings were held in western states, and its final report focused on regional imbalance. A national economy, that report noted, was a fiction. Rather, the American economy was a composite of regional economies, each with its special problems. "Our Southern states were agricultural and the West a wilderness when industrialization began," the report noted. "Since then, our major industries have fought a ruthless battle to deny the West and South the industries they can support and to which they have every right." The West and the South accounted for 65 percent of the nation's mineral production in 1940 but only 20 percent of its manufactures, whereas the East produced 65 percent of all manufactures. To that kind of centralization the committee was opposed. Moreover, it was hostile to the large-scale importation of strategic minerals, which would further weaken American producers. The committee also advocated a policy of contract termination to promote decentralization of industry. That meant federal disposal of surplus war plants to encourage new industries in the West, enough perhaps to employ one and a half million new workers. And the committee called for the aggressive development of Asian markets. "The impulse to centralization is basically anti-capitalistic," the committee declared, sharing McCarran's views. "The result is a system more feudal than capitalistic, with emphasis upon control, rather than freedom, authoritarian, rather than rational government."[41]

As viewed from Washington, the West was a region whose economic destiny was to be largely determined by the federal government. That, of course, was not a new perspective. From the days of early western exploration—the days of the Lewis and Clark expedition—through the period of initial settlement—the territorial stage—the West to a considerable extent had been the creature of the national government. Such a symbiotic relationship could be terminated no less suddenly than that between a parent and a growing adolescent. Thus, the NRPB and the Department of the Interior prepared comprehensive plans for the region's economic development in which the national government would continue to play a dominant, determining role and in which the department and the NRPB would set the parameters and pace of change. In essence, they hoped to dictate directions for the future. In Congress the sentiment for centralized direction was far less developed. There the leading advocates of western economic expansion envisaged more of an equal partnership between the federal government and the West—more like the relation between a parent and an offspring that had grown to adulthood. To congressional leaders like Murray and McCarran, the national government still had a vital role, but as a response to the wishes of westerners and not as a determining force.

In spite of differences in goals and styles the advocates of western economic expansion in 1945 agreed in significant areas. They believed that the West was on the threshold of a new economic era in which it would finally shed its colonial status. They believed that the disposal of federal surplus properties held the key to the further industrialization of the West. They believed that a gradual process of contract termination would preserve many of the wartime economic gains. They espoused the hope that competitive enterprise—small business and small agriculture—would continue to have a significant role in the economic life of the region. They felt that economic diversification was essential, not only for the economic stability of the region but also for that of the nation. If the view from Washington was not ultimately to prevail, it nevertheless became part of an emerging consensus that was taking shape elsewhere in the nation, and on the state and local levels in the West.

CHAPTER 9

Visions of the Future:
The View from Western
States and Cities

ENTHUSIASM for planning the future of the West was not confined to Washington, D.C. It was a genuine grass-roots movement that affected millions of westerners in the region. It stimulated regional cooperation, produced statewide plans to turn dreams into reality, and created a very active phase of city planning. Not all of the dreams for the future West were realized, but substantial portions of the vision came into being during the next generation. The westerners of 1945 had hopes for a region with a burgeoning population, dynamic new cities, and a prosperous, more diversified economy with full employment. By the 1980s much of that vision had become a reality.

But during World War II a wide-ranging debate ensued over the best means to achieve these goals. One approach was suggested by the NRPB and the adherents of centralized planning. It was their belief that comprehensive planning by the federal government—in cooperation with states and localities—was the most effective way to reshape the West. At the opposite end of the ideological spectrum were advocates of laissez-faire, who believed that the responsibility for the new West lay largely in the hands of individuals and private enterprise. Perhaps the most widely held views were somewhere between these two polarities. This consensus held that the industrialization of the West was a task for private entrepreneurs, but with the support of governments at all levels wherever feasible. To a considerable extent this reflected the position of the Roosevelt administration, which had evolved during the New Deal to a stance slightly left of center. If the action of the electorate was any indication, this too was where a majority of the American people found themselves. And it was this view that underlay much of the planning for the West in the 1940s by cooperative state efforts, by individual states, and by the cities.

The earliest efforts to stimulate postwar planning by the states were made by the NRPB. That body had been trying since 1935 to gain wider acceptance of the idea of national planning, without much success. By 1941 its attempts were already encountering considerable opposition in Congress and in the business community, where its members were seen as left-wing ideologues intent on foisting centralized planning programs on the rest of the nation. In fact, it was this perception that led Congress to abolish the NRPB in 1943.

Nevertheless, in the two years before its expiration the NRPB created a foundation for state planning programs directed toward postwar growth. Although the range and scope of such efforts differed widely, they provided an outlet for the hopes and aspirations that many westerners had for the future of their region. By 1942 forty-five states had established special committees to engage in planning and had provided them with staffs to work out detailed programs. The NRPB—reflecting Roosevelt's own special concerns—was determined to prevent the chaos that had occurred after World War I in the transition from war to peace. As the NRPB declared: "Our experience after the last war makes us determined not to relinquish the fight to win the peace. We in the planning movement . . . have as heavy a responsibility to prepare plans for the postwar period . . . as for wartime planning." And to bolster its policy of seeking to supervise state planning programs—already under fire—the board added, "A decade of state planning has proved the utility of state planning boards as arms of planning management for State functions in our Federal system." Meanwhile, in 1939 the Council of National Defense had suggested to governors that their state planning boards should also operate as research and planning agencies for formulating postwar plans in spheres such as economic growth, employment, housing, urban development, and industrial expansion. A detailed analysis of these manifold plans as they embraced visions of the future is beyond the scope of this volume and remains to be written. Suffice it to say that most of the western states envisaged a more diversified economy, greater affluence, full employment, and an expanded population.[1]

Utah was one of the first states to prepare an extensive program under the prodding of the NRPB. Reflecting its Keynesian vision, the NRPB virtually mandated a comprehensive program of public works to provide for the thousands of returning service men and women and war workers it expected would flood the labor market. In addition, the NRPB em-

190

phasized the expansion of conservation policies, all to be administered under close federal supervision.[2]

Once the NRPB went out of existence, the momentum for state planning was assumed by professional organizations, such as the Council of State Governments, but most of all by concerned individuals, such as Senator McCarran. As a prime mover, he was in constant touch with governors and other state officials throughout the West, quite apart from his home state of Nevada. In fact, the *San Francisco News* wondered why he was making himself a national spokesman for the West.[3] In addition to his activities on the national scene he sought to unify the West by encouraging regional conferences and closer cooperation among state officials concerned with economic issues. He was also active in addressing state legislatures on the need to reshape their economies, and he advised individual governors on shaping their plans for industrialization. Not all his efforts were successful, since the forces making for regional diversity often proved stronger than those making for unity in ensuing years. But his activities did bear fruit in the World War II era.

Within the next year representatives of the western states met in San Francisco, Carson City, and Salt Lake City to prepare blueprints of economic plans. The San Francisco conference in October 1943 laid the foundations for a unified approach to significant issues affecting the West, such as the disposal of federally owned war plants, the anticipated unemployment problem, and the expansion of public works. The delegates at the meeting made plans for another session scheduled for February 1944 in Carson City, Nevada.[4] There the representatives of California, Nevada, Oregon, Washington, and Utah assembled, about sixty strong, to map out policies for the immediate future. McCarran told them, "The West has been treated as a colonial institution with little more than colonial rights." He urged the West to unite with the South to keep eastern industrialists from choking new wartime industries. California's dynamic attorney general, Robert W. Kenny, echoed McCarran. "The East cannot strangle the West's growing might," he declared. "It has been a tough struggle for the West to achieve what already has been gained. . . . The West should not . . . be at the feudal mercy of the industrial monarchs of the East." And Nevada's governor, E. P. Carville, summarized the feelings of many of the delegates when he said, "The very foundations of postwar planning for the western region must be built around the conservation, development, and preservation of all our natural resources [and] the retention and development of already established war plants by private enterprise." In particular, he was thinking of Basic Magnesium and the Geneva Steel Works. The conference representatives enacted a series of resolutions urging the transfer of federal war plants to private ownership, the addition of westerners to the staffs of the War Production Board and other federal agencies dealing with economic matters, and greater cooperation among western governors to attract new industries and to develop regional markets.[5]

Soon McCarran was off to Salt Lake City where a conference of eleven western states was held in June 1944 to consider their economic future. He had already spoken of what he called "the blueprint of a new frontier." He argued that his plan should serve the same purpose as had the old frontier of the West, "providing employment and opportunity for all comers, and infusing new blood into the nation's economic and industrial arteries." Then he presented a six-point program for consideration. It included policies for conserving the West's resources and for improving western transportation by a far-reaching new road network and a vast expansion of airfields and air traffic. He also advocated extensive urban renewal programs, increased mineral production, and closer political cooperation among the western states. As McCarran noted, his was a middle-of-the-road approach. He did not favor federal direction of postwar reconstruction of the West because it would result in regimentation. At the other extreme were advocates of laissez-faire, with whom he did not sympathize either. His alternative was to emphasize regional and state planning, together with government-sponsored public works to prevent large-scale unemployment. Instead of relying on haphazard relief programs in the postwar years, he felt it essential that the West prepare comprehensive plans to develop the region in an orderly fashion and to secure long-term economic benefits. Such planning could best be accomplished by the states, McCarran felt.[6]

Within these broad parameters McCarran made specific suggestions. To secure full employment, the West should place projects dealing with dam and river development high on the list. Expanding transportation was also a "must." "The short-line railroad has been relegated to the past," he declared. In its place were highways and aircraft. Howard Hughes had inspired his generation, for as McCarran noted: "Huge cargo planes will become commonplace, and millions of tons of cargo will move by air. . . . The skies will be filled with cargo vessels, plying a true course through that greatest sea of all—the Aerial Ocean. . . . The inland regions of the west will not be inland, so to speak, because every airline and every airport facility brings these inland regions to the coast." As for diversified public works, these should be pursued "with a view to undertaking reconstruction and new construction by the States, or by Regions if possible, yet enlisting the cooperation of the federal government whenever necessary or desirable." They embraced projects for power, irrigation, housing, sewers, streets, schools, and public buildings. None of these aims could be achieved, however, without closer cooperation among the western states. He urged western politicians to join together on regional issues without regard to party lines. "The Governors of the eleven western states should get together at scheduled, frequent intervals to discuss common interests, problems, to advise and council [*sic*] each other, and to cooperate as state representatives of a great region with common interests, in the development and conservation and expansion of the West."[7]

McCarran developed his philosophy further in an address to a joint session of the California legislature. "The trend to centralization," he said, "constitutes the greatest threat to democracy. The parallel trend to centralize the reconversion problem, if it is not checked, will provide the favorable conditions for the total and fatal subversion of our democratic form of government. . . . Should the reconversion problem be left overwhelmingly to the Federal Government, the result will be a Federal apparatus that will prove fatal to the position of the State governments and the whole question of States' rights." McCarran believed that the economic development of the West would bring incalculable benefits to the entire nation.

> Everything argues for the intelligent development of this area, including reasons of national security. Our security in the Pacific demands a larger population in the Western States, demands more industry, more agriculture. . . . In addition . . . a better balanced economy also demands the development of the West. A larger urban population in the West would open new prospects to the agricultural states of the Middle West, would prove a boon to Eastern industries, too. . . . Finally . . . the West offers new prospects and new opportunities for millions of people who have reached the zenith of their hopes and possibilities in the overcrowded and overdeveloped East. . . . Think of what would happen should 10,000,000 new settlers be attracted to the West.

And, concluding his plea, he declared, "I would venture to say that an intelligent policy of developing the West would open to this whole country a new era of prosperity and would go far to add much needed stability to our national economy."[8]

McCarran made a deep impression on the California lawmakers, some of whom had attended the regional conferences on future planning. One of these was Gardiner C. Johnson, a member of the California assembly and a member of the California Commission on Interstate Cooperation, a regional body. "I have seen the day in 1940," he said, "when hundreds, and even thousands of people came to our State Capitol and lined themselves outside demanding relief, and when the State Police had to go before us and clear our way, so that we could get into the State Capitol. We don't want to see that happen again. But it will happen . . . unless some constructive policy is worked out by which the millions of people who are now located in the West are given employment. . . . We take the position that whether we like it or not, regions have already been created, and that our effort is to bring about equality in those regions." Johnson shared McCarran's views on colonialism. "As far as the West is concerned . . . we have been treated industrially as colonial possessions . . . we have never been given equality, and it is for that equality that we are working together today."[9]

California legislators like Johnson were concerned about the loss of federally owned war plants.

> We urge the proposition that governmentally owned war plants should not be removed from the West. . . . It is our belief that these plants should be operated in the post-war period by the inclusion of some guaranty of the operations in the disposal contract. To elaborate upon that, rugged individualists though we are in the West, we believe that the Federal Government may render us a service by stepping in and providing the contracts of disposal whether they be agreements of sale . . . or otherwise, by inserting some clause which will require that the purchaser actually operate these plants. We believe that is essential to bringing about full employment for our people.

Johnson also felt that monopolistic enterprises in the West should be restrained by government. And if markets for goods produced by former war plants were still inadequate, he hoped the government would keep the plants on a standby basis until sufficient consumer demand had developed for their operation by private enterprise. So much for rugged individualism.[10]

From California McCarran spread his message on national radio, coast to coast. In August 1944 he told Americans, "Our aim . . . is to open the West to a new era of industrial development and large-scale settlement." To accomplish that he urged the retention of war industries in the West, including steel manufacturing. At the same time he proposed more federal reclamation to stabilize a larger farm population in the West. He also advocated the exploitation of western coal to provide the basis for a new synthetic fuel and chemical industry in the West. "I am determined that this impulse . . . to independent and individual economic achievement . . . shall not be stultified." And he urged systematic scientific research to adapt technical advances to western resource exploitation. "In the development of the vast empire of the West, this country's last and greatest frontier, our nation will find a new outlet for its energies . . . and a new stepping stone to heights of permanent prosperity beyond anything we have known," he concluded.[11] His predictions showed his remarkable prescience.

In addition to regional planning movements, individual states in the West attempted to work out their own economic development programs for the future. If there were common bonds in the West, there was also much diversity. Thus, Gail Ireland, Colorado's representative on the State Council on Interstate Cooperation, emphasized that the problems of his state differed from those in California, Utah, or Nevada. Since Colorado had had fewer industrial plants than California, he expected his state's reconversion to be less traumatic. Colorado, traditionally conservative, standpat, and cautious, did not expect great changes after the war, in contrast to other western states. He believed that reliance on federal reclamation projects like the Big Thompson system, along with public works and road building, would cushion the shock of readjustment. In addition, he expected that the mining and cattle industries would continue to be a foundation for the state's economy. "We must necessarily look to the East in some of our transactions," he said, somewhat apologetically. "We must necessarily find markets for some of our agricultural products and our cattle and meat products." Still, Coloradans did not abjure cooperation with more ambitious neighbors. "Our sympathies and our interests are voluntarily as well as necessarily to the West. One reason is because we belong to the group of 17 Western reclamation states. . . . [W]e have been drawn together for the last 2 or 3 years with a common purpose, because of the constant legislation being proposed in Washington which does not show any too much sympathy toward the arid and semi-arid regions when it comes to the management and control of our waters. These things naturally bring these Western states together."[12]

In Nevada the entrepreneurial spirit was much stronger, and the state's business leaders eagerly looked forward to extensive diversification. Robert Allen, Nevada's highway engineer, was a member of the Governors' Committee on Post-war Industrial Development in the Western States. That group developed a thirteen-point program for the future, one that called for the stockpiling of strategic minerals by the federal government to sustain western mining and for federal reclamation, highway, forestry, and public works projects. It also urged the orderly disposal of manufacturing and processing plants in the region and special inducements for manufacturers to stay in the West. It advocated an improved transportation network for the West and the removal of discriminatory railroad freight rates by the Interstate Commerce Commission and Congress. The group saw manufacturing as the key to diversification. "It seems silly to us," said Allen, "that copper mat should move from the mines in the Western region to the East coast, be refined, fabricated, and then move back to the markets of the West coast. . . . We think it would be more economic to move some of those facilities . . . to the Pacific Coast. . . . It is high time that we started to look out for our own interests in the West. We want the entire West to be developed as a regional unit."[13]

The state of Washington formulated its own program but, like Nevada, saw its relation to the region. P. Hetherton, the executive officer of the Washington State Planning Council, expressed his sentiment. "For quite some time," he said, "I had held the hope that economic forces in themselves would be sufficient to continue the expansion of the West. Unfortunately, economic forces are also being used to deter its expansion, hence I am convinced that political action is also necessary. . . . [We], the people, should use our Government to advance our economic interest." He used historical analogies to make his point, citing Jefferson's dispatch of the Lewis and Clark expedition in 1804, federal railroad subsidies in the 1860s, the building of the Panama Canal in 1904–14, and the Columbia River development during the New Deal. With incentives such as a favorable tax structure, private investment capital could do much to develop the state—and the region. The future would see more joint private-federal partnerships, he was convinced, and more regional cooperation among eleven western states.[14]

Of all the states in the West, California established the most extensive state planning program. In 1943 the state legislature created the California Reconstruction and Reemployment Commission. Governor Earl Warren appointed Colonel Alexander Heron its executive director. A former San Francisco businessman, Heron embarked on hundreds of detailed studies relating to the postwar economic environment of California. His staff ranged widely throughout the state and consulted closely with economic interest groups in seeking to secure an accurate impression of their visions of California's economic future.[15]

Although a staunch proponent of private enterprise, Heron was typical of most westerners in favoring a strong role for the federal government in reshaping the regional economy.

> The war emergency, which sent a huge wave of people into the State, creates an obligation on the part of the Federal Government that California's war industries be not left broken, crippled victims of the war. Private industry in local and State-wide [efforts] is busy planning realistically for reconversion to a post-war economy. The State and its cities are now making ready with private and public works to help meet the challenge of the transition from war to peace. But beyond that there is a Federal responsibility to cushion the shock of readjustment and to aid post-war industrial development. We shall need a high

order of teamwork by private enterprise and by Federal, State, and local governments to bring about the post-war industrialization of California and the West necessary to provide employment for their large populations.[16]

Heron had a sound grasp of the economic situation in California. Noting that more than two million civilians had moved into eleven Western states during the war, he said in 1944, "The war has brought huge expansion of shipbuilding and aircraft manufacturing industries to California together with a relatively large increase in other industries manufacturing special equipment." With pride he added:

> It has also brought to California a large basic steel processing plant, a magnesium plant, and an aluminum processing plant, all of which were new to the state's industry. The war induced expansion of manufacturing industries in California and the West has created larger opportunities for peacetime industrial development . . . with increased expansion of mining and mineral industries. Potentially, California and other Western states stand at the threshold of a more diversified economic growth. Not only has the war telescoped into a few years the normal industrial progress of two decades in the West, it has brought new types of industries that heretofore have been lacking in the Western economy. A new economic frontier, made possible by the broader industrial base built during the war has opened up. . . . The impact of wartime industry in California and other Western states has been so heavy that its imprint will remain on the post-war economy.

And like other business leaders in the West, Heron associated western economic growth with the expansion of Oriental trade.[17]

In fact, Heron viewed the development of trade with the Pacific rim as an essential ingredient in the West's future prosperity.

> California and the West are in a strategic position to serve the nation in the coming era of the Pacific. With their present expanded economies and closer integration with the rest of the Nation the far West states should be viewed as the American coast of the Pacific as well as the Pacific coast of America. These states are . . . the gateway of trade with the Orient after the war. The Western States' new importance as a defensive area requires that the Army, Navy, and Air Force bases be maintained. . . . The larger and more industrialized economy of the far West states must . . . be preserved as a guaranty of national safety. In a peacetime Pacific, the Nation and the Western States can develop an increasing two-way trade with the great potential markets of China, India, Netherlands East Indies, Australia, and Southeast Asia.

Interestingly enough, in the heat of war Heron and many of his contemporaries did not expect Japan to become a leading trade partner with the United States. "Development loans to help industrialize these countries," Heron advocated, "would bring a demand for machinery, railroad equipment, and other products of American factories. The return route of this trade would find the West Coast the logical workshop to which trans-

Pacific and Alaskan materials can be brought, in which they can be processed."[18]

In California Heron viewed the new metals industries as spearheading the drive for diversification. "Preservation and continued operation of the new basic steel and light metal plants built during the war in California and the West are vital to the post-war economy of the state," he declared. "These plants will be extremely important . . . not merely as isolated producers of basic metals, but for the broad field of new opportunities they will open up for a large diversified expansion of secondary manufacturing and processing plants in the West. Many of these opportunities lie in the field of intermediate manufacturing of durable goods. . . . It is in this field of durable goods industries that California's economy has been notably deficient in the past."[19]

Heron believed that the postwar transition would not be easy. "Private operators may be reluctant to . . . operate these basic metal plants because their surveys may indicate that the immediate postwar market in the West may not be of sufficient size to justify the investment required. . . . It will take some time to expand peacetime consumer markets to their full potentialities." But, he noted, alluding to historical analogy, "The new basic metal plants of California and the West . . . stand in somewhat the same relation to future economic growth that the first transcontinental railroads did to earlier development." Both were built before their full potential could be realized. "However, the railroads created the traffic necessary for their support. They opened up a great Western empire and eventually they became self-sustaining. Not only the West but the Nation will benefit if these basic plants are provided with the necessary additional facilities and produce a partial output pending the time when there will be demands sufficient to insure profitable operation. This would furnish . . . the economic impetus by which California and the West could gradually develop more diversified manufacturing."[20]

Heron emphasized that he was not arguing for complete self-sufficiency for California. "With its highly specialized production in agriculture, minerals, and service industries," he said, "California cannot and is not striving for economic self-sufficiency. The State's larger population will depend more than ever upon Nation-wide and worldwide markets to absorb more of its specialized products. At the same time, post-war expansion of manufacturing in California is essential for economic balance and for high-level peacetime employment. . . . It is recommended that federal policies be established that will permit and encourage private financing of such enterprises possibly under guaranteed loans such as FHA and the G.I. Bill."[21]

California's planning was far more extensive than that of other western states. Yet, throughout the region many state officials were rethinking the shape of the economy to come. The war provided an opportunity they had not had for half a century and transported the depression-wracked economies of the West into a new era.

A similar ferment in planning for a new West affected the cities of the region. There a debate ensued that was reminiscent of discussions at the national and the state levels. Should city planning for the future be conducted by government under centralized control? Or should much of such planning be undertaken primarily by private enterprise with some support by government? That conflict became apparent quite early in the war years. Among those favoring a centralized approach were notable city planners such as Lewis Mumford and Charles W. Eliot. Eliot was executive director of the NRPB and after 1943 became director of the John W. Haynes Foundation in Los Angeles, an urban affairs institute. Opposing their viewpoint were powerful figures such as Robert Moses, New York City's famous planning consultant. Moses supported urban planning by private enterprise, albeit in conjunction with public works. The controversy became heated in 1943 when the November issue of *Fortune* featured these divergent approaches. Moses lashed out at his critics in the following year in an attack in the *New York Times Magazine* in which he especially lambasted European city planners such as Eero Saarinen and Walter Gropius, whom he accused of being social and ideological visionaries seeking to undermine American values.[22]

In the West, both views had their adherents, although the pragmatists were achieving dominance by the war's end. Their visions of future western cities were rarely embodied in grandiose schemes for elaborately planned communities. Rather, they preferred to leave urban expansion primarily to private developers, with some consideration for government programs in public works, the conversion of war industries, and the improvement of housing and transportation. But by 1945 the idea of postwar planning was beginning to lose the New Deal onus that even the mention of the word *planning* had entailed earlier. A historian of the Sunbelt has aptly written: "The long-term impact of post-war planning was in fact more significant than its immediate accomplishment. The process itself helped to legitimize the idea of urban planning. It anticipated the thrust of public policy in sunbelt cities during the next two decades. Agreement on the need to make encouragement of growth an explicit aim of city government and on the importance of metropolitan land use planning . . . constituted a framework for post-war agendas in the majority of sunbelt cities."[23]

The wartime planning experience of Los Angeles illustrated these trends. As one of its students has noted, "The war years provided a rich opportunity for local planners and federal officials to establish programs that could serve as a basis for post-war urban renewal." Municipal authorities, professional planners, and business and civic leaders participated in the process while also looking to Washington, D.C. for financial support. Between 1941 and 1943 the NRPB attempted to lead city officials in making plans for the reconversion period. But the vigor of the board's efforts to stimulate centralized planning alienated the power structure in Los Angeles, as it did in Portland, Oregon, and in other western cities. The Los Angeles Chamber of Commerce was not alone in fearing the NRPB's brand of "Socialistic" planning.[24]

Instead, Mayor Fletch Bowron and the business community favored the pragmatic approach to postwar planning in which private enterprise would play a more significant role. "Our planning must be intelligent, constructive, and based on all known factors," the mayor said. "The future position of Los Angeles among the great cities of the world will be largely determined by how we plan and how intelligently we put our plans into operation following the war." His sympathies lay with the business leaders who also sat on the city planning commission. They viewed urban sprawl as an inevitable consequence of healthy economic growth and hoped to rehabilitate older neighborhoods, but not revamp them. In contrast, professional city planners and admirers of Lewis Mumford envisioned a reorientation of city growth along comprehensive, orderly guidelines with rigid regulation of land use. The clashes between these alternative views of Los Angeles's future were reflected in the controversies that came before the city planning commission in the 1940s. At the same time, the need for some federal aid led both sides to adapt their visions to conform to federal standards. Although the NRPB was gone by 1943, its ghost continued to dominate the planning process in most western cities.[25]

The postwar planning experience of San Francisco reflected some of the same themes. By 1942 opposition to the NRPB's efforts to stimulate planning became intense, as local government officials and business groups disdained close federal supervision. "We don't like to feel that . . . we have to take your suggestions," declared the district attorney of Contra Costa County, responding to the California State Planning Board, which was affiliated with the NRPB. And in 1943 the California legislature abolished the State Planning Board altogether, replacing it with the State Reconstruction and Reemployment Commission, which was dominated by business interests.[26]

In Oregon, the experience of Portland followed that of California's cities. By 1942 those planners who had been close to the NRPB were being eased out of their positions. Mayor Robert E. Riley merely bypassed planning agencies with which they were associated and created new advisory commissions on which business interests were dominant. To allow them to have greater influence, Riley in 1943 created a Portland Areas Postwar Development Commission chaired by David Simpson, the president of the chamber of commerce. Simpson promptly invited Robert Moses to come from New York to devise a postwar plan for Portland that could guide the city's growth during the next decade.[27]

Smaller cities, like Las Vegas, Nevada, also opted for decentralized planning at the hands of private enterprise. By 1943 the Las Vegas development commission was making plans to convert the Basic Magnesium plant into some type of minerals processing facility. The commission was hoping for an industrial base for the town of about eight thousand. Meanwhile, several entrepreneurs were utilizing wartime conditions to develop tourism. Las Vegas found itself a weekend retreat for the millions of war workers and service men and women in southern California, Nevada, and adjoining states. The first large hotel was not completed until 1941. Within a year hotel magnate Thomas Hull had built the El Rancho Vegas, which featured entertainment as well as legalized gambling. This enterprise was a huge success, and by 1946 many other hotels and restaurants had been developed, including the lavish Flamingo Hotel built by mobster Bugsy Siegel. Planning in Las Vegas was, in the next decade, largely in the hands of the kings of the tourist industry who put Las Vegas on the map.[28]

In the states and cities the sentiment for centralized planning was much weaker than in the nation's capital. Westerners were not so much opposed to planning per se as to centralized direction in which they had little voice. This may have been as much a reaction against the centripetal tendencies of the New Deal as it was a traditional distrust of the federal bureaucracy. Every western state and scores of cities established planning boards to chart directions for their immediate economic future. But though these cities and states envisaged substantial aid from the federal government, they also hoped to exercise the levers of political control themselves rather than to let Congress, the executive departments, or the federal bureaucracy set the pace. This view was reinforced by the realistic belief that economic interests—whether business of agriculture—could often influence state legislatures and city governments far more effectively than they could the more distant authorities in Washington. In 1944 and 1945 the champions of decentralization decisively bested the advocates of centralized planning, such as those in the NRPB and on state and city planning commissions, and replaced them with more pragmatic and less doctrinaire individuals who felt that planning should be determined by the practical needs of local economic interests. In the emerging consensus on the economic future of the West, state and city planning groups were to play an important role.

The proponents of these diverging views on planning differed considerably about ends and means, yet they also met on some common ground concerning postwar policy. That government should play an important part in maintaining economic stability was rarely questioned. Even the most fervent advocates of local control agreed that public works programs would be necessary not only to provide full employment but also to rebuild and expand the cities in view of the rapid population growth experienced in wartime. The scope and pace of such growth, however, was to be determined by state and local governments, with federal support but with significant decision-making powers in the hands of private enterprise. Through a process of co-optation this approach was to be gradually integrated into the national consensus on the economic future of the West that was beginning to emerge at the end of World War II.

CHAPTER 10

Visions of the Future:
The Private Sector

GOVERNMENTS did not have a monopoly in planning the reshaping of the West, for thousands of private groups representing a myriad of economic interests were also engaged in hammering out a consensus about the future shape of the region's economy. As Raymond Miller, chief of the industrial section of the Bonneville Power Administration, said, "The promotion and growth of industry . . . in the post-war period . . . has received the attention of every businessman and of every public agency interested in the region, city and state planning councils, chambers of commerce, committees of industrial and economic development, post-war committees, state colleges and universities, public and private utilities [and] private industries."[1] Moreover, farm organizations and labor unions participated in the process as well as newly organized economic research groups, such as the Committee for Economic Development. A unified or centralized plan did not emerge from these efforts, but the debates resulted in the formation of broad guidelines for reshaping the West. In contrast to many government planners, the overwhelming majority of private groups favored a flexible, pragmatic approach to planning. CIO unions were an exception to this trend, since they opted for centralized, national planning. But most economic interests—including business, agriculture, labor, and research groups—hoped for a West shaped largely by private enterprise, although with government assistance to achieve an affluent society with full employment.

Certain areas of agreement emerged from the discussions on how to pursue this goal. That the postwar West should have a diversified economy came to be an article of faith. And despite much rhetoric about free enterprise, most westerners favored extensive government involvement in reshaping the region. A substantial number believed that the removal of discriminatory railroad freight rates and the expansion of air transport would be keys to an economic boom. Like generations before them, many westerners saw the future of the area tied closely to the Far East and what they were sure would be a vast expansion of trade with the Orient.

Additionally, most westerners in 1945 were determined not to permit the chaos that unplanned demobilization had brought in 1919 and 1920. Harrison S. Robinson, president of the California State Chamber of Commerce in 1945, made that point well. In considering his own experience after World War I, he said, "In view of what occurred . . . if it is any precedent for what will occur after World War II, the Western States will have to be on their toes or they will get the short end of the stick." He recalled particularly the sudden cancellation of shipbuilding contracts by the U.S. Shipping Board in 1919. "It took a group of Western and Mountain Senators and Representatives, and the most urgent recommendations from the civic and business interests of the West to change that order." Although strongly emphasizing the role of private enterprise in reshaping the West, he declared, "It surely is the responsibility of every organized society to provide the leadership and . . . the machinery for meeting conditions which are beyond the scope and power of individuals, and which, if not successfully dealt with, will seriously hurt substantial numbers . . . of people in the West."[2]

Full employment was clearly a prime goal of the postwar West, as of the nation. As Oliver Wheeler, director of research for the Federal Reserve Bank for the Twelfth District, noted:

> It is the task of leaders in business, finance, labor and government to see to it that the immense natural resources of this region with their tremendous trade and industrial potential are brought together with the greatly expanded population and labor force in such a way as to produce something approaching full employment. . . . It is not true that any industry which is not now established here, but whose products may be marketable here, is a good prospective industry for this region, and should be started here. We must give due thought to problems of geographical specialization and consider economic feasibility regardless of local pride, regardless of a desire to assert ourselves out of the so-called "colonial" stage of development.

Edward Landells, representing the California State Chamber of Commerce, expressed a similar sentiment. "I think it can be said," he declared, "that there is . . . unanimity . . . as to what our post-war objectives are, even though there may be a difference as to means. . . . We all want to see everyone in productive employment after the war who desires and is able to work." The chamber, in fact, prepared an extensive report on postwar policies in which it made bread-and-butter proposals, including a workable contract cancellation law and the rapid disposal of federal surplus properties into the hands of private operators.[3]

Full employment was also a prime goal of one of the important regional associations representing diverse business interests, the Builders of the West. Rex Nicholson, a former New Deal official, was executive secretary of the group. He made frequent appearances before congressional committees during 1944 and 1945 and kept up a running correspondence with advocates of western industrialization such as Senator Pat McCarran. "The development of new industries and businesses is essential to the future economy of the West," Nicholson noted at one of his many congressional appearances. "These 11 Western States have experienced a considerable percentage of decrease in the number of businessmen since 1929. Studies of post-war needs indicate that we must regain this loss and increase it over the all time high in order to process our own raw products and maintain a proper balance between small business and the population of the West." Nicholson thought that this might be achieved through tax incentives and the abolition of wartime controls. But "the No. 1 problem with which we are confronted in the West is to provide jobs for the returning servicemen. . . . A large program of public works offers the best solution for this problem." The Builders of the West urged a $10-billion public works program for the region.[4]

In addition to stressing full employment, business interests yearned for more economic diversification and greater opportunities for small business. That would move the West away from the raw materials economy that had predominated in the prewar years. Diversification could be achieved through a variety of means, from the disposal of federal war plants to the expansion of service industries such as tourism and the increase of foreign trade. Representatives of small as well as large business reiterated these themes. As C. T. Bateman, director of industrial development for the Puget Sound Power and Light Company in Seattle, explained, "The most immediate and pressing post-war need of the Northwest is the development of a large number of small manufacturers of finished goods that will provide employment opportunities for . . . war workers . . . and . . . servicemen." In cooperation with other utilities, his company was involved in a national advertising campaign to bring such new enterprises to the region. And he suggested that diversification could be speeded by tax incentives for venture capital, the prompt disposal of federal plants, rapid contract termination, and the expansion of foreign trade.[5]

The Washington Manufacturer's Association expressed similar views. The unbalanced economy of the past had been practically eliminated by war-induced developments. "The heretofore thinly populated Pacific coast area has developed its agricultural production, its service industries, and its tourist business aggressively and effectively," as a result of mobilization, the association noted. Before 1941, markets had been preempted by older manufacturers in the East and the Midwest while sparseness of population had held back local manufacturers. By 1945, they declared with enthusiasm, this situation had finally changed. "The war has brought to the Pacific area such substantial increases in population, plant facilities, skilled workers, engineering, and management ability that Pacific coast industries can now make a stronger competitive bid for manufacturing business and the markets upon which it depends." Nevertheless, the association believed it was vital that the federal government "insure equality of competitive opportunity between the new manufacturing industries of the West and the entrenched industrial firms of the Middle West and the East."[6]

Diversification through the encouragement of small business was also a prime concern expressed by David Simpson, president of the Portland Chamber of Commerce. "We hold that a continuing high level of national income is wholly essential after the war," he said.

> To attain it, we state unhesitatingly that we believe . . . there should be specific encouragement given to the men and women of America to venture their time and money into new fields of business enterprise. . . . There is a smaller percentage of our population willing to risk their time and resources to create wealth by manufacturing and processing. They are the job creators. They open the avenues for employment. . . . The ambitions of those willing to take a chance in business enterprise have been somewhat dulled by the uncertainties of pre-war economic conditions, both here and abroad. . . . This western country . . . is far from its ultimate goal. There is not a State among them incapable of greater contribution to national wealth. Unknown to some of our eastern friends we have great areas of rich and fertile land now growing only luxuriant sagebrush.[7]

In the interior the desire for diversification was just as great. "We anticipate . . . one of the outstanding potential resources is tourist business," declared Clifford Steib, secretary of the Kalispell, Montana, Chamber of Commerce. "This Nature's wonderland will be a mecca for the vacationists. . . . These things make for business opportunities."[8]

Newly formed economic research groups such as the Committee for Economic Development also placed great emphasis on diversifying the western economy through the encouragement of small business. Hal C. Thomas, regional manager of the CED from Los Angeles, reiterated the organization's view when he noted that it "is dedicated to the single objective of stimulating, encouraging, and assisting business enterprises to reach maximum levels of employment through maximum production and distribution. . . . Our entire approach is by and through businessmen and business organizations, but with the friendly cooperation of governmental agencies." That was the gist of a consensus voiced by many business leaders. Small businesses, Thomas declared, "provide one of the Nation's greatest laboratories for new ideas and new products." They would spearhead the diversification that the West would undergo, exclaimed F. N. Belgrano, regional chairman of the CED.

> We here in the West feel strongly that as a result of nationally directed war production, the destiny of all our Western states has been pushed far ahead and our economy has been changed. Whether our manpower utilization and productivity remain with us after the war will depend in large measure upon whether or not we grasp the opportunity before us to hold our present industrial facilities and promote new industries in competition with the rest of the world. These Western States are favored. They have the advantage of geographical position for both domestic and foreign commerce. They have the most favorable climate for employment and production. . . . To achieve the destiny which we visualize . . . we must have the cooperation of industry, business, agriculture, labor, and government.[9]

In addition to full employment, economic diversification through small business, and related issues, most business groups placed great hope in the expansion of Far Eastern trade. These expectations were clearly voiced by Robert Brady, a noted economist at the University of California. "I am of the opinion that we are going to see over the next fifty years the industrialization of the whole of the Orient to a level which in many places will compare quite favorably with the contemporary levels in America." Brady was referring mainly to China and Russia. In explaining the benefits that such a development might bring to the West, he declared: "Industrialization in a new area always takes place at the latest technical level. . . . In this connection, the United States is the one country in the world that will come out of this war with a large scale . . . industrial system . . . and of a size to cope with the problem that will arise in connection with the industrialization of the Orient. I think this means that this country is more apt to be the country whose methods will be copied, whose experts will be wanted, to whom contracts will be let, from whom they will want to purchase goods, from whom they will want to borrow their ideas." That was particularly important for the West, he believed. "The west . . . must recognize that market," he noted. "We are the closest to it. We have had the most experience with the Orient. . . . I think there is still something left in the West . . . of a pioneering attitude."[10]

The Los Angeles Chamber of Commerce was enthusiastic about trade expansion. Under the guidance of its World Trade Department manager, Stanley Olafson, it appointed a special committee on postwar world trade to make specific proposals. "Up to the outbreak of this war," said Olafson, "the industrial economy of southern California consisted primarily of a comparatively few large concerns in three major industries—petroleum, aircraft, and motion pictures—and several thousand small [manufacturing] plants. . . . War and subsequent developments saw our industrial economy undergo radical changes. A sharp increase took place in the total number of our industries . . . and in our population." In view of such changes the chamber hoped for rapid conversion of war industries to take advantage of international commerce. "In the past years the western ports have been major shipping centers, the outlets overseas for products of the hinterland. Because of their geographical isolation they have been forced to seek markets beyond our shores for an important part of the output of their farms, forests, mines, and industries. This need will be increasingly important in post-war years with an awakening of a fuller appreciation of the importance of foreign trade." In that appreciation Olafson hoped Los Angeles would play a vital role for the entire West. "Trade and industrial interests are fully cognizant of the hinterland," he said. "Not only are these regions important markets for products of local industries, but they are extremely important sources of many of the raw materials not formerly consumed that will be needed by domestic industrial activities."[11]

Although business groups were most vocal in planning the economic future of the West, organizations representing farmers joined in the great debate. Like business people, farmers believed that diversification of the western economy was essential for prosperity. "We believe," said John A. Sutherland, master of the Montana State Grange, "[that] the establishment of canneries . . . will make it possible to process the many kinds and varieties of fresh fruit and vegetables raised; . . . egg-drying plants, sugar beet refineries, woolen mills, pulp mills . . . plywood . . . plants." With approval he noted the criticisms that A. S. Goss, master of the National Grange, had leveled at the Baruch-Hancock Report on Reconversion, which gave little attention to agriculture. Recalling the farm depression of the 1920s Sutherland noted: "Apparently the report is built upon the fallacy which was chiefly responsible for the collapse following the last war. We refer to the widespread belief that if labor and industry are prosperous, the whole Nation will prosper. They forget that for a decade following the last war labor and industry enjoyed the greatest . . . income . . . in history [while] farming was conducted at a loss . . . and that finally this great unbalance in income and the failure to maintain the purchasing power of our people resulted in our greatest economic crack-up." Sutherland sounded a warning lest history repeat itself. "If there is to be a post-war program that lives and endures, it must include every group. If in this planning the farmer's income is cut, . . . it . . . will make it impossible to reconstruct America or the world on a sound economic basis."[12]

One quick means of achieving diversification, in the view of some farm organizations, was the rapid disposal of surplus federal properties. H. S. Bruce of the Montana Farmers' Union declared that his organization favored the distribution of such properties by the Department of Agriculture to needy farmers, whether in the form of land, equipment, or supplies. The union also supported regional power programs, such as a Missouri Valley Authority. Cheap power, he declared, was essential to a diversified and integrated postwar economy for Montana and the West.[13]

Labor leaders in the West were divided over the goals, and the means, to reshape the region's economy. Some favored highly centralized national planning, whereas others accorded a larger role to private enterprise. Mervyn Rathbone, for example, the secretary-treasurer of the California C.I.O., believed that national planning for the region was essential for its growth.

> The special problems of the various regions can best be protected by the creation of a National Planning Board. . . . We believe that the so-called States' rights approach to the problem of reconversion and reemployment is a blind alley which will lead us only into the darkness of another depression. We also believe that the proponents of the States' rights program are not really serious in their proposals. . . . Certain governors of Western States have come out for both States' rights and for building of the West . . . a regional problem. The 11 Western States are 11 times removed from States' rights in their common aim and nothing less than national planning will integrate the plans of the various regions. Nothing less than national planning will enable us to do justice to the West.[14]

Not all C.I.O. leaders were as strongly committed to national planning, but most shared a mistrust of business groups. Virgil Burts, a representative of the Washington State C.I.O. in Seattle, declared: "We have built huge war plants and brought new industries into the Pacific Northwest . . . and we must maintain these plants after the war. These plants were built with the people's money . . . [and] should not be turned over to a monopoly. . . . There is a vast industrial frontier in the Northwest which will take just as much courage to open as when our forefathers crossed the plains. It will take money and planning." And then he concentrated on his vision, which included "free enterprise, meaning free competition in business, dissolving international cartels, a national income

209

that will allow consumers to buy the goods produced, conserving natural resources, and proper disposal of defense plant holdings. We have allowed big business and monopolies to run the country too long."[15]

Western leaders of the A. F. of L. were far more inclined to let private enterprise take much of the initiative for reshaping the West. This attitude was held by Robert E. Noonan, secretary of the San Diego County Federated Trades and Labor Council. "Our membership refuses to believe that the depression and its attendant ills are inevitable in post-war America. The same energy and brain power which has achieved the war production miracle can operate in a peacetime economy and produce a standard of living beyond anything this world has ever seen." But Noonan also envisaged an active role for government in this scenario. "Private enterprise, however successful in employing our total work force in the long run, cannot be depended upon to bridge the gap between a war economy and a peace economy."[16]

Other A. F. of L. officials made this same assumption. Edward F. Skagen, business representative of the International Association of Machinists, in Los Angeles said quite plainly: "To reestablish a just and workable return to a peacetime economy it seems to me that Government must necessarily become the guiding factor. That means control and regulation. That does not mean a socialistic state." Looking to the future, Skagen said: "With the proper governmental direction the problem of reconversion in the Western States would be simple. We have the raw materials, the war has brought us the machinery and the technical help needed. . . . Given the combined agricultural-industrial economy that has sprung up during the war . . . we will be able to support a much larger population than we now have. We have seen the heavy goods industries moving west. We have seen the miracles of production brought about by our workers. We know what we can do. It is the job of Government to see that we go on performing those miracles for peace."[17]

In the euphoria of the later stages of the war even Communist labor leaders temporarily dropped their calls for revolution. Carl Winter, executive secretary of the Communist Association of Los Angeles, was the soul of moderation as he advocated centralized planning for the creation of a new West. Economic stability, he said, required "a planned and controlled transition from wartime to peacetime mobilization of our economy and manpower." Particularly in the West, he said, "the problem is so vast and complex . . . that it demands the unified cooperation of industry . . . , labor, and the farmers—all working together with the Government for its solution." He supported the Full Employment Bill then pending in Congress, comprehensive public works and river valley developments, and special benefits for World War II veterans.[18]

Underlying the myriad of details in the varied programs for the reshaping of the western economy by government officials and by private interests were shifting psychological assumptions. The war wrought enormous changes in the self-image of westerners. In the everyday hustle and bustle of work and wartime activities Americans rarely stopped to analyze themselves, to examine these often subtle changes of mood. Yet one of the most significant consequences of the war was the transformation of the image westerners had of themselves. When the West first participated in the domestic mobilization program in 1940, it was a self-doubting, depression-wracked region painfully aware of its limitations. But in 1945 the West emerged with an ebullient air of self-confidence, determined to reach new heights in economic development and envisioning unlimited horizons—horizons as wide as the western sky. If it can be argued that the psychological orientation of a society is a prime determinant of economic change, that attitudes and motivation are more important than capital, raw materials, or the labor force, then this was clearly the most important result of the war for the reshaping of the western economy.

Although the participants in the great debate over the future of the West only infrequently stopped to reflect on the more subtle changes initiated by the war, a group of writers and social critics did document them. The decade of the 1940s saw an outpouring of speculation about the future of the West. Most critics were not concerned so much with the details of reconversion as they were with the larger contours of change. They were seeking to document the decline, if not the end, of colonialism in the West and the emergence of a young, vibrant, pacesetting economy. If in 1945 the dimensions of the postwar economy were not yet visible, the social critics were nevertheless able to discern and document the profound psychological changes that had taken place and that were resulting in a transformed self-image for the West.

A bevy of writers sought to articulate visions of the future West during the war, but William Allen White, Vannevar Bush, John Kinsey Howard, A. G. Mezerick, Wendell Berge, and Bernard DeVoto were among the more widely read. Invariably, they placed the immediate future of the West into the broad context of national development. Disturbed about the growth of large corporations and the concentration of capital in twentieth-century America, they saw the West as providing another opportunity for a new start—just as the frontier had done a hundred years earlier. Their hope was for diversified economic growth characterized by small enterprise and an egalitarian social structure. In fact, their vision of the future West was distinctly Brandeisian.

In *The Changing West,* one of his last books, the famous journalist William Allen White addressed the question of the West's future. "Certainly the constantly moving frontier which was a hundred years going from Pittsburgh to Los Angeles," wrote the Sage of Emporia, "did make a civilization of its own kind, a golden age here in the West. . . . The West became what it was because of a vast increment of wealth from the rising price of the virgin land. . . . This tremendous increment transmuted by the democratic process into fluid capital . . . was distributed economically and digested socially, also by the democratic processes, by literate people who were as nearly absolutely free as it was possible in the nineteenth century." White hoped that the development of technology—instead of land—would provide the context for a truly democratic West in the immediate future. "Time and again in the West," he declared, "has it been made clear that a social order may be erected and maintained under the capitalist profit system. . . . But as our old West worked fairly well despite the rascal . . . in the distribution of the unbelievable billions of dollars of increment from the land, so the new West will work if it is underpinned with the democratic faith. We can, if we will, create an equitable order for the distribution of the stupendous increase in human wealth that is rising from the enlargement of mechanical power with the increase of production." White was reflecting his generation's faith in the miraculous power of science and technology, a faith shared by most Americans.[19]

Distinguished scientists, no less than journalists like White, saw technology as the key to a new golden age for the West. A good example was Vannevar Bush, director of the Office of Scientific Research and Development and one of the nation's leading scientific minds. Bush was convinced that science would create new frontiers for the West in the twentieth century, just as land and natural resources had brought prosperity to the region in the nineteenth century. In a well-known report, also published as a book entitled *Science: The Endless Frontier,* Bush urged government support of science because the U.S. government had always been in the vanguard in creating new frontiers. "It has been basic United States policy," Bush wrote, "that government should foster the openings of new frontiers. It opened the seas to clipper ships and furnished land for pioneers. Although these frontiers have more or less disappeared, the frontier of science remains. It is in keeping with the American tradition—one which made the United States great—that new frontiers shall be made accessible for development by all American citizens." In essence, Bush was reiterating the basic democratic faith that the economic development of the nation's youngest region would provide an optimum of equal opportunity.[20]

That such equal opportunity in the economic sphere had often been stifled by corporate monopolies in the West was the substance of anguished cries from the Great Plains. In 1943 Joseph Kinsey Howard wrote an angry book, *Montana, High, Wide, and Handsome*, which won him a Pulitzer Prize that year. Howard bitterly wrote of what he regarded as the rapacious exploitation of Montana and its mineral wealth by the Anaconda Copper Company in the preceding half century. Such exploitation, Howard warned, should serve as a dire warning in the future against allowing corporate monopoly to dominate the economic growth of the West. In Montana Anaconda created uneven economic development characterized by the ruthless extraction of minerals that were processed in the East. This led to corporate domination of political life and culture and created an unbalanced social structure with great extremes in wealth and poverty. Meanwhile, this colonial domination resulted in an unprecedented desecration and ravaging of the natural environment. Howard pulled few punches. "The reason for singling out a state whose economy seems most precarious," he wrote, was "that discussion of its experience may encourage sympathetic understanding" of its plight and prevent a similar disaster from befalling the entire West. Howard fervently hoped that if the problems of regional exploitation could be more fully recognized throughout the United States, and if Americans could build a more balanced and diversified economy, the future of the West could be bright indeed.[21]

The economic subservience of the West to the East was more stridently decried by A. G. Mezerick, a journalist who specialized in economic affairs. In a stream of articles and an impressive book Mezerick called attention to the new economic opportunities the war was bringing to the West. "Why at this time a book which stresses the divisions within our country?" asked Mezerick in *The Revolt of the South and West*. In response he noted: "The internal stresses which existed before the war are still with us, and more significantly, the war . . . was the instrument with which the corporate clique in the East strengthened its grip on the economic life of the South and West. There can be no internal harmony as long as Eastern corporate power enforces . . . centralized control of major industry, banking and distribution," he wrote. "The South and West are denied the industries which they could readily support and to which they have every right. . . . [They] have been held in the vise of a raw materials economy fashioned by that Eat." But World War II was providing a unique

213

opportunity for the West to emancipate itself from eastern economic bondage. "Western America has a post-war plan," he declared with a degree of bombast. "Simply stated, it is to wage war against the financial monopoly now held by the East. The goal is industrial self-determination." His view of the West's economic future was grandiose. "The West is playing for a new empire—not only to supply the needs of its own five and one-half million people with manufactured articles, but by utilizing Alaska and its alliance with the undeveloped Canadian Northwest, to become self-sufficient for almost all of its raw materials. Then boldly it expects to ship finished products through the Panama Canal to undersell the East in the South and Southwest, and finally to hit the jackpot—the domination of the world's greatest market, Asia. It will be a breathtaking fight that may change the pattern of our economy." Mezerick's vision of empire was no less grandiose than the dreams of European explorers in the New World in the sixteenth century. And it was obviously overblown with an excess of hyperbole. Yet to the generation that had just lived through World War II, anything seemed possible.[22]

Or so it seemed also to Wendell Berge, the assistant attorney general in the U.S. Department of Justice. Berge had been Thurman Arnold's assistant in the antitrust campaign waged during the final phases of the New Deal. Intellectually and emotionally he was heavily involved in the broadly based effort of many westerners to diversify their economy. He articulated his views in 1945, writing an eloquent little book, *Economic Freedom for the West.* Quite accurately, Berge perceived the changing self-image of westerners in the course of the war years. "Historians have told us that the vanishing of the geographic frontier constituted a major turning point in our evolution," Berge wrote. "All too often in the years before the war it was assumed that the passing of the geographic frontier also meant the disappearance of broad opportunities for economic development." But that had been a short-range view inspired by the pervasive pessimism of the Great Depression. "Far from being mature or senile, our economy had been asleep to its own powers, both in terms of technical progress . . . and of the fields awaiting exploration and enterprise," he noted with considerable prescience. Like some of his contemporaries, Berge saw the end of the war as a crucial juncture in the economic development of the West. In 1945, he declared: "The economic future of the West has a critical significance. . . . If the West is denied a chance to develop its resources . . . our economy could then not look forward to expansion but would once more risk contraction and depression. The West is once more the frontier on which the question of America's economic expansion will be decided. All of its trails have not been blazed . . . the full economic greatness of the West is undiscovered. It need not remain so. . . . The development of the West will constitute a magnificent addition to industrial strength and economic welfare of America."[23]

The themes so well articulated by Berge, Mezerick, Howard, and others were even more cogently addressed by Bernard DeVoto. A distinguished literary critic who wrote for a large popular audience in his regular column for *Harper's Magazine*, DeVoto often used the column between 1944 and 1947 to analyze significant issues concerning the West's future economic growth. Born in Utah and having lived much of his early life in the West, DeVoto in his middle years became increasingly concerned with the fate of his native region. Although he had wide literary interests, his increasing preoccupation with the national economic role of the West perhaps represented a search for identity and self-fulfillment in his own life, a search for roots. That may explain the passionate spirit with which he approached the subject. "War industries have given the West a far greater and more widely distributed prosperity than it has ever had before," he wrote in 1946. "Moreover, during the war a fundamental revolution took place; power and industrial developments in the West have made a structural change in the national economy . . . [and] if the developments that have occurred are revolutionary those already planned and sure to be carried out are even more revolutionary and some of those which so far are only dreams but may be achieved stagger the mind. Finally, the world movements which are working out a long-term reorientation of human societies whose focus is the Pacific Ocean will be increasingly favorable to the West." DeVoto believed that westerners had waited a long time for this moment. "The West sees all of this in terms of its historical handicaps; colonial economic status and absentee control. The ancient Western dream of an advanced industrial economy . . . is brighter now than it has ever been before. For the first time there are actual rather than phantasmal reasons for believing that the dream can be realized."[24]

But DeVoto was concerned that westerners might not seize their unique opportunity. He detected a split in the western psyche. On the one hand, westerners were striving for economic independence. On the other, they seemed all too willing to allow eastern capitalists to undertake ruthless exploitation and despoliation of the West's natural resources. Until westerners could resolve such conflicting desires, DeVoto warned, the future of the West was in jeopardy, and the best dreams would remain unfulfilled. "Realization that the dream can be fulfilled has made the West all but drunk," DeVoto wrote. "I cannot list here the sectional and interstate associations and committees engaged in implementing the dream, the plans they are working out, the measures they are preparing. . . . Enough that the West understands the opportunity . . . the possibilities of success and failure. . . . Whether the great dream will fail or be fulfilled depends on how that split works out." Thus, DeVoto posed some of the key issues for westerners conscious of being on the brink of momentous economic changes.[25]

Through their books and articles the social critics of the West helped to define problems, clarify options, and generally raise the consciousness of Americans about the future of the West. Their varied writings not only revealed that the West was at a crossroads but also provided a context within which policy makers would operate in the coming decade, supplying much food for thought about possible approaches to future western economic growth.

The war years, then, spawned a comprehensive effort by westerners to plan for the future of their region. During the Great Depression the demands of crisis—the sheer battle for survival—had dampened western planning for the future. Only a small group of New Dealers, ensconced in the NRPB and elsewhere, had visions about the future of the West, which they embodied in a stream of reports between 1939 and 1943. But fears about the growth of centralized government, as well as increasing opposition to the New Deal, led Congress to abolish the NRPB in 1943. Amidst growing affluence in wartime the efforts of idealistic planners were distrusted more than ever, particularly by business people and those who preferred a decentralized, pragmatic approach to planning. This approach emphasized decentralization of the economy and promotion of voluntary efforts and private enterprise. Government might assist such efforts, but not too obtrusively.

But whatever their orientation, the dreams and hopes of westerners for the future were reflected in an unprecedented outburst of planning activities between 1944 and 1946. In charting blueprints for the economic future of the region westerners demonstrated their preference for practical and pragmatic proposals rather than large-scale, comprehensive abstract designs. Planning activities were carried out by thousands of postwar reconstruction or redevelopment commissions. This was a broadly based, genuinely grass-roots movement. Some of these activities were sponsored by federal, state, or local governments; others were conducted by chambers of commerce, trade associations, business groups, farm organizations, and labor unions. In many ways, they were a striking illustration of democracy at work, of the process by which Americans went about restructuring their economic life. The war years thus witnessed one of the most significant planning movements in twentieth-century America. Although diverse and fragmented, it deserves to be recognized as one of the milestones in the reshaping of the West.

CHAPTER 11

Conclusion: World War II
and Western
Economic Growth

IF NOT ALL the dreams of west-
erners in 1945 were to be fulfilled in the next generation, still many of
their hopes and aspirations were realized. The economy of the West became far more diversified in the second half of the twentieth century than
it had been in the first. If the West still had not caught up with the older
regions in its economic development, that was due partly to its youth,
rather than to the colonial type of exploitation that had been demonstrated
in discriminatory freight rates and wanton extraction of raw materials. As
the West now developed bustling new urban centers where there had
been few before, these became the hub of the postindustrial economy of
the region. The sizable population increase in the trans-Mississippi West
created significant new markets that made the region less dependent on
the East. And it stimulated a bevy of service industries, of which tourism
came to be among the most important. Much of this growth was fueled
by the vast expansion of the military-industrial complex, which would
constitute an important component of the western economy. Frequently
it was intertwined with an expanding science-technology complex that
was on the cutting edge of new innovations. After World War II the West
was obviously a very different place than it had been before.

The patterns that developed during World War II created the parameters for western economic growth during the next generation. In the years
from 1945 to 1980, apart from its agricultural and mining base the West
could boast a small but significant network of manufacturing industries.
The region became more involved with the fabrication of raw materials,
chemicals, petroleum, and aluminum. Increasingly the service sector became more important as tourism, education, health care industries, and
financial institutions blossomed. Beyond these mainstays the region also

218

attracted new technological industries involving computers, electronics, and information-processing systems. These became a vital and dynamic element of the regional economy. California's Silicon Valley came to symbolize the most important advanced forms of American technology, and similar research and manufacturing complexes dotted many other western cities, including Phoenix, Tucson, Denver, and Albuquerque. In addition, the West retained a significant share of the military-industrial complex fathered by World War II. Such national defense industries embraced rocketry and missiles and scores of components for the nation's large new military establishment as well as for the space program. Not quite as dramatic or glamorous but no less significant was the extensive network of military installations. Air bases, supply depots, and training sites became an essential part of the economies of most western states, contributing jobs and income. The fact that the two major wars of this period—Korea and Vietnam—were fought exclusively in the Pacific was clearly felt in the western states, whose proximity to the Pacific theater of war emphasized their new strategic importance as staging and supply areas. In addition, the West was a prime beneficiary of vast federal expenditures for the environment. This was the age of giant dam and water projects such as those in the Central Valley of California, Big Thompson in Colorado, and central Arizona.[1] The heritage of World War II endowed the West with a new economic structure that would serve it for a generation.

By the 1980s, however, this economic structure was clearly eroding. Raw material industries such as copper and cattle were beset by declining domestic demand and increasing foreign competition and now faced serious difficulties. Manufacturing and fabrication industries such as steel—so laboriously built during World War II—faced tough foreign competition that created hardships serious enough to threaten their very existence. Even the younger aluminum industry fell on hard times. Processing industries such as petroleum were also directly affected by the downturn as the American economy increasingly relied on foreign imports and cheap wage levels overseas. And these trends affected the region's service industries, banks, tourist-oriented enterprises, and educational institutions, which now faced a more slowly expanding economy. As western natural resource industries slackened, as jobs were lost in these as well as in the fabricating industries, the service sector was also affected. And declining revenues led most state governments in the West to embark on financial retrenchment.

Even the West's proudest hope for affluence—the technological and electronics industries—began to face serious setbacks by 1980 when international competition, particularly from Japan, brought depression to

Silicon Valley and similar enclaves. At the same time, the slowing of the federal government's space exploration program and the more cautious dispersal of federal funds for national security dampened public expenditures for military purposes in the West. Moreover, by 1980 the Bureau of Reclamation and the Corps of Engineers had dammed over many of the more obvious power sites in the West, so that the prospects for major new federal reclamation projects seemed less bright than they had a half century before. By the 1980s it was clear that the patterns set by World War II were disintegrating in the face of new technologies and foreign competition, slackening productivity, and other influences.[2] If westerners wanted to retain economic affluence, some reshaping of their economy was an imminent necessity.

In the last decades of the twentieth century, therefore, westerners, like other Americans, began to grope for ways to restructure their faltering economy. Their hope was that they could regain the competitive edge they seemed to have lost to Japan and other Asian and European nations.[3] Although Americans might admire aspects of these competing economic systems, it was hardly practical to imitate them, since each was rooted within a particular cultural context. More relevant was previous American experience with restructuring the economy, such as the rebuilding of the western economy during World War II.

Of course, the 1980s presented a set of problems very different from those of this earlier era. The influence of big business in the region's economy was greater than it had been in 1940. Although opportunities for economic innovation had by no means disappeared, perhaps they were more restricted in some areas of the economy. The pace of technological innovation—as measured by patents issued by the Patent Office to Americans—had clearly atrophied, and other nations had gained preeminence in many fields. The heavy hand of bureaucracy in government, business, and labor affected the economy in many ways, augmented by a tax system that clearly inhibited economic innovation and risk taking. The military-industrial complex had become institutionalized in the national as well as the regional economy, absorbing at least 7 percent annually of the gross national product.[4] The psychological outlook of Americans in the 1980s was also very different from that in the 1940s. By the 1980s most Americans were preoccupied with consumption, hedonism, and the more equal distribution of wealth—with what the popular writer Tom Wolfe castigated as "Meism." A concern for problems of production and worker productivity was far more muted and rarely mentioned. Government policies reflected the popular mood. In the Tax Reform Act of 1987, the

U.S. government provided disincentives to investment in new enterprises and emphasized instead redistribution of existing wealth and transfer payments.

A growing chorus of critics bemoaned these tendencies. "We rationalize that we are a nation of service industries," declared Arthur A. Taylor, a former Columbia Broadcasting System executive who in 1988 served as dean of the Fordham University School of Business. "We let other nations manufacture, but no economy can thrive serving McDonald's hamburgers. The most important thing is that we need trained young people to cope with an America that no longer is sitting on the top. They must learn to be competitive and that it will be tougher to continue our standard of living."[5] Other economists were disturbed by increasingly large investments made by foreigners in the United States. In a trenchant critique of America's economic condition, economists Martin and Susan Tolchin declared that the prime reason for the selling of America was the American decision to have a standard of living higher than what its productivity permitted. In the public realm, Americans sought to enjoy consumption in spheres such as defense, social security, and medical care—without paying very high taxes. To raise the money to finance these programs, they were forced to sell their assets. In the private sphere, Americans were disinclined toward saving and sought to enjoy greater consumption than their incomes warranted. To finance such preferences, they also found it necessary to sell assets.[6]

If, as the Tolchins argue, the selling of America is not a good idea, the primary remedy is not so much in new laws as it is in changes of American behavior and attitudes that would preclude such sales. As the economist Lester C. Thurow has calculated, by 1988 Americans had already borrowed $500 billion, but would still need to borrow at least $200 billion annually to maintain their public as well as private levels of consumption. At such a rate, Americans will have used up all their assets in about fifty years. At the end of that time the rest of the world will have become the owners of the United States, whereas Americans will become the work force for the foreign owners. The nation will then be similar to a Third World economy, with a standard of living to match. And the democratic political process will be affected accordingly.[7]

What is to be done? The 1980s have witnessed a wide-ranging discussion of these problems that is likely to extend into the 1990s. If previous restructurings of the economy are an indication, the process will be neither easy nor smooth and is bound to be characterized by severe economic crises and dislocations. Prior experiences may not provide precise models, but they can point to significant parameters of economic change. Within such a context, the experience of westerners in rebuilding their economy in World War II may have some relevance.

In that restructuring, westerners placed a high priority on technological innovation. This was reflected in many aspects of their economic life but particularly in the shipbuilding and aircraft industries. In shipbuilding, the rapid adaptation of prefabrication and mass production to replace the craft mode of production was striking. The transition was easier in the West than in the East because accumulated institutional experience was far less firmly established there than in the older regions. Consequently, western shipyards were able to set new production records and to pace the industry nationwide throughout the war. Moreover, western shipbuilders like the Kaisers, the Bechtels, or McCone simply were not burdened by the morass of tradition that enveloped the older shipbuilders. They were managers and entrepreneurs rather than craftsmen, innovators rather than traditionalists.

Innovation was also spectacular in the western aircraft industry. Unlike shipbuilding, this was still a young industry in which pioneering entrepreneurs rather than managerial technocrats played a dynamic and dominant role. Douglas, Ryan, Boeing, and Hughes were men who relished the opportunity to innovate in the quantity and quality of production that the war provided. Like shipbuilding, airplane manufacture had been a craft. But these men jumped at the chance to transform it into a mass-production industry. By pioneering with research and development, they gave the industry a competitive edge with which they paced the world for the next generation.

A belief in the need to maintain competition in the American economic system was another characteristic of the reshapers of the western economy in World War II. One manifestation of this conviction was the effort to limit the influence of big business to preserve competitiveness and free enterprise. A fundamental goal of many of the leading advocates of small business in wartime, men like Ickes, Murray, Arnold, Maverick, O'Mahoney, and Berle, was the preservation of small business not only to preserve the ideal of economic equality but above all to encourage economic creativity and innovation. Those qualities had contributed to the greatness of the American economy before 1940, and these men hoped to continue the tradition. It was not that innovation, imagination, and economic creativity were exclusively rooted in small business; these could often be found in big business as well. But proponents believed that small business symbolized the competitive system in the United Stated that, even in an oligopolistic economy, could prevent calcification and smugness and could ensure dynamism and change.

A third characteristic of economic restructuring in the West during World War II was a decided determination to limit the deadening influence of pervasive bureaucracy. The creative competition that Roosevelt encouraged in his subordinates inspired a spirit of energy in the enormously expanded wartime bureaucracy that made it work. Even then, however, the torpor of excessive bureaucratic regulation often impeded the efforts of some of the most innovative business leaders, such as Edgar Kaiser. By 1943 he was becoming increasingly concerned about this trend and gave vent to his doubts. In a lengthy letter to Daniel Ring of the U.S. Maritime Commission, Kaiser articulated some of the dilemmas of his and later generations.

> Unknowingly and perhaps unavoidably, as time passes, more governmental procedures and controls are creeping in—building up—and it all centers back on this question of what the General Accounting Office will say or what the Audit section will say, and management is now reaching a point where its very thinking is controlled and limited by these factors. . . . I understand what has happened—a gradual building up of regulations so that the yards will operate identically to governmental agencies. If you accomplish this, you will lose incentive, initiative, and the very things for which you hired the contractors to do this job. . . . Again, I say . . . we either operate as a government agency or we go back to freedom of management.[8]

Somewhat unintentionally, Kaiser had defined a dilemma that was to confound him and later leaders in both business and government.

The economic restructuring that westerners undertook in World War II included a new element in the increasingly significant role of military spending by the armed services and their contractors. It is true, of course, that expenditures by military agencies had been a significant factor in the western economy since the first settlements in the nineteenth century. At that time the establishment of forts housing U.S. Army troops engaged in warfare against the Indians had already affected the economies of many localities and states. Supplying such installations, especially in sparsely populated areas, provided significant income for individuals and communities. During the nineteenth century the level of such expenditures remained remarkably constant. Thereafter, military installations had a decided effect in shaping the growth of western cities.[9]

Thus, the influence of World War II in expanding federal spending for national security was not unique. What was distinctive was the scope and scale of such military expenditures and their effect on the regional economy. In many western towns, cities, and states, defense spending accounted for an increasing percentage of total income. Military installations, training camps, and air bases proliferated on an unprecedented scale. Related testing and scientific research centers, like Los Alamos, Livermore, Hanford, or Sandia, and western state universities under federal contracts added to the flow of government funds, not to speak of private contractors whose work was oriented primarily toward national security. This new military-industrial complex became a significant additional source of income for the region and an integral part of its economy, not only in wartime but also in the succeeding four decades. At its best, it could invigorate selected sectors of the economy. At its worst, as the Canol Project indicated, it could result in great wastefulness and inefficiency—always under the guise of protecting the national security.

The World War II experience indicated that attitudes toward restructuring played a vital part in the mobilization process. The psychological outlook of westerners in World War II, their "can do" attitude, was an important ingredient in the successful revamping of the depression-wracked economy in which they found themselves at the beginning of the war. Even so, a cultural lag was evident in the early stages of mobilization. All Americans did not at first share the new sense of confidence—the positive self-image. That was evidenced by the old-time shipbuilders and by the leaders in the steel and aluminum industries who tended to think small rather than big and who were weighed down by a depression psychology favoring limited output and growth potentials of the economy. It was only with phenomenal new production records that these older attitudes gradually began to change, sweeping away the cultural lag in regard to the potential of the western, and the American, economy. If somewhat more intangible than production schedules, such attitudes and perceptions about the future were an important element in the broad process of economic restructuring.

The World War II experience underlined the importance of government leadership in reshaping the regional economy. Government played a significant role in the entire process. The extraordinarily large sums expended by the federal government provided much of the capital that fueled western economic growth. In addition, other key measures were crucial in enabling private enterprise to undertake the formidable task. Apart from deficit spending, these measures included the establishment of the Smaller War Plants Corporation, which enabled small business to maintain a place in the expanded wartime production program. The various projects of the Defense Plant Corporation not only created entire new industries for the West, such as aluminum processing, but also laid foundations for the aircraft and shipbuilding industries, which provided

224

a more balanced industrial base for the region. The G.I. Bill of 1944 eased the transition of war veterans and civilian workers into the labor force and avoided the sudden shock of millions entering the job market within a short period of time. This was particularly crucial for areas, such as southern California, that had large concentrations of war-related industries.[10] The Surplus Property Act provided for the federal industrial establishment built during the war to be gradually transferred into private hands with a minimum of disruption. And the Contract Termination Act prevented the shocks to the economy that had contributed to the post–World War I depression, by providing a more orderly and gradual process of reconversion. Americans had learned much from their experience between 1917 and 1921, and these lessons benefited the West's transition to a peacetime economy in 1945.

The primary goal of westerners, as of other Americans in World War II, was to stimulate the productive capacity of their region. That was in contrast to the post-1945 decades, when Americans increasingly emphasized consumerism and the more equitable distribution of wealth. By the 1970s, it was clear, this trend had dulled the competitive edge of American management and workers. By the 1980s the United States could no longer boast the world's preeminent economy. When Jean Servan Schreiber published *The American Challenge* in 1973 he was describing America's experience in the three decades after World War II. Underlying this affluent society was a belief that it had solved most problems of production and that it should devote prime attention to the more equitable distribution of wealth. But, even if imperceptibly, the decline of the American economy was already under way. A decade later the appearance of books by authors who suggested that Americans emulate the Japanese economic experience indicated that the torch had passed, that Americans were no longer the model for the world's leading economic system.[11] As in the Great Depression, once more the efficacy of the American economy was open to question.

The reshaping of the economy posed a significant challenge to political leadership, whose task it is to energize the creativity of the American people. It was easy in World War II, as it was at a later time, to point to weaknesses and inconsistencies in the Roosevelt administration's war mobilization program. The overlapping functions of wartime agencies were often maddening. And yet despite such very real shortcomings in his program, Roosevelt met the highest challenge of leadership: to stimulate the American people to bend their best efforts to mass production for the war effort. In the last analysis, national and regional economies are only as strong as the abilities, imaginations, training, and motivation of the people who compose them. In World War II westerners, like other Americans, were at their best. Perhaps their example cannot be duplicated by another generation. But the experience of westerners in rebuilding their economy in World War II provides a model, and sets a standard, that later generations could well emulate as they seek to cope with equally pressing economic issues of their own day.

Notes

Short citations are used in the notes. For full bibliographical information, see the bibliography.

1. Introduction: Reshaping the Western Economy

1. For general background on these economic cycles see Merrill Jensen, *The New Nation*, 147–53, 335; Curtis P. Nettels, *Emergence of a National Economy, 1775–1815*, 1–44; George R. Taylor, *The Transportation Revolution*, 3–6, 384–98; Edward C. Kirkland, *Industry Comes of Age*, 1–12, 406–8; Adolf A. Berle, *The Twentieth Century Capitalist Revolution*, 9–24; John Kenneth Galbraith, *The New Industrial State*, 1–10, 388; and Alfred D. Chandler, *The Visible Hand*.

2. Gerald D. Nash, *The American West in the Twentieth Century*, 9–41; Gene M. Gressley, "Colonialism and the American West," 1–8; Walter P. Webb, *Divided We Stand*, 3, 4, 26, 30; A. G. Mezerick, *The Revolt of the South and West*, 50–76, 112–273. See also Gerald D. Nash, "Reshaping Arizona's Economy," in Beth Luey and Noel J. Stowe eds., *Arizona at Seventy-Five*, 127–33. For contemporary observations on western colonialism see John Gunther, *Inside U.S.A.*, 151–53; Ellis Arnall, *The Shore Dimly Seen*, 165–85; and idem, *What the People Want*.

3. Frank L. Kidner, *California Business Cycles*, 1–8, 65; Forest G. Hill, "An Analysis of Regional Economic Development," 8; J. J. Parsons, "California Manufacturing," 229–41; Sterling J. Brubaker, "The Impact of Federal Government Activities on California's Economic Growth," 6–7, 47–51, 155–68. See also Abner Hurwitz and Carlyle P. Stallings, "Inter-regional Differentials in Per Capita Real Income Change"; and Simon J. Kuznets, *National Product in Wartime*. For a general survey see Harold G. Vatter, *The U.S. Economy in World War II*.

4. See the table compiled from U.S. Department of Commerce, Bureau of the Census, *Census of Manufactures*, 1947 (Washington, 1947), 21, 30, 603, in Leonard J. Arrington and Anthony T. Cluff, *Federally Financed Industrial Plants Constructed in Utah During World War II*, 69; Morris E. Garnsey, *America's New Frontier*, 5, 134–36, 163–65.

5. Leonard J. Arrington and Thomas G. Alexander, "Supply Hub of the West,"

227

Notes to Pages 5–9

99, 100, 103. See also John D. Millett, *U.S. Army in World War II—The Army Service Forces*, 302. A general survey is in Leonard J. Arrington and George Jensen, *The Defense Industry of Utah*, 4–13.

6. Leonard J. Arrington, Thomas G. Alexander, and Eugene A. Erb, Jr., "Utah's Biggest Business," 9–10; Wesley Frank Craven and James Lea Cate, eds., *Army Air Forces in World War II*, 128–29, 378.

7. Leonard J. Arrington and Thomas G. Alexander, "They Kept 'Em Rolling," 3, 5, 6, 12. See also Harry Thomsen and Lida Mayo, *The Ordnance Department*, 375–76. The situation was similar in other western states. When the army decided to expand Camp Kit Carson in Colorado by spending $22,875,000, the *Colorado Springs News* of January 9, 1942, declared that it was one of the biggest events ever to occur in that area.

8. Leonard J. Arrington and Thomas G. Alexander, "World's Largest Military Reserves," 324, 325, 327.

9. Leonard J. Arrington and Thomas G. Alexander, "Sentinels on the Desert," 32–36.

10. Leonard J. Arrington and Archer L. Durham, "Anchors Aweigh in Utah," 111–12; Thomas G. Alexander, "Ogden's Arsenal of Democracy, 1920–1955," 240–45; Thomas G. Alexander, "Brief Histories of Three Federal Military Installations in Utah," 124–26. For similar trends in Colorado see Leroy Hafen, ed., *Colorado and Its People*, 3: 592–98. Hundred of unpublished histories of federal installations are available in air force and private library collections. For an example see Jean Provence, "Luke Field During World War II," manuscript in Arizona Collection, Arizona State University Library, Tempe.

11. Thomas G. Alexander and Leonard J. Arrington, "Utah's Small Arms Ammunition Plant During World War II," 185–96. The five counties were Box Elder, Weber, Davis, Tooele, and Salt Lake.

12. James Phinney Baxter III, *Scientists Against Time*, 20, 174, 179–81, 203–4, 210, 261, 265; Clayton Koppes, *JPL and the American Space Program*, 9–29; Gerald D. Nash, *The American West Transformed*, 153–77.

13. The literature on Los Alamos is extensive. For the official history see Richard G. Hewlett and Oscar Anderson, *The New World*, 1:229–52; James W. Kunetka, *City of Fire*; and Frank Szasz, *The Day the Sun Rose Twice*. A contemporary personal account is in Ernest O. Lawrence, "History of the University of California Radiation Laboratory (1945)," manuscript in Ernest O. Lawrence Papers, Bancroft Library, University of California, Berkeley. On Lovelace see Jake Spidle, *The Lovelace Medical Center*.

14. Bernard Jaffe, *Men of Science in America*, 476.

15. 79th Cong., 2d sess., 1946, Senate, Special Committee to Study the Problems of American Small Business (hereafter cited as SB Committee), *Report of the Smaller War Plants Corporation: Economic Concentration and World War II*, also issued as *Senate Document* no. 206, 51, 53 (hereafter cited as *Economic Concentration and World War II*). See also Press Release by Senator James E. Murray on presentation of report, June 14, 1946, mimeograph, 1–5, in James E. Murray Papers, University of Montana, Missoula.

16. *Economic Concentration and World War II*, vii; see also James E. Murray, "What About Small Business?" manuscript speech (1944) in Murray Papers. See also James E. Murray to Franklin D. Roosevelt, August 16, 1942; and Franklin D. Roosevelt to James E. Murray, August 31, 1942, Murray Papers, in which Roosevelt noted, "The problem is one that has concerned me for some time and I wish very much that a solution might be found."

17. *Economic Concentration and World War II*, 21, 25. See also James E.

Murray, "Problems of Small Business Enterprises," Address at 15th Annual Meeting of Gray Iron Founders' Society Inc., Cincinnati, Ohio, October 5, 6, 1943, manuscript in Murray Papers. James E. Murray, "Remarks at Army-Navy E Award Ceremony—Central California War Industries," (Fresno, California, 1943); Murray Papers.

18. Compiled from tables in *Economic Concentration and World War II*, 30, 31; see also ibid., 27, 29, and on government-operated plants see 49–50. Smaller War Plants Corporation, *18th Report* (April-May 1945) (Washington, 1945), 7; *19th Report* (June-July 1945) (Washington, 1945), 9; *Survey of Current Business* (July 1943), 6.

19. *Economic Concentration and World War II*, 48; 77th Cong., 2d sess., 1942, Senate, Committee on Banking and Currency, *Hearings on Smaller War Plants Corporation—S. Bill 2250* (hereafter cited as *Hearings on S. Bill 2250*), 52, 100, 167; 77th Cong., 2d sess., 1942, SB Committee, *Senate Report* no. 479, part 2, pp. 18 ff., contains many examples of how small businesses were neglected in the mobilization program. Donald Nelson objected to the interference of antitrust activities with war production; see Donald Nelson to Thurman Arnold, September 5, 1942; Thurman Arnold to Donald Nelson, September 9, 1942, denying interference; and Donald Nelson to Francis Biddle, September 19, 1942, complaining about Arnold's "meddling," in Thurman Arnold Papers, University of Wyoming, Laramie. At one point Roosevelt was so frustrated with Nelson that he offered the chairmanship of the War Production Board to Bernard Baruch; see Franklin D. Roosevelt to Bernard Baruch, February 5, 1943, Franklin D. Roosevelt Papers, Franklin D. Roosevelt Library, Hyde Park, New York (hereafter cited as FDR Papers).

20. See compilation in *Economic Concentration and World War II*, 48; on the Defense Plant Corporation see Gerald T. White, *Billions for Defense*; Jesse Jones, *Fifty Billion Dollars*; and Frederick C. Lane, *Ships for Victory*.

21. In October 1941 Donald Nelson, chairman of the Office of Production Management (and of its successor in 1942, the War Production Board), made a survey of his key men in the Priorities Division. The study revealed that almost all of these eighteen officials, at least 90 percent, were from New York, Boston, Washington, D.C., or Chicago. See OPM, Priorities Division, Personnel and Organization Survey, "Key Men and Promotable Youngsters," October 14, 1941 (mimeographed), in Donald A. Nelson Papers, Henry L. Huntington Library and Art Gallery, San Marino, California. See also "Dollar-A-Year and Without Compensation Personnel in the War Production Board and Predecessor Agencies, May, 1940–September 30, 1944," A report for Donald Nelson Prepared by Edwin A. Locke, Jr., manuscript in Nelson Papers, which revealed that of five hundred such individuals only three came from west of the Mississippi River.

22. Text of Murray statement in *New York Times*, January 2, 1942. On Murray's background see Donald E. Spritzer, "New Dealer from Montana: The Senate Career of James E. Murray" (Ph.D. diss., University of Montana, 1980), 1–41, 146–47, also published as *The New Dealer From Montana*.

23. James E. Murray memo to Franklin D. Roosevelt, July 24, 1940, FDR Papers; James E. Murray, "The Murray Committee's Approach to the Small Business Problem," *Congressional Digest* (February 1942), 47–49; 79th Cong., 2d sess., 1947, Senate, Special Committee to Study Problems of American Small Business, *The Future of Independent Business: Progress Report of the Chairman to the Members of the Committee*, 148–51 (hereafter cited as *Independent Business*); on Taft, see *Hearings on S. Bill 2250*, part 2, pp. 291, 309.

24. Library of Congress, Legislative Reference Service, "Resolutions Creating,

Continuing . . . Funds for the Senate Special Committee . . . Small Business,"
manuscripts in Murray Papers; "13 Years—741 Bills," *Small Business Quarterly*
1 (November 1946): 13 ff.; on Dewey Anderson see Spritzer, "New Dealer," 148–
49, 220–21, and sketch of his career dated December 19, 1946, Murray Papers.
See also "Murray's Megaphones," *Newsweek* (February 26, 1945), 62.

25. See 77th Cong., 2d sess., 1941–47, SB Committee, *Hearings* (hereafter
SB Committee, *Hearings*); see also Carl Hayden to James E. Murray, August 30,
1944, on the importance of the committee's work in the West, in Carl Hayden
Papers, Arizona State University Library, Tempe. On the effort of the Small
Business Committee to be a prime spokespiece for small business, see Jonathan
Daniels to Sam Rosenman, November 12, 1943, FDR Papers. Jim Heath, "Ameri-
can War Mobilization and the Use of Small Manufacturers, 1939–1943," 295–319.

26. The Murray Papers contain scores of letters dealing with Murray's intervention with federal agencies on behalf of small businesses. See James E. Murray
to Charles A. Weaver, February 11, 1942; Murray to E. T. McCanna, April
27, 1942; Murray to Oscar Horsford, September 24, 1942; S. Abbott Smith to
Murray, June 7, 1943; Pat A. Kelley to Murray, January 26, 1943; Paul Raver to
Murray, November 27, 1944; and Harold W. Wright to Murray, May 14, 1946,
Murray Papers.

27. Lou Holland to Harry S. Truman, August 20, 1940; Truman to Holland,
August 31, 1940, in Harry S. Truman Papers, Harry S. Truman Library, Independence, Missouri.

28. Holland to Truman, September 19, 1940; Truman to Holland, September
20, 1940; Truman to Holland, February 1, 1941; see also Truman to Holland,
February 4, 1941, Truman Papers.

29. Remarks of Davis in U.S. Temporary National Economic Committee, *Final
Report and Recommendations of the Temporary National Economic Committee*
(Washington, 1943), 57, Appendix E.

30. Truman to Holland, June 20, 1942, Truman Papers. Jim Heath, "Frustrations of a Missouri Small Businessman," 299–316.

31. SB Committee, *Hearings*, Part 1, 1, 129, 153; *Hearings on S. Bill 2250*,
8–11, 18–20, 239, 253, 268–76; *New York Times*, February 5, March 24, 25, 1942;
John M. Blair and Harrison F. Houghton, "History of the Smaller War Plants
Corporation" (hereafter cited as "SWPC History"), compiled and written by the
agency's staff in 1945, 11 volumes, manuscript in Records, U.S. Smaller War
Plants Corporation, National Archives, Washington, D.C. (hereafter cited as
SWPC Records). See 1: 1, 3, 5–6, 10, 19, on "why the SWPC was indispensible
to the American economy."

32. Coronado W. Fowler, "Congress Creates the Smaller War Plants Corporation," in "SWPC History," 23–24, 27, 31, 38–48, 56–59; 77th Cong., 2d sess.,
1942, SB Committee, *Senate Report* no. 457, part 2, p. 25, and *Senate Report*
no. 479, 1–5. For an analysis of problems on the local level in the West, see John
W. Hedges, "History of the Smaller War Plants Corporation—Region IX (Denver)," typescript, 1–6, in World War II Records. Collection, Colorado Historical
Society, Denver. Small plants in Colorado had been doing repair work for ranchers
and were not well equipped to handle precision work such as the army and the
navy demanded.

33. *New York Times*, April 1, 2, 1942; *Cong. Rec.*, 77th Cong., 2d sess. (March
31, 1942), 3223–33, 3241 and (May 26, 1942), 4578. Of seventy-seven men recommended for the Board of Directors of the SWPC Murray named eleven, and
together with Truman he chose Holland as chairman. See Sidney Weinberg memo

for Small Business Committee, SWPC Records. See also Spritzer, "New Dealer," 158. U.S., *Statutes at Large*, 56:351–57.

34. SB Committee, *Hearings*, part 5, pp. 1047, 1077; Murray to Donald Nelson, May 11, 1942, Murray Papers; Donald E. Spritzer oral history interview with Bertram Gross (staff director of the Small Business Committee), 2, in Murray Papers; Murray to Holland, December 11, 1942; Holland to Murray, January 14, 1943, SWPC Records. See also *Washington Star*, November 22, 1942.

35. Wright Patman to Roosevelt, December 16, 1942, FDR Papers.

36. James E. Murray Press Release, December 15, 1942, Murray Papers; *New York Times*, January 10, 1943; SB Committee, *Hearings*, part 5, pp. 1148–52, 1337–48; 78th Cong., 1st sess., 1943, SB Committee, *Senate Report* no. 12.

37. Roosevelt memo to James F. Byrnes, December 18, 1942, FDR Papers.

38. Roosevelt memo to Patman, December 22, 1942; Byrnes memo to Roosevelt, January 11, 1943, FDR Papers.

39. Byrnes memo to Roosevelt, January 14, 1943, FDR Papers.

40. Patman to Byrnes, March 20, 1943, FDR Papers. An examination of the Day File of Letters of the chairman of the SWPC in the SWPC Records reveals that Johnson's correspondents were almost exclusively in the East; see Day File of the Chairman for April, May, June, and July 1943, SWPC Records. Johnson tried to appease Murray; see his dinner invitation in Johnson to Murray, June 28, 1943, SWPC Records. On the other hand, Johnson was not obliging westerners by granting loans to their constituents; see Murray to Johnson, January 26, 1943; and Johnson's apologetics in Johnson to Murray, March 17, 30, 31, 1943, SWPC Records. Senator Carl Hayden of Arizona was also upset; see Hayden to Albert Carter (a director of the SWPC), March 9, 1943; and Johnson to Murray, March 11, 1943, on Hayden's complaint concerning the Pine Top Asbestos Mine in Arizona, SWPC Records. Johnson did try to make contact with antitrust advocates like Thurman Arnold; see Johnson to Arnold, August 11, 1942, Arnold Papers. See also Robert W. Johnson, *But, General Johnson*, an apologia; *New York Times*, March 4, August 11, September 17, 1943.

41. A detailed narrative is in "SWPC History," 112–36; see also Johnson to Roosevelt, February 24, 1944 [1943]; and Roosevelt to Johnson, March 2, 1944 [1943], FDR Papers. The only field offices in the West were in Denver and San Francisco. In June 1943 Johnson opened field offices also in Seattle and Los Angeles. See SWPC Report in 78th Cong., 1st sess., 1943, *Senate Report* no. 98, 2–28. Johnson defended himself against regional discrimination toward the West in Johnson to Murray, June 24, 1943, SWPC Records. See also 78th Cong., 1st sess., 1943, *Senate Document* no. 6, 1, 4–6, and 78th Cong., 1st sess., 1943, *Senate Report* no. 134, 1, 2–5, 10, 17–29, for SWPC progress reports. Murray's friend, C. W. Fowler, a SWPC director, was sending unfavorable confidential reports on Johnson to Murray. See Fowler to Charles A. Murray (the senator's son and assistant), July 22, 1943; Fowler to James E. Murray, August 28, 1943; Johnson to James E. Murray, August 30, 1943, Murray Papers.

42. Senator Tom Stewart to Wright Patman, August 3, 1943, Murray Papers. Stewart jestingly noted that the agency might be designated as the "Larger War Plants Corporation." See also Stewart to Murray, August 20, 1943; and Robert K. Lamb (staff director of the Small Business Committee) to Murray, August 24, 1943, Murray Papers. "Administration of the Smaller War Plants Corporation: Confidential Memo from Sub-Committee on Complaints to Small Business Committee," September 18, 1943, Murray Papers. See also Murray to Roosevelt, December 17, 1943, Murray Papers. Drew Pearson in *Washington Post*, October

29, 1943; Murray seems to have been in regular contact with Pearson whenever he "leaked" news.

43. Roosevelt memo to Byrnes, September 20, 1943; Byrnes memo to the President, September 23, 1943, FDR Papers. Murray and Patman also wanted Cooke as the next chairman of the SWPC; see Murray to Roosevelt (telegram), December 17, 1943, copy in Murray Papers, original in FDR Papers.

44. E. M. Watson memo for the President, December 18, 1943; Watson memo to FDR, January 5, 1944; Nelson to Byrnes, January 3, 1944, FDR Papers.

45. The voluminous records of the SWPC in the National Archives have not yet attracted a historian to write a detailed history of that remarkable agency. A detailed account of Maverick's administration is in "SWPC History," 137–50, 158–584, SWPC Records. In addition to the history of the Washington office, these unpublished volumes contain detailed histories of the fourteen regional offices. Regions 8–14 deal directly with western states. On the increase of orders for western business, see 78th Cong., 2d sess., 1944, *Senate Document* no. 246, 28. On Maverick's efforts to secure more orders for the West, see Maverick to Frank Knox, June 25, 1943; Nelson to Maverick, July 11, 1944; Maverick to J. J. Underwood, August 8, 1944, in Maury Maverick Papers, University of Texas, Austin. On Maverick's administrative style as it related to the West, see Maverick to Murray, October 9, 1945; Maverick to Murray, June 21, 1945; Murray to Maverick, February 22, 1944; Murray to Maverick, May 25, 1945, SWPC Records. Ickes originally thought Maverick too volatile, but came to like him better. See Harold L. Ickes Diary, 4476 (June 12, 1940), 7161–62 (November 7, 1942), 7559 (March 20, 1943), 8013 (July 25, 1943), 9147 (August 6, 1944), Library of Congress, Manuscripts Division, Washington, D.C.

2. The Western Mining Industry at War

1. Although the literature on mining in the nineteenth-century West is extensive, for the twentieth century it is spotty. As yet there is no comprehensive history of mining in the West after 1890. For background see Lewis Atherton, "Structure and Balance in Western Mining History," 55–84; Robert G. Cleland, *A History of Phelps Dodge, 1834–1950*; K. Ross Toole, "A History of the Anaconda Mining Company: A Study in the Relationship Between a State and Its People and a Corporation, 1880–1950" (Ph.D. diss., UCLA, 1954); Russell R. Elliott, *Nevada's Twentieth Century Mining Booms*; Robert F. Campbell, *The History of Basic Metals Price Control*, 67–70; Thomas R. Navin, *Copper Mining and Management*, 139–45; Michael Malone, "The Collapse of Western Metal Mining," 455–64; and Gerald W. Thompson, "Frontier West," 373.

2. 77th Cong., 1st sess., 1942, Senate, Sub-Committee of the Committee on Public Lands and Surveys, *Hearings Pursuant to Senate Resolution no. 53* (hereafter cited as *Hearings on S. 53*) 1:780, see also 1:781–86; see also Charles B. Henderson, "Report on Activities of the Metals Reserve Corporation, 28 June 1940 to November 1, 1940," 1–3, 6–10, 16–17, manuscripts in Records, U.S. Metals Reserve Corporation, National Archives, Washington, D.C.; War Production Board (Maryclaire Macauley), "Evolution of the Metals and Minerals Policy of the War Production Board," 13–14, manuscript in Nelson Papers (September 4, 1943), and in-house administrative history of the agency (hereafter cited as "WPB Minerals Policy"). C. K. Leith Memo to M. B. Folsom, October

Notes to Pages 19–25

4, 1940, on Strategic Minerals Procurement Plans, in Records, U.S. War Production Board, National Archives, Washington, D.C. (hereafter cited as WPB Records); Governor Sam Ford (Montana) to Office of Production Management, November 28, 1941, urging more domestic production, in Secretary's File, U.S. Department of the Interior, National Archives, Washington, D.C. (hereafter cited as DI Records). See also Campbell, *Basic Metals Price Control*, 32–35, 86–87, 90, 101, 171; and *Engineering and Mining Journal* (November 1940), 60.

3. SB Committee, *Hearings*, part 27, pp. 3489, 3493; 78th Cong., 2d sess., 1944, Senate, Sub-Committee on Mining and the Minerals Industry, *Senate Sub-Committee Print no. 6*, 16–31 (hereafter cited as *Sub-Committee Print no. 6*); Stephen Rauschenbush memo for J. L. Sayers, August 26, 1942, DI Records.

4. SB Committee, *Hearings*, part 27, pp. 3491–92; *Sub-Committee Print no. 6*, 31–51; Senator Carl Hayden was already badgering Donald Nelson to accommodate the small miners in the West; see Nelson to Hayden, December 23, 1942; and Hayden to James E. Murray, December 31, 1942, Hayden Papers.

5. SB Committee, *Hearings*, part 26, p. 3351; "Transcript of meeting of Assistant Secretary of the Interior Oscar Chapman with miners in Butte, Montana, March 16, 1942," 1–8, DI Records. Chapman was making a tour to meet with western miners; see transcripts of meetings with miners in Reno, Nevada, March 12, 1942, 1–9; in Portland, Oregon, March 14, 1942, 1–5; in Laramie, Wyoming, March 20, 1942, 1–10, DI Records.

6. SB Committee, *Hearings*, part 26, p. 3455; "Transcript of meeting of Assistant Secretary of the Interior Oscar Chapman with miners of Colorado in Denver, March 18, 1942," DI Records; Ickes Diary, 6402 (March 7, 1942), and 6497 (April 5, 1942).

7. SB Committee, *Hearings*, part 27, p. 3364; Roosevelt to Dennis Chavez (New Mexico), August 16, 1940, on utilizing minerals in that state, FDR Papers. See also "Small Mine Operators v. Strategic Minerals," *Mining Journal* (May 15, 1942).

8. SB Committee, *Hearings*, part 27, p. 3472; Thurman Arnold was concerned about what he considered WPB favoritism to large mining companies; see Ickes Diary, 6898 (August 8, 1942).

9. SB Committee, *Hearings*, part 27, p. 3544; see also Pat McCarran to Carl Hayden, March 10, 1043, Hayden Papers.

10. SB Committee, *Hearings*, part 27, pp. 3530–31; *Washington Post*, October 16, 1942. Ickes intervened for small miners to secure processing facilities in the Pacific Northwest; see Ickes to William Knudsen, December 15, 1941, DI Records. The WPB did not view itself in this light, judged by its own account of these policies; see "WPB Minerals Policy," 1–34.

11. SB Committee, *Hearings*, part 27, p. 3531; Carl Hayden to Ralph Henderson, January 25, 1944, Hayden Papers; "WPB Minerals Policy," 30, notes ruefully that the WPB staff had to defend itself before the Small Business Committee on March 30, 31, 1943, including Frank Ayer, Harry King, E. F. Hatch, and Andrew Leith.

12. *Sub-Committee Print no. 6*, 72–75; SB Committee, *Hearings*, part 26, p. 3392, and part 27, pp. 3541, 3572, 3582, 3594; U.S. Bureau of Mines, *Minerals Yearbook*, 1941 (Washington, 1942), 67; Maryclaire Macauley for U.S. Civil Production Administration, "The Closing of the Gold Mines," 1–4, unpublished administrative history, available on microfilm from Research Publications in "Administrative Histories of World War II" series. Original in WPB Records.

13. Macauley, "Closing Gold Mines," 9, 15; 77th Cong., 2d sess., 1942, Senate, Sub-Committee of Special Committee on Investigation of Silver, *Hearings* (May 5, 6, 8, 28, 1942), 562; *New York Times*, March 16, October 7, 9, 1942.

14. McCarran, quoted in Macauley, "Closing Gold Mines," 33; Stephen Rauschenbush to J. L. Sayers, August 26, 1942, DI Records; Pat McCarran and 20 Western U.S. Senators to Roosevelt, October 10, 1942, protesting the closing, FDR Papers. *Denver Post*, August 13, October 9, 10, 12, 18, 1942; *Rocky Mountain News*, October 6, 7, 1942.

15. Letter is reproduced in Macauley, "Closing Gold Mines," 43–44; Donald Nelson to Roosevelt, October 16, 1942; Roosevelt to Carl Hatch, October 17, 1942, FDR Papers. U.S. War Production Board, *Minutes*, meeting 34, October 6, 1942.

16. Memorandum is reproduced in Macauley, "Closing Gold Mines," 45; *Rocky Mountain News*, October 14, 1942. McCarran charged that his life was threatened because of his stand. *Denver Post*, December 16, 1942.

17. *New York Times*, October 15, 1942. Western Congressmen introduced bills to reverse L-208, without success. See *Cong. Rec.*, 78th Cong., 1st sess., S. 27 (January 7, 1943), S. 344 (January 14, 1943), and H.R. 3009 (June 19, 1943).

18. *New York Times*, May 25, June 16, 1943; WPB, *Minutes*, meeting 61, June 15, 1943.

19. Text of memo in Macauley, "Closing Gold Mines," 50.

20. Ibid., 52.

21. WPB, *Minutes*, November 23, 1942, record of Inter-Division meeting of Divisions Concerned with Mineral Production; Wilbur Nelson memo to H. W. Dodge, November 24, 1942, noted in Macauley, "Closing Gold Mines," 56–58; for Donald Nelson's defense, see his statements in SB Committee, *Hearings*, part 18, pp. 2446–48.

22. Harold L. Ickes to Joseph C. O'Mahoney, February 6, 1942, DI Records, but also reproduced in 77th Cong., 2d sess., 1942, *Senate Report* no. 838, 1, 3, 4, 5; Abe Fortas to E. P. Carville, February 18, 1942 in Pat McCarran Papers, Nevada State Historical Society, Reno. I examined these papers at the Nevada State Archives in Carson City before they were moved to Reno. The *Engineering and Mining Journal*, March 1942, had caustic editorials on Ickes's plans, which it likened to Joseph Stalin's five-year plans. See also R. S. Dean to Stephen Rauschenbush, March 27, 1942, DI Records. Ickes tried hard to win Roosevelt to his program "to yield from this country's own natural resources . . . the minerals and metals necessary for prosecution of the war"; see Ickes memo for the President, March 10, 1942, DI Records. See also Ickes to John Boettiger, February 5, 1941, on the need to hold western liberals together, in Harold L. Ickes Papers, Library of Congress, Manuscripts Division, Washington, D.C.; *Time* (February 23, 1942), 34.

23. *Hearings on S. 53*, 5–6; Press Release, Department of the Interior, February 16, 1942, "Minerals and Power to Win the War and Develop the West," 1–8, in E. P. Carville Papers, Nevada State Archives, Carson City.

24. *Hearings on S. 53*, 6; Abe Fortas to E. P. Carville, February 9, 1942, McCarran Papers, assuring him that the Department of the Interior would seek maximum development of western minerals resources. See also Abe Fortas to Carville, February 17, 1942, DI Records.

25. *Hearings on S. 53*, 6; although westerners like Carville supported Ickes's minerals program, they emphasized that the states should have a significant

role in their development; Carville to Abe Fortas, March 13, 1942, McCarran Papers.

26. *Hearings on S. 53*, 7; Ickes Speech File, 3215–38, Ickes Papers.

27. SB Committee, *Hearings*, part 13, pp. 1802–4; see also Ickes's remarks in part 18, p. 2397–98.

28. Ibid., part 13, p. 1803 and part 18, pp. 2400–2401.

29. Ibid., part 13, p. 1804.

30. Ibid., 1808–10, 1816.

31. Ibid., part 18, pp. 2397–98.

32. *Hearings on S. 53*, 327–28; on Slattery see J. Leonard Bates, *The Origins of Teapot Dome*, 3–7.

33. *Hearings on S. 53*, 333; *New York Times*, August 21, 22, 1941.

34. *Hearings on S. 53*, 334.

35. Ibid., 406.

36. Ibid., 405, 410.

37. Ibid., 185–207.

38. Ibid., 248.

39. Ibid., 435, 437, 438, 439, 446.

40. SB Committee, *Hearings*, part 26, pp. 3293–96; James E. Murray to Roosevelt, February 19, 1943, FDR Papers, also reprinted in ibid., part 27, pp. 3521–22; see also Murray to Joseph Guffey, May 1, 1943, in Elbert D. Thomas Papers, Franklin D. Roosevelt Library, Hyde Park, New York.

41. SB Committee, *Hearings*, part 29, pp. 3834, 3836, 3838; see also part 13, p. 1801.

42. Ibid., part 27, p. 3467, and part 28, pp. 3606, 3607, 3608.

43. Ibid., part 27, pp. 3477–78.

44. Ibid., part 29, p. 3904.

45. *Hearings on S. 53*, 18; on sentiment for stockpiling, see Julian Conover (secretary of the American Mining Congress) to Elbert Thomas, February 20, 1943, Thomas Papers.

46. *Hearings on S. 53*, 22, 38.

47. Murray to Roosevelt, February 19, 1943, in SB Committee, *Hearings*, part 27, p. 3522; Murray to Nelson, May 24, 1943, Hayden Papers; Roosevelt to Nelson, March 11, 1943, Nelson Papers; "WPB Minerals Policy," 27, 31–33.

48. Nelson to Roosevelt, April 17, 1943, Nelson Papers, also reprinted in SB Committee, *Hearings*, part 27, pp. 3522–23. See also Roosevelt to Murray, April 24, 1943, Murray Papers (a copy was also found in the McCarran Papers and the FDR Papers) and Pat McCarran to Thomas, March 10, 1943, Thomas Papers. Macauley noted in "WPB Minerals Policy," 2, that Nelson prepared the policy statement only under intense pressure from Murray and that it required a departure from prevailing WPB policies by placing greater emphasis on domestic production.

49. SB Committee, *Hearings*, part 27, pp. 3523–25; Nelson in ibid., part 18, pp. 2438–42, 2444; Senator Scrugham of the Small Business Committee said, "It is clear that Mr. Nelson followed the Committee's suggestions nearly to the letter" (quoted in "WPB Minerals Policy," 33).

50. Harold L. Ickes to Sam Rayburn, May 21, 1943, McCarran Papers. Ickes pleaded: "It is essential to the proper administration of the lands that some satisfactory disposition be made of the large number of invalid and speculative claims which exist on the public domain. . . . The situation calls for legislative action." Rayburn sent a copy to McCarran, who was negatively inclined to the suggestion.

3. Wartime Industries in the West: Shipbuilding

1. 76th Cong., 1st sess., 1939, House, Committee on Merchant Marine and Fisheries, *Hearings on Dry Dock Facilities on the West Coast*, 19–23; 78th Cong., 2d sess., 1944, House Sub-Committee on Production in Shipbuilding Plants, Committee on Merchant Marine and Fisheries, *Executive Hearings*, part 3, pp. 533, 550 (hereafter cited as *PSP Hearings*); Lane, *Ships for Victory*, is the official history of the U.S. Maritime Commission in World War II. Shipbuilding in the West has not yet attracted the attention it deserves.

2. 76th Cong., 2d sess., 1942, House, Committee on Merchant Marine and Fisheries, *Hearings on Higgins Contracts, July 22–25, 1942*, 47, 57, 67–72 (hereafter cited as *Higgins Hearings*); *Time*, July 27, 1942, pp. 71, 74.

3. SB Committee, *Hearings*, part 21, pp. 2945, and part 30, pp. 4055–63; for photographs of Denver shipyards, see part 30, pp. 4124–26, 4170–89; *Denver Post*, August 16, 23, 1942; *Rocky Mountain News*, August 19, 23, 1942; Arnold S. Lott, *A Long Line of Ships*, 212–14.

4. In announcing an emergency shipbuilding program Roosevelt advocated building a minimum of two hundred ships that year. *New York Times*, January 17, 1941; 78th Cong., 2d sess., 1944, House, Sub-Committee on Shipyard Profits of Committee on Merchant Marine and Fisheries, *Hearings on House Resolution no. 52*, 85–86 (hereafter cited as *Ship Profits Hearings*). On Marinship, see 78th Cong., 1st and 2d sess., 1944, House, Committee on Merchant Marine and Fisheries, *Executive Hearings on Rheem Manufacturing Company*, 55, 59–61, 63–65 (hereafter cited as *Rheem Manufacturing Co. Hearings*). Professor Carroll Pursell has written an unpublished manuscript on aspects of the Marinship operation in World War II. See also "Marin City, California," *Architectural Forum* (December 1943), 67–74. Quote in *New York Times*, December 11, 1940.

5. *PSP Hearings*, part 3, pp. 915–16; for detailed maps of the West Coast shipyards, see Records, Oregon Shipbuilding Company, Oregon Historical Society, Portland.

6. Vickery in *PSP Hearings*, part 3, p. 916. See also Land in *Higgins Hearings*, 73, 82; Vickery in *Rheem Manufacturing Co. Hearings*, 61–63, 92; and Land in *Ship Profits Hearings*, 6, 8, 11.

7. *PSP Hearings*, part 3, p. 916; Lane, *Ships for Victory*, 463–66.

8. Bechtel in *PSP Hearings*, part 3, pp. 691–95, 697, 699–708; *Calshipbuilding Company* (San Pedro, 1947), 13, 28, copy in Oregon Historical Society.

9. *Rheem Manufacturing Co. Hearings*, 63–65, 94.

10. *PSP Hearings*, part 3, pp. 891–93, 905; *Rheem Manufacturing Co. Hearings*, 251–52.

11. *PSP Hearings*, part 4, pp. 919–25, for Henry J. Kaiser and Oregonship operations. Mark Foster generously let me read the manuscript of his forthcoming biography of Henry J. Kaiser. See also *Current Biography*, 1942, pp. 431–35; *Time* (March 3, 1941), 67–68, and (September 21, 1942), 171; on Todd-Kaiser problems, see Kaiser to John Reilly (President, Todd Shipyards), March 20, 1941; and also transcript of telephone conversation, Kaiser and Reilly, June 4, 1941, in Henry J. Kaiser Papers, Bancroft Library, University of California, Berkeley.

12. *Higgins Hearings*, 252–53; *PSP Hearings*, part 3, p. 905; Kaiser to Tom Corcoran, June 16, 1941, Kaiser Papers, on reluctance of Jesse Jones to expand Kaiser shipbuilding operations.

13. *PSP Hearings*, part 3, p. 915.

14. *PSP Hearings*, part 3, p. 905; see also *New York Times,* January 3, February 8, 1942.

15. *PSP Hearings*, part 3, p. 622, part 4, p. 1100; Charles Mann, "Emergency Shipyards of the Pacific Northwest," *Marine Engineering and Shipping Review,* (October 1942), 199; "Shipbuilding Activity in Portland, Oregon," *The Log* 37 (June 1942): 37; *Monthly Labor Review* 55 (November 1942): 926–27. See also Records, Oregon War Industries, Oregon Historical Society, Portland. This was a consortium of small companies in the area who collaborated to become a prime contractor for the U.S. Maritime Commission. See also remarks of Edgar Kaiser, October 19, 1941, in Edgar Kaiser Papers, Oregon Historical Society, Portland.

16. *Rheem Manufacturing Co. Hearings,* 94; Margery E. Moore, "Brief History of Oregonship Company," manuscript in Edgar Kaiser Papers, 1–2; *Transactions of the Northeast Coast Institute of Engineers and Shipbuilders,* 59:D 47–64; *The Log* 37 (October 1942): 25; Van Rensselear Sill, *American Miracle,* 161.

17. *PSP Hearings*, part 3, p. 691, and part 4, pp. 1000, 1015; "Sources of Labor Supply in West Coast Shipyards and Aircraft Parts Plants," *Monthly Labor Review* 55 (November 1942): 926–27; *The Log* 37 (June 1942): 37.

18. 79th Cong., 2d sess., 1946, House, Committee on Merchant Marine and Fisheries, *Hearings on House Resolution no. 38,* 7–9 (hereafter cited as *Hearings no. 38*); *Ship Profits Hearings,* 7–9. Hannay, Jr., in *PSP Hearings,* part 4, pp. 926–28, 930; Hannay, Sr., in ibid., 1002.

19. Lane, *Ships for Victory,* 139–40, based on an analysis of Maritime Commission work sheets.

20. 77th Cong., 1st sess., 1941–47, Senate, Special Committee Investigating the National Defense Program, *Hearings,* part 12, pp. 5177–98 (hereafter cited as *Truman Committee Hearings). PSP Hearings,* part 3, p. 916; *Rheem Manufacturing Co. Hearings,* 96; *Journal of Commerce,* April 28, 1942; 77th Cong., 2d sess., 1943, House, Committee on Merchant Marine and Fisheries, *Interim Report on Investigation of South Portland Shipbuilding Company, 1942,* 5, 11–12. Lane, *Ships for Victory,* 465–66.

21. Flesher in *PSP Hearings,* part 3, pp. 578, 583; see also 561–62, 571–73, 582; Moore in ibid., part 3, p. 633.

22. *Marine Engineering and Shipping Review* (April 1943), 182–90; Lane, *Ships for Victory,* 220.

23. *The Log* 37 (June 1942): 30, 64; *PSP Hearings,* part 4, pp. 1110–12.

24. G. Guy Via, "The Wartime Training of Shipbuilders," Society of Naval Architects and Marine Engineers, *Transactions,* 1942, p. 325.

25. *Truman Committee Hearings,* part 23, pp. 9998, 10,000–10,024.

26. Ibid., 10,027, 10,029, 10,030–32; and on Wilson see 9977. See also ibid., 9993.

27. Ibid., 10,201, 10,202.

28. Ibid., 9942–43. "Wonder Man Hit: Henry J. Kaiser Replies to Charges of Faulty Construction," *Business Week* (March 27, 1943), 30.

29. *New York Times,* January 18, 1943; Simon Lubin memo for Roosevelt, March 23, 1945, FDR Papers, notes that despite the bad publicity surrounding the ship crack-ups, Kaiser was still a hero to American troops, and General Eisenhower asked him to visit the front lines in Europe to boost morale. *Truman Committee Hearings,* part 23, pp. 9951–52.

30. *Truman Committee Hearings,* part 23, pp. 9949–50, 10,066, 10,108.

31. *Washington Evening Star*, January 20, 1944; *Marine Engineering and Shipping Review* (April 1943), 207–8; *Truman Committee Hearings*, part 18, pp. 7148–75, 7179–94, and part 23, pp. 9938–40, 10,011–13.

32. 78th Cong., 2d sess., 1944, House, Committee on Merchant Marine and Fisheries, "Investigation of Plate Fractures on Welded Ships," *House Report* no. 1685, 1–19; see also *New York Times*, January 21, 1943.

33. *Truman Committee Hearings*, part 18, pp. 7179–94, and part 23, p. 9937.

34. Ibid., part 23, pp. 10,160–61, 10,171.

35. Ibid., part 23, p. 10,198; for Stubbs see 9942–43, and for Bedford, 10,200.

36. "Union Agreements in Shipbuilding," *Monthly Labor Review* 51 (September 1940): 597–99, and "Characteristics of Shipbuilding Labor Hired During First Six Months of 1941," ibid. 53 (February 1942): 393; John A. Yancy, "Training a Democracy to Build Liberty Ships," *Marine Engineering and Shipping Review* (November 1943), 188–89; *PSP Hearings*, part 1, pp. 67, 120, 134; *Truman Committee Hearings*, part 4, p. 1237, and part 18, pp. 7381–84. See also Frank J. Taylor, "Builder no. 1," 11.

37. "Collective Bargaining on the Pacific Coast," *Monthly Labor Review* 64 (April 1947): 551; American Federation of Labor, Metal Trades Department, *Proceedings of the 32d Convention*, November 11, 1940, 31–36, and also *Proceedings of the 35th Convention*, September 27, 1943, p. 132; *Truman Committee Hearings*, part 4, pp. 1143–47, 1237; *New York Times*, March 18, 1942.

38. *PSP Hearings*, part 1, p. 2; *Truman Committee Hearings*, part 18, p. 7384, for Frey; A.F. of L., Metals Trades Department, *Proceedings of 32d Convention*, 32–33, and *Proceedings of 35th Convention*, 131; Lane, *Ships for Victory*, 278–83.

39. William Green to Roosevelt, November 21, 1942, FDR Papers, explaining his appraisal of Master Agreement. Green was president of the A.F. of L. *PSP Hearings*, part 1, pp. 3, 6–10; see 88–97 for a copy of the Master Agreement; *New York Times*, April 20, 1942.

40. H. A. Millis (chairman of the National Labor Relations Board) acquainted Roosevelt with the Oregon case in a letter of December 9, 1942, whereas John Green (president of the C.I.O.'s Industrial Union of Marine and Shipbuilding Workers of America) presented his side in a letter to Roosevelt, January 22, 1943, FDR Papers. *New York Times*, May 15, 1943.

41. *PSP Hearings*, part 1, pp. 67, 75, 120, 134; *Truman Committee Hearings*, part 18, pp. 7303–55.

42. American Federation of Labor, International Brotherhood of Boilermakers, *Proceedings of the 17th Convention*, January 31–February 9, 1943, pp. 154–56, 175; Marvin McIntire to A. A. McAdam, February 6, 1944; and McIntire to L. M. Russell, February 6, 1944, FDR Papers. Roosevelt instructed McIntire to inform others that he had not made a final disposition of the issues. Frey's version in *PSP Hearings*, part 1, pp. 4–7, 8–10, 12–16.

43. Text of resolution in *PSP Hearings*, part 1, p. 20; see also 17–19, 80–85, 101–7.

44. 78th Cong., 1st sess., 1943, House, Sub-Committee on Appropriations, Appropriation Bill for 1944, *Hearings*, part 1, pp. 323–24; *Truman Committee Hearings*, part 18, pp. 7381–88; Lane, *Ships for Victory*, 296–97.

45. See Moore in *PSP Hearings*, part 3, p. 631; Katherine Archibald, *Wartime Shipyard*, 104–5.

46. Boilermakers, *Proceedings of the 17th Convention*, 295–98; Malcolm Ross, *All Manner of Men* (New York: Reynal and Hitchcock, 1948), 142–46, 149–52.

47. Fair Employment Practices Committee, "California Shipbuilding Company *v.* International Brotherhood of Boilermakers," in Records of the Fair Employment Practices Committee, Region 12, Federal Records Center, San Bruno, California (hereafter cited as FEPC Records); and Harry Kingman to Barney Mayes, January 25, 1944, FEPC Records. James *v.* Marinship, 25 Cal 2d 721; 78th Cong., 1st sess., 1944, House, Sub-Committee of Committee on Naval Affairs, *Hearings on Congested Areas*, part 4, pp. 857–63 (hereafter cited as *Congested Areas Hearings*).

48. *Oregon Journal,* February 26, March 13, 1942; *PSP Hearings,* part 1, p. 309.

49. *PSP Hearings,* part 1, p. 314.

50. Agnes Meyer wrote about the dissatisfactions of women in the Portland yards in the *Washington Post,* March 28, 1943; see also Augusta Clawson, *Shipyard Diary of a Woman Welder;* Dorothy K. Newman, "Employing Women in the Shipyards," U.S. Women's Bureau, *Bulletin* no. 192 (Washington, 1944); *PSP Hearings,* part 1, pp. 73–74.

51. Roosevelt was concerned about working conditions in shipyards and on December 22, 1943, wrote Admiral Land about the need for more cafeterias, rest rooms, and locker facilities. See Lane, *Ships for Victory,* 449, and Land's testimony in 78th Cong., 2d sess., 1945, Senate, Committee on Appropriations, Independent Offices Appropriation Bill for 1945, *Hearings,* 189; *PSP Hearings,* part 1, p. 414; Philip Drinker, "Health and Safety in Shipyards," American Merchant Marine Conference, *Proceedings,* 1944, p. 111, touches on the pinkeye epidemic in West Coast yards in 1942–43.

52. *PSP Hearings,* part 4, p. 1156.

53. Adolf A. Berle and Gardiner C. Means, *The Modern Corporation and Private Property.*

54. *Hearings no. 38,* 107, 129; on Kaiser see ibid., 40–66. On Berle's role, see Jordan A. Schwarz, *Liberal.*

55. *Hearings no. 38,* 2–4.

56. Ibid., 6, 7, 9, 11; some of Kaiser's contracts were later renegotiated. 79th Cong., 1st sess., 1945, House, Committee on Ways and Means, *Hearings on 1945 Extension of Termination Date of Renegotiation Act,* 135, 138.

57. *Hearings no. 38,* 40, 41. In the November 1944 elections Kaiser organized a Non-Partisan Association for encouraging voter participation. Roosevelt was grateful for the effort, which he felt had been beneficial for the Democrats. See Roosevelt to Kaiser, January 10, 1945, FDR Papers; *Truman Committee Hearings,* part 42, pp. 25,508–15. Lane, *Ships for Victory,* 802–6.

58. *Hearings no. 38,* 4, 25, 43; 79th Cong., 2d sess., 1946, House, Committee on Merchant Marine and Fisheries, *Hearings on the Accounting Practices of the War Shipping Administration and U.S. Maritime Commission,* 129–31, 210.

59. *Hearings no. 38,* 131.

60. Ibid., 13, 14, 17.

4. The Western Aircraft Industry

1. A good history of the western aircraft industry has not yet been written. But see John B. Rae, *Climb to Greatness;* William G. Cunningham, *The Aircraft Industry,* 75–77; J. Carlyle Sitterson, *Aircraft Production Policies;* Craven and Cate, eds., *Army Air Forces in World War II;* Tom Lilley et al., *Problems of*

Accelerating Aircraft Production in World War II, 4–13; U.S., President's Air Policy Commission, *Survival in the Air Age*, 51–52, 67–68; J. J. Croston, "Expansion of the Aircraft Industry to Meet War Demands," *Monthly Labor Review* 52 (February 1941): 327; Michael S. Sherry, *The Rise of American Air Power;* for Roosevelt's call for fifty thousand planes, see *New York Times*, May 17, 1940; for General George C. Marshall's statement, see U.S. Army, Chief of Staff, *Biennial Report*, July 1, 1943, to June 30, 1945, p. 117.

2. Frank J. Taylor and Lawton Wright, *Democracy's Air Arsenal*, 46; Cunningham, *Aircraft Industry*, 49–55, 75–97; T. P. Wright, "America's Answer," *Aviation* (June 1939), 6.

3. Cunningham, *Aircraft Industry*, 53. *New York Times*, August 9, 1942.

4. *Truman Committee Hearings*, part 6, pp. 1859, 1860, 1861. *New York Times*, January 13, May 1, June 8, 1941, and June 26, August 15, 16, 1942.

5. *Truman Committee Hearings*, part 31, p. 15,449; see also remarks of Gage H. Irving, vice-president of Northrop, in *Truman Committee Hearings*, part 6, p. 1875; for a list of airplane projects initiated during the war see *Truman Committee Hearings*, part 43, p. 27,221.

6. Taylor and Wright, *Democracy's Air Arsenal*, 98; *Truman Committee Hearings*, part 31, pp. 15,366–74; Boeing Company, *Pedigree of Champions. New York Times*, November 5, 1941, and June 6, 26, 1942.

7. *Truman Committee Hearings*, part 40, pp. 24,298–99.

8. U.S. Surplus Property Administration, *Aircraft Plants and Facilities*, 7. The DPC financed about 75 percent of the expansion undertaken by aircraft companies. See White, *Billions for Defense*, 68–71; Taylor and Wright, *Democracy's Air Arsenal*, 167–73.

9. *Truman Committee Hearings*, part 6, pp. 1856–57.

10. Ibid., 1865.

11. Monroe in ibid., 1870–71, and Douglas in *ibid.*, 1854; Washington State University, Bureau of Business Research, *The Impact of World War II Subcontracting*, 9–20, 22–48; John S. Day, *Sub-contracting Policy in the Airframe Industry*, 20–25.

12. Glenn Hotchkiss, "Modification Centers: An American Military Innovation," *Aviation* (April 1943), 134–36; "Modification Centers Fit Military Planes for Combat," *Aero Digest* (September 1943), 128; for a particular center, see Jesse R. Wood, "Wings for the U.S. Army Air Forces—Review of Continental Denver Modification Center," 4, manuscript in World War II Records Collection, Colorado State Historical Society, Denver. This facility modified 2,073 B-17 and 402 B-29 bombers. See also Taylor and Wright, *Democracy's Air Arsenal*, 98–100, and Cunningham, *Aircraft Industry*, 94–95, 132–35.

13. *Truman Committee Hearings*, part 6, p. 1865.

14. Taylor and Wright, *Democracy's Air Arsenal*, 44–45.

15. Lilley et al., *Aircraft Production*, 37–44, 46–49, 50–52; Taylor and Wright, *Democracy's Air Arsenal*, 46–47. *New York Times*, October 3, 5, 1942.

16. Taylor and Wright, *Democracy's Air Arsenal*, 47; Cunningham, *Aircraft Industry*, 89, n. 30; see also the charts of Boeing Aircraft Company concerning increased engineering man-hours, design, and aerodynamic development, in *Truman Committee Hearings*, part 31, p. 15,577; see also table showing floor area of Consolidated Aircraft Company in ibid., 15,588; U.S. Department of Commerce, Office of Aviation Information, *U.S. Military Aircraft Acceptances, 1940–1945, Aircraft, Engine and Propeller Production* (Washington, 1945).

17. Leonard G. Levenson, "Wartime Development of the Aircraft Industry,"

Monthly Labor Review 59 (November 1944): 910–11, 915; Cunningham, *Aircraft Industry,* 79–81.

18. *Truman Committee Hearings,* part 31, pp. 15,367–71.

19. Statistics in *Monthly Labor Review* 59 (November 1944): 911–13; for figures on turnover, see ibid., 922–25; Taylor and Wright, *Democracy's Air Arsenal,* 107–9.

20. Cunningham, *Aircraft Industry,* 21–24, 39–44, 130–35, 169–70; Douglas in Taylor and Wright, *Democracy's Air Arsenal,* 115, 116–18. Arthur P. Allen and Betty V. Schneider, *Industrial Relations in the California Aircraft Industry.*

21. National Negro Congress, Los Angeles Council, *Jim Crow in National Defense,* 13; Lester B. Granger, "Negroes and War Production," *Survey Graphic* 31 (November 1942): 470; Memo of Clarence Johnson to Robert C. Weaver, January 17, 1942, concerning employment of Negroes and minorities at Boeing, FEPC Records, Region 12; Charles P. Clark Interview with Rayford Logan, July 11, 1941, in Records, U.S. Senate, Special Committee to Investigate the National Defense Program, 1941–47, National Archives, Washington, D.C. (hereafter cited as Truman Committee Records). See also Archibald, *Wartime Shipyard,* 58–99.

22. Quote in *Congested Areas Hearings,* part 2, p. 469; see also pp. 449–53, 524; Memo of H. C. Legg to Corrington Gill, April 27, 1944, on food problems at Consolidated Vultee, in Records, U.S. Committee for Congested Production Areas, National Archives, Washington, D.C. See also *Monthly Labor Review* 59 (November 1944), 909, 913, 915–16, 919–27; Nash, *American West Transformed,* 58–61.

23. Lilley et al., *Aircraft Production,* 19, 22–25, 32–38, 39–49, 72–73; 77th Cong., 2d sess., 1942, Senate, Special Committee to Investigate National Defense Expenditures, *Report* no. 480, part 5, p. 62; Cunningham, *Aircraft Industry,* 78–80.

24. According to recollections of Glenn Odekirk, a designer of the Hughes transport, in *New York Times,* January 15, 1987; a fine, detailed account of the project is in Charles Barton, *Howard Hughes and His Flying Boat.* Donald Nelson to G. Loening, August 10, 1942, inviting him to join a committee to help Kaiser prepare designs, in *Truman Committee Hearings,* part 40, p. 23,546; and Loening to Nelson, August 12, 1942, in ibid., 23,546; Nelson to Kaiser, August 10, 1942, in ibid., 24,430.

25. Roosevelt to William D. Leahy, July 27, 1942, asking him to make preliminary cost estimates; Leahy to Marvin McIntire, August 1, 1942, noted that all the army and navy officers to whom he spoke thought that such planes might be desirable, "but I have found nobody who believes Mr. Kaiser can do what he promises," FDR Papers. Roosevelt was more optimistic and in a memo to McIntire noted, "I am trying to get order out of the Kaiser problem and things are going quite well" (Roosevelt to McIntire, August 12, 1942, FDR Papers). *Truman Committee Hearings,* part 40, pp. 23,580–83, 23,741–48. *New York Daily Mirror,* July 30, 1947, reported that the daughter of Donald Douglas married General Hap Arnold's son, creating an interesting relationship; Kaiser telegram to Grover Leoning, August 18, 1942; and Loening to Kaiser, August 19, 1942, in *Truman Committee Hearings,* part 40, pp. 23,542–43, 24,388.

26. *Washington Times Herald,* July 29, 1942; *New York Times,* July 29, 30, 31, 1942; Kaiser in *Truman Committee Hearings,* part 40, pp. 23,585–86. Ickes was strongly in favor of the project; see Ickes Diary, 6901–2 (August 8, 1942). Martin in part 40, p. 23,761; quote on 23,688; Kaiser on 23,587–92; exhibits on

23,515, *Truman Committee Hearings.* Kaiser Press Release, July 29, 1947, Kaiser Papers.

27. Martin in *Truman Committee Hearings,* part 40, p. 23,693, and Kaiser, 23,601, 23,612–20; report of meeting held in office of Donald Nelson, July 27, 1942, ibid., 24,386; *Washington Post,* August 24, 1942; *Truman Committee Hearings,* part 14, pp. 5759–69; Harold E. Talbott to Jesse Jones, September 15, 1942, recommending a contract, FDR Papers.

28. For Kaiser see part 40, pp. 23,621–25; for Hughes, 24,257; a copy of the contract is on 24,433; Jesse Jones to Donald Nelson, September 17, 1942, p. 24,442; and discussion by Jones, 23,625, 23,699–703, *Truman Committee Hearings.* I have examined a voluminous file of correspondence on the Kaiser-Hughes plane between Jones, Truman, and Nelson in WPB Records, Box 192.

29. For a detailed account of WPB policy on the plane, see Nelson to Truman, February 11, 1944, FDR Papers. *Truman Committee Hearings,* part 40, p. 23,740; Patterson's memo on ibid., 23,741; Patterson to Nelson, July 30, 1942, details the opposition of the Joint Chiefs of Staff to the plane, ibid., 24,449. For Jones see ibid., 26,631; for a detailed account of Kaiser's role as seen by his staff, Frank O'Conner memo to Vance Fawcett, July 24, 1947, Kaiser Papers, is good.

30. *Truman Committee Hearings,* part 40, pp. 24,257, 24,345–48. On the close monitoring of his progress, see W. R. Morgan to W. E. Joyce, December 2, 1942, pp. 23,760–62; D. A. Gannon memo for C. W. Comstock, August 27, 1943, pp. 23,762–64; H. R. Edward to William E. Joyce, February 19, 1944, pp. 24,451–52; Sam Husbands to Hughes, February 22, 1944, p. 23,775, all in *Truman Committee Hearings,* part 40.

31. Ibid., 24,357, 24,362–65. Loening to Nelson, February 22, 1943, p. 24,392; Loening memo to Charles E. Wilson, September 29, 1943, p. 24,396; and Loening memo to Wilson, October 6, 1943, p. 24,405, all in *Truman Committee Hearings,* part 40.

32. Ibid., 24,267, 24,280, 24,367. A typical popular account is Albert B. Gerber, *Bashful Billionnaire,* 37–86.

33. *Truman Committee Hearings,* part 40, pp. 24,368–69, 24,371, 24,374, 24,377–79; Hughes in ibid., part 43, pp. 26,463–67, 26,471–75; Nelson to Jones, February 12, 1944, FDR Papers; Jones to Nelson, February 16, 1944, FDR Papers; and memo of Jones conversation with Roosevelt, February 18, 1944, in *Truman Committee Hearings,* part 40, p. 24,444.

34. *Truman Committee Hearings,* part 40, pp. 24,299, 24,303, 24,304, 24,305; Minutes of Aircraft Production Board, October 4, 1943, on p. 24,408, and October 11, 1943, reaffirming cancellation, and meeting of November 1, 1943, p. 24,410; A. C. Strickland to Donald Wilson, March 24, 1942, pp. 23,663–64; Donald Nelson to Harry Truman, February 11, 1944, p. 24,415, all in *Truman Committee Hearings,* part 40. *New York Herald Tribune,* July 30, 1947; see also extensive clipping file in Kaiser Papers.

35. *New York Times,* November 1, 2, 1947; Hughes in *Truman Committee Hearings,* part 40, pp. 24,356, 24,357. Hughes Aircraft to Frank Ronan, February 10, 1946, p. 24,472; G. W. Lewis to G. Loening on future possibilities of plane, January 27, 1944, p. 24,414; James V. Forrestal to John W. Snyder, August 24, 1945, rejecting further testing, pp. 23,726–27, *Truman Committee Hearings,* part 40.

36. *Truman Committee Hearings,* part 40, pp. 24,367–70. Jones memo for Roosevelt, June 27, 1942, and Roosevelt memo for General H. H. Arnold, July 7, 1942, ibid., p. 24,445; Arnold to Roosevelt, July 8, 1942, ibid., 24,446–47. Drawings of the plane are in ibid, part 43, p. 27,162.

37. Ibid., part 40, pp. 24,370, 24,450. Vice-president, Hughes Aircraft to Chief, Materiel Division, Army Air Corps, December 5, 1939, p. 24,473; B. E. Meyers to Wright Field, April 11, 1941, p. 24,475; negative views of Lieutenant Colonel Paul H. Kemmer are in memo of October 3, 1941, p. 24,476, and of Brigadier General George C. Kenney, 24,477; B. E. Meyers to Assistant Chief of Staff, June 30, 1942, p. 23,811; transcript of telephone conversation between O. P. Echols and F. O. Carroll, July 29, 1942, p. 24,480; on the formal contract for the F-11, see L. S. Robinson to Hughes Tool Company, October 11, 1943, p. 24,531, all in *Truman Committee Hearings*, part 40.

38. On Elliott Roosevelt see his *As He Saw It*, 225, which is not helpful. *New York Times*, November 15, 1944, and August 2, 3, 4, 1947. *Washington Star*, November 15, 1944; *New York Times*, August 8, 1947; *Truman Committee Hearings*, part 40, pp. 23,972–80; Cable, July 3, 1943, from Washington to Commanding General, 12th Air Force, Algiers, requesting return of Elliott Roosevelt for reconnaissance plane program, ibid., 24,608; D. E. Riley memo, August 10, 1944, reporting on aircraft conference on F-11, ibid., 24,500; transcript of telephone conversation between B. W. Chidlaw and Orval R. Cook on development costs of D-2 in *Truman Committee Hearings*, part 43, p. 26,210–12; Report of Conference, February 24, 1944, by officials of Procurement Division, Army Air Forces, Wright Field and Hughes Aircraft on D-2 and F-11, ibid., 27,155–56.

39. *Truman Committee Hearings*, part 40, pp. 23,390, 24,009, 24,034, 24,450. O. P. Echols to B. W. Chidlaw, August 31, 1943, p. 23,823; Echols memo for Arnold, September 2, 1943, p. 24,486; H. A. Craig memo to Assistant Chief of Air Staff, Materiel, September 3, 1943, p. 24,488; negative views were expressed by F. O. Carroll to Commanding General, Matériel Command, September 17, 1943, p. 24,490; for expense account of John Meyer, see 24,536, all in *Truman Committee Hearings*, part 40.

40. *Washington News*, August 5, 1947; *New York Times*, August 5, 6, 7, 1947, reporting on his testimony; and Elliott Roosevelt in *Truman Committee Hearings*, part 40, pp. 24,031, 24,037–39. On expenses of his wedding party, see W. D. Rouzer, (manager of El Tovar Hotel, Grand Canyon National Park), to F. D. Flanagan, March 12, 1947, p. 24,630; on military opposition to the Hughes plane, see Echols memo to Chief of Air Staff, August 13, 1943, p. 24,484; Chidlaw for Commanding General, Wright Field, August 21, 1943, p. 23,821; memo of Carroll to Hughes Aircraft, November 7, 1941, pp. 24,494–95, all in *Truman Committee Hearings*, part 40. Carroll to Chief of Production, Wright Field, March 14, 1944, on D-2 in ibid, part 43, p. 27,156.

41. For further extensive inquiry into the Hughes operations, see *Truman Committee Hearings*, part 43, which also contains a large number of primary sources gathered by the committee's staff.

42. *Truman Committee Hearings*, part 31, pp. 15,366–67; see also the statement of C. L. Egtvedt, chairman, Boeing Company, on postwar plans, August 24, 1945, in ibid., 15,578.

43. Ibid., 15,368.

44. Ibid., 15,371–77, 15,382–86. Similar views were expressed by Robert E. Gross, president of Lockheed Aircraft Company; see his comments on August 24, 1945, in ibid., 15,592.

45. Ibid., 15,589–90; see also Donald Douglas's letter to James Mead, August 21, 1945, on postwar plans in ibid., 15,588.

46. Douglas in ibid., 15,590, and Raymond, 15,402.

47. Ibid., 15,386–90; see also Albert Lombard's testimony, ibid., 15,390–94, 15,399, and the editorial in *American Aviation*, August 15, 1945.

48. *Truman Committee Hearings*, part 31, pp. 15,443, 15,602–4 for Kindelberger. For Northrop, 15,449, 15,609–10, 15,540, and the statements of Kindelberger, 15,600–15,605, and of Northrop, August 24, 1945, 15,606,15,610; similar views were expressed by T. Claude Ryan in telegram to Andrew Haley, August 23, 1945, p. 15,613, all in *Truman Committee Hearings*, part 31.

5. New Basic Industries for the West: Aluminum

1. Temporary National Economic Committee, *Monograph* no. 29, pp. 1489, 1514–21, also entitled *The Distribution of Ownership in the 200 Largest Nonfinancial Corporations*. See also 78th Cong., 2d sess., 1944, Senate, Sub-Committee on War Mobilization of the Committee on Military Affairs, *Senate Committee Print no. 1, Economic and Political Aspects of International Cartels*, 1–11; Donald H. Wallace, *Market Control in the Aluminum Industry*, 85–87; Ervin Hexner, "International Cartels in the Postwar World," 121. A thorough history of the aluminum industry in the West remains to be written.

2. Charlotte F. Muller, *The Light Metals Monopoly*, 50–67; Wallace, *Market Control*, 9–14, 24–43; "Aluminum—Have or Have Not," *Fortune* 28 (December 1943): 258–61; Charles M. Wiltse, *Aluminum Policies of the War Production Board and Predecessor Agencies, May, 1940 to November, 1945*, 145, quotes a memo from Lieutenant General Brehon Somervell (chief, Army Service Forces), April 4, 1942, in which he noted that a "shortage of aluminum . . . will, of course, wreck the whole strategy of the War Department. Will you please put the best people you have on this problem?"

3. Muller, *Light Metals Monopoly*, 243–44; 44 Fed. Supp. 97.

4. Aluminum Co. of America *v.* U.S., 302 U.S. 230; 148 Fed.(2) 416 (1945); *Truman Committee Hearings*, part 3, pp. 236–38; when the court adjudged Alcoa to be a monopoly, the decision broke its power because in the following year the courts forced the company to make its formerly exclusive patents available to competitors without royalties. This led competitors like Reynolds Metals to expand and induced newcomers like Henry J. Kaiser to enter the industry. By 1956 Alcoa's share in the industry had declined to 43 percent; Kaiser accounted for 27 percent and Reynolds 26 percent. See White, *Billions for Defense*, 106–7.

5. Ickes in *Truman Committee Hearings*, part 3, p. 879; Ickes Diary, 5236 (February 22, 1941). Ickes consulted Thurman Arnold on what he considered to be Harriman's favoritism to Alcoa; see ibid., 5244 (February 22, 1941). *New York Times*, November 29, December 24, 29, 1940, and January 15, 1941.

6. *Truman Committee Hearings*, part 3, pp. 882, 883–84; Ickes Diary, 6408–9 (March 7, 1942). Ickes shared Arnold's concern that the War Department would seek immunity from antitrust laws for its suppliers. See also Senator O'Mahoney's charges against Alcoa, *New York Times*, January 13, 1941. For Harry Truman's views, see *Truman Committee Hearings*, part 3, p. 713.

7. *Truman Committee Hearings*, part 3, p. 881; Ickes Diary, 6686 (June 7, 1942); Wiltse, *Aluminum Policies*, 1–35; *New York Times*, November 28, 1940.

8. *Truman Committee Hearings*, part 3, p. 1880; Abe Fortas to Harold Ickes, August 20, 1942, opposing Alcoa's policies, Ickes Papers.

9. *Truman Committee Hearings*, part 3, pp. 881–82; Ickes Diary, 5224 (February 16, 1941). Ickes clashed with Secretary of War Henry L. Stimson over awarding unlimited electric power from Bonneville to Alcoa. Henry L. Stimson, *On Active Service in Peace and War* (New York: 1948), ignores the subject.

10. *New York Times,* January 13, 1941; *Truman Committee Hearings,* part 3, pp. 882–83.

11. *Truman Committee Hearings,* part 7, pp. 2112, 2113, 2114.

12. Ibid., 2115, 2121, 2123.

13. Ibid., part 3, pp. 878, 879; see also 713.

14. *New York Times,* June 26, 1941; *Truman Committee Hearings,* part 3, pp. 752, 753, and part 7, pp. 2123–24.

15. *Truman Committee Hearings,* part 3, pp. 749, 750, 753, 755; Roosevelt to Reynolds, January 12, 1942, FDR Papers. *New York Times,* January 30, February 4, 19, 1941.

16. *Truman Committee Hearings,* part 3, pp. 901, 894, 900; see Davis in ibid., 940–43, and see Marion Folsom of OPM in ibid., 824–25; *New York Times,* November 28, 29, December 24, 29, 1940.

17. *Truman Committee Hearings,* part 3, pp. 894, 900, 901, 902, and part 7, p. 2313.

18. *New York Times,* May 15, 1941; *Truman Committee Hearings,* part 3, p. 812; Wiltse, *Aluminum Policies,* 55–75; Harold Stein, ed., *Public Administration and Policy Development,* 319; "The War Goes to Mr. Jesse Jones," *Fortune* 24 (December 1941): 189–90.

19. *Truman Committee Hearings,* part 3, pp. 713, 721; Wiltse, *Aluminum Policies,* 36–84, 121–65; I. F. Stone, *Business As Usual.*

20. *New York Times,* July 13, 14, 15, 1940, on meeting of Northwest congressional delegation; ibid., December 24, 1940, on shortages at Northrop, and January 15, 1941, at Martin. O'Mahoney charged Alcoa with holding down production; see *New York Times,* January 13, 1941. See also *SB Committee, Hearings,* part 57, pp. 6804–5, and part 58, p. 6975; *Cong. Rec.,* 77th Cong., 1st sess. (December 14, 1942), 9863.

21. *New York Times,* May 15, 16, 17, June 16, 24, 26, 27, 1941; *Truman Committee Hearings,* part 3, contain the relevant hearings.

22. Jones, *Fifty Billion,* 329; White, *Billions for Defense,* 42–43, 72–73; Muller, *Light Metals Monopoly,* 196–225.

23. Arrington and Cluff, *Industrial Plants,* 17–32; U.S. Bureau of Mines, *Alunite Resources of the United States,* Report no. 3561 by J. Thoenen (Washington, 1941); see also 77th Cong., 1st sess., 1941, Senate, Sub-Committee of the Committee on Public Lands and Surveys, *Mineral Resources of the Public Lands of the United States and their Development,* Senate Report no. 838, 11.

24. "Aluminum—Have or Have Not," *Fortune* 28 (December, 1943): 262; *Truman Committee Hearings,* part 3, p. 885; *Salt Lake Tribune,* July 30, August 7, 1940 and March 14, June 7, 1941.

25. *Hearings on S. 53,* 394; *Truman Committee Hearings,* part 3, pp. 883–85, and part 7, pp. 2125–39, 2143; *Salt Lake Tribune,* July 17, 21, 1943; other western states desired alumina pilot plants, especially Montana. See Roosevelt to Burton K. Wheeler, August 28, 1943, denying Wheeler's request for a pilot plant in Missoula, Montana, FDR Papers. Nelson to Charles A. Murray, August 23, 1943, turning down a similar request originating with the Missoula Chamber of Commerce, and Charles E. Wilson to James E. Murray, November 1, 1943, Murray Papers.

26. 77th Cong., 2d sess., 1942, House, Sub-Committee of Committee on Irrigation, *Hearings on Columbia River,* 1513; and 79th Cong., 1st sess., 1947, *Senate Report* no. 94. *Truman Committee Hearings,* part 3, p. 787, and 77th Cong., 1st sess., 1941, *Senate Report* no. 480, 6, for Truman Committee's report.

27. *Salt Lake Tribune*, August 24, 1941.

28. *Hearings on S. 53*, 394; *Salt Lake Tribune*, July 25, August 7, 8, 1941.

29. 77th Cong., 1st sess., 1941, *Senate Report* no. 480, 3, 6; *Salt Lake Tribune*, August 17, 19, 22, 23, 30, 1941.

30. Arrington and Cluff, *Industrial Plants*, 26–29; U.S. Bureau of Mines, *Minerals Yearbook*, 1943, p. 696, and ibid., 1944, p. 680; *Salt Lake Tribune*, September 26, October 25, 1941, and January 22, February 3, 1942; J. R. Mahoney, "Economic Changes in Utah During World War II," *Utah Economic and Business Review* 4 (June 1946): 11.

31. For background, see Muller, *Light Metals Monopoly*, 50–67, 97–119. *New York Times*, January 31, 1943.

32. The Metals Reserve Corporation signed four contracts with Alcan. It canceled the first two, which were superseded by Contract P-702 on March 1, 1942, and Contract P-794 on April 1, 1942. It amended these on April 15, 1944, deferring delivery of 100 million pounds, and on August 9, 1944, deferring delivery of 250 million pounds after June 30, 1945. See *SB Committee, Hearings*, part 57, pp. 6828–30, for P-794 and deliveries under P-702; see also Harvey Gunderson to Aluminum Company of Canada, January 20, 1945, in ibid., 6831–33; Jones, *Fifty Billion*, 424–28; *New York Times*, March 24, April 27, May 15, 1943.

33. See *SB Committee, Hearings*, part 57, pp. 6803, 6869–71 for details, 6869 for Cordon, and 6892 for Batt; see also ibid., part 58, p. 6975; *New York Times*, July 15, 1940.

34. *New York Times*, May 2, 1941; *Washington Post*, July 14, 1941; *Portland Oregonian*, August 31, 1942, and February 13, 1943, contains a summary of the Shipshaw situation. See also *Portland Oregonian*, September 5, 1943. Secretary of the Interior, *Annual Report*, 1941, pp. 15, 38, and ibid., 1942, p. 72.

35. Jones, *Fifty Billion*, 326; *Portland Oregonian*, August 15, 1943. Privately, Roosevelt was rather concerned. In a memo to Milo Perkins, the president noted, "This . . . is rather serious," referring to Shipshaw. March 26, 1943, FDR Papers. See also Jones to Roosevelt, July 28, 1943, detailing the Shipshaw contracts. "We made the best trades we could," Jones wrote, "not being a buyer's market," FDR Papers. Ickes complained bitterly to the president about Shipshaw; see Ickes to Roosevelt, May 31, 1943, FDR Papers. Roosevelt forwarded his letter to Attorney General Francis Biddle on June 5, 1943, since Biddle was also critical of certain specific provisions; Biddle to Roosevelt, June 25, 1943, FDR Papers.

36. *SB Committee, Hearings*, part 60, pp. 7104–5. Ickes Diary, 7525 (May 13, 1943), 7534 (May 14, 1943), 7590 (May 22, 1943), 7607 (May 24, 1943).

37. *SB Committee, Hearings*, part 60, pp. 7105, 7116, 7120, 7123, 7133, 7142, 7144.

38. Ibid., 7154; Ickes Diary, 9538, 9628 (October 1944).

39. *SB Committee, Hearings*, part 60, pp. 7154, 7157, 7158, 7166, and part 51, pp. 6404, 6409, 6410, 6412.

40. Ibid., part 57, p. 6860.

41. Cordon in ibid., 6803, 6808, 6961. Cordon had lobbied for Northwest aluminum plants as early as 1940; DeLacey in ibid., 6810.

42. Ibid., 6811.

43. Ibid., part 60, p. 7147.

44. Ibid., 7152.

45. Ibid., part 57, p. 6814; see also ibid., part 58, pp. 6975, 6976.

46. Ibid., part 58, p. 6996.

47. Ibid., 7000, and part 57, p. 6928.

48. DeLacey in ibid., part 58, pp. 7036–37. *Portland Oregonian*, August 15, 1944; *SB Committee, Hearings*, part 57, pp. 6807–9.

49. *SB Committee, Hearings*, part 57, p. 6833; Roosevelt to Reynolds, January 12, 1942, FDR Papers.

50. *SB Committee, Hearings*, part 57, pp. 6862, 6864.

51. Ibid., 6864–65.

52. Ibid., 6893.

53. Ibid., 6894; *New York Times*, May 17, 18, 19, 1941; *New York Journal of Commerce*, May 17, 1941.

54. *SB Committee, Hearings*, part 57, pp. 6906–7.

55. Ibid., 6926, 6998, and part 58, p. 6962.

56. Ibid., part 60, p. 7166. Jones, *Fifty Billion*, 326–27.

57. Wiltse, *Aluminum Policies*, 299–327, presents the official view. U.S. Surplus Property Board, *Aluminum Plants and Facilities*, 40–46; see also 79th Cong., 1st sess., 1945, Senate, Committee on Military Affairs, Sub-Committee on Surplus Property, *Joint Hearings on Aluminum Plant Disposal*. *SB Committee, Hearings*, part 60, pp. 1742, 7166, and part 51, pp. 6406, 6412.

58. U.S. Attorney-General, *Report of the Attorney-General on the Aluminum Industry*, 1945, pp. 2–12.

59. *SB Committee, Hearings*, part 55, pp. 6677–79.

60. Ibid., part 49, pp. 6187, 6261.

61. Ibid., part 52, p. 6528.

62. Ibid., part 49, p. 6263. Bernard Baruch noted in a letter to Roosevelt, June 18, 1943, FDR Papers: "He also has some wonderful practical ideas about postwar conditions. Whatever faults he may have—imagination and lack of courage are not in his composition." On Kaiser's early interest in aluminum, see Jones to Kaiser, August 18, 1941, Kaiser Papers.

63. *SB Committee, Hearings*, part 49, pp. 6264–70.

64. Ibid., part 52, pp. 6483, 6486, 6496.

65. Ibid., 6530, 6534, 6537, 6541, 6544, 6548.

66. Ibid., 6549, 6551, 6554.

67. Ibid., 6555, 6558.

68. Ibid., part 55, pp. 6651, 6653.

69. Ibid., 6659; Ickes to Roosevelt, June 9, 1944, Ickes Papers, opposes appointment of Bunker for disposal of surplus plants. "I know that the Senators of the Western states who are interested in aluminum and magnesium war plants feel very bitterly about Mr. Bunker's activities," Ickes wrote. His impression was correct. On August 30, 1944, for example, Representative John Coffee of Washington telegraphed the acting chairman of the WPB, Julius Krug, "If the War Production Board is influenced by the wishes of the dominant Eastern producers of aluminum and magnesium and thereupon takes any ill advised steps to shut down our plants it will certainly lead to a volume of protest which will jeopardize the standing of the Roosevelt Administration in this section of the country" (quoted in Wiltse, *Aluminum Policies*, 293).

6. Sinews of War: Magnesium, Steel, and Oil

1. Muller, *Light Metals Monopoly*, 150–95; "Magnesium—Newcomer among the Industrial Metals," *Mining World* (July 1942), 3–4; *Truman Committee Hearings*, part 17, pp. 12–13; Jones, *Fifty Billion*, 331–33; 77th Cong., 1st sess., 1942,

Senate, Committee on Patents, *Hearings on S. 2303 and Patents,* part 2, exhibit 10, deals with magnesium patents; "Magnesium by the Ton," *Fortune* 29 (March 1944): 184–87, 194–96; see also *SB Committee, Hearings,* part 49, on magnesium. *Life* (January 10, 1944), 55–60, reflects how magnesium caught popular fancies in World War II.

2. On the pre–World War II history of the area, see essay in *Nevada: The Silver State,* 2: 677–93, by Elbert B. Edwards, "Clark County: From Wilderness to Metropolitan Area." See also Russell R. Elliott, *History of Nevada,* 307–10.

3. On the early history of magnesium in Nevada, see "A Statement by Basic Magnesium, Inc., Relative to Its Magnesium Project in Nevada," in *Truman Committee Hearings,* part 13, pp. 5671–74; for a detailed chronology of the development of the Las Vegas magnesium project, see ibid., 5674–80; Howard P. Eels, president of Basic Magnesium, describes the negotiations of 1941 in ibid., 5621–27, 5645–48, and for construction problems see 5648–51. H. C. Mann, project manager for Basic Magnesium, discusses his difficulties in ibid., 5626, 5629–51. An excellent brief history of Basic Magnesium can be found in 78th Cong., 2d sess., 1944–45 Senate, Special Committee to Investigate the Centralization of Heavy Industry in the United States, *Hearings,* part 5, pp. 519–21 (hereafter cited as *McCarran Committee Hearings*). See also 77th Cong., 1st sess., 1944, Senate, Special Committee Investigating the National Defense Program, *Report* no. 10, part 17; a detailed account of Willard Dow's role in establishing Basic Magnesium is in his testimony in *Truman Committee Hearings,* part 24, pp. 10,285–323; for a copy of the contract between the DPC and Basic Magnesium, and amendments, see *McCarran Committee Hearings,* part 5, pp. 654–73.

4. *Truman Committee Hearings,* part 13, pp. 5671–80. According to Ickes, at a stormy cabinet meeting Roosevelt ordered Jones to finance a small magnesium plant for Kaiser, who had retained Tom Corcoran as counsel and advocate for the project. See Ickes Diary, 5224 (February 16, 1941) and 5231 (February 22, 1941). Jones, *Fifty Billion,* 333.

5. On negotiations between the DPC and Basic Magnesium as Jones described them, see his statement of August 1, 1941, Exhibit no. 532, *Truman Committee Hearings,* part 12, Appendix, 5369, and part 13, pp. 5566–75, 5681; testimony of Eels in ibid., part 13, pp. 5576–608; the rather severe housing problems are discussed in ibid., 5608–27.

6. Roosevelt to Pat McCarran, July 9, 1941, and McCarran to Joe McDonald, July 11, 1941, McCarran Papers. *Las Vegas Age,* August 15, 1941; *Las Vegas Review Journal,* September 23, 1941; *Pioche Record,* September 25, 1941; *Nevada State Journal,* November 26, 1941. McCarran kept up his lobbying for other facilities as well. See *Reno Gazette,* November 25, 1941, and McCarran to Dave Dotta, June 1, 1943; McCarran to Frank Tiltines, June 22, 1943; and McCarran to J. C. Magee, October 2, 1943, McCarran Papers.

7. The Basic Magnesium operation deserves a book-length study. Ample primary materials are available at the Nevada Historical Society, at the Nevada State Archives, in newspapers, and at the Nevada Archives. On brief accounts concerning the functioning of Basic Magnesium, see *McCarran Committee Hearings,* part 5, pp. 455–76; *Truman Committee Hearings,* part 13, pp. 5676 ff. Quotation is from *Las Vegas Review Journal,* November 20, 1941.

8. *Production Achievements and the Reconversion Outlook: Report of the Chairman, War Production Board,* October 9, 1945, pp. 62–64; Truman Committee, *Additional Report no. 10,* part 17, pp. 12–14; "The War Goes to Mr. Jesse Jones," *Fortune* 24 (December 1941): 192; see also Building and Construction Trades Council, A. F. of L., Clark and Lincoln Counties, Nevada, to Truman

Committee, April 24, 1942, in *Truman Committee Hearings*, part 13, pp. 5689–90.

9. McCarran in *Las Vegas Review Journal*, November 20, 1942; McCarran to Joe McDonald, July 11, 1941, McCarran Papers. See also Kaiser in *SB Committee, Hearings*, part 49, pp. 6265–66.

10. Jones, *Fifty Billion*, 333.

11. Ickes suggested to Roosevelt that he let Kaiser manufacture magnesium, although Jones was opposed. See Ickes Diary, 5224 (February 16, 1941) and 5233, 5244 (February 22, 1941); Jones, *Fifty Billion*, 333; Jones let his personal dislike of Kaiser cloud his judgment; Hugh Fulton, counsel of the Truman Committee, was more accurate when he noted on March 13, 1944: "The production by Henry J. Kaiser has been of great value to the program because it was obtained when the scarcity was great. Future production will be very valuable because in this particular type of process the magnesium is first produced in powder form and can be used directly in incendiary bombs" (*Truman Committee Hearings*, part 17, p. 19). Hansgirg was a highly respected Hungarian engineer who had operated plants in Europe. Henry J. Kaiser gave him an affadavit to emigrate to the United States and hired him to manage his California facility. See "Confidential F.B.I. Report on Henry J. Kaiser," FDR Papers. Roosevelt ordered such an investigation after various complaints were made, but no incriminating evidence surfaced. On Hansgirg see F. J. Hansgirg, "Thermal Reduction of Magnesium Compounds," *Iron Age* 153 (November 25, 1943), 54; H. A. Doerner, *Magnesium—Present Outlook for a Magnesium Metal Industry in the Northwest*, 24.

12. *McCarran Committee Hearings*, part 5, pp. 454, 607, 630; Philip D. Wilson to Case, April 4, 1944, in ibid., 513; Clinton Golden memo to A. H. Bunker, April 4, 1944, in ibid., 514; Case to J. R. Hobbins, September 6, 1944, in ibid., 516–17; Sam Husbands to Case, December 31, 1944, ibid., 516; Robert H. Ramsay, "Magnesium Production at the World's Largest Plant," *Chemical and Metallurgical Engineering* (October 1943), 100.

13. *McCarran Committee Hearings*, part 1, pp. 1–10; parts 1–5 contain extensive testimony; 78th Cong., 1st sess., 1944, Senate Resolution no. 190.

14. *McCarran Committee Hearings*, part 1, pp. 13–27.

15. Ibid., 1–10; Ickes to Nelson, February 28, 1944, in ibid., 11–12; E. F. Scattergood to McCarran, March 13, 1944, in ibid., 12. This was one of the few issues on which Ickes and McCarran were in complete agreement. McCarran also urged other western senators to protest. See Herbert Maw to Elbert D. Thomas, March 16, 1944, Thomas Papers. Other plants the WPB ordered closed included Permanente, Amco, Mathiesen, International Minerals and Chemicals, Ford, Electro-Metallurgical in Spokane, and three Dow Magnesium plants in Marysville, Utah, Ludington, Michigan, and Velasco, Texas. *New York Times*, July 16, November 25, 1944.

16. See "Outline of Potential Chemical Products Development for Boulder Dam Area," in *McCarran Committee Hearings*, part 5, p. 486; F. O. Case to McCarran, December 1, 1944, in ibid., 500; a detailed analysis of this report by the DPC is in ibid., 500–508; for comments by Willard Dow see *SB Committee, Hearings*, part 49, pp. 6228–31, 6237.

17. Maverick discusses the postwar prospects for magnesium in *SB Committee, Hearings*, part 55, pp. 6690–92; *Portland Oregonian*, July 31, 1944, discusses the Maverick Plan for war plants disposal.

18. *Liberty* (November 11, 1944); *McCarran Committee Hearings*, part 5, p. 638.

19. On aspects of the western steel industry, see Howard Lee Scamehorn,

Pioneer Steelmaker in the West; on basing points, Fritz Machlup, *The Basing Point System,* 61–90; Webb, *Divided We Stand,* 3, 4, 26, 30; Garnsey, *America's New Frontier,* 168–89.

20. "Fourth Report of the Attorney-General on Western Steel Plants and the Tin-Plate Industry, June 29, 1945," 79th Cong., 1st sess., 1945, *Senate Document* no. 95, iii, 1, 2, 34; Ewald T. Grether, *The Steel and Steel Using Industries of California,* 112; Clifford M. Zierer, "Iron and Steel Production and Related Industries," in Clifford M. Zierer, ed., *California and the Southwest,* 298–301.

21. Grether, *Steel and Steel Using Industries,* 93–104; J. R. Mahoney, "The Western Iron and Steel Industry," 3–5, 27; H. F. Bain, "A Pattern for Western Steel Production," in U.S. Bureau of Mines, *Information Circular* no. 7315 (Washington, 1945), 1–5. The productive capacity of western steel manufacturers can be gleaned from the *Annual Statistical Reports* of the American Iron and Steel Institute for the war years. Abe Murdock to Roosevelt, April 28, 1941; Roosevelt to Murdock, May 9, 1941, FDR Papers, on steel manufactures in Utah.

22. Mark S. Foster, "Giant of the West," 15–16; Richard A. Lauderbaugh, *American Steelmakers and the Coming of the Second World War,* 3, 20–22.

23. *New York Times,* September 19, December 21, December 22, 1940; *Truman Committee Hearings,* part 7, pp. 2085, 2091–94, 2108–10; ibid., part 14, pp. 5838–40, 5907–32; 79th Cong., 1st sess., 1945, Senate, Sub-Committee on Surplus Property of the Committee on Military Affairs and the Industrial Reorganization Sub-Committee of the Special Committee on Postwar Economic Policy and Planning, *Hearings on War Plants Disposal—Iron and Steel Plants,* 3–5.

24. *New York Times,* January 12, February 1, March 1, 1941.

25. Ibid., February 23, 1941; *Report to the President of the United States on the Adequacy of the Steel Industry for National Defense,* February 22, 1941.

26. *New York Times,* May 8, 23, 29, June 4, 14, 1941; Foster, "Giant of the West," 16.

27. *New York Times,* June 5, 1941; Jones, *Fifty Billion,* 332–34; Donald W. Nelson, *Arsenal of Democracy,* 355. Congressional delegations from western states were urging expansion of western steel; see *Colorado Labor Advocate* (A.F. of L.), December 17, 1942. Roosevelt was very favorable to steel expansion in the West; see Early J. Beaudry to Samuel L. Stratton, February 21, 1941; and Roosevelt to Steve Early, February 21, 1941, FDR Papers, urging him to "get behind it," the effort to secure western steel facilities.

28. *Salt Lake Tribune,* April 13, 1941; Arrington and Cluff, *Industrial Plants,* 36–38.

29. *Truman Committee Hearings,* part 14, pp. 5765, 5766; "Kaiser Plans a Steel Plant," *Time* (April 28, 1941), 77–78; S. R. Fuller to E. M. Watson, May 12, 1941, FDR Papers, noted that the president had telephoned to say that Kaiser's proposal for steel plants on the Pacific Coast should be seriously considered. Roosevelt memo to Ickes, May 16, 1941; Kaiser to Fuller, June 9, 1941; and also Kaiser to Fuller, June 11, 1941, FDR Papers. Foster, "Giant of the West," 7–8.

30. *Salt Lake Tribune,* May 24, 1941; *New York Times,* April 23, 1941; Arrington and Clough, *Industrial Plants,* 37–38. See also A. P. Heiner to E. E. Trefethan, September 30, 1942, Kaiser Papers. In addition, also useful are "Kaiser's Steel?" *Business Week* (May 3, 1941), 24–26; *New York Times,* April 23, May 24, 1941; *Salt Lake Tribune,* May 24, 1941; Marvin McIntire memo for E. M. Watson, April 17, 1941, FDR Papers, in which he noted that Senator Murdock would bring Kaiser in to see the president on April 22, 1941, to discuss Utah and western steel.

31. *Salt Lake Tribune*, June 20, July 20, 25, October 2, 22, November 27, 1941, and February 9, March 19, May 12, 1943; Mahoney, "Western Iron and Steel Industry," 67; "Utah's Big Baby," *Saturday Evening Post* (May 15, 1948), 154; Herbert Maw to Roosevelt, March 14, 1944, noted, "The November election will prove our gratefulness for what you have done [to expand steel in Utah]," FDR Papers. Even in 1943 McCarran was still seeking to expand the steel industry in the West; see McCarran to Elbert D. Thomas, July 2, 1943, Thomas Papers.

32. Walter Malthesius, "The Growth of Western Steel," *American Society for Metals and American Institute of Mining and Metallurgical Engineers* (September 24, 1951), 24. Malthesius directed the Geneva Steel Works in wartime. Jones, *Fifty Billion*, 332–33; Foster, "Giant of the West," 14–19.

33. Kaiser to Marvin McIntire, October 5, 1942, FDR Papers. Jones, *Fifty Billion*, 333.

34. At the dedication of his first blast furnace at Fontana on December 30, 1942, Kaiser said: "The Westward movement which began so long ago on the Asiatic plains did not come to an end on the Pacific slope of North America. It is posed for the next great thrust. The day of the West is at hand. Westward, the course of empire takes its way" (quoted in Foster, "Giant of the West," 17–18).

35. Grether, *Steel and Steel Using Industries*, 112–14; Morris E. Garnsey, "Future of the Mountain States," 333; Lester Velie, "The Truth About Henry Kaiser," 11–12, 24–26; "The Arrival of Henry Kaiser," *Fortune* 44 (July 1951): 68–73, 141–54.

36. Kaiser to Walter Lippmann, (n.d.), quoted in Foster, "Giant of the West," 20.

37. On post-1945 events, see ibid., 15–20.

38. For background, see Harold F. Williamson et al., *The American Petroleum Industry*, 2:747–94; Gerald D. Nash, *United States Oil Policy, 1890–1964*, 157–79; John W. Frey and Chandler Ide, *A History of the Petroleum Administration for War, 1941–1945*; John G. Clark, *Energy and the Federal Government*, 316–47, which provides a somewhat jaundiced view; Martin Melosi, *Coping With Abundance*.

39. Roosevelt to William P. Cole, March 4, 26, November 29, 1940; Cole to Roosevelt, March 7, 1945, FDR Papers; Roosevelt to Cole, March 22, 1941, DI Records. Nash, *Oil Policy*, 158–59.

40. *New York Times*, June 15, 19, July 13, 1941; Roosevelt to Ickes, May 28, 1941, DI Records; Harold L. Ickes, *Fightin Oil*.

41. Ickes to Roosevelt, June 4, 1941, FDR Papers; *New York Times*, November 30, 1941; *Oil and Gas Journal*, December 18, 1941.

42. Ickes to Smith Brookhart, June 27, 1941, DI Records; J. S. Grover, "15 Hours Ahead of Schedule: How Railroads Rush Oil Across the Continent," *Nation's Business* 30 (November 1942): 30–32; "Wartime Revolution in Oil Transportation," *Business Week* (April 17, 1943), 57; Williamson et al., *American Petroleum Industry*, 2:763–66; "Oil Rechannelled: Vast New Pipeline Pattern Evolved by Industry," *Business Week* (May 9, 1942), 17–18; F. B. Dow, "The Role of Petroleum Pipelines in the War," 93–100.

43. Ickes to Roosevelt, January 19, 1942, Ickes to Roosevelt, June 2, 1942, DI Records; Nash, *Oil Policy*, 167–69; Frey and Ide, *Petroleum Administration for War*, 178–89; for operation in western local areas, see Records, U.S. Petroleum Administration for War, Region X (California), Organizational Chart, in Henry L. Huntington Library and Art Gallery, San Marino, California, and see Petroleum Administration for War, Region X, Production Committee, Minutes of California

Allocation Sub-Committee, in Records, U.S. Petroleum Administration for War, National Archives, Suitland, Maryland.

44. Statistics are based on figures taken from the annual reports of the U.S. Bureau of Mines. An extensive literature has developed concerning U.S. efforts to develop foreign oil sources. See Michael B. Stoff, *Oil, War, and American Security*, and Anthony Sampson, *The Seven Sisters*.

45. A brief, incomplete account is in Donald H. Riddle, *The Truman Committee*, 101–21; William D. Leahy, *I Was There*, 127.

46. U.S. Army, Office of Quartermaster General, "Historical Summary— Canol Project," September 20, 1943, in Truman Committee Records. See 1–19 of this report and also *Truman Committee Hearings*, part 22, p. 9388, 9454.

47. *Truman Committee Hearings*, part 22, pp. 9381–406; for Graham's role, ibid., 9492, 9573–76, 9640, 9842–43; Le Sueur's letter is reprinted in ibid., 9855–57.

48. "Oil from the Arctic," *Lamp* (October 1943), 3–7; Riddle, *Truman Committee*, 105.

49. Text of letter in *Truman Committee Hearings*, part 22, pp. 8889–90.

50. Ibid., 9528; Ickes to Stimson, October 29, 1942, Ickes Papers; Ickes to Stimson, December 9, 1942, protesting infringement on his authority, and Ickes to Truman, December 1, 1943, Truman Committee Records—Canol Project, complaining about Stimson.

51. For Ruby report, see *Truman Committee Hearings*, part 22, p. 9531; Riddle, *Truman Committee*, 108; W. A. Hunter to James M. Mead, September 5, 1946, noting that he accompanied consultants to Alaska who urged abandonment of the project, Truman Committee Records—Canol Project.

52. *Truman Committee Hearings*, part 22, pp. 9865, 9875–78, 9890, and see also 9552; L. J. Logan, "Canadian Wartime Project is Herculean Undertaking," 13–19. Nelson to Truman, December 11, 1943, Truman Committee Records— Canol Project, noted that on December 9, 1943, Knox called a conference with Ickes, Patterson, and Nelson and that Knox, Nelson, and Ickes opposed continuation of Canol.

53. *Truman Committee Hearings*, part 22, pp. 9875–78 for Searls, and 9571 for Whitney. Riddle, *Truman Committee*, 110–11.

54. *Truman Committee Hearings*, part 22, pp. 9900–9901; Truman Committee, *Fifth Annual Report*, 23, in 79th Cong., 2d sess., 1946, *Senate Report* no. 110, part 7; Truman to Eugene Meyer, November 30, 1943, Truman Committee Records—Canol Project.

55. *Truman Committee Hearings*, part 22, p. 9596; Patterson to Harold Smith, July 27, 1943, Truman Committee Records—Canol Project. Patterson was brash and noted: "Military necessity requires that the Canol Project be completed as rapidly as possible. . . . The success of the Canol Project may well be the determining factor which will control the size and extent of an air offensive aimed at the heart of the Japanese Empire through Alaska and Siberia."

56. *Truman Committee Hearings*, part 22, p. 9680; Wilbur D. Sparks to George Meader, September 24, 1946, recalled the Joint Chiefs of Staff meeting, October 2, 1943, General George C. Marshall approved the decision, Truman Committee Records—Canol Project.

57. *Washington Post*, October 2, 1946; William D. Leahy to James M. Mead, July 22, 1946, Truman Committee Records—Canol Project, defends the Joint Chiefs of Staff decision in some detail. See also Truman Committee, *Third Annual Report*, 460, in 78th Cong., 1st sess., 1943, *Senate Report* no. 10, part 14.

58. *Truman Committee Hearings*, part 22, pp. 9900–9901, and part 39, pp. 22,991 and 23,010; Truman to Hugh Fulton, December 21, 1943, Truman Committee Records—Canol Project, noted, "We shall have a showdown with the Admiral." See also Truman to Ernest J. King, December 27, 1943, in Truman Committee Records—Canol Project.

59. Richard L. Neuberger, "The Great Canol Disaster," 421. At the time, Neuberger was aide to the commanding general of the Northwest Service Command. Truman Committee, *Fifth Annual Report*, 25.

60. Department of State, Foreign Liquidation Committee, "Report to Congress on U.S. Owned Petroleum Facilities Abroad," April 6, 1946, pp. 1–109, in Truman Committee Records—Canol Project, and also U.S. Bureau of the Budget, "Report on the Canol Project in Northwest Canada and the Territory of Alaska," September 5, 1944, in Truman Committee Records—Canol Project. See as well Harley Kilgore to Ickes, July 31, 1946, Ickes Papers.

7. World War II and the Western Environment

1. Department of the Interior, *Annual Report*, 1941, p. iii; O'Mahoney to Ickes, January 7, 1942; Ickes to O'Mahoney, February 6, 1942, DI Records, War Resources Council File; Nevadans wanted the western states to have a greater part in the development of regional resources. See E. P. Carville to Abe Fortas, March 13, 1942; Fortas to Carville, February 17, 1942; and Stephen Rauschenbush's memo for Ickes, January 16, 1942, DI Records.

2. Department of the Interior, *Annual Report*, 1941, p. iv; Ickes to Michael W. Straus, February 6, 1942, DI Records. Straus had prepared a draft of the departmental program for Ickes. R. S. Dean to Rauschenbush, March 27, 1942, also enclosing an editorial from the *Engineering and Mining Journal* criticizing the Ickes plan for the West, DI Records.

3. Department of the Interior, *Annual Report*, 1943, p. vi; comments of Ivan Bloch at meeting of Oscar Chapman with western miners in Reno, Nevada, March 12, 1942, particularly on industrial development, in Transcript of Meeting, 1–7, DI Records; see also Chapman to J. L. Morrill, March 5, 1942, DI Records; *Laramie Daily Bulletin*, March 20, 1942, and Chapman to M. F. Coolbaugh, March 4, 1942, DI Records.

4. Department of the Interior, *Annual Report*, 1942, p. v; Ickes demanded absolute compliance with his views. "This war program . . . is a matter of public interest . . . and I expect all to support it," he wrote. Ickes memo to all Bureaus, February 9, 1942, DI Records.

5. F. C. Walcott to Ickes, January 21, 1942; Walter Onslow to Ickes, January 22, 1942; quote from Ickes to Walcott, January 30, 1942; Rauschenbush to Fortas, February 17, 1942, arranging meeting with McCarran and the Committee on Public Lands concerning the department's plan for western economic development; Ickes to Frank Knox, January 30, 1942, urging creation of an interdepartmental board to settle conservation problems, an idea Knox did not relish; Walter Onslow to Ickes, January 22, 1942, urging a public campaign for conservation, all in DI Records.

6. Department of the Interior, *Annual Report*, 1941, pp. 30–31. Early in the war the department created the War Resources Council to coordinate internal policies, and from that evolved the Western War Resources Council to deal with issues of special interest to the region. See Rauschenbush memo for Ickes, June

2, 1942, outlining membership and functions, DI Records. The minutes of the council meetings are in the DI Records. See also Ickes administrative order no. 1636 creating the War Resources Council, January 14, 1942, DI Records.

7. Department of the Interior, *Annual Report*, 1941, pp. 35, 38, 40; ibid., 1942, pp. xx, 126; ibid., 1944, p. xiv; see also Ickes to John Boettiger, January 7, 1942, Ickes Papers.

8. Department of the Interior, *Annual Report*, 1941, p. 38; ibid., 1942, p. 26.

9. Ibid., 1943, pp. x, xi, 2, 38, 43.

10. Chapter 7 of the "Wartime History of the Bureau of Reclamation," manuscripts in DI Records, 222–300, provides a detailed account of selected wartime activities written by the bureau's staff. Their hostility to the Army Corps of Engineers is reflected on 258–72.

11. John C. Page (Commissioner of Bureau of Reclamation) to Carl Hayden, February 24, 1943, describes plans for the resumption of irrigation projects, DI Records. A copy is also in Hayden Papers.

12. "Wartime History of the Bureau of Reclamation," 276–88; William E. Warne memo to Ickes, January 25, 1944; and Kenneth A. Reid (Executive Secretary of the Izaac Walton League) to Ickes, August 2, 1944, opposing more dam building in the West, Ickes Papers. At the annual meeting of the National Reclamation Association in Denver, October 28, 1943, Commissioner Harry Bashore said: "The West will face a problem that calls for heroic measures. The Bureau of Reclamation is determined to help meet this crisis . . . the Bureau has been stripped for action" (Department of the Interior, *Annual Report*, 1944, p. 2). *Denver Post*, October 29, 1943; Department of the Interior, *Annual Report*, 1943, pp. ix–x; ibid., 1944, p. 2, reprints Roosevelt's letter; ibid., 1945, pp. 10, 14.

13. A comprehensive study of western fisheries still needs to be written. But see Gerald D. Nash, *State Government and Economic Development*, 201–5, 292–307, and Arthur F. McEvoy, *Ecology and Law in the California Fisheries, 1850–1980*, for background. See also "A Report of the War Activities of the Office of Coordinator of Fisheries in the Interests of Food Production," 1–2, 3–5, manuscripts (1946) in DI Records—Fisheries File (hereafter cited as Fisheries Report).

14. Department of the Interior, *Annual Report*, 1941, pp. xxi, 186, 188, 197; Ickes to Chester Bowles, June 14, 1945, DI Records, seeking increase of ceiling prices for canned tuna.

15. Ickes to Roosevelt, November 2, 1942, FDR Papers, requesting expanded powers. Department of the Interior, *Annual Report*, 1941, p. xxi; ibid., 1942, pp. xxviii, xxix, 229–31.

16. Fisheries Report, 15–20; Coordinator of Fisheries, "Coordinator of Fisheries and Food Production," 1–21, manuscript in DI Records (hereafter cited as "Coordinator of Fisheries"); "Wartime History of the United States Fish and Wildlife Service," 62–65, manuscript in DI Records (hereafter cited as "Wartime History"); Ickes to David Oliver, (Secretary of California Sardine Products Institute) February 16, 1944, DI Records; Ickes Diary, 6881 (August 1, 1942); Department of the Interior, *Annual Report*, 1942, p. 269, and 1943, pp. xxvi, 200–201.

17. Fisheries Report, 13–14; "Coordinator of Fisheries," 21–27.

18. Ickes was consistent in seeking higher prices for fish. See, for example, Ickes to Bowles, June 14, 1945, DI Records. Characteristically, Ickes noted, "The responsibility for meeting the canned fish production requirements of the War Food Program has been delegated to [me]." See also Charles E. Jackson to Ickes, May 30, 1944; and Fortas to Ickes, June 2, 1944, DI Records. Fisheries Report,

36–47 on salmon; 48–52 on sardines; and 51–52 on halibut. Petition of Boat Owners to Coordinator of Fisheries, January 28, 1944, seeking fishing permits under pilchard plan and for fishing for shark off Oregon and Washington coast, and Ickes Decision M33539; DI Records; Department of the Interior, *Annual Report*, 1943, pp. 200–201, 204–5; ibid., 1944, pp. 200, 202; "Wartime History," 82–83.

19. Fisheries Report, 52–58; detailed statistics on the fisheries in "Wartime History," 87–101; Charles E. Jackson memo for Ickes, August 31, 1945, DI Records. "Coordinator of Fisheries," 44–59; Ickes Diary, 9306 (February 6, 1944).

20. 74th Cong., 1st sess., 1935, Senate, Committee on Public Lands and Surveys, *Hearings on Taylor Grazing Act*, part 2, pp. 36–45, 50–54, 69–74; Department of the Interior, *Annual Report*, 1939, pp. x–xi; Commissioner of General Land Office to Ickes, July 26, 1940, alerting him to McCarran's impending attack on grazing policies, DI Records. E. Louise Peffer, *The Closing of the Public Domain, 1900–1950*, 248.

21. Ickes to McCarran, January 6, March 28, 1942, DI Records; Departmental War Records Project, "Grazing Service," manuscript in DI Records (hereafter cited as "Grazing History"). Ickes Diary, 8390 (November 27, 1943). Ickes wrote that he considered McCarran a one-man circus.

22. Ickes generally maintained a conciliatory tone toward the cattle growers. See Ickes to F. E. Mollin, June 8, 1942, acknowledging discontent in the industry; see also Ickes to Carl Hayden, February 3, 1945; Ickes to McCarran, February 3, 1945; and Oscar Chapman memo for Ickes, February 21, 1945, DI Records. Philip O. Foss, *Politics and Grass*, 62–98; Peffer, *Closing*, 252–57; Wesley Calef, *Private Grazing and Public Lands*, and Gary Libecap, *Locking Up the Range*, provide broad context.

23. McCarran actually urged the American National Livestock Association to lobby for the hearings he was conducting. E. S. Haskell to Lawrence F. Mollin, (Assistant to Executive Secretary of American National Livestock Association), January 8, 1943; Haskell to George C. Wilson, January 21, 1943; Haskell to Horace Hening, February 1, 1943; (Executive Secretary, New Mexico Cattle Growers Association), Haskell to Paul Etchepare, February 2, 1943; and McCarran to Murray, January 28, 1943, McCarran Papers. Ickes suspected him, as noted in Ickes Diary, 9702 (May 6, 1945). On 10,111 Ickes noted that McCarran was an SOB-plus, "and I don't mean Senate Office Building, either." "Grazing History," 43. In a personal letter to Harold Smith, director of the Bureau of the Budget, Ickes lamented: "McCarran has outplayed us. He has held a number of hearings in all parts of the West to which we have had to send witnesses on our depleted funds" (Ickes to Smith, January 31, 1945, DI Records).

24. Note quote in "Grazing History," 14. By 1944 Ickes had less sympathy for cattle growers. See Ickes to McCarran, December 28, 1944; and Ickes to O'Mahoney, January 23, 1945, DI Records. Senator Hayden also protested Grazing Service policies; see Michael Straus to Hayden, February 28, 1945; and Oscar Chapman to Ickes, February 21, 1945, DI Records. Claude Wickard (secretary of agriculture) to Carl Hatch, June 24, 1944, McCarran Papers, blasted McCarran as a tool of the American National Livestock Association. 79th Cong., 1st sess., 1945, Senate, Sub-Committee of Committee on Public Lands and Surveys, *Hearings on Administration and Use of Public Lands*, 6–10.

25. For opposition to the grazing bill, see Fortas to Hatch, August 16, 1944, McCarran Papers. James A. Hooper to Haskell, December 12, 1944, McCarran Papers, complained about the Grazing Service "men in the local offices . . .

becoming arrogant, dictating with considerable vindictiveness. There is plenty of resentment regarding the raising of grazing fees." Sheepherders were concerned about army and navy appropriation of their grazing lands; see A. E. Lawson (Washington Wool Growers Association) to McCarran, February 8, 1943; and C. K. Williamson to McCarran, February 17, 1943, McCarran Papers. 78th Cong., 1st sess., 1943, *Senate Report* no. 404, Appendix B, 83; 79th Cong., 2nd sess., 1944, *Senate Report* no. 808, part 2, pp. 9–14; 80th Cong., 1st sess., 1947, *Senate Report* no. 10, 9–11; and 80th Cong., 1st sess., 1947, House, *Hearings on Interior Department Appropriations Bill for 1948*, part 1, pp. 1228–29 (hereafter cited as *Appropriations Bill 1948*).

26. *American Cattle Producer* 27 (September 1946): 14, quoted in Peffer, *Closing*, 262, n. 27; Ickes Diary, 9628 (March 31, 1945); McCarran also intervened directly with Grazing Service and Forest Service officials to secure expansion of grazing rights for individuals; see Haskell to Benjamin Casey, March 31, 1943, and Haskell to H. Hutchins, March 23, 1943, McCarran Papers. "Grazing History," 82–102.

27. On Nevada's reaction see *Cong. Rec.*, 79th Cong., 1st sess. (February 16, 1945), Appendix, 665–66; a detailed analysis was made by the Central Committee of Nevada State Grazing Boards and Gordon Griswold, Nevada's representative on the National Advisory Council of the U.S. Grazing Service. Forsling met in Salt Lake City on November 23–25, 1944, with the National Advisory Council, where he surprised them with the announcement of an intended increase. See *Salt Lake Tribune*, November 24, 26, 1944; Gordon Griswold to Pat McCarran, December 5, 1944, and the Press Release of the National Advisory Council, November 25, 1944, McCarran Papers. By this time Ickes viewed McCarran as a major troublemaker. He even suggested to Roosevelt that he appoint McCarran to a Federal District Court judgeship, admitting "it's terrible to use a judgeship to buy a man off" (Ickes Diary, 8633 [February 12, 1944]). Roosevelt refused, as Ickes noted in his diary, 9587 (March 4, 1945).

28. A table listing Grazing Service appropriations for 1936–1946 is in 79th Cong., 2d sess., 1944, *Senate Report* no. 808, part 2, p. 21, and in Peffer, *Closing*, 266. 78th Cong., 1st sess., 1943, *Senate Report* no. 404, p. 38. 73d Cong., 1st sess., 1934, House, Committee on Public Lands, *Hearings on Taylor Grazing Act*, 127, 139. Ickes noted in his diary on November 14, 1945, p. 10,114, that McCarran used his subcommittee to intimidate the Department of the Interior. "He doesn't use this so much for investigation as for a club to beat us over the head," he wrote. "I'm pretty completely fed up with this man who isn't fit to be an alderman from a river ward in Chicago."

29. 79th Cong., 2d sess., 1944, *Senate Report* no. 808; 80th Cong., 1st sess., 1947, *Senate Report* no. 10.

30. 79th Cong., 2d sess., 1947, *House Report* #241, p. 7; Johnson in *Cong. Rec.*, 79th Cong., 2d sess., 4634, quoted in Peffer, *Closing*, 268; "Grazing History," 8, 15–18; a copy of Nicholson report (November 12, 1946) is in Ickes Papers.

31. *Cong. Rec.*, 79th Cong., 2d sess. (May 10, 1946), 4834–39, 4663; Marion Clawson, *The Western Range Livestock Industry*, 11–13, 381–82; J. Russell Penny and Marion Clawson, "Administration of Grazing Districts," 23–34.

32. 79th Cong., 2d sess., 1946, House, Committee on Appropriations, Sub-Committee, *Hearings on Interior Department Appropriation Bill for 1947*, 1252–54, 1260–65; *American Cattle Producer* 28 (September 1946): 13; *Appropriations Bill 1948*, part 1, pp. 463, 487, 1235–36.

33. *Appropriations Bill 1948*, part 1, pp. 455, 517; *American Cattle Producer* 28 (September 1946): 14; Peffer, *Closing*, 274–78.

34. "National Park Service War Work, December 7, 1941 to June 30, 1944," manuscript written by the staff and edited by Charles W. Porter III, DI Records, also available on microfilm in *Administrative Histories of World War II*, 1–2, 23–24 (hereafter cited as NPS History). Newton Drury, "What the War is Doing to National Parks and Where They Will Be at Its Close," *Living Wilderness* (May 1944), 11–12; Department of the Interior, *Annual Report*, 1941, pp. vii–ix, 159–64; ibid., 1942, p. 218; ibid., 1944, p. 212.

35. NPS History, 2–4; Department of the Interior, *Annual Report*, xx, 159–61; ibid., 1942, p. 202.

36. Department of the Interior, *Annual Report*, 1942, p. 203.

37. NPS History, 7–11, 14–21, and for a purported conversation between Drury and Greeley, 19–20; F. H. Brundage, western log and lumber administrator for the War Production Board, wrote to Ickes on January 20, 1943, stressing the urgent need for such cutting, very likely at the behest of W. B. Greeley, executive secretary of the West Coast Lumbermen's Association. Drury met with representatives of the chamber of commerce in Port Angeles, Oregon, on May 6, 1943, and at Gray's Harbor to dissuade them. See letters of Ickes to Nelson, September 14, 1943; and Nelson to Ickes, September 23, 1943, reproduced in NPS History, 11. See also Anna Boettiger Roosevelt to Ickes, June 7, 24, 1943, Ickes Papers. Department of the Interior, *Annual Report*, 1942, pp. xxvi, 198, 203; ibid., 1943, p. 208.

38. In Colorado, cattle growers wanted to graze in Mesa Verde National Park. See Haskell to Mancos Cattlemen's Association, August 23, 1944, McCarran Papers. Haskell wrote, "I think you perhaps know pretty well my opinion of the sophistry involved in the policy of the Park Service . . . members of this subcommittee hold similar views." See also Haskell to Don H. Biggers, September 9, 1944, McCarran Papers. On the rejection of the California Cattlemen's Association to graze in Yosemite National Park, see Oscar Chapman to Hiram Johnson, May 12, 1944, DI Records. Ickes to Anna Boettiger Roosevelt, July 21, 1944, Ickes Papers. In a letter to Ickes on July 7, 1944, DI Records, Drury noted that the members of the committee were from the Sierra Club, the Save the Redwoods League, the California Conservation Council, and the Federation of Western Outdoor Clubs. They were obviously stacked and rejected all thirty-one applications at their June 22, 1944, meeting in San Francisco. See also Department of the Interior, *Annual Report*, 1941, p. 164; ibid., 1942, p. 203; ibid., 1943, p. xxviii, 209–10.

39. NPS History, 29–30, 39–41, 55–62; Department of the Interior, *Annual Report*, 1942, p. 204; ibid., 1943, p. 210.

40. Ickes Diary, 7382 (January 17, 1943), 7460, 7466–67 (February 20, 1943), 7648 (April 17, 1943); Ickes to Roosevelt, September 17, 1943; and Roosevelt memo to Ickes, September 22, 1943, FDR Papers. Some Forest Service personnel opposed a national monument at Jackson Hole; see Ickes to Roosevelt, November 1, 1943, FDR Papers. For background see David J. Saylor, *Jackson Hole, Wyoming*, 117–18; Nathaniel Burt, *Jackson Hole Journal*, 9; Department of the Interior, *Annual Report*, 1942, pp. 210–17.

41. Ickes Diary, 8924 (May 27, 1944), 8950 (June 3, 1944), 8965, 8974 (June 4, 1944), 8976 (June 10, 1944); Irving Brant, "The Fight Over Jackson Hole," 13–14; Katherine Boyd, "Heard About Jackson Hole?," 102–6; Raymond D. Fos-

dick, *John D. Rockefeller, Jr.*, 313–16; John Ise, *Our National Park Policy*, 329; 78th Cong., 1st sess., 1943, House, Committee on Public Lands, *Hearings on H. R. 2241—To Abolish Jackson Hole*, 76 (hereafter cited as *Jackson Hole Hearings*).

42. Ickes Diary, 7985 (July 20, 1943), 8110 (August 29, 1943), 9709 (May 19, 1945); Ickes in 78th Cong., 2d sess., 1943, *House Report* no. 1303, 6–7; and *Jackson Hole Hearings*, 51–61, 81, 87, 111, 137–41, 162; Ise, *Our National Park Policy*, 506; Bernard De Voto, "Sacred Cows and Public Lands," 44–55, and Lester Velie, "They Kicked Us Off Our Land," 20–21, 40–42; J. B. Wilson, "De Voto Distorts Facts," *National Wool Grower* (August 1948), 7, 32, 37; Burt, *Jackson Hole Journal*, 129, 141; Frank Calkins, *Jackson Hole*, 161–78.

43. Lee Muck memo to Rauschenbush, May 1, 1942; and E. N. Kavanagh to M. E. Musgrave, April 21, 1942, DI Records, discuss land management and soil conservation programs respectively. Department of the Interior, *Annual Report*, 1941, pp. 129–30; ibid., 1942, p. 161; ibid., 1945, p. 149.

44. On the role of the important revested Oregon and California Railroad grant lands, see W. H. Horning, "Report on Contributions from the Revested Oregon and California Railroad Grant Lands and the Coos Bay Wagon Road Grant Lands to the U.S. War Production Program," 1–8, 30–41, 67–74, manuscript in DI Records. Department of the Interior, *Annual Report*, 1943, p. 186; ibid., 1945, pp. 149–51, 155–59.

45. Ickes and McCarran were united in supporting McCarran's bill S. 1634 (1945) to create a Natural Resources Council to formulate a national resources policy. See draft of bill in McCarran Papers. President Truman mentioned it in a speech on September 6, 1945, and McCarran lobbied for it unsuccessfully. See McCarran to Hatch, November 30, 1945, McCarran Papers. He sent drafts to about fifty other people. See list attached to Hatch letter. McCarran wanted Hatch to appoint him as chairman of a subcommittee to hold hearings on the bill. See memo for Eva (McCarran's aide), December 4, 1945; and Nathan Koenig (Executive assistant to Harold Ickes) to McCarran, December 5, 1945, McCarran Papers, on Ickes's support. Department of the Interior, *Annual Report*, 1941, p. 131; ibid., 1942, p. 171; ibid., 1943, pp. xxv, 147–48; ibid., 1944, p. xxvi; ibid., 1945, p. 161.

46. The Department of the Interior encouraged local organizations in the West to stimulate mining, such as the Albuquerque, New Mexico, Chamber of Commerce. See Ed Pierson to Director, Grazing Service, Salt Lake City, April 30, 1942, DI Records. Department of the Interior, *Annual Report*, 1944, pp. v, vii–viii, xli. *Albuquerque Tribune*, April 27, 29, 1942.

47. "War Record of the U.S. Geological Survey," manuscript in DI Records, 1–11, 17–28, 29–87, on metals, and 102–81 on other activities; Rauschenbush to R. R. Sayers, August 25, 1942, DI Records, on increasing minerals production; for an estimate of U.S. minerals deposits, see *Mining and Metallurgy* (April 1945), 204–14. Rauschenbush and the Department of the Interior officials were hostile to the Mining Division of the War Production Board, particularly its head, C. K. Leith, whom they accused of usurping their authority. Rauschenbush to Oscar Chapman, September 8, 1942, DI Records, urging a showdown. Both the Bureau of Mines and the Geological Survey were sluggish in the first year of the war. "I think that the two Bureaus have simply not brought themselves to the place yet where they are willing to realize that the Secretary wants them to undertake a very large job," wrote Rauschenbush to Oscar Chapman, March 4, 1942, DI Records.

48. Department of the Interior, *Annual Report*, 1941, pp. v–viii, 63, 70, 74–75, 81; ibid., 1942, pp. viii, 8–11, 67–68, 73, 76.

49. Ibid., 1941, p. 81; ibid., 1942, p. x; ibid., 1943, pp. 68, 72; Ibid., 1944, pp. viii, 73, 84.

50. Ibid., 1944, pp. ix–x, 71; Ickes to John Boettiger, February 23, 1943, Ickes Papers, on political problems and interregional competition.

51. Department of the Interior, *Annual Report*, 1944, p. xi.

8. Visions of the Future: Westerners in Washington

1. *Vital Speeches* 10 (May 1, 1944): 432. Warren recruited prominent individuals such as Donald Nelson for the new California State Reconstruction and Reemployment Commission; see Nelson to Warren, August 22, 1945; Nelson to Warren, October 5, 1945; and Warren to Nelson, November 13, 1945, Nelson Papers.

2. Alvin Hansen, *After the War*; Alvin Hansen and Guy Greer, "Toward Full Use of Our Resources," 130–33; Creighton J. Hill, "The National Resources Planning Board and Its Work," 14; idem, "Alvin Hansen," 15; Philip W. Warken, *A History of the National Resources Planning Board, 1933–1943*, 190–94.

3. Warken, *National Resource Planning Board*, 182, 199; 88, 110 on Watkins; and 110 on Blaisdell. Marion Clawson, *New Deal Planning*, 21–29, 176–88, and also 50, 70, 122, 132, 149, 153, 159, 206; "New Deal Plans Industry Control," *Business Week* (March 20, 1943), 15–17; and Myron W. Watkins, "Post-war Plan and Program," 397–414.

4. U.S. National Resources Planning Board, *Industrial Location and National Resources*, iii–iv; on Delano see Clawson, *New Deal Planning*, 58–60; K. C. Stokes, *Regional Shifts in Population, Production, and Markets, 1939–1943*, 1–34.

5. U.S. National Resources Planning Board, *Pacific Northwest Region—Industrial Development*, vi, 2, 4, 29–33, 36, 39, and a related publication, idem, *Development of Resources and of Economic Opportunity in the Pacific Northwest*. Clawson, *New Deal Planning*, 168, 170.

6. U.S. National Resources Planning Board, *Pacific Southwest Region—Industrial Development*, pp. 1–6, 54.

7. U.S. National Resources Planning Board, *Mountain States Region*, iv, 1–5.

8. Warken, *National Resources Planning Board*, 135, 140–81; Taft quote in Clawson, *New Deal Planning*, 231–32, and see also 45, 53; U.S. National Resources Planning Board, *National Resources Development: Postwar Plan and Program*, 4, 29; Maury Maverick to Frederick A. Delano, December 24, 1942, Maverick Papers.

9. Harold L. Ickes, *The Secret Diary of Harold Ickes*, 1:171, 2:664–69; Warken, *National Resources Planning Board*, 44, 55, 82, 98, 135; Clawson, *New Deal Planning*, 18, 42–47, 49–53, 55–57, 111–13, 119–26, 146–49, 232.

10. *Hearings on S. 53*, 5, 15, and see also 8, 13; Press Release of Department of Interior Information Service, February 16, 1942, pp. 3–14, DI Records; Robert H. Jackson to Ickes, June 3, 1941, urging continuation of antitrust enforcement; and Ickes to Jackson, June 4, 1941, Arnold Papers.

11. *Hearings on S. 53*, 6. As Ickes was becoming more tired and frustrated, in December 1944 he submitted another of his resignations, which, as usual,

Roosevelt declined. See Ickes to Roosevelt, December 13, 1944; and Roosevelt to Ickes, December 9, 16, 1944, FDR Papers.

12. *Hearings on S. 53*, 15; see also Harold L. Ickes, "America's Post-War Frontier," speech before Commonwealth Club of California, April 14, 1944, Ickes Speech File, 4300–4314, Ickes Papers. *San Francisco Chronicle*, April 15, 1944.

13. Department of the Interior, *Annual Report*, 1942, p. vii; ibid., 1944, p. viii.

14. Ibid., 1945, p. xii. Ickes promoted McCarran's bill, S. 1634 (1945), a copy of which is in McCarran Papers. Nathan W. Koenig to McCarran, December 5, 1945, McCarran Papers, in which Ickes's executive assistant asked for McCarran's support. McCarran also solicited Bernard Baruch's views on this proposal; J. G. Sourwine to Baruch, November 8, 1945, McCarran Papers. But the Bureau of the Budget at the time was anxious to secure passage of the Employment Act of 1946 first and planned to integrate the McCarran Bill; see J. B. Hudson to Hatch, December 14, 1945, McCarran Papers. As Assistant Director of the Budget F. J. Bailey noted, "Planning for the conservation . . . of natural resources should be closely related to the machinery to be . . . set up for planning the national budget under the Full Employment Bill." McCarran also solicited the president's support for decentralization of industry; see McCarran to Roosevelt, May 11, 1944; and Roosevelt to McCarran, May 22, 1944, FDR Papers. The last cited letter was drafted by James F. Byrnes.

15. *Hearings on S. 53*, 400, 405, 406, 408, 410, 417. See also Michael Straus in *SB Committee, Hearings*, part 40, pp. 4722–26; Department of the Interior, *Annual Report*, 1941, pp. 30–31, 38, 40; ibid., 1943, pp. ix–x, 1–2, 35; ibid., 1944, pp. xiii, xiv, 2, 13, 49.

16. Department of the Interior, *Annual Report*, 1944, pp. 4–6; ibid., 1945, pp. 12–15.

17. Ibid., 1943, p. 35.

18. Ibid., 1944, p. 2.

19. Ibid., 14.

20. Bernard Baruch and John Hancock, *War and Post-War Adjustment Policy*, 8–10, 23, 25, 32–36, also published as 78th Cong., 2d sess., *Senate Document* no. 154. On Maverick, the biography by Richard B. Henderson, *Maury Maverick: A Political Biography* (Austin: University of Texas Press, 1970), completely ignores the World War II era and is useless for that period. See *Current Biography*, 1944, pp. 454–58, for a short sketch. I have utilized the extensive Maverick Papers.

21. 78th Cong., 2d sess., 1944 House, Special Committee on Post-War Economic Policy and Planning, *Hearings*, part 1, pp. 55–63; and *New York Times*, June 14, 1944; *SB Committee, Hearings*, part 35, pp. 4335–85.

22. Copy of speech, July 14, 1944, pp. 2, 3, 4, 6, 7, 15, 16, 28, Maverick Papers; *New York Times*, July 15, 1944.

23. Speech by Honorable Maury Maverick in Biltmore Bowl, Los Angeles, July 11, 1944, pp. 2, 3, 4, 15, Maverick Papers. See also Maverick to Murray, October 9, 1945, on small business policies; and Maverick to Murray, April 15, 1944, in SWPC Records. Maverick suggested to Roosevelt that he supervise settlement of war veterans in Alaska, which provoked a bitter and vitriolic response from Ickes, who considered this to be in his domain. See Maverick to Roosevelt, November 1, 1944; Roosevelt to Maverick, November 21, 1944, and the biting letter of Ickes to Maverick, December 20, 1944, charging him with making job applications, FDR Papers. Truman to Maverick, May 2, 1945; and Maverick to Maurice Latta, May 9, 1945, Truman Papers.

Notes to Pages 180–84

24. Maury Maverick, "Post-War Plan for the West—Seattle, Portland Region," July 19, 1944, pp. 1, 2, 3, 4, 5, Maverick Papers; *Portland Oregonian*, July 31, 1944; George Moscrip to A. B. Walker, August 4, 1944, reports on reaction to the plan in Portland, Maverick Papers. See also "Speech to Association of Washington Cities," April 21, 1943, Seattle, Maverick Papers.

25. Maury Maverick, "A Report on Reconversion Problems and Post-War Development on the Pacific Coast Presented Before Seattle Chamber of Commerce," July 18, 1944, pp. 2, 3–5, 7, 22, 27–28, 29–31, Maverick Papers; Arthur H. Langlie to Maverick, January 15, 1942; John Boettiger to Maverick, March 1, 1943; and Maverick to J. J. Underwood, August 8, 1944, Maverick Papers. Maverick explains his small business policy proposals in greater detail in Maverick to Murray, November 15, 1944, SWPC Records.

26. Maverick, "Report on Reconversion," 29, 30, 31, and "Description of Super-Highway and Super-Airport System for entire United States" (1944), 1–4, manuscripts in Maverick Papers. Hayden had already talked directly with Roosevelt about postwar highway construction; see Hayden to Donald L. Greer, December 10, 1943; and Hayden to Greer, February 11, 1944, in Hayden Papers. See also Maverick to Arnold, April 11, 1943, Arnold Papers.

27. *Hearings on S. 53*, 534–39. The Arnold Papers contain extensive speeches by Arnold in the same vein. See also Arnold to Roosevelt, May 17, 1941; Arnold to Robert H. Jackson, September 9, 1942; and Arnold to Jackson, September 10, 1942, in Gene Gressley, ed., *Voltaire and the Cowboy: The Letters of Thurman Arnold*, 320–22, 330–34, 334–38. By 1942 Kaiser came to Arnold to complain bitterly about Nelson, although Arnold felt that his views on antitrust policies were close to those of Nelson; see Arnold to Nelson, August 29, 1941, Nelson Papers.

28. *SB Committee, Hearings*, part 40, p. 4806, and part 42, p. 5166; Murray to Alben Barkley, July 10, 1942, described the work of his committee. The president encouraged his efforts, noting: "I am glad that you have called my attention to the hardships that may be suffered by many small businesses. The problem is one that has concerned me for some time and I wish very much that a solution might be found" (Roosevelt to Murray, August 31, 1942, Murray Papers). Murray attacked the Committee for Economic Development's emphasis on big business; see his memo, October 20, 1943, Murray Papers. He also rejected charges of the *Wall Street Journal*, July 4, 1944, that he was sharpening sectionalism by setting off the West against the East; see his letter to the *Wall Street Journal*, July 6, 1944.

29. *SB Committee, Hearings*, part 44, p. 5572. Murray was a frequent radio speaker. See, for example, "Small Business in the War Effort," Murray with Howard P. Costigan, February 20, 1942, Murray Papers.

30. *SB Committee, Hearings*, part 42, p. 5166, part 40, p. 4806, and part 44, p. 5572.

31. Ibid., part 41, p. 4969, and part 43, p. 5328.

32. Ibid., part 41, p. 4969, and part 40, pp. 4720, 4806.

33. Ibid., part 43, p. 5328; "Address of James E. Murray to Harvard University Graduate School of Business," February 12, 1944, pp. 13–16, expresses similar views, manuscripts in Murray Papers.

34. 78th Cong., 1st sess., 1944, Senate, Sub-Committee on Military Affairs, *Hearings on Problems of Contract Termination*, 30–35; Murray to Francis Biddle, October 5, 1943; Murray to Truman, September 30, 1943; and Murray to Truman, October 11, 1943, Truman Papers. *New York Times*, October 12, 1943,

and February 12, May 3, 4, 5, 1944; James E. Murray, "Contract Settlement Act of 1944," Spring, 1944, manuscript in Murray Papers. Baruch to Murray, July 17, 1944, Murray Papers, noted that he thought the act to be a significant contribution to reconversion. See also Stephen K. Bailey, *Congress Makes a Law*, 30–32; Roland Young, *Congressional Politics in the Second World War*, 200, and Allen Drury, *A Senate Journal, 1943–1945*, 157.

35. U.S. Office of Contract Settlement, "War Contract Termination and Settlement," 1–3, 188–92, manuscript in Murray Papers; Murray to Sheldon E. Davis, September 13, 1943; and Alfred J. Van Tassel to Murray, September 23, 1944, Murray Papers. Drury, *Senate Journal*, 228–38; *Wall Street Journal*, June 23, 1944; *New York Times*, May 13, August 26, 1944; *Washington Post*, August 2, 5, 8, 1944; Spritzer, "New Dealer," 193–209, 216–59, 305–56; *Independent Business*, 15, 29; Memorandum on American Forum of Air Radio Broadcast, December 7, 1943, and Murray's discussion with Maverick about the role of small business in the postwar era, June 16, 1944, Murray Papers.

36. 78th Cong., 1st sess., 1943, Senate, Sub-Committee of Special Committee on Post-War Economic Policy and Planning, Sen. Res. no. 102, *Hearings*, 2, 3, 5 (hereafter cited as *O'Mahoney Hearings*). I have also consulted the extensive correspondence of Joseph C. O'Mahoney at the University of Wyoming, Laramie.

37. McCarran deserves a full-scale biography. Jerome Edwards, *Pat McCarran, Political Boss of Nevada*, deals competently with McCarran's role in state politics.

38. *McCarran Committee Hearings*, part 4, pp. 188–89. Murray enthusiastically supported the movement for decentralization; see Murray memo and Press Release on Industrial Decentralization, January 21, 1943, Murray Papers. McCarran also solicited Maverick's views; see Maverick to McCarran, July 14, 1944, Maverick Papers. McCarran's statement, November 16, 1944, on industrial decentralization, for colleagues, typescript in McCarran Papers, and also "Remarks of Honorable Pat McCarran on Industrial Decentralization at a Joint Meeting of the Members of the House and Senate held October 4, 1943," typescript McCarran Papers.

39. *McCarran Committee Hearings*, part 4, pp. 183–84. He received widespread national support. Southern senators were enthusiastic; see Walter F. George to McCarran, July 3, 1943; Lister Hill to McCarran, July 3, 1943; Alben Barkley to McCarran, July 5, 1943; Harry Truman to McCarran, July 9, 1943, noting, "I believe you have something"; and Harley Kilgore to McCarran, July 19, 1943, McCarran Papers.

40. *McCarran Committee Hearings*, part 4, p. 184. McCarran to William Hopkins, June 15, 1944, McCarran Papers, soliciting grass-roots support.

41. 78 Cong., 2d sess., 1944, Senate, Special Committee to Investigate Industrial Centralization, *Report*, 2, 3, 5; *New York Times*, October 8, 1944.

9. Visions of the Future: The View from Western States and Cities

1. U.S. National Resources Planning Board, *State Planning*, vi, vii, viii, 2, 4, 5, 25, 30, 36, 40, 41, 48, 53, 58; Clawson, *New Deal Planning*, 189–98.

2. Utah Department of Publicity and Industrial Development, *After Victory: Report of Cooperative Planning Program for Utah and the Wasatch Front* (n.p., 1943), 5–7, 13, 17, 25, copy in Robert W. Kenny Papers, Bancroft Library, University of California, Berkeley.

3. *San Francisco News*, February 14, 1944, clipping in McCarran Scrapbooks, McCarran Papers.

4. *San Francisco News*, October 2, 3, 1943; Western Conference on Postwar Problems in the States, sponsored by Council of State Governments, Tentative Program, Brief Resume, and Attendance List, 1–5, typescript in Kenny Papers. Kenny was chairman of the conference while also attorney general of California.

5. Brief Resumé, Interstate Conference on Post-War Industrial Developments of the West, held February 11, 12, 1944, Carson City, Nevada, 9–10, McCarran Papers. *Carson City Star*, February 12, 13, 1944.

6. McCarran's "Blueprint for a New Frontier" for governors of eleven western states is in his letter to Utah's Governor Herbert Maw, April 9, 1943, pp. 1–2, 6–9, typescript in McCarran Papers. McCarran to Maw, April 2, 1943; and McCarran Press Release, April 9, 1943, McCarran Papers. On September 29, 30, 1944, another Western Conference on Post-War Problems convened in Salt Lake City; see typescript of proceedings in Kenny Papers. States represented were California, Colorado, Idaho, Nevada, New Mexico, Oregon, Utah, and Wyoming. Sponsorship came from the Council of State Governments and Utah Commission on Interstate Cooperation. See also *McCarran Committee Hearings*, part 4, pp. 282–84.

7. McCarran, "Blueprint for a New Frontier"; *McCarran Committee Hearings*, part 4, pp. 205–7.

8. Pat McCarran, "The West—Key to Full Employment and Our Post-War Prosperity," Address before Special Joint Session of California State Legislature, June 9, 1944, 2, 3, 4, McCarran Papers; *Sacramento Union*, June 10, 1944. Kenny was instrumental in convening a "Statewide Emergency Legislative Conference," in Sacramento, January 5, 6, 1946, to draw up plans for the state; a copy of "Proceedings" is in Kenny Papers. Richard Neutra, the famous architect, served as chairman of the California State Planning Board in 1946 and provided his expertise. Esther McCoy, *Richard Neutra*; Neutra magazine clipping, Kenny Papers.

9. *McCarran Committee Hearings*, part 4, p. 280.

10. Ibid., 284, 285.

11. "Speech of Senator Pat McCarran Delivered on radio stations KOH and KENO on August 30, 1944," pp. 1, 3, McCarran Papers.

12. *McCarran Committee Hearings*, part 4, p. 286.

13. Ibid., 287, 289.

14. Ibid., 332, 343.

15. On Heron see ibid., 295. The library of the Institute of Governmental Studies at the University of California has the most complete collection of this agency's unpublished as well as published materials.

16. *McCarran Committee Hearings*, part 4, p. 295; Alexander Heron to Nelson, October 8, 1945; and Nelson to Heron, October 15, 1945, Nelson Papers.

17. *McCarran Committee Hearings*, part 4, p. 293; Heron to Nelson, November 21, 1945, Nelson Papers.

18. *McCarran Committee Hearings*, part 4, p. 293; Heron to Nelson, October 20, 1945, Nelson Papers.

19. *McCarran Committee Hearings*, part 4, pp. 293–94.

20. Ibid., 294–95.

21. Ibid., 294.

22. Fuller discussions of this subject can be found in Gerald D. Nash, "Planning for the Postwar City: The Urban West in World War II," 99–112, and idem,

"Urban Development in the Southwest," 471–80; "City Planning: Battle of the Approach," *Fortune* 28 (November 1943): 164–68, 222–23; "Mr. Moses Dissects the 'Long Haired' Planners," *New York Times Magazine* 6 (June 1944): 16–17. Moses further explained his views in 78th Cong., 2d sess., 1944, House, Special Committee on Post-War Economic Policy and Planning, *Hearings*, part 6, pp. 1780–84.

23. Carl Abbott, *The New Urban America*, 118–19.

24. Martin Schiesl, "City Planning and the Federal Government in World War II," 127, 140.

25. Ibid., 129–35. The papers of the Los Angeles mayor Fletcher Bowron contain scores of letters reflecting similar sentiments; see Fletcher Bowron to Morgan Adams, September 25, 1942, in Fletcher A. Bowron Papers, Henry L. Huntington Library and Art Gallery, San Marino, California.

26. Quoted in Mel Scott, *The San Francisco Bay Area*, 246–48.

27. Carl Abbott, "Portland in Pacific War," 12–24. The letters of Robert E. Riley at the Oregon Historical Society in Portland provide ample illustration of Abbott's thesis. Robert Moses, *Portland Improvement*, 1–3. "How Cities are Preparing for the Post-War Era: Portland," *Planning* (1944), 78–80.

28. Perry Kaufman, "The Best City of Them All: A City Biography of Las Vegas, 1930–1960" (Ph.D. diss., University of California, Santa Barbara, 1974), and idem, "City Boosters," 46–60; Edwards, "Clark County," *Nevada*, 2:677–93; Las Vegas Chamber of Commerce, "Conditions in Business and Real Estate and their Dependency Upon the Local Defense Industries," 1–7, manuscripts in McCarran Papers. See also "Minutes of the Business and Industry Committee of Clark County Economic Council," July 28, 1943, Carville Papers.

10. Visions of the Future: The Private Sector

1. *SB Committee, Hearings*, part 42, p. 5182.

2. *McCarran Committee Hearings*, part 4, pp. 190–92, 196.

3. Wheeler in *SB Committee, Hearings*, part 43, pp. 5341–42; Landells in ibid., 5425–27, 5429–33; see also Louis B. Lundborg in ibid., 5442–43; and C. N. Coffing in *McCarran Committee Hearings*, part 4, pp. 298–99.

4. *McCarran Committee Hearings*, part 4, pp. 185–86; Nicholson in *SB Committee, Hearings*, part 41, pp. 4970–74. Rex Nicholson, "The Importance to the West of Conversion and Expansion," speech given to Council of State Governments meeting in Salt Lake, September 29, 1944, typescript in McCarran Papers; Nicholson to McCarran, July 10, 1944; and McCarran to Nicholson, July 15, 1944, McCarran Papers; Pat McCarran, "Build the West to Build the Nation," speech for Builders of the West delivered on June 9, 1944, at Palace Hotel in San Francisco, McCarran Papers.

5. *SB Committee, Hearings*, part 41, pp. 5026, 5028. The Industrial West Foundation was a group similar to the Builders of the West and also recruited prominent individuals like Donald Nelson. See George N. Malone to Nelson, October 25, 1944; and Nelson to Malone, November 13, 1945, Nelson Papers.

6. *SB Committee, Hearings*, part 41, pp. 5122–24; see also F. L. McGovern in *McCarran Committee Hearings*, part 4, pp. 352–58; and for similar views of the Reno Chamber of Commerce see ibid., 412–16.

7. *Small Business Hearings*, part 42, pp. 5197–98.

8. Ibid., part 40, pp. 4744, 4747, 4748.

9. Ibid., part 44, p. 5660; *McCarran Committee Hearings*, part 4, pp. 215–17. See also Harold Weber in *SB Committee, Hearings*, part 43, pp. 5458–60.

10. *SB Committee, Hearings*, part 43, pp. 5407–11; see 5411–15 for his detailed plans to expand trade with the Orient.

11. Ibid., part 44, pp. 5634–35, 5636–43.

12. Ibid., part 40, p. 4837.

13. Ibid., part 41, p. 4766.

14. Ibid., part 43, pp. 5530–31, and part 44, pp. 5678–79, 5687.

15. Ibid., part 41, pp. 5136–37; see also John F. Shelley in *O'Mahoney Hearings*, 186.

16. *SB Committee, Hearings*, part 44, pp. 5675–77; *O'Mahoney Hearings*, 46–47; and Cornelius Haggerty, in *Truman Committee Hearings*, part 31, pp. 15,089–90.

17. *SB Committee, Hearings*, part 44, pp. 5686–87.

18. Ibid., 5688.

19. William Allen White, *The Changing West*, 136–37.

20. Vannevar Bush, *Science*, 11.

21. Joseph Kinsey Howard, *Montana, High, Wide, and Handsome*, 6, 7, 321. See also Garnsey, "Future of the Mountain States," 329–36; and manuscript of an article, "Montana Twins," by Howard for *Harper's*, Joseph Kinsey Howard Papers, University of Montana, Missoula.

22. A. G. Mezerick, *The Revolt of the South and West*, ix, xiv, 290; see also A. G. Mezerick, "West Coast versus East," 48–52. Mezerick to Murray, February 25, 1946, requesting data for his writings, Murray Papers. "Postwar Hopes and Fears on the West Coast," *Business Week* (November 20, 1943), 20.

23. Wendell Berge, *Economic Freedom for the West*, x, 148, 149.

24. Bernard De Voto, "The Anxious West," 489, 490; Wallace Stegner, *The Uneasy Chair*.

25. Bernard De Voto, "The West Against Itself," 13.

11. Conclusion: World War II and Western Economic Growth

1. For a survey of these broad trends see Nash, *American West in the Twentieth Century*, 213–89; and Nash, "Reshaping Arizona's Economy," in Luey and Stowe, eds., *Arizona at Seventy-Five*, 127–33.

2. Robert Reich and Ira C. Magaziner, *Minding America's Business*.

3. Christopher Freeman, *Technological Policy and Economic Performance*; and R. A. Morse, "Japan's Drive to Preeminence," 3–21.

4. See Paul A. C. Koistinen, *The Military-Industrial Complex*; and Seymour Melman, *The Permanent War Economy*.

5. *New York Times*, March 29, 1988.

6. Martin and Susan Tolchin, *Buying Into America*. See also Benjamin Friedman, *The Consequences of American Economic Policy Under Reagan and After*.

7. *New York Times*, February 24, 1988.

8. Kaiser quoted in Lane, *Ships for Victory*, 485–86.

9. On the nineteenth century, see Leonard J. Arrington, *The Changing Economic Structure of the Mountain West, 1850–1950*, 54 ff.; on the twentieth century, see Roger W. Lotchin, "The Metropolitan-Military Complex in Comparative

Perspective," in Gerald D. Nash, ed., *The Urban West*, 19–30; and Roger W. Lotchin, ed., *The Martial Metropolis*.

10. Sar Levitan, *Swords into Plowshares*; and Keith W. Olson, *The G.I. Bill*.

11. Allen C. Kelley and Jeffrey G. Williamson, *Lessons from Japanese Development*; Robert Reich, *The Next American Frontier*; and James C. Abegglen, *Management and Worker*.

Bibliography

Archival Sources

Arizona State University Library, Tempe
  Arizona Collection
  Carl Hayden Papers
Bancroft Library, University of California, Berkeley
  Henry J. Kaiser Papers
  Robert W. Kenny Papers
  Ernest O. Lawrence Papers
Colorado State Historical Society, Denver
  World War II Records Collection
Federal Records Center, San Bruno, California
  Fair Employment Practices Committee, Region 12, Records
Henry L. Huntington Library and Art Gallery, San Marino, California
  Fletcher A. Bowron Papers
  Donald A. Nelson Papers
  U.S. Petroleum Administration for War, Region X, Records.
Library of Congress, Manuscripts Division, Washington, D.C.
  Harold L. Ickes Diary
  Harold L. Ickes Papers
University of Montana, Missoula
  James E. Murray Papers
  Joseph Kinsey Howard Papers
National Archives and Records Service, Suitland, Maryland
  U.S. Petroleum Administration for War, Records
National Archives And Records Service, Washington, D.C.
  U.S. Committee for Congested Production Areas, Records
  U.S. Department of the Interior, Secretary's File
  U.S. Metals Reserve Corporation, Records
  U.S. Senate, Special Committee to Investigate the National Defense Program, 1941–47, Records
  U.S. Smaller War Plants Corporation, Records
  U.S. War Production Board, Records

Bibliography

Nevada State Archives, Carson City
   E. P. Carville Papers
Nevada State Historical Society, Reno
   Pat McCarran Papers
Oregon Historical Society, Portland
   Edgar Kaiser Papers
   Oregon Shipbuilding Company, Records
   Oregon War Industries, Records
   Robert E. Riley Papers
Franklin D. Roosevelt Library, Hyde Park, New York
   Franklin D. Roosevelt Papers
   Elbert D. Thomas Papers
University of Texas, Austin
   Maury Maverick Papers
Harry S. Truman Library, Independence, Missouri
   Harry S. Truman Papers
University of Wyoming, Laramie
   Thurman Arnold Papers
   Joseph C. O'Mahoney Papers

Government Documents

U.S. Attorney-General. *Report of the Attorney-General on the Aluminum Industry, 1945.* Washington, 1945.
U.S. Bureau of Mines. *Minerals Yearbook, 1940–46.* Washington, 1940–46.
U.S. Congress. *Congressional Record, 1940–46.* Washington, 1940–46.
———. 73d Cong., 1st sess., 1934, House, Committee on Public Lands, *Hearings on Taylor Grazing Act.*
———. 74th Cong., 1st sess., 1935, Senate, Committee on Public Lands and Surveys, *Hearings on Taylor Grazing Act.* 2 parts.
———. 76th Cong., 1st sess., 1939, House, Committee on Merchant Marine and Fisheries, *Hearings on Dry Dock Facilities on the West Coast.*
———. 76th Cong., 2d sess., 1942, House, Committee on Merchant Marine and Fisheries, *Hearings on Higgins Contracts, July 22–25, 1942.*
———. 77th Cong., 1st sess., 1942, Senate, Committee on Patents, *Hearings on S. 2303 and Patents.* 2 parts.
———. 77th Cong., 1st sess., 1941–47, Senate, Special Committee Investigating the National Defense Program, *Hearings.* 43 parts.
———. 77th Cong., 1st sess., 1942, Senate, Sub-Committee of the Committee on Public Lands and Surveys, *Hearings Pursuant to Senate Resolution no. 53.* 4 parts.
———. 77th Cong., 2d sess., 1943, House, Committee on Merchant Marine and Fisheries, *Interim Report on Investigation of South Portland Shipbuilding Company, 1942.*
———. 77th Cong., 2d sess., 1942, House, Sub-Committee of Committee on Irrigation, *Hearings on Columbia River.*
———. 77th Cong., 2d sess., 1942, Senate, Committee on Banking and Currency, *Hearings on Smaller War Plants Corporation—S. Bill 2250.*
———. 77th Cong., 2d sess., 1941–47, Senate, Special Committee to Study the Problems of American Small Business, *Hearings.* 99 parts.

Bibliography

———. 77th Cong., 2d sess., 1942, Senate, Sub-Committee of Special Committee on Investigation of Silver, *Hearings*.

———. 78th Cong., 1st and 2d sess., 1944, House, Committee on Merchant Marine and Fisheries, *Executive Hearings on Rheem Manufacturing Company*.

———. 78th Cong., 1st sess., 1943, House, Committee on Public Lands, *Hearings on H.R. 2241—To Abolish Jackson Hole*.

———. 78th Cong., 1st sess., 1944, House, Sub-Committee of Committee on Naval Affairs, *Hearings on Congested Areas*. 8 parts.

———. 78th Cong., 1st sess., 1943, House, Sub-Committee on Appropriations, Appropriation Bill for 1944, *Hearings*.

———. 78th Cong., 1st sess., 1943, Senate, Sub-Committee of Special Committee on Post-War Economic Policy and Planning, Sen. Res. no. 102, *Hearings*.

———. 78th Cong., 1st sess., 1944, Senate, Sub-Committee on Military Affairs, *Hearings on Problems of Contract Termination*.

———. 78th Cong., 2d sess., 1944, House, Special Committee on Post-War Economic Policy and Planning, *Hearings*. 9 parts.

———. 78th Cong., 2d sess., 1944, House, Sub-Committee on Production in Shipbuilding Plants, Committee on Merchant Marine and Fisheries, *Executive Hearings*. 4 parts.

———. 78th Cong., 2d sess., 1944, House, Sub-Committee on Shipyard Profits of Committee on Merchant Marine and Fisheries, *Hearings on House Resolution no. 52*.

———. 78th Cong., 2d sess., 1944, Senate, Committee on Appropriations, *Hearings*.

———. 78th Cong., 2d sess., 1945, Senate, Committee on Appropriations, Independent Offices Appropriation Bill for 1945, *Hearings*.

———. 78th Cong., 2d sess., 1944, Senate, Special Committee to Investigate Industrial Centralization, *Report*.

———. 78th Cong., 2d sess., 1944–45, Senate, Special Committee to Investigate the Centralization of Heavy Industry in the United States, *Hearings*. 5 parts.

———. 78th Cong., 2d sess., 1944, Senate, Sub-Committee on Mining and the Minerals Industry, *Senate Sub-Committee Print no. 6*.

———. 78th Cong., 2d sess., 1944, Senate, Sub-Committee on War Mobilization of the Committee on Military Affairs, *Economic and Political Aspects of International Cartels*.

———. 79th Cong., 1st sess., 1945, House, Committee on Ways and Means, *Hearings on 1945 Extension of Termination Date of Renegotiation Act*.

———. 79th Cong., 1st sess., 1945, Senate, Committee on Military Affairs, Sub-Committee on Surplus Property, *Joint Hearings on Aluminum Plant Disposal*. 5 parts.

———. 79th Cong., 1st sess., 1945, Senate, Sub-Committee of Committee on Public Lands and Surveys, *Hearings on Administration and Use of Public Lands*.

———. 79th Cong., 1st sess., 1945, Senate, Sub-Committee on Surplus Property of the Committee on Military Affairs and the Industrial Reorganization Sub-Committee of the Special Committee on Postwar Economic Policy and Planning, *Hearings on War Plants Disposal—Iron and Steel Plants*.

———. 79th Cong., 2d sess., 1946, House, Committee on Appropriations, Sub-Committee, *Hearings on Interior Department Appropriation Bill for 1947*.

Bibliography

————. 79th Cong., 2d sess., 1946, House, Committee on Merchant Marine and Fisheries, *Hearings on House Resolution no. 38.*

————. 79th Cong., 2d sess., 1946, House, Committee on Merchant Marine and Fisheries, *Hearings on the Accounting Practices of the War Shipping Administration and U.S. Maritime Commission.*

————. 79th Cong., 2d sess., 1947, Senate, Special Committee to Study Problems of American Small Business, *The Future of Independent Business: Progress Report of the Chairman to the Members of the Committee.*

————. 79th Cong., 2d sess., 1946, Senate, Special Committee to Study Problems of American Small Business, *Report of the Smaller War Plants Corporation: Economic Concentration and World War II.*

————. 80th Cong., 1st sess., 1947, House, *Hearings on Interior Department Appropriations Bill for 1948.*

U.S. Department of the Interior. *Annual Reports, 1941–46.* Washington, 1941–46.

U.S. President's Air Policy Commission. *Survival in the Air Age.* Washington, 1946.

U.S. Smaller War Plants Corporation. *Reports, 1942–1946.* Washington, 1942–46.

U.S. Surplus Property Administration. *Aircraft Plants and Facilities: Report of the Surplus Property Administration to the Congress, January 14, 1946.* Washington, 1946.

U.S. Surplus Property Board. *Aluminum Plants and Facilities.* Washington, 1945.

U.S. Temporary National Economic Committee. *The Distribution of Ownership in the 200 Largest Nonfinancial Corporations.* Washington, 1940.

————. *Final Report and Recommendations of the Temporary National Economic Committee.* Washington, 1943.

U.S. War Production Board. *Minutes, 1942–1945.* Washington, 1945.

————. *Production Achievements and the Reconversion Outlook: Report of the Chairman, October 9, 1945.* Washington, 1945.

U.S. Women's Bureau. *Bulletin.* Washington, 1919–45.

Newspapers

Albuquerque Tribune, 1941–46.
Colorado Labor Advocate, 1942.
Colorado Springs News, 1940–45.
Denver Post, 1940–46.
Journal of Commerce (New York), 1941–4
Las Vegas Age (Nevada), 1941–42.
Las Vegas Review Journal, 1941–42.
Nevada State Journal, 1941–44.
New York Daily Mirror, 1947.
New York Herald Tribune, 1942–47.
New York Times, 1939–47.
Pioche Record, 1941.
Portland Oregonian, 1941–46.
Reno Gazette, 1941–43.
Rocky Mountain News, 1942.
Salt Lake Tribune, 1941–46.

Bibliography

San Francisco Chronicle, 1941–46.
San Francisco News, 1943–44.
Wall Street Journal, 1944–46.
Washington Post, 1940–46.
Washington Star, 1940–46.
Washington Times Herald, 1940–46.

Periodicals

Aero Digest, 1941–46.
American Aviation, 1945.
American Cattle Producer, 1940–46.
Architectural Forum, 1940–46.
Aviation, 1941–46.
Business Week, 1941–46.
Congressional Digest, 1940–46.
Current Biography, 1944.
Engineering and Mining Journal, 1940–46.
Fortune, 1940–46.
Lamp, 1941–46.
Liberty, 1944.
Life, 1941–46.
Log, 1940–46.
Marine Engineering and Shipping Review, 1943.
Mining Journal, 1940–46.
Mining World, 1941–46.
Monthly Labor Review, 1940–46.
Nation's Business, 1940–46.
Newsweek, 1940–47.
Oil and Gas Journal, 1940–46.
Planning, 1944.
Saturday Evening Post, 1941–46.
Small Business Quarterly, 1942–46.
Survey Graphic, 1941–46.
Survey of Current Business, 1940–46.
Time, 1940–46.
Utah Economic and Business Review, 1946.
Vital Speeches, 1944.

Books

Abbott, Carl. *The New Urban America: Growth and Politics in Sunbelt Cities*. Chapel Hill: University of North Carolina Press, 1982.
Abegglen, James C. *Management and Worker: The Japanese Solution*. New York: C. E. Tuttle, 1988.
Allen, Arthur P., and Betty V. Schneider. *Industrial Relations in the California Aircraft Industry*. Berkeley: Institute of Industrial Relations, University of California, 1956.

271

Bibliography

American Merchant Marine Conference. *Proceedings*. New York: American Merchant Marine Association, 1941–46.

Archibald, Katherine. *Wartime Shipyard*. Berkeley: University of California Press, 1947.

Arnall, Ellis. *The Shore Dimly Seen*. Philadelphia: J. B. Lippincott Co., 1947.

———. *What the People Want*. Philadelphia: J. B. Lippincott Co., 1948.

Arrington, Leonard J. *The Changing Economic Structure of the Mountain West, 1850–1950*. Logan: Utah State University, 1963.

Arrington, Leonard J., and Anthony T. Cluff. *Federally Financed Industrial Plants Constructed in Utah During World War II*. Logan: Utah State University, 1969.

Arrington, Leonard J., and George Jensen. *The Defense Industry of Utah*. Logan: Utah State University, 1965.

Bailey, Stephen K. *Congress Makes a Law: The Story of the Employment Act of 1946*. New York: Columbia University Press, 1950.

Barton, Charles. *Howard Hughes and His Flying Boat*. Fallbrook, Calif.: Aero Publishers, 1982.

Baruch, Bernard, and John Hancock. *War and Postwar Adjustment Policy*. Washington: U.S. Government Printing Office, 1944.

Bates, J. Leonard. *The Origins of Teapot Dome*. Urbana: University of Illinois Press, 1963.

Baxter, James Phinney, III. *Scientists Against Time*. Boston: Little, Brown and Co., 1946.

Berge, Wendell. *Economic Freedom for the West*. Lincoln: University of Nebraska Press, 1946.

Berle, Adolf A. *The Twentieth Century Capitalist Revolution*. New York: Harcourt, Brace, 1954.

Berle, Adolf A., and Gardiner C. Means. *The Modern Corporation and Private Property*. 2 vols. New York: Macmillan Co., 1933.

Boeing Company. *Pedigree of Champions: Boeing Since 1916*. 4th ed. Seattle: Boeing Company, 1977.

Burt, Nathaniel. *Jackson Hole Journal*. Norman: University of Oklahoma Press, 1983.

Bush, Vannevar. *Science: The Endless Frontier*. Washington: U.S. Government Printing Office, 1945.

Calef, Wesley. *Private Grazing and Public Lands*. Chicago: University of Chicago Press, 1960.

Calkins, Frank. *Jackson Hole*. New York: Random House, 1973.

Calshipbuilding Company. San Pedro: n.p., 1947.

Campbell, Robert F. *The History of Basic Metals Price Control*. New York: Columbia University Press, 1948.

Chandler, Alfred D. *The Visible Hand*. Cambridge: Harvard University Press, Belknap Press, 1977.

Clark, John G. *Energy and the Federal Government: Fossil Fuel Policies, 1900–1946*. Urbana: University of Illinois Press, 1987.

Clawson, Augusta. *Shipyard Diary of a Woman Welder*. New York: Penguin Books, 1944.

Clawson, Marion. *New Deal Planning: The National Resources Planning Board*. Baltimore: Johns Hopkins University Press, 1981.

———. *The Western Range Livestock Industry*. New York: McGraw-Hill, 1950.

Bibliography

Cleland, Robert G. *A History of Phelps Dodge, 1834–1950.* New York: McGraw-Hill, 1952.

Craven, Wesley Frank, and James Lea Cate, eds. *Army Air Forces in World War II.* 7 vols. Chicago: University of Chicago Press, 1948–58.

Cunningham, William G. *The Aircraft Industry: A Study in Industrial Location.* Los Angeles: L. L. Morrison, 1951.

Day, John S. *Sub-Contracting Policy in the Airframe Industry.* Boston: Harvard Graduate School of Business Administration, 1956.

Doerner, H. A. *Magnesium—Present Outlook for a Magnesium Metal Industry in the Northwest.* State College of Washington, Mining Experiment Station, *Bulletin P.* Pullman: State College of Washington, 1943.

Drury, Allen. *A Senate Journal, 1943–1945.* New York: Da Capo, 1972.

Edwards, Jerome. *Pat McCarran, Political Boss of Nevada.* Reno: University of Nevada Press, 1982.

Elliott, Russell R. *Nevada's Twentieth Century Mining Booms: Tonopah-Goldfield-Ely.* Reno: University of Nevada Press, 1966.

Elliott, Russell R., with William Rowley. *History of Nevada.* 2d ed. Lincoln: University of Nebraska Press, 1987.

Fosdick, Raymond D. *John D. Rockefeller, Jr.* New York: Harper, 1956.

Foss, Philip O. *Politics and Grass: The Administration of Grazing on the Public Domain.* Seattle: University of Washington Press, 1960.

Freeman, Christopher. *Technological Policy and Economic Performance: Lessons from Japan.* New York: Columbia University Press, 1987.

Frey, John W., and Chandler Ide. *A History of the Petroleum Administration for War, 1941–1945.* Washington: U.S. Government Printing Office, 1946.

Friedman, Benjamin. *The Consequences of American Economic Policy Under Reagan and After.* New York: Random House, 1988.

Galbraith, John Kenneth. *The New Industrial State.* Boston: Houghton Mifflin and Co., 1967.

Garnsey, Morris E. *America's New Frontier: The Mountain West.* New York: Knopf, 1950.

Gerber, Albert B. *Bashful Billionaire.* New York: Lyle Stuart, 1967.

Gressley, Gene, ed. *Voltaire and the Cowboy: The Letters of Thurman Arnold.* Boulder: Colorado Associated University Press, 1977.

Grether, Ewald T. *The Steel and Steel Using Industries of California.* Berkeley: University of California Press, 1946.

Gunther, John. *Inside U.S.A.* New York: Harper and Brothers, 1947.

Hafen, Leroy, ed. *Colorado and Its People.* 4 vols. New York: Lewis Historical Publishing Company, 1950.

Hansen, Alvin. *After the War: Full Employment.* Washington: U.S. Government Printing Office, 1943.

Hewlett, Richard G., and Oscar Anderson. *The New World.* 2 vols. University: Pennsylvania State University Press, 1962.

Howard, Joseph Kinsey. *Montana, High, Wide, and Handsome.* New Haven: Yale University Press, 1943.

Ickes, Harold L. *Fightin Oil.* New York: A. A. Knopf 1943.

———. *The Secret Diary of Harold Ickes.* 3 vols. New York: Simon and Schuster, 1953–54.

Ise, John. *Our National Park Policy.* Baltimore: Johns Hopkins University Press, 1961.

Bibliography

Jaffe, Bernard. *Men of Science in America*. New York: Simon and Schuster, 1944.

Jensen, Merrill. *The New Nation: A History of the United States During the Confederation, 1781–1789*. New York: Knopf, 1950.

Johnson, Robert W. *But, General Johnson*. Princeton: Princeton University Press, 1944.

Jones, Jesse. *Fifty Billion Dollars: My Thirteen Years with the Reconstruction Finance Corporation*. New York: Macmillan Company, 1951.

Kelley, Allen C., and Jeffrey G. Williamson. *Lessons from Japanese Development: An Analytical Economic History*. Chicago: University of Chicago Press, 1974.

Kidner, Frank L. *California Business Cycles*. Berkeley: University of California Press, 1946.

Kirkland, Edward C. *Industry Comes of Age: Business, Labor, and Public Policy, 1860–1897*. New York: Holt, Rinehart and Winston, 1961.

Koistinen, Paul A. C. *The Military-Industrial Complex: An Historical Perspective*. New York: Praeger, 1979.

Koppes, Clayton. *JPL and the American Space Program: The Jet Propulsion Laboratory, 1936–1976*. New Haven: Yale University Press, 1982.

Kunetka, James W. *City of Fire: Los Alamos and the Birth of the Atomic Age*. Englewood Cliffs, N.J.: Prentice-Hall, 1978.

Kuznets, Simon J. *National Product in Wartime*. New York: National Bureau of Economic Research, 1945.

Lane, Frederick C. *Ships for Victory: A History of Shipbuilding under the U.S. Maritime Commission in World War II*. Baltimore: Johns Hopkins University Press, 1951.

Lauderbaugh, Richard A. *American Steelmakers and the Coming of the Second World War*. Ann Arbor: University of Michigan Research Press, 1980.

Leahy, William D. *I Was There*. New York: Whittlesey House, 1950.

Levitan, Sar. *Swords into Plowshares: Our G.I. Bill*. Salt Lake City: Olympus Publishing Co., 1973.

Libecap, Gary. *Locking Up the Range: Federal Land Controls and Grazing*. Cambridge: Cambridge University Press, 1981.

Lilley, Tom, et al. *Problems of Accelerating Aircraft Production in World War II*. Boston: Harvard Graduate School of Business Administration, 1946.

Lotchin, Roger W., ed. *The Martial Metropolis: U.S. Cities in War and Peace 1900–1970*. New York: Praeger, 1984.

Lott, Arnold S. *A Long Line of Ships*. Annapolis: U.S. Naval Institute, 1954.

Luey, Beth, and Noel J. Stowe, eds. *Arizona at Seventy-Five*. Tucson: Arizona Historical Society, 1987.

McCoy, Esther. *Richard Neutra*. New York: G. Braziller, 1960.

McEvoy, Arthur F. *Ecology and Law in the California Fisheries, 1850–1980*. Cambridge: Cambridge University Press, 1986.

Machlup, Fritz. *The Basing Point System*. Philadelphia: Blakiston Co., 1949.

Melman, Seymour. *The Permanent War Economy: American Capitalism in Decline*. Rev. ed. New York: Touchstone, 1985.

Melosi, Martin. *Coping with Abundance: Energy and Environment*. Philadelphia: Temple University Press, 1985.

Mezerick, A. G. *The Revolt of the South and West*. New York: Duell, Sloan and Pearce, 1946.

Millett, John D. *U.S. Army in World War II—The Army Service Forces: The*

Bibliography

Organization and Role of the Army Service Forces. Washington: U.S. Government Printing Office, 1954.

Moses, Robert. *Portland Improvement.* Portland: The Oregon Journal, 1943.

Muller, Charlotte F. *The Light Metals Monopoly.* New York: Columbia University Press, 1947.

Nash, Gerald D. *The American West in the Twentieth Century.* Albuquerque: University of New Mexico Press, 1977.

———. *The American West Transformed: The Impact of World War II.* Bloomington: Indiana University Press, 1985.

———. *State Government and Economic Development: A History of Administrative Policies in California, 1849–1933.* Berkeley: Institute of Governmental Studies, University of California, 1964.

———. *United States Oil Policy, 1890–1964.* Pittsburgh: University of Pittsburgh Press, 1968.

———, ed. *The Urban West.* Manhattan, Kans.: Sunflower University Press, 1980.

National Negro Congress, Los Angeles Council. *Jim Crow in National Defense.* Los Angeles: n.p., 1940.

Navin, Thomas R. *Copper Mining and Management.* Tucson: University of Arizona Press, 1978.

Nelson, Donald W. *Arsenal of Democracy.* New York: Harcourt, Brace, and Co., 1946.

Nettels, Curtis P. *Emergence of a National Economy, 1775–1815.* New York: Holt, Rinehart and Winston, 1962.

Northeast Coast Institution of Engineers and Shipbuilders. *Transactions.* Newcastle-upon-Tyne and London: Northeast Coast Institution of Engineers and Shipbuilders, 1940–46.

Olson, Keith W. *The G.I. Bill.* Lexington: University of Kentucky Press, 1974.

Peffer, E. Louise. *The Closing of the Public Domain, 1900–1950.* Stanford: Stanford University Press, 1951.

Rae, John B. *Climb to Greatness: The American Aircraft Industry, 1920–1960.* Cambridge: MIT Press, 1968.

Reich, Robert. *The Next American Frontier.* New York: Times Books, 1983.

———, and Ira C. Magaziner. *Minding America's Business: The Decline and Rise of the American Economy.* New York: Harcourt Brace Jovanovich, 1982.

Riddle, Donald H. *The Truman Committee.* New Brunswick: Rutgers University Press, 1964.

Roosevelt, Elliott. *As He Saw It.* New York: Duell, Sloan and Pearce, 1946.

Sampson, Anthony. *The Seven Sisters: The Great Oil Companies and the World They Made.* New York: Viking Press, 1975.

Saylor, David J. *Jackson Hole, Wyoming.* Norman: University of Oklahoma Press, 1970.

Scamehorn, Howard Lee. *Pioneer Steelmaker in the West: The Colorado Fuel and Iron Company, 1872–1903.* Boulder: Pruett Publishing Co., 1976.

Schwarz, Jordan A. *Liberal: Adolf A. Berle and the Vision of an American Era.* New York: Free Press, 1987.

Scott, Mel. *The San Francisco Bay Area: A Metropolis in Perspective.* Berkeley: University of California Press, 1959.

Sherry, Michael S. *The Rise of American Air Power: The Creation of Armageddon.* New Haven: Yale University Press, 1987.

Bibliography

Sill, Van Rensselear. *American Miracle*. New York: Odyssey Press, 1947.

Sitterson, J. Carlyle. *Aircraft Production Policies under the National Defense Advisory Commission and Office of Production Management, May, 1940 to December, 1941*. Washington: Civilian Production Administration, Bureau of Demobilization, 1946.

Society of Naval Architects and Marine Engineers. *Transactions*. New York: Society of Naval Architects and Marine Engineers, 1940–46.

Spidle, Jake. *The Lovelace Medical Center: Pioneer in American Health Care*. Albuquerque: University of New Mexico Press, 1987.

Spritzer, Donald E. *The New Dealer from Montana: The Senate Career of James E. Murray*. New York: Garland Publishing Co., 1986.

Stegner, Wallace. *The Uneasy Chair: A Biography of Bernard De Voto*. Garden City, N.Y.: Doubleday, 1974.

Stein, Harold, ed. *Public Administration and Policy Development*. New York: Harcourt, Brace, 1952.

Stoff, Michael B. *Oil, War, and American Security: The Search for a National Policy on Foreign Oil, 1941–1947*. New Haven: Yale University Press, 1980.

Stokes, K. C. *Regional Shifts in Population, Production, and Markets, 1939–1943*. Washington: Bureau of Foreign and Domestic Commerce, Department of Commerce, 1943.

Stone, I. F. *Business as Usual*. New York: Modern Age Books, 1941.

Szasz, Frank. *The Day the Sun Rose Twice*. Albuquerque: University of New Mexico Press, 1985.

Taylor, Frank J., and Lawton Wright, *Democracy's Air Arsenal*. New York: Duell, Sloan and Pearce, 1947.

Taylor, George R. *The Transportation Revolution, 1815–1860*. New York: Holt, Rinehart and Winston, 1951.

Thoenen, J. *Alunite Resources of the United States*. Washington: U.S. Government Printing Office, 1941.

Thomsen, Harry, and Lida Mayo. *The Ordnance Department: Procurement and Supply*. Washington: U.S. Government Printing Office, 1960.

Tolchin, Martin, and Susan Tolchin. *Buying into America: How Foreign Money is Changing the Face of Our Nation*. New York: Times Books, 1988.

U.S. National Resources Planning Board. *Development of Resources and of Economic Opportunity in the Pacific Northwest*. Washington: U.S. Government Printing Office, 1942.

———. *Industrial Location and National Resources*. Washington: U.S. Government Printing Office, 1943.

———. *Mountain States Region*. Washington: U.S. Government Printing Office, 1943.

———. *National Resources Development: Postwar Plan and Program*. Washington: U.S. Government Printing Office, 1943.

———. *Pacific Northwest Region—Industrial Development*. Washington: U.S. Government Printing Office, 1942.

———. *Pacific Southwest Region—Industrial Development*. Washington: U.S. Government Printing Office, 1943.

———. *State Planning*. Washington: U.S. Government Printing Office, 1942.

Vatter, Harold G. *The U.S. Economy in World War II*. Irvington, N.Y.: Columbia University Press, 1988.

Bibliography

Wallace, Donald H. *Market Control in the Aluminum Industry.* Cambridge: Harvard University Press, 1937.

Warken, Philip W. *A History of the National Resources Planning Board, 1933–1943.* New York: Garland Publishing Co., 1979.

Washington State University, Bureau of Business Research. *The Impact of World War II Sub-contracting by the Boeing Airplane Company Upon Pacific Northwest Manufacturing.* Seattle: Bureau of Business Research, University of Washington, 1954.

Webb, Walter P. *Divided We Stand: The Crisis of a Frontierless Democracy.* New York: Farrar and Rinehart, 1937.

White, Gerald T. *Billions for Defense: Government Financing by the Defense Plant Corporation During World War II.* University: University of Alabama Press, 1982.

White, William Allen. *The Changing West.* New York: Macmillan Company, 1939.

Williamson, Harold F., et al. *The American Petroleum Industry.* 2 vols. Evanston, Ill.: Northwestern University Press, 1959–63.

Wiltse, Charles M. *Aluminum Policies of the War Production Board and Predecessor Agencies, May, 1940 to November, 1945.* Washington: Civilian Production Administration, Bureau of Demobilization, 1946.

Young, Roland. *Congressional Politics in the Second World War.* New York: Columbia University Press, 1956.

Zierer, Clifford M., ed. *California and the Southwest.* New York: Wiley, 1956.

Articles

Abbott, Carl. "Portland in the Pacific War: Planning from 1940 to 1945." *Urbanism Past and Present* 11 (Winter–Spring 1981): 12–24.

Alexander, Thomas G. "Brief Histories of Three Federal Military Installations in Utah: Kearns Army Air Base (1942–1948)." *Utah Historical Quarterly* 34 (Spring 1966): 123–26.

———. "Ogden's Arsenal of Democracy, 1920–1955." *Utah Historical Quarterly* 31 (Summer 1963): 240–45.

———, and Leonard J. Arrington. "Utah's Small Arms Ammunition Plant During World War II." *Pacific Historical Review* 34 (May 1965): 185–96.

Arrington, Leonard J., and Thomas G. Alexander. "Sentinels on the Desert: The Dugway Proving Ground (1942–1963) and Deseret Chemical Depot (1942–1955)." *Utah Historical Quarterly* 32 (Winter 1964): 32–43.

———. "Supply Hub of the West: Defense Depot Ogden, 1941–1964." *Utah Historical Quarterly* 32 (Spring 1964): 99–112.

———. "They Kept 'Em Rolling: The Tooele Army Depot, 1942–1962." *Utah Historical Quarterly* 31 (Winter 1963): 3–14.

———. "World's Largest Military Reserves: Wendover Air Force Base, 1941–1963." *Utah Historical Quarterly* 31 (Fall 1963): 324–32.

Arrington, Leonard J., Thomas G. Alexander, and Eugene A. Erb, Jr. "Utah's Biggest Business: Ogden Air Materiel Area at Hill Air Force Base, 1938–1965." *Utah Historical Quarterly* 33 (Winter 1965): 9–16.

Arrington, Leonard J., and Archer L. Durham. "Anchors Aweigh in Utah: The U.S. Naval Supply Depot at Clearfield, 1942–1962." *Utah Historical Quarterly* 31 (Spring 1963): 109–18.

Bibliography

Atherton, Lewis. "Structure and Balance in Western Mining History." *Huntington Library Quarterly* 30 (1966): 55–84.

Boyd, Katherine. "Heard About Jackson Hole?" *Atlantic Monthly* 175 (April 1945): 102–6.

Brant, Irving. "The Fight Over Jackson Hole." *Nation* 161 (July 7, 1945): 13–14.

DeVoto, Bernard. "The Anxious West." *Harper's* 193 (December 1946): 481–91.

———. "Sacred Cows and Public Lands." *Harper's* 197 (July 1948): 44–55.

———. "The West Against Itself." *Harper's* 194 (January 1947): 1–13.

Dow, F. B. "The Role of Petroleum Pipelines in the War." *Annals of the American Academy of Political and Social Science* 230 (November 1943): 93–100.

Edwards, Elbert B. "Clark County: From Wilderness to Metropolitan Area." *Nevada: The Silver State.* 2 vols. Carson City: Western States Historical Publishers, 1970.

Foster, Mark S. "Giant of the West: Henry J. Kaiser and Regional Industrialization, 1930–1950." *Business History Review* 59 (Spring 1985): 15–30.

Garnsey, Morris E. "Future of the Mountain States." *Harper's* 191 (October 1945): 329–36.

Gressley, Gene M. "Colonialism and the American West." *Pacific Northwest Quarterly* 54 (January 1963): 1–8.

Hansen, Alvin, and Guy Greer. "Toward Full Use of Our Resources." *Fortune* 26 (November 1942): 130–33.

Hansgirg, F. J. "Thermal Reduction of Magnesium Compounds." *Iron Age* 153 (November 25, 1943): 54–55.

Heath, Jim. "American War Mobilization and the Use of Small Manufacturers, 1939–1943." *Business History Review* 46 (Autumn 1972): 295–319.

———. "Frustrations of a Missouri Small Businessman: Lou E. Holland in Wartime Washington." *Missouri Historical Review* 68 (April 1974): 299–316.

Hexner, Ervin. "International Cartels in the Postwar World." *Southern Economics Journal* 10 (October 1943): 114–35.

Hill, Creighton J. "Alvin Hansen: Hard Headed Prophet." *Scholastic* 42 (February 1, 1943): 15.

———. "The National Resources Planning Board and Its Work." *Scholastic* 42 (April 5, 1943), 14.

Hill, Forest G. "An Analysis of Regional Economic Development: The Case of California." *Land Economics* 31 (February 1955): 1–12.

Hurwitz, Abner, and Carlyle P. Stallings. "Inter-regional Differentials in Per Capita Real Income Change." *Regional Income.* Vol. 21 of *Studies in Income and Wealth* (Princeton: Princeton University Press, 1951).

Kaufman, Perry. "City Boosters: Las Vegas Style." *Journal of the West* 13 (July 1974): 46–60.

Logan, L. J. "Canadian Wartime Project is Herculean Undertaking." *Oil Weekly* 110 (August 9, 1943): 13–19.

Lotchin, Roger W. "The Metropolitan-Military Complex in Comparative Perspective: San Francisco, Los Angeles, and San Diego, 1919–1941." In Gerald D. Nash, ed., *The Urban West* (Manhattan, Kansas: Sunflower University Press, 1980), 19–30.

Mahoney, J. R. "Economic Changes in Utah During World War II." *Utah Economic and Business Review* 4 (June 1946): 5–13.

———. "The Western Iron and Steel Industry." *Utah Economic and Business Review* 3 (June 1944): 3–5, 27.

278

Bibliography

Malone, Michael. "The Collapse of Western Metal Mining: An Historical Epitaph." *Pacific Historical Review* 55 (August 1986): 455–64.

Mezerick, A. G. "West Coast versus East." *Atlantic Monthly* 173 (May 1944): 48–52.

Morse, R. A. "Japan's Drive to Preeminence." *Foreign Policy* 69 (Winter 1987–88): 3–21.

Moses, Robert. "Long Haired Planners: Common Sense vs. Revolutionary Theories." *New York Times Magazine* (June 25, 1944), 16–17.

Nash, Gerald D. "Planning for the Postwar City: The Urban West in World War II." *Arizona and the West* 27 (July 1985): 99–112.

———. "Reshaping Arizona's Economy: A Century of Change." In Beth Luey and Noel J. Stowe, eds., *Arizona at Seventy-Five* (Tucson: Arizona Historical Society, 1987), 127–47.

———. "Urban Development in the Southwest." *Journal of Urban History* 11 (August 1985): 471–80.

Neuberger, Richard L. "The Great Canol Disaster." *American Mercury* 66 (April 1948): 415–21.

Parsons, J. J. "California Manufacturing." *Geographical Review* 39 (April 1949): 229–41.

Penny, J. Russell, and Marion Clawson. "Administration of Grazing Districts." *Land Economics* 29 (April 1953): 23–34.

Schiesl, Martin. "City Planning and the Federal Government in World War II: The Los Angeles Experience." *California History* 62 (May 1979): 127–40.

Taylor, Frank J. "Builder #1." *Saturday Evening Post* 213 (June 7, 1941): 11.

Thompson, Gerald W. "Frontier West: Process or Place." *Journal of the Southwest* 29 (Winter 1987): 364–75.

Velie, Lester. "They Kicked Us Off Our Land." *Colliers* 120 (July 26, 1947): 20–21, 40–42.

———. "The Truth about Henry Kaiser." *Colliers* 118 (July 27, 1946): 11–12, 24–26.

Watkins, Myron W. "Post-war Plan and Program." *Journal of Political Economy* 51 (March 1943): 397–414.

Dissertations

Brubaker, Sterling J. "The Impact of Federal Government Activities on California's Economic Growth." Ph.D. diss., University of California, Berkeley, 1959.

Kaufman, Perry. "The Best City of Them All: A City Biography of Las Vegas, 1930–1960." Ph.D. diss., University of California, Santa Barbara, 1974.

Spritzer, Donald E. "New Dealer from Montana: The Senate Career of James E. Murray." Ph.D. diss., University of Montana, 1980.

Toole, K. Ross. "A History of the Anaconda Mining Company: A Study in the Relationship Between a State and Its People and a Corporation, 1880–1950." Ph.D. diss., UCLA, 1954.

Index

Index

Index

Index

Index

Index

Index

Index